WRITING
THE NEWS

WRITING THE NEWS

Douglas A. Anderson
Arizona State University

Bruce D. Itule
Arizona State University

Portions of this book previously appeared in *News Writing and Reporting for Today's Media.*

 Random House / New York

First Edition
987654321
Copyright © 1988 by Random House, Inc.

All rights reserved under International and Pan-American Copyright Conventions. No part of this book may be reproduced in any form or by any means, electronic or mechanical, including photocopying, without permission in writing from the publisher. All inquiries should be addressed to Random House, Inc., 201 East 50th Street, New York, N.Y. 10022. Published in the United States by Random House, Inc., and simultaneously in Canada by Random House of Canada Limited, Toronto.

Library of Congress Cataloging-in-Publication Data

Anderson, Douglas A.
  Writing the news.

  Includes index.
  1. Reporters and reporting. 2. Journalism—Authorship. I. Itule, Bruce D., 1947-
II. Title.
PN4781.A595 1987   070.4′3   87-28483
ISBN 0-394-37419-3

Book Development: Domenig and Henry; Acquisitions Editor: Roth Wilkofsky

Book Design: Karin Batten

Cover Design: Eric Baker

Manufactured in the United States of America

Since this page cannot legibly accommodate all the copyright notices, the following pages constitute an extension of the copyright page.

Permissions Acknowledgments

For permission to use personal quotations and printed material, we are grateful to the following:

Chapter 3: *32–34:* Reprinted with permission from the *Washington Journalism Review*. *35–39:* Copyright © 1985 by Don Fry; reprinted with permission. *39–48:* Adapted from Robert Gunning, "The Technique of Clear Writing," rev. ed. (New York: McGraw-Hill, 1968), used with permission of the Gunning-Mueller Clear Writing Institute, Inc. *40:* Reprinted with permission of *The Arizona Republic*; permission does not imply endorsement. *41:* Greta Tilley, *Greensboro* (N.C.) *News & Record*. *47: The Orlando Sentinel*.

Chapter 5: *81–82:* Reprinted wth permission of the *Tempe* (Ariz.) *Daily News Tribune*.

Chapter 6: *98, 99, 100, 101: Chicago Tribune*. *108–109:* Reprinted with permission from *The Philadelphia Inquirer*, January 9, 1985.

Chapter 7: Quotes and paraphrases by Art Geiselman are used with his permission. *120, 121:* Reprinted with permission of *The Dallas Morning News*.

Chapter 9: All material from the *New Haven Register* is reprinted with permission of the *New Haven* (Conn.) *Register*. *152, 153:* Reprinted with permission of the *Tempe* (Ariz.) *Daily News Tribune*. *161, 162:* Reprinted with permission of the *Fairbanks* (Alaska) *Daily News-Miner*. *164:* Reprinted with permission of *The Observer*, La Grande, Ore. *165, 166:* Reprinted with permission of *The Gleaner*, Henderson, Ky. *172:* Reprinted with permission of *The Arizona Republic*. *173:* Reprinted with permission of *The Phoenix Gazette*.

Chapter 11: *214, 215:* Reprinted with permission of the *Tempe* (Ariz.) *Daily News Tribune*. *215:* Reprinted with permission of the *State Press*, Arizona State University.

Chapter 12: *224, 225, 226, 227, 228, 232:* Reprinted with permission of the *Topeka* (Kan.) *Capital-Journal*. *239–240:* Reprinted with permission of the *Tempe* (Ariz.) *Daily News Tribune*. *248, 249, 250, 251, 252, 253:* Reprinted with permission of the *Mesa* (Ariz.) *Tribune*.

Chapter 13: *271–272:* Reprinted with permission of the *Mohave Valley News*, Bullhead City, Ariz. *279: Chicago Tribune*.

Chapter 14: Quotes and paraphrases by Topy Fiske are used with her permission. *290, 291, 292, 294–295, 296:* Reprinted by permission from *The State Journal*, Frankfort, Ky. *292, 293:* Reprinted by permission from the *Chicago Sun-Times*; copyright © with permission of the Chicago Sun-Times, Inc., 1987. *299:* Reprinted by permission from the *San Francisco Examiner*; copyright © 1986 the *San Francisco Examiner*.

Chapter 15: *307:* From "Synopsis of the Law of Libel and the Right of Privacy," by Bruce W. Sanford; used with permission of Scripps-Howard Newspapers. *316–*

PERMISSIONS ACKNOWLEDGMENTS

317: New York State Newspapers Foundation. *322–323:* Reprinted by permission from John C. Merrill.

Appendix B: Portions of the Associated Press Stylebook are used by permission of The Associated Press.

Appendix C: *359–361:* Reprinted with permission of the author, William F. Thomas, *Los Angeles Times*.

Preface

Writing the News introduces students to basic news writing skills and concepts. We wanted also to introduce students to current journalistic issues and to reporters and editors who provide down-to-earth advice. We sought to kindle an excitement by challenging students to master the rudiments of news writing.

We think our book will help students learn the basics while examining the work of professionals. For example, students will be with *Topeka* (Kan.) *Capital-Journal* reporter Roger Aeschliman as he covers a major fire; *Tempe* (Ariz.) *Daily News Tribune* reporter Adrianne Flynn as she writes about local government; *Chicago Tribune* reporter Mark Eissman as he compiles facts for a story on a dramatic rescue of a woman dangling 16 stories above a busy street; and *Chicago Sun-Times* feature writer Mary Gillespie as she works on a personality profile of the superintendent of the Illinois State Lottery.

The list of reporters gracious enough to participate in making this book possible can go on and on. Our focus is on real reporters in real situations, but the story telling does not cloud the lessons of the text. We have woven the experiences of journalists into the pedagogical fabric of our book.

Throughout the book, we use reporters and editors as instructional models. Their experiences, and our own as working journalists and journalism educators, show students how principles and issues work in practice.

FEATURES OF THE BOOK

To write a comprehensive, lively news writing text, we chose to feature the following:

- *First-person accounts from reporters and editors.* We show how concepts and principles work in real situations and we explore the problems, philosophical questions and issues that journalists face on the job. First-person accounts from reporters and editors help to breathe life into the book.
- *Numerous, current story examples from a wide range of newspapers.* We use story examples from large metros, medium-circulation dailies, small-circulation dailies and student newspapers.

- *Detailed, comprehensive chapters on the rudiments of news writing.* After a brief overview of how newspapers operate, we provide thorough, solid chapters on the basics of news writing: how to write summary leads; how to organize stories; how to conduct interviews; how to use quotes and attribution effectively; how to gather information; and how to write special leads. The basics are carefully and completely spelled out early in the book. Later, students are introduced to common types of stories such as obituaries, press releases, speeches and features.

ORGANIZATION OF THE BOOK

Because the chapters are self-contained, this text should be flexible enough to meet the needs of most news writing classes.

Chapter 1 introduces students to contemporary newspapers by exploring how reporters cover the news. It examines the primary jobs held by print journalists, discusses the organizational structures of newsrooms and distinguishes between coverage of stories by morning and afternoon newspapers.

Chapter 2 discusses the evolution of news treatment. It outlines traditional criteria that determine news, examines the factors that affect news treatment and discusses the roles of gatekeepers.

Chapter 3 provides instruction on the qualities of good writing. It features advice from Roy Peter Clark and Donald Fry of the Poynter Institute for Media Studies in St. Petersburg, Fla. Clark takes a look at the common traits of good writers. Fry provides practical advice on how to construct clear, open sentences. Examples are used to illustrate each of Robert Gunning's "Ten Principles of Clear Writing."

Chapter 4 shows students how to write summary leads. Examples are provided and instruction is given on writing lead paragraphs for news stories. Students also are shown how to rate the primary elements—who, what, why, when, where and how—for inclusion in the lead paragraph.

Students are told in Chapter 5 that strong, vivid quotations can make an ordinary story a special one. The chapter analyzes the types of quotations—direct, partial and indirect—and discusses when and how to use them. Guidelines for when to use quotes, how to punctuate them and how to attribute them are presented.

Chapter 6 shows how to organize news stories. It calls attention to the steps to use when organizing an inverted pyramid. It also takes a look at the hourglass style, in which the writer provides the major news in the first few paragraphs of the story before using a transitional paragraph to introduce a chronology of events.

Chapter 7 underscores the importance of interviewing: conducting research, setting up an appointment, asking the right questions at the right time, establishing rapport, taking notes and asking follow-up questions.

Chapter 8 surveys standard newsroom and library sources. It emphasizes that background information is essential to good reporting and writing.

Chapter 9 provides instruction on how to write basic stories: obituaries,

PREFACE

weather and sports. The first section of the chapter stresses that obituaries are among the most widely read items in newspapers. The section outlines basic information contained in obits and provides advice on how to humanize them with anecdotes and quotations. The second section of the chapter shows how to write weather stories, with particular attention given to forecasts, hard news and year-end summaries. The final section of the chapter explores the evolution of sportswriting and provides practical advice on deciphering statistics and writing about games.

Chapter 10 discusses press releases and provides tips on how to decide if the releases are of interest to readers. The chapter shows how to rewrite press releases.

In Chapter 11 students are given a front-row seat at a press conference and speech by lawyer F. Lee Bailey. The chapter explains how to prepare for press conferences and speeches, how to cover them and how to organize the information into a coherent story.

Chapter 12 shows how to write stories while covering common beats: police and fire, local government and the courts. The first section of the chapter presents strategies for effective coverage of police and fire departments. Advice is provided on writing fire, arrest and accident stories. The second section of the chapter explores the various forms of municipal governments—mayor-council, council-manager and commission. It also provides advice on writing stories about city council meetings. The third section of the chapter introduces students to the federal and state judicial systems. Advice on how to write stories at various junctures of a criminal case is presented. Advice also is given on reporting civil cases.

Chapter 13 discusses alternatives to the summary lead. It explains and provides examples of the following leads: narrative, contrast, staccato, direct address, question, quote and "none of the above." The chapter closes by illustrating how several types of leads can be written for the same story.

Chapter 14 stresses that the main functions of features are to humanize, to add color, to educate, to entertain, to illuminate and to analyze. The chapter distinguishes between hard and soft news. It also discusses types of features: personality profiles, human interest stories, trend stories, in-depth stories and backgrounders. It provides advice on finding a theme, developing a story and using effective transition.

The first section of Chapter 15 introduces students to the tort of libel. It discusses libel defenses and provides practical advice to reporters on how to avoid libel actions and how to respond to sources who threaten to file libel suits. The second section of the chapter stresses that society increasingly is calling for journalistic accountability. The section focuses on the ethics of journalism. It considers some of the most important issues facing journalists today: fairness and objectivity, reporter misrepresentation, conflicts of interest and the use of anonymous sources.

WORKBOOK AND INSTRUCTOR'S MANUAL

We also have written an accompanying workbook that does not rely on Springdale, U.S.A.–type exercises. To the greatest extent possible, the exercises are based on real news events. Students are given facts from actual news stories; then they are asked to construct their own versions. In our Instructor's Manual we have reprinted the stories as they appeared in various newspapers. The Instructor's Manual also provides supplementary exercises.

The Workbook exercises are built around stories that were published in newspapers of various circulations, including: *The Birmingham* (Ala.) *News*; the *Fairbanks* (Alaska) *Daily News-Miner*; the *Mesa* (Ariz.) *Tribune*; *The Arizona Republic* in Phoenix; the *Santa Cruz* (Calif.) *Sentinel*; the *Colorado Springs* (Colo.) *Gazette Telegraph*; *The Hartford* (Conn.) *Courant*; *The Idaho Statesman* in Boise, Idaho; the *Chicago Tribune*; *The Gleaner* in Henderson, Ky.; the *Star-Herald* in Scottsbluff, Neb.; *The Beaumont* (Texas) *Enterprise*; and *The Dallas Morning News*.

In addition to devising realistic exercises based on stories published in the newspapers listed above, we also based exercises on stories disseminated by The Associated Press.

The Workbook chapters also contain review questions for the corresponding chapters in the text.

ACKNOWLEDGMENTS

Some of the journalists interviewed for this book have moved to other jobs. References to them, however, remain within the context of their jobs at the time their articles were published or at the time they were interviewed.

Many people contributed to the research and preparation of our text. Individuals who were helpful through their insights, counsel and willingness to provide examples include the entire staff of the *Chicago Tribune*, but in particular Managing Editor Dick Ciccone, who allowed us to use whatever stories and resources we needed; *Beaumont* (Texas) *Enterprise* Managing Editor William Mock; *Birmingham* (Ala.) *News* Managing Editor Thomas Bailey; *Dallas Morning News* night news editor Kenneth Bowling; *Dayton* (Ohio) *Journal Herald* and *Daily News* reporter Marie Dillon; Ron Jenkins, editor of *The Gleaner*, Henderson, Ky.; *Mesa* (Ariz.) *Tribune* Executive Editor Max Jennings and reporters Maren Bingham and Mike Padgett; *Omaha* (Neb.) *World-Herald* reporters Lee Barfknecht and Terry Henion; *Phoenix* (Ariz.) *Gazette* sports news editor Dennis Brown and reporter Tom Spratt; Cynthia Scanlon, reference librarian at the Phoenix Public Library; and Poynter Institute for Media Studies Associate Directors Roy Peter Clark and Donald Fry, St. Petersburg, Fla.

In addition, we would like to thank *San Antonio Express-News* reporter Kym Fox; *Santa Cruz* (Calif.) *Sentinel* reporter Denise Franklin; Publisher Marc Anthony of the *Star-Herald* in Scottsbluff, Neb.; Southern Illinois University-Carbondale Professor Emeritus Harry W. Stonecipher; *Tempe* (Ariz.) *Daily News Tribune* Managing Editor Lawn Griffiths and reporters Adrianne Flynn and Gail Maiorana; NBC News correspondent Mark Nykanen; *Fresno* (Calif.) *Bee* copy editor Jerry Guibor; *Topeka* (Kan.) *Capital-Journal* reporter Roger Aeschliman; Jack Williams, a weather page editor

PREFACE

for *USA Today*; *Albuquerque* (N.M.) *Journal* reporter Art Geiselman; and *San Francisco Examiner* feature editor Topy Fiske.

Several of our colleagues at Arizona State University contributed examples, advice and encouragement: administrative assistant Salima Keegan and Professors Donald Brown, Frank Hoy, Richard Lentz, Richard McCafferty, W. Parkman Rankin, Dennis Russell, Ben Silver, Edward Sylvester and Sharon Bramlett-Solomon.

We also would like to acknowledge those professors who reviewed all or parts of our previous text, *News Writing and Reporting for Today's Media,* from which we drew so heavily for this book: Fred Bales, The University of New Mexico; Jerry Chaney, Ball State University; Carolyn Stewart Dyer, The University of Iowa; Wallace B. Eberhard, University of Georgia; Thomas Fensch, University of Texas, Austin; Gilbert Fowler, Arkansas State University; Bruce Garrison, University of Miami; John R. Hetherington, California State University, Chico; Bruce E. Johansen, University of Nebraska at Omaha; Mike Kautsch, University of Kansas; Cecil Leder, Mott Community College; Thomas B. Littlewood, University of Illinois; Sue A. Lussa, San Diego State University; Donald Morrisseau, Florida Junior College; Marlan Nelson, Oklahoma State University; Edith Pendleton, Edison Community College; Jane W. Peterson, Iowa State University; Humphrey A. Regis, Hampton University; Schyler Rehart, California State University, Fresno; and Marshel D. Rossow, Mankato State University.

We would like to thank those professors who reviewed all or parts of this text: R. Thomas Berner, The Pennsylvania State University; James L. Baughman, University of Wisconsin-Madison; Bernard DeHoff, University of Northern Iowa; Carole M. Gorney, Lehigh University; Jon Hughes, University of Cincinnati; and Terry J. Vander Heyden, Western Kentucky University.

We would like to thank our primary editors in the College Department at Random House: Roth Wilkofsky, executive editor, humanities and social sciences, who has helped to steer us through publication of three books; Kathleen Domenig, the editor who conceived of this project and who efficiently guided us through it; and Fred H. Burns, editorial supervisor, who saw to it that the galleys and page proofs for the text and workbook came together in coordinated fashion.

Special appreciation goes to our families for their patience and understanding while we wrote this book: Claudia, Laura and Mary Anderson, and Priscilla, Dena and Justin Itule. This book is dedicated to them and to two people who made a lasting impression on us and our work: Marjorie Smith, retired journalism adviser at Superior (Neb.) High School, and Frank Johnson, the retired managing editor of the *Arizona Daily Star* in Tucson.

Douglas A. Anderson and Bruce D. Itule
Arizona State University
Tempe, Ariz.

Contents

1. THE NEWSROOM — 3

    Meeting the Challenge — 4
        From Metros to Main Street 4

    How Reporters Cover the News — 5
        General Assignment 5
        Working a Beat 6
        Specialty Reporting 6

    The Newspaper Newsroom — 7
        Inside the News Huddle 10
        AM vs. PM Coverage 10
        One Story, Two Angles 12

2. INGREDIENTS OF NEWS — 15

    Evolution of News Treatment — 16
        Changing Habits of Readers 16

    The Gatekeepers — 17
        How the Gates Open and Close 17

    What Makes News? — 18
        Timeliness 19
        Proximity 20
        Conflict 20
        Eminence or Prominence 21
        Consequence or Impact 22
        Human Interest 22

    Factors That Affect News Treatment — 23
        Instincts of Editors and Reporters 23
        The Audience 24

  The News Hole 25
  Availability of News 25
  Philosophy of the Media Outlet 26
  Pressure From Publishers 26
  Influence of Advertisers 27
  The News Mix 27
  Competition Among Media 28

3. QUALITIES OF GOOD WRITING   31

Roy Peter Clark's Common Traits of Good Writers   33
The Foundation of Writing: The Sentence   34
Don Fry's Guide to Writing Clear Sentences   35
  How to Construct Open Sentences 35
  Keeping Stuff Together 38
  Two Basic Principles 39

Robert Gunning's "Ten Principles of Clear Writing"   39
  Keep Sentences Short, on the Average 40
  Prefer the Simple to the Complex 40
  Prefer the Familiar Word 41
  Avoid Unnecessary Words 42
  Put Action in Your Verbs 44
  Write the Way You Talk 45
  Use Terms Your Reader Can Picture 45
  Tie in With Your Reader's Experience 46
  Make Full Use of Variety 46
  Write to Express Not Impress 48

Newspaper Style   48
  Who Needs a Stylebook? 48

4. SUMMARY LEADS   51

Topping an Inverted Pyramid   52
The Five W's and H   53
  Rating the Primary Elements 53
  The Thought Process Behind the Lead 54

Writing a Summary Lead   55
Multiple-Element Summary Leads   57
How Many Words?   58
Making Them Better   59
  Avoid Clutter Leads 60
  Avoid Buried Leads 61
  Determine the Focal Point 62

CONTENTS

No Two Are the Same	**64**
Where to Put the Time Element	**64**
After the Verb 65	
In a "Comfortable" Spot 65	
At the End 65	
After the Object of the Verb 66	
After an Adverb or Prepositional Phrase 66	
Writing in Active Voice	**66**

5. QUOTES AND ATTRIBUTION — 69

Types of Quotations — 71
 Using Direct Quotes   71
 Using Partial Quotes   71
 Using Indirect, or Paraphrased, Quotes   72

When to Use Quotes — 72
 Guidelines for the Use of Direct Quotes   73

Quotation Pitfalls to Avoid — 76
Observing Taste in Quotations — 78
 Handling Offensive Language   79
 Use of Dialect   79

Attribution — 79
 Verbs of Attribution   80
 Identification in Attribution   82
 Placement of Attribution   84
 Guidelines for Handling Attribution   84

Punctuation for Quotes and Attribution — 86
Anonymous Sources — 90
 Guidelines to Observe   90
 Making Decisions on a Case-by-Case Basis   91
 Some Policies on Anonymous Sources   93

6. ORGANIZING A NEWS STORY — 95

An Inverted Pyramid — 96
 Should a Suicide be Covered?   97
 Working the Phones   97
 Breaking Down the Story   98

Reorganizing and Improving a Bland Story — 101
 The Initial Version   101
 What's Wrong With It?   103

The Rewrite   104
Why It's Better   105

Steps to Follow in Organizing an Inverted Pyramid   105
Write a Terse Lead   106
Provide Background   106
Handling Chronology   106
Sprinkle Quotes Throughout   106
Use Transition   106
Avoid "The End"   107
Do Not Editorialize   107

An Alternative to the Inverted Pyramid   107
Advantages of the Hourglass Style   107
An Example   108
Organizing an Hourglass   109
When to Use the Hourglass   109

7. INTERVIEWING   111

The Research   112
Using the Morgue   112
Using Campus or Public Libraries   113
Other Sources of Information   113

Setting Up the Interview   114
Make an Appointment if Possible   114
Identify Yourself   115
Make It Convenient for the Source   115
Describe the Story   115
Do Not Be Late   115
Dress the Part   116

On the Interview   116
Closed-Ended Questions   116
Open-Ended Questions   116
Funnel Interview   117
Inverted-Funnel Interview   118
Memorizing Questions   118
Using the Telephone   118
Framing Questions to Fit the Story's Purpose   119
Establishing Rapport   121
Observation   122
Personal Questions   124
Follow-Up Questions   127
Handling Hostile Sources and "No Comment"   128
Taking Notes   130

When It Ends   132

CONTENTS *xvii*

8. GATHERING INFORMATION — 135

Standard Sources — 136
Newsroom Sources 136
Library Sources 138
Sources on Law 143

9. WRITING BASIC STORIES — 147

Obituaries — 148
Selecting Obits to Publish 148
Basic Information in Obits 149
Sources for Obit Information 149
Importance of Accuracy 150
Hoaxes 150
Obituary Styles 150
Capturing the Flavor of the Decedent's Life 152
Writing Interesting Leads 153
Providing Additional Information 157
Terminology and Other Obit Hangups 158

Weather — 158
Local Weather Coverage 159
Coverage of a Snowstorm in Fairbanks 160
Steps to Follow When Writing About Weather 162
Types of Weather Stories 163
Consulting the AP Stylebook 166

Sports — 167
Getting Away from Clichés 167
Contemporary Sports Pages 168
Deciphering the Statistics 168
Writing Sports Contest Stories 170
Some Sportswriting Tips 173

10. PRESS RELEASES — 177

Determining Their Value — 179
Which Releases Make It? — 179
No Strict Rules 180

Boiling Down a Handout — 180
Finding the Lead 181
The Result 182
Eliminate the Fluff 182

CONTENTS

How to Avoid Free Ads — 183
Handouts with Local News Value — 184
An Example 185

On the Job in Evansville — 187
Steps to Follow 187
Rewriting a Typical Handout 188

11. PRESS CONFERENCES AND SPEECHES — 193

Press Conferences — 194
Media Events 194
Before It Begins 195
The Questions and Answers 199
Picking Out the News 202

Speeches — 204
The Preparation 204
Covering a Speech 205
Examining a Reporter's Notebook 207

Writing the Story — 210
Organizing the Information 211
The Result 212
Same Event, Different Stories 214

12. BEAT REPORTING — 217

Covering Police and Fire — 218
Staffing the Beat 218
Coverage of Departments 219
Developing Sources 219
A Day on the Beat With Roger Aeschliman 221
Writing Stories From Department Records 229
Tips for Police and Fire Reporters 232

Covering City Government — 234
Learning the System 235
A Day on the City Beat With Adrianne Flynn 237
Coverage of City Council Meetings 238
Importance of Preparation 241
Tips for Covering City Government 241

Covering the Courts — 243
The Judicial System 244
Types of Court Cases 246
Criminal Cases 246
Steps to Follow When Covering the Courts 253

CONTENTS

    Civil Cases 254
    The Challenge of Covering the Courts 257

13. SPECIAL LEADS   261

Narrative   262
    The Nut Graph 263
    Using Observation 264
    Keeping It Going 264
    Developing Raw Material into a Narrative Lead 265

Contrast   266
    Keep It Brief 267
    Good and Bad Examples 267
    The Need for Observation 268
    Strong "Turn Words" 268
    On a Hard News Story 269

Staccato   269
    Get the News Peg High 270

Direct Address   271
    Use It Sparingly 272
    Be Prepared to Rewrite 272

Question   273
    Teasing an Audience 274
    Combining Question with Direct Address 274

Quote   274
    Do Not Misrepresent 275
    Beware of Libel 275

None of the Above   276
    Combining Several Leads 276

The Need for Strong, Vivid Verbs   276
    Examples 277

Which One and When?   278
    One Story, Several Leads 279

14. FEATURES   283

The Importance of Features   284
Hard and Soft News   285
    "Jell-O Journalism" 287

Types of Features — 287
Personality Profile 288
Human-Interest Story 288
Trend Story 288
In-Depth Story 288
Backgrounder 288

Finding a Theme and Developing a Story — 289
Feature Leads — 289
From Start to Finish — 290
The Beginning 290
The Body 290
The Conclusion 291

Steps to Follow — 292
The Mechanics of a Feature — 292
Transition 294
Using Voice 296

What an Editor Looks for in a Feature — 298
A San Francisco Story 298
A Love Affair with Words 300

15. LAW AND ETHICS — 303

The First Amendment: Not an Absolute — 304
Libel — 305
Libel Law Boundaries 306
Words to Handle With Care 306
Responsibility for Quoting Others 307
Classes of Libelous Words 308
Libel Defenses 310
The New York Times Rule 312
First Consideration: Public or Private? 313
Impact of the *Gertz* Case 313
Advice for Reporters 315
Guidelines for Potential Libel Defendants 316

Reporters and Their Sources — 317
The *Branzburg* Case 317
Shield Laws 318

Responsibility of the Press to Society — 318
Theories of Press Systems — 319
The Authoritarian System 319
The Libertarian System 319
Social Responsibility Theory 319

An Increase in Press Criticism — 320
The Press Responds — 321
The Press Critic 321
The Ombudsman 321

The Ethics of Journalism — 322
Codes of Ethics — 323
The Issue of Enforcement 324

Ethical Issues — 325
Fairness and Objectivity 325
Reporter Misrepresentation 326
Privacy Rights vs. the Public's Right to Know 327
Conflicts of Interest 328
Anonymous Sources 329
"Freebies" 330
Ticklish Times: When Compassion Collides With Policy 331

"A Swampland of Philosophical Speculation" — 332

APPENDIX A STORY PROCESSING — 333
APPENDIX B THE ASSOCIATED PRESS STYLE RULES — 340
APPENDIX C CODES OF ETHICS — 357

GLOSSARY — 363
INDEX — 375

WRITING THE NEWS

Reporters who are on deadline often telephone sources to get the latest news into stories. (Photo by Alan Carey/The Image Works)

1/ The Newsroom

In most newspaper newsrooms the city desk is where plans originate for local news stories covered by reporters. Here is where some stories are praised and others killed.

In this chapter you will be introduced to the following terms:

news story
feature story
general assignment reporter
spot news
beat reporter
specialty reporter
editor
managing editor
byline
news editor
copy desk
makeup editor
copy editor
slot editor

city editor
editorial news hole
state (area, suburban) editor
national and/or foreign editor
photo editor
sports editor
lifestyle editor
financial editor
AMs
AM cycle
PMs
PM cycle
paper of record

"City desk."

People always are calling a newspaper's city desk to offer news tips, to seek help from a reporter to solve their problems, to ask questions, to settle arguments or to find out news before they read it in the paper.

In most newsrooms the city desk is center stage. Here is where plans originate for all of the local news stories that go into the newspaper. Here is where all local stories must pass.

Reporters are guided by the city desk, and it is up to the editor or editors on the desk to get the best stories possible into the newspaper. A give and take between the city desk and a newspaper's reporters goes on throughout the day.

At smaller newspapers a single person in charge of the city desk guides reporters, edits their stories and also answers the telephone. That person may lay out pages and write headlines. At a metropolitan newspaper there are several editors at the city desk who supervise reporters and edit their copy before sending it to the copy desk, where it will be edited again and a headline will be written for it.

MEETING THE CHALLENGE

A city desk is one of many similarities between large and small newspapers. There also are similarities among reporters in any size market:

- The biggest challenge all reporters face is to give readers the information they want and need in a limited amount of time and space. All journalists must meet their deadlines.
- Wherever they work, reporters must be aggressive yet diplomatic enough to handle any type of interview, willing to give up their home and social life when a newsworthy event occurs, consistently ethical and as objective as possible. They must write so that their readers understand them, never hesitate to ask a question more than once and understand the legal framework within which they work.

FROM METROS TO MAIN STREET

Often, when aspiring journalists think of where they would like to work, they think of the huge newspapers that pay the best wages and have scores of "specialists" traveling around the world. The truth is, most reporters never will work in New York, Chicago, Los Angeles or Washington, D.C. The majority will work for the hundreds of community newspapers throughout the United States. Some reporters use their first jobs as springboards to a medium-size metropolitan newspaper; then they will move up to a major U.S. city. Others will spend their careers in a small community, learning every aspect of journalism. They will cover social club meetings; they will interview presidential candidates in town for a whirlwind tour; they even may sell ads, do production work and answer the telephone.

THE NEWSROOM

Today's reporters must be able to handle a wider variety of stories than those of a few years ago, and they need more than just journalism training. For instance, newspapers are conducting more polls than ever, which requires not only someone to make the survey, but also someone trained to interpret it for readers.

Today's reporters are interviewers and writers, historians and lawyers, mathematicians and economists. Still, the prerequisites of being a good reporter are curiosity and enthusiasm. A good reporter also must know how to spell and write in simple sentences.

HOW REPORTERS COVER THE NEWS

Reporting takes three forms:

- General assignment
- Beats
- Specialties

Each of these areas has distinct characteristics, but their borders are fuzzy. News stories simply do not fall neatly into a single category. They tend to spill over into all three. That means that good reporters must be able to operate effectively in any of these areas. They also must cover and write both news stories and feature stories. *News stories* chronicle the five W's and H—who, what, where, when, why and how—of timely occurrences. *Feature stories*, which will be discussed in Chapter 14, often analyze the news, entertain readers or describe people, places or things in or out of the news.

GENERAL ASSIGNMENT

General assignment reporters cover breaking news or feature stories as they come up. Their assignments usually come directly from an editor or assistants. Story ideas come from many sources: the mail, the wires, other publications, public relations people, other editors or reporters or people who telephone the newsroom.

General assignment reporters—they are called GAs—cover mainly *spot news*, which is occurring now. They are important to any newsroom operation because they are there when a story breaks. For example, there may be a report on the radio that a group of 50 protesters is marching on the local Planned Parenthood office to demonstrate against abortions. A GA is sent to the scene immediately. Later in the day, the same GA may cover a parade downtown, then a community meeting in which political candidates are questioned.

The most successful GAs are excellent and quick writers who know their communities well. The stories they write range from crime to crops, from weather to widgets. They must know what is going on and who the main players are around town.

WORKING A BEAT

Beat reporters cover breaking news and features in specific geographic and subject areas every day, such as police and fire, county and federal courts, and city, county and state governments. They generally come up with their own story ideas, based on knowledge of their beats and constant contact with sources. They also may be given assignments by their editors. Beat reporters usually write at least one story a day.

"I'm responsible for any spot news that occurs on my beat while I'm at work," said Kym Fox, who covers the police beat for the *San Antonio* (Texas) *Express-News*. "I listen to police and fire scanners (radios) all day and I make the rounds to all police and criminal investigations offices, the sheriff, fire department and medical examiner. I check with them to see if I missed anything. I have my favorite sources in every office who I can call on whenever I hear anything."

Fox is a typical beat reporter. She is responsible for letting her newsroom know when a story breaks. She comes up with her own ideas and usually covers the stories she chooses. Her newspaper relies heavily on her; she cannot afford to miss a story.

"Beat reporting is more stressful than general assignment," said Fox, who was a GA when she first came to the *Express-News*. "GAs never are accused of missing something. They are reacting to the city editor. If something happens on the police beat and the competition gets it and I don't, it's my butt."

Fox knows the key to being a successful beat reporter is covering as much of the beat as possible each day. Beat reporters have to budget their time carefully. Besides covering spot news and features, they must constantly cultivate sources and potential sources.

"Beat reporters make sure a newspaper is getting all the news," Fox said. "If it didn't have someone in city hall or the police station who knew all the important people, things would get by. You would never know if something was wrong."

SPECIALTY REPORTING

Specialty reporters cover breaking news and features in even more specialized areas than beat reporters, such as transportation, energy, education, law and aviation. Like beat reporters, they are responsible for finding and writing the stories that originate in their areas.

Their story ideas come from contacting sources and from public relations people, the wires and other editors, reporters and publications. While general assignment and beat reporters are concerned with spot news, specialty reporters often are interested in long-range stories, the roots of problems and the reasons behind the news. That means they often operate under the most flexible deadlines.

For instance, if there is a serious contamination problem in the largest lake in town, the environmental reporter first will write a spot news story reporting it. Then the reporter may study the problem in depth over a period of time to find out what caused the contamination, how it will affect the community in years to come, what can be done about it and what lessons it has taught city officials.

Specialty reporters have to talk to experts in a specialized field and then write stories in language readers will understand. That means that they must be experts as well as skilled news writers.

They also must be excellent reporters who can cross over into many areas. In the story on the contamination of the lake, the environmental reporter will have to talk to people at city hall to find out why it happened, sources in the medical field to check on the health effects, police and fire officials who are keeping people away from the lake and researchers who are studying long-term effects of water pollution.

THE NEWSPAPER NEWSROOM

Most newspaper newsrooms are structured the same. At the top is the *editor*, whose role changes depending on the size of the paper. At a community newspaper the editor also may be a publisher, a business manager, a reporter, a photographer and an advertising salesman. At a metro the editor may have nothing to do with the day-to-day editorial process; the *managing editor* is in charge.

At the other end of the ladder are the beginning reporters, who are trying to make their mark on the profession and hoping to get their name—a *byline*—on a Page One story. The number of newsroom personnel between the beginning reporter and the top editor is determined by the circulation of the newspaper and its budget.

At most newspapers the managing editor runs the newsroom. It is his or her job to make sure that the newspaper is out on time each day and that costs are kept within a budget. The managing editor usually is responsible for hiring and firing newsroom personnel and serves as a spokesperson for the paper. At smaller newspapers the managing editor also is involved in story, photo and graphics selection; assignments; laying out pages; and editing copy and writing headlines.

In a typical newsroom the managing editor has a number of subeditors, each responsible for one facet of putting out the paper.

• **The news editor.** This editor is in charge of the *copy desk*, where *makeup editors* and *copy editors* work. Their job is to dummy (lay out) pages and write headlines for the wire and locally written copy (stories) that goes on the news pages each day. At larger papers there is a national copy desk that handles stories from other cities, a foreign copy desk that edits copy from other countries and a local copy desk that handles stories by "cityside" reporters. Individual departments, such as sports and lifestyle, also may have their own copy desks. Some newspapers have a "universal copy desk," which edits stories from every department.

Most daily newspapers are members of The Associated Press (AP) and/or subscribe to United Press International (UPI) and several supplemental news services, which give them a steady flow of stories from cities and battlefields throughout the United States and the world. Once the news editor decides which "wire stories" and which cityside stories go into the paper, they are sent to a makeup editor, who positions them on a page and assigns the size and style of the headline. Then each story is sent to the *slot editor* on the copy desk. The slot editor distributes the story to a copy editor who edits it and writes the headline. The copy desk is the last desk to handle the story before it appears in print.

• **The city or metropolitan editor.** This editor runs the city (or metropolitan) desk and is in charge of the cityside general assignment, beat and specialty reporters. Assistant city editors may help hand out assignments and review stories. Reporters come to the city desk for ideas, with ideas, for counseling and with stories ready for editing.

It is the city editor's job to make sure that the news in the city (or metropolitan area) is covered and as many local stories as possible get into each edition. There is only so much space between the first and last pages of a newspaper, and ads fill up much of that space. What is left is called the *editorial news hole*. The city editor and the other subeditors at the paper are hoping to fill as much of the editorial news hole as possible with stories or photographs from their staffs, so much of their job is spent trying to sell their material to the managing and news editors.

The number of reporters reporting to the city editor is determined by the size of the newspaper. Major metropolitan newspapers have hundreds of reporters; community newspapers may have only a few.

• **The state editor.** Alternatively called the area or suburban editor, this person supervises reporters who cover communities and areas outside of the city in which the newspaper is published. At a big newspaper, reporters may staff bureaus in communities throughout the state. They write news and feature stories about events and people in those communities, then call them in or send them via computer to the state editor, who edits the stories and finds space for them in the newspaper. Even small newspapers have state or area desks, but instead of covering the entire state, they often cover only other communities in the county or in the circulation area of the paper. Coverage of neighboring communities or other cities in the state is important to newspapers because they always are trying to increase their circulation and advertising base.

• **The national and/or foreign editor.** Metropolitan newspapers usually have one or two editors who work much like the state editor, but they supervise reporters in bureaus throughout the country and/or world. Some newspapers may have reporters in Washington and New York. Others may have fully staffed bureaus in Washington, New York and other major U.S. cities. They may also have reporters in London, Rome, Moscow, Peking and other major foreign cities. Community newspapers generally do not have national and foreign correspondents; they depend on the wire services to supply them with national and foreign news and features.

• **The photo editor.** This editor supervises a newspaper's photographers. At many papers the photo editor sits at or near the city desk, assigning photographers to accompany reporters on news and feature assignments.

THE NEWSROOM

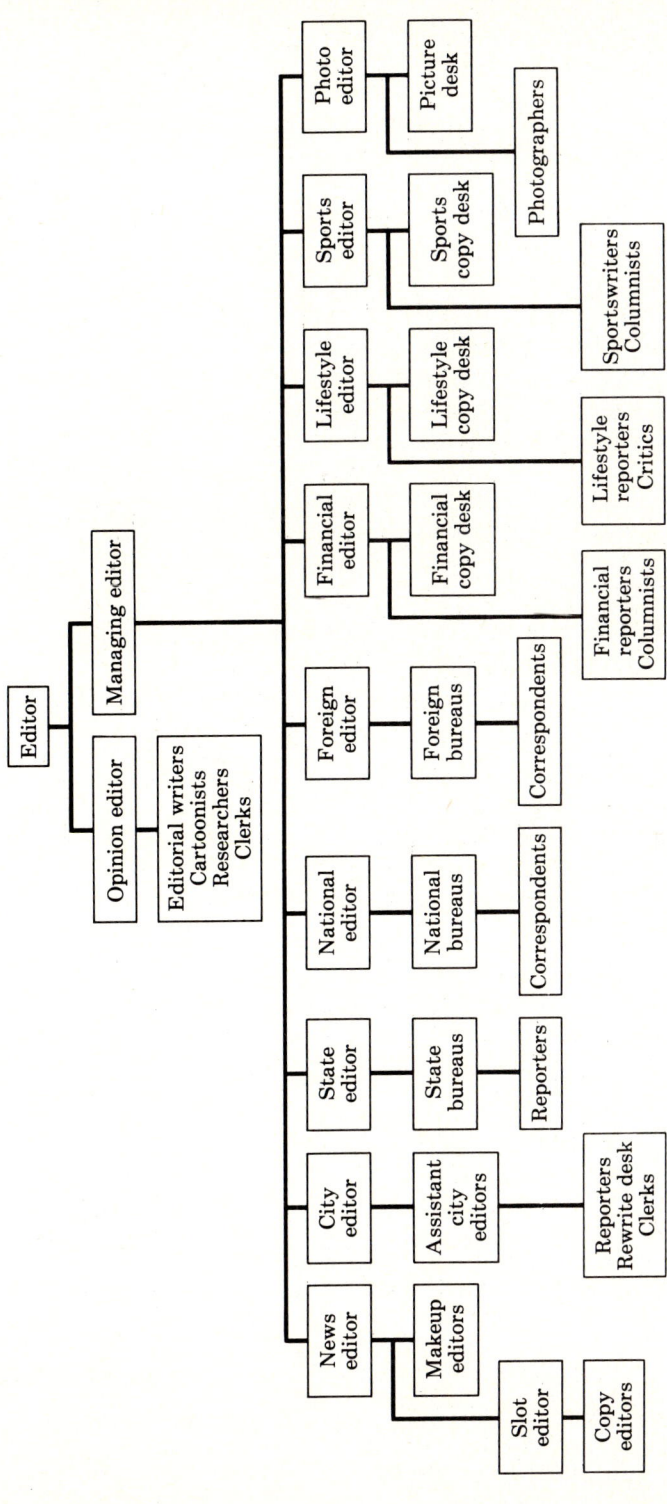

Figure 1.1 A typical metropolitan newsroom

Some papers have one photographer who handles everything, including pictures for advertisements. Others have several who divide assignments; a few have dozens who are specialized in the types of events they cover. Sometimes the photo editor is also a "graphics editor," although many newspapers today have a separate editor in charge of the maps, charts, informational graphics and other illustrations that accompany stories. An artist or staff of artists works for the graphics editor.

   • **The sports editor.** This editor is in charge of sportswriters and the desk people who process their copy. The writers cover sports events and features in a community's high schools and colleges. They also cover professional sports in their area. The desk people on the sports staff edit stories and lay out the daily sports pages. The sports editor often writes a column.

   • **The lifestyle editor.** This person, who also might be called "features editor," heads what usually is a paper's main features section. The section may include articles by lifestyle writers, a food editor, an entertainment writer, a drama critic, a television writer and other reviewers and critics. It may include engagement and wedding announcements. The lifestyle editor, like the sports editor, also is responsible for editing and laying out pages each day.

   • **The financial editor.** This editor is in charge of the business news that goes into the newspaper. Most papers have a business page or section each day, and many have a staff of financial reporters who cover area businesses. Financial news has grown in popularity in recent years, and many papers are expanding their staffs to cover it. Newspapers always have printed closing stock averages and press releases on business openings, expansions and closings, but now they are assigning their own reporters to cover financial news as aggressively as other news is covered.

INSIDE THE NEWS HUDDLE

At least once each day, the foreign, national, state, city, news and photo editors meet with the managing editor in what may be called a news huddle, doping session, budget meeting, news conference, editors meeting or editorial conference. In this meeting they discuss the top foreign, national, state and local stories and photographs. They will decide in the conference which stories will make it into the paper and which of those will be on Page One. A breaking news story could change their plans, but after about 20 minutes of give and take, these editors have determined what their readers will get that day. The sports, lifestyle and financial editors also meet with the managing editor each day, and they will be called into the meeting if they have stories that are being considered for the news section.

AM VS. PM COVERAGE

Morning newspapers are called *AMs*. They report news that breaks on the *AM cycle,* generally from noon to midnight, as well as other non-breaking stories. Their news huddles are held in the late afternoon because deadlines are in the evening and the papers are printed and delivered during the night, while most people are sleeping. Beat reporters for an AM generally work during the day, but many staff members work during the evening.

Evening newspapers are called *PMs*, and the *PM cycle* runs from about midnight to noon. Editors at PMs hold their news huddles in the morning because their deadlines are usually before noon. PMs try to get the latest news to their readers, but they realize that by the time the paper is printed and distributed in the afternoon, most of their readers will have had a chance to hear the news on radio or watch it on television. Therefore, they try to offer their readers a bigger and more comprehensive news report and more local feature stories than radio or television can. Larger evening papers also have more than one edition each day, which helps them deliver the latest news possible.

Evening newspapers are fighting an uphill battle, however. PMs still outnumber AMs in the United States—most newspapers in small, one-paper cities are PMs—but many have shut down or switched to AM. (People still like to look at their morning newspaper before work each day, while they are drinking coffee, to find out what happened since they went to bed the night before.) There are many complicated reasons for the fall of evening newspapers, but one reason can be attributed to changing lifestyles. In most households today both the man and woman are wage earners, and they are bombarded by radio and television throughout the day. When they get home, they often want to use their leisure time in some other way than reading an evening newspaper.

Work on an evening paper is done primarily during the day, and by late afternoon, when the last edition is out, many of the staffers are off work.

For the most part, morning and afternoon newspapers cover the same news events, but the writing angles are different. Traditionally, a morning newspaper is a *paper of record*, offering straightforward news accounts of what happened in the world, nation, state and community since the last edition. A paper of record also is a source for future historical reference. It often prints texts of speeches or court decisions that other papers summarize in a few paragraphs.

Reporters at AMs generally cover newsworthy events that break during the day or night before the next morning's edition. Readers who open their newspaper first thing in the morning might not know anything about the event; they want to know the essential ingredients, the who, what, where, when, why and how. That means AMs usually report the news firsthand.

By contrast, reporters working for afternoon newspapers generally are covering events that occur after their deadlines for that day's paper. That means news that breaks in the afternoon or evening must be reported the following afternoon, after morning newspapers and radio and television already have provided the essential ingredients. Because they are writing about events that already have been well covered, reporters for PMs often write comprehensive stories that encompass not only the essential ingredients but also a unique angle. Their accounts should not be a rehash of what already was reported. They often have time to analyze events and look for angles not covered in AMs or by the electronic media.

ONE STORY, TWO ANGLES

When the Arizona Board of Education ruled on a proposal to toughen the state's high school graduation requirements, Jacquee Petchel of the morning *Arizona Republic* and Michael Murphy of the afternoon *Phoenix Gazette* were there to cover it. The board ruled in the afternoon, on the AM cycle, which meant Petchel wrote the breaking story. Her account began:

> The state Board of Education on Monday narrowly rejected a proposal to toughen Arizona's standards for earning a high school diploma—a defeat that one board member called "appalling."
> Board member C. Diane Bishop, a math teacher at University High School in Tucson who led the attempt to set new standards, also told the board that its decision was a "travesty."
> "We should all be ashamed," she said after the 5–4 vote.

Because the breaking news already had been reported by the time the story appeared the next afternoon, Murphy had to look for an angle that did not merely rehash old news. His "featurized" account began:

> Members of the state's high school class of '89 who are returning to school can relax—at least for a little while.
> The state Board of Education delayed action Monday that would have required this fall's freshman class to meet increased high school graduation requirements.
> By a 5–4 vote, the board defeated a controversial proposal that would have made students complete at least 22—instead of 20—credits.

Stories do not always break on the AM cycle, of course. When they occur early in the morning, on the PM cycle, afternoon newspapers are the first to report them. In these cases, reporters for AMs would look for a different angle.

Editors at *The Gleaner* in Henderson, Ky., confer on the news budget for the next day's newspaper. From left: news editor Donna Stinnett, managing editor Dave Dixon, editor Ron Jenkins and chief copy editor Kathy Meadows. (Photo by Chuck Stinnett)

2 / Ingredients of News

Each day, journalists decide which news stories they will disseminate. These journalists select stories that are most relevant and interesting to readers. There is no scientific formula to measure news values, but traditional elements of news help to guide reporters and editors who make the selections.

In this chapter you will be introduced to the following terms:

hard news
soft news
gatekeeper
wide-open pages

tight pages
dummy
news mix

In 1957 the U.S. Supreme Court said obscenity was not protected by the First Amendment. That declaration, in turn, placed a burden on the court: it had to define *obscenity*. Through the years the court has attempted to structure a workable definition. Justice Potter Stewart, in 1964, summarized the court's frustration. He said obscenity might be difficult to define, but "I know it when I see it."

A definition of *news* is equally elusive. The stock answers are easy: news is when man bites dog; news is something you haven't heard before; news is what editors and reporters say it is.

One thing is clear: News is different things to different people. Certainly, geography plays a role. News of unemployment in the steel industry will be on the front page in Pittsburgh but might not receive a mention in Great Bend, Kan. Conversely, a 15-cent increase in wheat prices will get front-page treatment in Great Bend but not rate a brief mention in Pittsburgh.

EVOLUTION OF NEWS TREATMENT

People always have been hungry for news. Colonial Americans scurried to arriving ships to pick up letters and newspapers from the mother country. The first attempt to publish a colonial newspaper was on Sept. 25, 1690, when Benjamin Harris of Boston issued *Publick Occurrences Both Foreign and Domestick*. His unauthorized paper was shut down by Massachusetts Bay officials after the first issue—and the next newspaper in the colonies was not printed until 1704—but *Publick Occurrences* began a wave of American newspapers that over the last three centuries has brought readers news of diverse happenings.

In *Publick Occurrences* Harris said that he would furnish his readers "with an account of such considerable things as have arrived unto our notice."

In today's media-conscious world, news comes from many sources. Sometimes news is bad; sometimes it is good. It can be hard; it can be soft.

Hard news events, such as killings, city council meetings and speeches by leading government officials, are timely and are reported almost automatically by most newspapers.

Soft news events, such as a luncheon to honor a retiring school custodian or a car wash by fourth-graders to raise money for a classmate with cancer, usually are not considered immediately important or timely to a wide audience. These events still contain elements of news, however, and newspapers often report them. (A more complete discussion of hard and soft news is in Chapter 14.)

CHANGING HABITS OF READERS

In 1978 researcher Ruth Clark reported the results of a study she conducted for the American Society of Newspaper Editors and United Press International. The study, "Changing Needs of Changing Readers," reported that readers wanted more local news and "how-to" pieces "to help them cope" with day-to-day activities. They also wanted the material presented in an easy-to-read form that did not demand too much of their time.

In the mid-1980s Clark again was commissioned by ASNE and UPI to determine what readers wanted on their news pages. She found that reader desires had changed. She reported that readers want more hard news and less emphasis on the softer, lifestyle pieces they had cited little more than a half decade earlier. According to an article in *Editor & Publisher* magazine, Clark told ASNE: "When people were asked what they like best about newspapers, 73 percent said keeping up with the news. Only 27 percent said they preferred interesting stories about people, places and things to do."

Clearly, there is a place for hard news and soft news. Newspapers strive to present both.

THE GATEKEEPERS

Selection of news, like a pass-interference call in football, is subjective. Communication researchers refer to persons in positions to make news decisions as *gatekeepers*. These editors and reporters can open the gate to let news flow; they can close the gate to keep it from oozing out. Of course, sources also can be considered gatekeepers. If they refuse to supply information, there possibly would be no story.

David M. White was the first researcher to study the gatekeeping process at newspapers. His case studies of the early 1950s have been replicated many times; the findings show that "Mr. Gates" is alive and well at American newspapers.

HOW THE GATES OPEN AND CLOSE

One person seldom has complete control over all the gates in the news-dissemination process. For example, a newspaper managing editor reads a story in a national news magazine about contemplated congressional action to cut benefits to military veterans. While mulling the possibility of developing a local angle, the managing editor notices that The Associated Press has just moved a similar national story. Seeing the AP story reinforces his belief that it should be further developed by one of his reporters.

The managing editor then talks to the city editor about assigning the story to a reporter. The managing editor suggests that the reporter interview some area veterans for their reactions to the contemplated cutbacks. The city editor, however, says he just saw a local television interview with an American Legion official about the cutback possibilities. The city editor says the interview was not enlightening, that the local official did not know enough about the issue to say anything more than "we all fought for our country and nobody should try to take our benefits away."

The city editor suggests that, rather than putting together a quick local story based on off-the-cuff emotional reactions, a reporter first conduct some interviews with state congressional representatives and review the specific proposals. Then, he could get reactions from local residents. The story would be held a day or so, but the managing editor agrees a stronger article would be worth the delay.

The city editor checks to see which reporters are available to write the story. He has three to choose from: one is a veteran of the Korean War; another was a conscientious objector during the Vietnam War; the third is just three years out of college and has had no contact with the military. The city editor decides—subjectively, of course—that the third reporter might approach the story more objectively than the other two. The young reporter gets the assignment, but he doesn't know a general from a corporal.

The gatekeeping process continues: The reporter must decide whom to interview and what to ask; he must decide which answers to include in his story; he must decide which element to play up in the lead; he must decide which sources are the most knowledgeable and quotable.

After the reporter makes his decisions, he writes his story and turns it in to an assistant city editor for review. The assistant city editor thinks more emphasis should be placed on comments made by a veteran's widow who was interviewed. The reporter obliges. The city editor determines that the story should run 20 inches and be given a four-column headline. It is to be a Page One story.

A copy editor reads the story and removes some of the material the assistant city editor asked the reporter to add. The reporter rants and raves about the cut. An assistant managing editor is called upon to resolve the dispute. A compromise is reached; the widow's quotes are left in the story, but because the article still must be cut, a comment from an American Legion member who says an area congressman is antimilitary is deleted. The assistant managing editor says the publisher is a good friend of the congressman, but claims that is not a factor in the decision to delete the remark.

Thirty minutes before deadline, a reporter calls the city desk to say the superintendent of schools has just been fired by the board of education. Her story will run 20 inches. The news editor decides to take the veterans' benefits story off the front page and move it to an inside news section. The managing editor intervenes; he says it should remain a Page One story—where readership is highest. He orders an international story shifted from the front page to an inside page.

The scenario could be extended, but the point is clear: There is no scientific formula for deciding what is news and where it should be placed in the newspaper. At several junctures in the news-gathering and writing process, decisions to include or exclude information are made. Reporters and editors, consciously or unconsciously, often rely on time-honored news elements to help them make decisions.

WHAT MAKES NEWS?

For decades, textbooks have discussed the classic elements of news. Criteria most often considered to determine newsworthiness include:

INGREDIENTS OF NEWS

- *Timeliness.* Is it a recent development or is it old news?
- *Proximity.* Is the story relevant to local readers?
- *Conflict.* Is the issue developing, has it been resolved or does anybody care?
- *Eminence or prominence.* Are noteworthy people involved? If so, that makes the story more important.
- *Consequence or impact.* What effect will the story have on readers?
- *Human interest.* Even though it might not be an earth-shattering event, does it contain unique, interesting elements?

Some examples will illustrate these classic news ingredients.

TIMELINESS

Freshness strengthens a news story. For example, when a storm hits, readers need to know immediately its effects. The first two paragraphs from an article in *The Evansville* (Ind.) *Press* illustrate the timely nature of the story:

> Tri-State roads called "hazardous at best" by the National Weather Service won't improve until at least tomorrow when sunny skies, temperatures near freezing and drying winds should help road clearing work.
>
> Police throughout the Tri-State urged residents to stay home as drifting snow closed roads throughout the Evansville area. Some could remain closed for days, weather officials said.

When a 25-year-old patient suffered a series of mild strokes after receiving an artificial heart, a search was accelerated to find a donor heart. When one was located, United Press International led its story with:

> TUCSON, Ariz.—A medical team flew to Texas Friday to fetch a donor heart to replace the Jarvik 7 mechanical organ that has kept a young Arizona man alive for more than a week.

When the president of the United States undergoes surgery, the public naturally wants to know his condition as soon as possible. The Associated Press, aware of the value of such a story, quickly gave readers the news:

> WASHINGTON (AP)—President Reagan, who will turn 76 in a month, underwent prostate surgery Monday in what the White House and his doctors described as a routine operation that showed "no suspicions of cancer."

Breaking news stories command space at most newspapers. Readers want to know what is happening *now*.

PROXIMITY

Close-to-home events naturally are of interest to media outlets. Note the following lead paragraph from *The Gleaner*, Henderson, Ky.:

> The city's stormwater management consultant Monday night unveiled a proposal designed to handle Henderson's stormwater problems and estimated cost of the plan at $26 million.

Henderson's stormwater problems might not be of interest to readers in Biloxi, Miss., or Laramie, Wyo., but they are deserving of Page One treatment in the Kentucky community.

Unemployment was running above the national average in Beaumont, Texas, so it was big news when that community was in the running for a new automobile plant. Here was another story with close-to-home relevance. The story in *The Beaumont Enterprise* began:

> Southeast Texas civic leaders are joining a crowd of suitors for a futuristic General Motors plant that offers 6,000 jobs.
>
> General Motors officials are looking for a place to build their planned Saturn subcompact car, and state Rep. Al Price said he hopes community leaders could unite to bring the carmaker to the Beaumont area.

The lead on a story published in the *Colorado Springs Gazette Telegraph* would not have raised the eyebrow of a reader anywhere but there. But it was news in that community:

> Two people who had been expected to run for the Colorado Springs City Council District 1 seat said Tuesday they will not be candidates.

CONFLICT

Conflict—whether it involves people, governmental bodies or sports teams—often is considered newsworthy. For example, note the lead on a story published in the *Star-Herald* of Scottsbluff, Neb.:

> A request from Nebraska Western College to install a storm sewer along the north side of East 27th Street was denied by the Scottsbluff City Council Monday night based on opposition from property owners in the area.

INGREDIENTS OF NEWS

Here is another lead from *The Gleaner* in Henderson, Ky.:

> Efforts to block the city's purchase of land that could be used to expand the city landfill appeared this weekend to be headed for defeat at Tuesday's city commission meeting.

The *Tempe* (Ariz.) *Daily News Tribune* recognized the news value in action taken by the Arizona Board of Regents in response to apartheid practices in South Africa:

> The Arizona Board of Regents Friday voted 4–3 to cut financial ties with South Africa "as soon as possible."

EMINENCE OR PROMINENCE

Some happenings simply are more newsworthy when well-known people are involved. Thousands of people chop firewood in this country each year. That generally would not be considered to be worth a news story. Nearly every time President Ronald Reagan split a log at his California vacation home, however, it made the news.

Stabbings in metropolitan areas normally do not receive Page One treatment—unless the victims are prominent. The lead paragraph from an *Evansville Press* story follows:

> A former Indiana State University Evansville basketball player was fatally stabbed and another ex-player was seriously hurt in a fight early today at the North Park Village parking lot.

Newspapers routinely publish obituaries. Only when a person of particular prominence dies, however, does the story make news in papers around the country. Here's the lead on a UPI story that was widely published:

> Robert W. Woodruff, the millionaire philanthropist who turned Coca-Cola from a drug store novelty to a soft drink known around the world, died last night at the age of 95.

CONSEQUENCE OR IMPACT

Few developments hit a community as hard—economically as well as emotionally—as mass layoffs by major employers. It is not surprising, then, that media give prominent play to these occurrences. Here are the first two paragraphs of a story published in *The Gleaner*, Henderson, Ky.:

> Alcan Aluminum Corp. announced Thursday it will shut down one of three potlines at its Sebree smelter, resulting in the layoff of about 250 employees.
>
> "Alcan has no proposed date when the employees might be called back," the company said in a statement.

The impact of layoffs is not limited to the employees and their families. An economic domino effect is felt throughout the area. Readers always are interested in stories that have considerable impact on their communities.

Projects that would involve millions of dollars naturally have a major impact on an area. Recognizing this, *The Evansville Press* led a story with:

> A group of Western Kentucky businessmen quietly is planning to build a Tri-State airport that would replace commercial airports in Evansville and Owensboro.

HUMAN INTEREST

It may be a cliché that there are a lot of interesting people in the world, but it is a fact that newspaper readers and television viewers like to hear about them. Human interest stories often appeal to the emotions of readers, pulling them into the lives of others or into subjects of broad concern. Bob Dvorchak wrote a story for The Associated Press that undoubtedly captured the interest of his readers in the first two paragraphs. The story was about an aide to a Pennsylvania state senator:

> On weekdays, Dennis Sciabica toils in politics as an aide to a state senator. In his free time, he's a professional cowboy, wrestling steers and riding snorting bulls.
>
> "Both are high risk businesses," Sciabica says. "I've had people tell me that I sling the bull during the week and ride it on weekends."

Ever wonder what happens to old soldiers who are nearly broke and who have medical problems? Chet Barfield of the *Mesa* (Ariz.) *Tribune* did. He found that they often end up in Veterans Administration Domiciliaries. He ventured to Prescott, Ariz., to a domiciliary and lured his readers into his story with this lead paragraph:

INGREDIENTS OF NEWS

> This is where they come, the old soldiers—sick, crippled, destitute and homeless. When there's no place else, they come here, to this sanctuary in the pine-covered hills.

FACTORS THAT AFFECT NEWS TREATMENT

In addition to the elements discussed above, other factors influence whether a story should be done. These include:

- *Instincts of editors and reporters.* To paraphrase Justice Stewart: They know news when they see it.
- *The audience.* Would inner-city residents of Los Angeles, for example, be interested in the death of a former governor of North Carolina?
- *The news hole.* Depending on available space, some stories could make the paper one day, but be left out on another.
- *Availability of news.* Depending on what is happening locally and in the world, there simply are more stories to choose from on some days. On slow news days, editors and reporters will scratch for stories of borderline value. On fast news days, relatively good stories don't merit dissemination.
- *Philosophy of the media outlet.* The business-oriented *Wall Street Journal*, for example, selects stories based on criteria different from those of a metropolitan arts and entertainment publication.
- *Pressure from publishers.* Most publishers try not to interfere openly with the news process, but most editors and reporters are aware of the political and social leanings of ownership.
- *Influence of advertisers.* Usually it is a subtle consideration, but some editors might think twice, for example, about giving prominent space to the formation of a "committee for decency in movies" if local theaters are major advertisers.
- *The news mix.* Media outlets often strive to balance hard news with soft news and to provide a local, national and international smattering of stories.
- *Competition among media.* To an extent, morning and afternoon newspapers supplement each other, as do the print and electronic media. Each medium has its strengths and weaknesses in coverage of news. But most media try to keep one step ahead of the competition and this sometimes affects handling of news.

An elaboration of these factors follows.

INSTINCTS OF EDITORS AND REPORTERS

William Mock, managing editor of *The Beaumont* (Texas) *Enterprise* (circulation: 71,000 weekdays), said that "gut instincts and common sense" often take over when making news decisions. "We have to second guess what our readers really want to know," he said.

If, for example, local teachers are threatening to strike and the wire services move a story about a school strike 2,000 miles away, the assumption is that local readers will be interested. If local teachers were not poised for a walkout, the instincts of the editor probably would be that local readers would not be interested in the far-from-home strike story.

Experienced editors and reporters develop a sense for what readers want. Readership surveys and demographic breakdowns, of course, provide editors and reporters with background information that can help hone their instincts.

THE AUDIENCE

"To determine news value, editors and reporters should put themselves in the reader's easy chair," Mock said. "You have to keep in mind that the reader probably is going to listen to the radio driving to and from work and he very likely will watch some television news. When he picks up his newspaper in the morning, he already has an idea of what is going on in the world. When the reader is getting ready for work and the rest of his family are getting ready for work or school, our newspaper must compete for his attention. We must compete not only with the radio and television news he has heard in the last 12 hours but with the scrambled eggs, bacon, toast, spilled orange juice and the kids jockeying for position in the bathroom. The reader may know what he saw on television the night before and what he heard on the radio that morning, but he may be confused about the details. We've got to tell him what is behind the news; we've got to put it in perspective for him."

Mock makes it a point to know his readers. Beaumont, a city of 120,000, has "a fairly good mix of socioeconomic demographics," according to Mock. The area is heavily dependent on the petrochemical industry. "Developments that in any way touch this industry, nationally or internationally, ripple down to many of our readers," Mock said. "Our unemployment rates often run above the average. When a company closes in Beaumont, that is a big story. It means more people will be out there competing for scarce jobs. The closing of a company might not be a big deal in areas with relatively low unemployment rates, but it means a lot to our readers and to our economy."

Mike Moscardini, national editor of the *St. Petersburg* (Fla.) *Times* (circulation: 268,000 weekdays), noted that many of his readers are elderly. "We naturally take an intense interest in such things as proposals to adjust Social Security benefits," Moscardini said. He also pointed out that knowledge of the audience allows editors and reporters to consider more subtle factors when making news decisions. "We'll carry a story on a sailboat accident in Europe, for example, simply because a lot of people around here have sailboats and might be interested," Moscardini said.

THE NEWS HOLE

The size of the news hole—the number of column inches available for news—varies at most publications from day to day. On days when the pages are *wide open* (where there are comparatively few advertisements and scores of column inches available for news) stories of borderline importance might be published. When pages are *tight* (if comparatively little space is available for news), stories that would be published on a day when even average space is available simply cannot be worked into the news hole.

The *Colorado Springs Gazette Telegraph*, in which advertisements sometimes fill less than 50 percent of the total space, has a big news hole on most days. On one Tuesday, for example, the 83-person news-editorial staff had 229 columns (more than 36 full pages) available for news and features. Of course, syndicated copy and wire service stories would fill a percentage of the hole.

The Gleaner in Henderson, Ky., is an 11,000-circulation Tuesday through Sunday publication. On most days, the paper runs 20 to 24 pages (with the equivalent of 10 to 12 full pages available for news); on Sundays, it averages 42. For the year, *The Gleaner* devotes about 48 percent of total space to news.

At some daily papers, when the news side is given the *dummy*, a page-by-page mock-up that has ads with specific sizes keyed in, editors are locked into the assigned space. At *The Gleaner*, however, editor Ron Jenkins has authority to get additional space when it is necessary.

"On a lot of days, it seems that we have 10 gallons of water to put in a 5-gallon bucket," Jenkins said. "When the news hole is really tight, the emphasis in our paper is on local news. We do a lot of cutting on national and international stories on those days. If we have five significant wire stories, but room to run only three of them, we'll slice all five at the bottom just to get them in the paper. On tight news days, we run a lot of national and international news briefs [summary accounts of longer news stories]."

AVAILABILITY OF NEWS

Some days are slower than others in terms of available news stories. News stories that would not merit publication on relatively brisk news days might make their way into print in a Saturday afternoon paper. Saturdays often are slow news days because government offices and other news-making institutions are closed.

Newspapers stockpile non-timely features and trend stories for use on these days.

Large-circulation newspapers naturally have more resources to gather news than do smaller operations. A large-circulation newspaper, for example, has scores of reporters and editors to gather and process news. It also subscribes to a wide variety of news services in addition to The Associated Press and/or United Press International. For a fee, newspapers can subscribe to scores of supplemental news services, such as Knight-Ridder, Gannett or *The New York Times* News Service. Because of budget restrictions, smaller newspapers do not subscribe to several supplemental services. Instead, they rely primarily on one of the major wire services and a skeleton news staff. Thus, available resources limit how media outlets gather and handle the news.

PHILOSOPHY OF THE MEDIA OUTLET

Some newspapers, such as *The New York Times*, consider themselves to be papers of record. It is not unusual for the *Times* to devote a full page to the text of a public official's speech or to verbatim excerpts from a significant U.S. Supreme Court decision. Most newspapers do not have the space to provide such detail. Instead, most American dailies would publish a story highlighting the speech or the court case.

PRESSURE FROM PUBLISHERS

Researcher Warren Breed, in an early study of socialization in the newsroom, determined that newspaper publishers have much to say in both long-term and immediate news policy decisions. His study, which was published in an article in *Social Forces* in 1955, concluded, however, that many publishers hesitate to issue direct commands to slant a news story. It is logical, however, that some subtle influence is always present, and low-key inferences or suggestions by publishers are philosophically and ethically more acceptable than open commands.

Managing editors of Kansas and Nebraska daily newspapers perceive little direct pressure from their publishers when making news and editorial decisions, according to a mail questionnaire survey in the two states.

The study, which was reported in the *Nebraska Newspaper* magazine, noted, however, that editors often respond to subtle suggestions from their publishers. The study showed a tendency of managing editors to consider the same persons (based on occupation) to be influential in the community that they perceive their publishers regard as influential.

The study showed that Kansas and Nebraska daily newspaper editors enjoy a certain management autonomy, a far greater freedom than "middle management" employees in other businesses. Still, there is a limit to an editor's management freedom when the most difficult decisions must be made: It oftens extends, in those circumstances, only to the publisher's door.

Publishers seldom pressure reporters directly about how to handle a news story. If they are pressured, however, reporters must react on a case-by-case basis. Naturally, their response depends on several factors. For

INGREDIENTS OF NEWS

example, does the publisher have a reputation for applying pressure to reporters? If so, how have other reporters dealt with it? What is the working relationship of the publisher, editors and reporters at the newspaper? Is the publisher one who might admire reporters who stand by their opinions in the teeth of pressure? Or, is the publisher one who would just as soon fire reporters as look at them?

Possibly the best way for reporters to deal with pressure from publishers, or advertisers, is to seek advice from experienced editors. They likely have encountered similar situations.

INFLUENCE OF ADVERTISERS

The potential always exists for advertisers to influence the dissemination of news. Theoretically, the news side of a media outlet is independent of the advertising arm. Most of the time, it works out that way.

Editors and reporters instinctively bristle at the thought of an advertiser attempting to economically blackmail the newspaper into running—or not running—a story. News organizations that would give in to blackmail are few and far between—particularly if a significant story hangs in the balance.

Suppression of major news events because of advertiser pressures is unlikely. For example, it is difficult to imagine a newspaper editor spiking a story about an investigation into alleged bid rigging by a local contractor simply because the contractor is a big advertiser.

The potential for spiking a story about a minor news event, however, probably is greater. An editor, for example, might exercise "news judgment" (by rationalizing that "no one really cares") not to publish a story if the same contractor were to be convicted of first-offense drunken driving.

Also, few newspapers delve deeply into consumer news reporting about local products and services. Some larger newspapers do, but they are in the minority. Reporters generally are more aggressive in tackling government issues than business issues.

Still, newspaper editors and reporters, for the most part, make every effort to avoid any appearance of catering to advertisers. This noble stand, of course, is economically less risky at large-circulation newspapers (where a single advertising account would not make a crucial profit-loss difference) than at smaller dailies and weeklies (where one large account could contribute a disproportionate share to overall revenue).

THE NEWS MIX

Most newspapers strive for a *news mix*—a combination of hard news stories and lighter, feature pieces. Also, these newspapers present a combination of local, regional, national and international news.

Editor Jenkins said *The Gleaner* uses a "smorgasboard approach" to the presentation of news. "We've had readership surveys show the appetite among readers is spread fairly evenly among local, national and international news," he said.

The Gleaner emphasizes local news, but Jenkins said the newspaper hopes to add a half page of national news each day. "We hope the advertising growth will allow us to do that," he said.

Managing editor Mock tries to put a "light piece" on the front page of *The Beaumont Enterprise* each day. "That page can get a little heavy at times with blood and mayhem," he said. "We try to lighten it a little to amuse or entertain our readers."

COMPETITION AMONG MEDIA

Competition has an effect on news coverage by various outlets. In Henderson, Ky. (population: 27,000), for example, editor Jenkins has to look over his shoulder at the metropolitan Evansville, Ind., newspapers, which are published just six miles up the road in a city of 130,000.

"We must provide our readers with the news that they won't get in the Evansville newspapers," Jenkins said. "Our policy is to keep the design of our newspaper simple, clean and inviting. But, when you open up the package, there has to be some substance in it."

The Gleaner publishes, for example, major stories at the end of every month about the number of building permits that were issued locally. "Following the trend in building permits is a way of monitoring our local economy," Jenkins said. "Sometimes the stories are played on Page One—if there is a significant upward or downward movement—but usually we play the story on the business page." The Evansville papers would be unlikely to carry the story at all.

Mock's *Beaumont Enterprise* is the dominant newspaper in his market. "We act like it, too," he said. "We don't let other newspapers influence us to a great degree." There are three other local dailies in the market, but the *Enterprise* has a 70 percent house saturation in its home delivery area. "The other newspapers compete with us more than we adjust our news flow to compete with them," Mock said.

Clearly, editors and reporters at local media react to one another in making their news judgments. It is common for reporters and editors to monitor not only other newspapers, but electronic media outlets as well. Some events, such as a press conference at which the mayor announces his intention to seek re-election, naturally would be covered by the print and electronic media.

Occasionally, however, a newspaper will cover an event that it normally would not simply because a television station is giving the event substantial attention. For example, a television station might do updates on its 6 p.m. and 10 p.m. newscasts about a 14-year-old who is attempting to break the world's record for sit-ups. Because television is giving so much attention to the event, a newspaper might also carry a picture and short story.

Editors would not want readers to believe that the newspaper missed a "big" story.

Editors and reporters at the newspaper might have felt that the teenager doing sit-ups wasn't really newsworthy, but because television gave it so much coverage, the newspaper had to provide some.

Roy Peter Clark, left, and Don Fry, associate directors of the Poynter Institute for Media Studies, St. Petersburg, Fla., discuss some of the qualities of good writing. (Photo Courtesy of the Poynter Institute for Media Studies)

3 / Qualities of Good Writing

Writing is hard work. After gathering information, the best writers draft, rewrite and edit their stories. During the writing process, they spend additional time just thinking about their stories. Good writers take pride in their work. They realize every story will not be a blockbuster, but they always do their best to serve their readers.

In this chapter you will be introduced to the following terms:

steady advance	independent clause
open sentence	complex sentence
dangling modifier	dependent clause
simple sentence	queue

Roy Peter Clark, who might be America's best known writing coach, described one of his first days in the newsroom of the *St. Petersburg* (Fla.) *Times.*

It was more than a decade ago; Clark had left behind a comfortable niche as a university professor to become a writing coach. Most of the reporters in the newsroom were not particularly impressed with his Ph.D. in English literature. He knew little of the day-to-day practicalities of journalism.

Writing in the *Washington Journalism Review* in 1985, Clark recalled the need he felt "to interview every reporter on the staff to learn much more than I could hope to teach." He told of an early experience:

One day, I found myself sitting beside Howell Raines, then political editor in St. Petersburg, now a Washington reporter for the *New York Times.* Howell had written a series of political profiles that became legendary in the newsroom. They were powerful and influential character studies so well written that other reporters could quote passages verbatim.

The week I interviewed Howell, *two* of his books had been published, a terrific novel called *Whiskey Man,* and an oral history of the civil rights movement, *My Soul Is Rested.* I felt humbled at the prospect of coaching him. What could I tell him, "Use more active verbs in your next novel, Howell"?

I decided to become student instead of teacher, and asked Howell a dozen questions about political reporting. I recorded his responses. Howell described how to write about politicians as human characters and not just authority figures. He got down to nitty-gritty matters of interviewing and lead writing.

Clark used portions of the interview in his in-house newsletter; it was well received. It occurred to him that advice from respected writers could be both instructional and inspirational to reporters.

Clark served as writing coach at the *St. Petersburg Times* for two years, worked as a reporter and then joined the staff of the Modern Media Institute, which in 1983 became the Poynter Institute for Media Studies. Nelson Poynter, publisher of the *St. Petersburg Times* and *Evening Independent,* willed the controlling stock of the Times Publishing Co. to the institute. Clark, who continues to function as a writing coach, directs the institute's Writing Center programs, which serve students of all ages and professionals from all over the nation.

In his *Washington Journalism Review* article, Clark told how he had interviewed dozens of reporters during writing seminars at the institute and during his years as editor or co-editor of "Best Newspaper Writing," which is published each year by the institute. The book features award-winning stories in the American Society of Newspaper Editors' annual writing contest.

Clark began to see similar qualities in the outstanding reporters he interviewed. In turn, he developed a list of common qualities often shared by good writers.

ROY PETER CLARK'S COMMON TRAITS OF GOOD WRITERS

Reprinted from the *Washington Journalism Review*, here is Clark's discussion of 14 of the common traits:

- Good writers see the world as their journalism laboratory, a storehouse of story ideas. If they can get out of the office, they can find a story. In fact, they can't walk down the street or drive to the mall or watch television without finding something to write about.
- They prefer to discover and develop their own story ideas. They have an eye for the off-beat and may find conventional assignments tedious. They appreciate collaboration with good editors but spend more time avoiding bad editors and what they perceive to be useless assignments.
- They are voracious collectors of information, which usually means that they take notes like crazy. They are more concerned with the quality of information than with flourishes of style. They more often describe themselves as reporters than writers.
- They spend too much time and creative energy working on their leads. They know that the lead is the most important part of their work, the passage that invites the reader into the story and signals the news. They are inclined to describe how they rewrote a lead a dozen times until they "got it right."
- They talk about "immersing themselves" in the story. They live it, breathe it and dream it. They plan and rehearse the story all day long, writing it in their heads, considering their options, talking it over with editors, always looking for new directions and fresh information.
- Most are bleeders rather than speeders. When they write, in the words of the great *New York Times* sports writer Red Smith, they "open a vein." This is because their standards are so high that their early drafts seem painful and inadequate. But when deadline comes or a big story breaks, adrenalin kicks them into a different warp factor. They can speed when they have to.
- They understand that an important part of writing is the mechanical drudgery of organizing the material, what the AP's Saul Pett describes as "donkey work." They may respond to this by developing careful filing systems. They also develop idiosyncracies that help them build momentum during the writing process: pilgrimages to the bathroom, chain smoking, taking walks, day dreaming, junk food orgies or self-flagellation.
- They rewrite. They love computer terminals because they permit maximum playfulness during revision. They move paragraphs around, invert word order for emphasis, find stronger verbs and occasionally purge the entire story to achieve a fresh start. Alas, they are rarely satisfied with their final stories and, burdened with imperfection, can hardly bring themselves to read their own work in the newspaper. Writing is an expression of ego, making the writer vulnerable and, at times, unsufferable.

- In judging their work, writers tend to trust their ears and their feelings more than their eyes. Some stare at the screen with their lips moving, praying that the inner music will reach their fingers. Editors "look for holes in the story." Writers want to "make it sing."
- They love to tell stories. They are constantly searching for the human side of the news, for voices that enliven the writing. Their language reflects their interest in storytelling. Rather than talk about the five W's, they are more inclined to discuss anecdotes, scenes, chronology and narrative. They tend to answer even the most theoretical questions during interviews with war stories, jokes and parables.
- They write primarily to please themselves and to meet their own exacting standards, but they also understand that writing is a transaction between writer and reader. Unlike many journalists, these writers have confidence that sophisticated work will not be lost on their readers. They treasure the reader and want to reward and protect and inform the reader and take responsibility for what the reader learns from a story.
- These writers take chances in their writing. They love the surprising and the unconventional approach to a story. They prefer failing in print on occasion because those failures are a test of their inventiveness. They love editors who tolerate experimentation but who will save them from falling on their faces. Their secret wish is to produce the best, most original piece in the newspaper every day.
- They are life-long readers, mostly of novels, and they like movies. They collect story ideas and forms from other genres. They love words, names and lists.
- They write too long, and they know it. Unlike other journalists, who stop caring for the reader after the lead is complete, these writers use transitions and endings to keep their readers going. Their endings are so good that it is almost impossible to cut stories from the bottom. They want their stories to be "seamless" or "connected by a single thread" or "to flow." They want readers to read every word.

THE FOUNDATION OF WRITING: THE SENTENCE

Stories fall apart without logically conceived paragraphs. Paragraphs deteriorate without solid, readable sentences. The foundation, then, of good writing is the sentence.

One person who recognizes and appreciates the importance of writing clear sentences is Dr. Donald Fry, associate director of the Poynter Institute for Media Studies. Fry, a former professor of English and comparative literature at the State University of New York at Stony Brook, is the author of scholarly volumes as well as popular articles. The next section (through p. 39), which was written by Fry, discusses how to carefully craft clear and open sentences.

DON FRY'S GUIDE TO WRITING CLEAR SENTENCES

Good news prose goes down like sweet iced tea. Readers read newspaper sentences only once. This need for *steady advance* dictates that news writers construct sentences so compelling, so controlled and so clear that the reader moves easily from the first word of a story to the last. We achieve such clarity by two principles:

- Lead the reader.
- Keep stuff together that belongs together.

Many news writers believe that clarity requires short sentences. Wrong. Clarity requires open sentences, regardless of their length. An *open sentence* presents no delays, no bumps and no confusing ambiguities to the reader. We can write open sentences if we lead the reader through them by presenting a clear path with reliable road signs. We convince our readers that we can serve as their guides when we get to the heart of the matter, the subject and verb, as quickly as possible.

HOW TO CONSTRUCT OPEN SENTENCES

Here are some suggestions for writing open sentences:

• Avoid preceding the subject and verb with distracting dependent clauses and phrases, as in this sentence:

When your sentence begins with dependent clauses or phrases, tending to delay the reader, especially when many such clauses intervene between the reader and the start of the thought of the sentence, and most especially with intervening material as long as this mess, then, just as you are annoyed at this sentence, the reader will regard you as a fool and stop reading your piece.

The best sentences start solidly with subject and verb:

Jones raced down the street.

• The passive voice should be used sparingly because it hides the agent of the action from the reader, as in this sentence:

The funds earmarked for student fellowships have been depleted.

The reader might pause and wonder who depleted the funds. The dean probably did and hid his action in the passive voice. A more honest but impolitic dean might choose the active voice:

    I spent the fellowship funds to redecorate my office.

The passive voice has legitimate uses, of course, such as blurring facts the reporter cannot substantiate:

    The house burned down when the kitchen curtains apparently were
accidentally set ablaze.

Ideally, good reporting solves this problem, but sometimes even the best reporters paper over the cracks in the information.
  The passive also can emphasize receivers of action, such as victims:

    A crippled 9-year-old girl was hit by an unidentified motorist
yesterday.

The sentence focuses on the victim but pays a price: the empty verb *was* and the need for a "by [agent]" phrase.

  • **Let punctuation guide the reader.** Good writers transcend mere rules (and style sheets) to provide a set of clear roadsigns. Commas tell readers what to expect next, especially in terms of clauses. An independent clause can stand alone as a sentence, but a dependent clause cannot. The conjunctions *and* or *but* connect two independent clauses in a compound sentence, and the comma before the conjunction tells the reader that a second clause has begun. Notice how smoothly the long sentences flow in this paragraph so far. Back up and study them, starting with "Commas tell readers . . ." The commas kept you as a reader on the track.
  On the other hand, leaving out the comma before the *and* in a compound sentence can cause confusion and disgust and chaos can result. See the problem in that last sentence? Does disgust go with *confusion*, or with *chaos* as the subject of *can result*? Not much at stake in that schoolteacher sentence, but try this one:

    The mayor got a ticket for illegal parking and drunken driving and
parking meters will rank high on his agenda.

Careful placement of the missing comma guides the reader to take *drunken driving* with *parking meters*, not with *illegal parking*. Leaving out that comma creates ambiguity, and ambiguity invites the libel lawyer.

QUALITIES OF GOOD WRITING 37

Commas also keep items in a series together for the reader, as in this sentence:

"The jail reports . . . including somebody's burning Styrofoam trays in his cell, a prisoner's throwing urine and feces at a guard and other inmates, and a third person who had cut both his wrists with a broken razor."

The careful placement of the comma before *and a third person* tells readers that the third item in the series has started. Otherwise readers might think *and other inmates* concludes the series. Try to sort out the various series in this badly punctuated mess:

"When the public criticizes press coverage of bad news, it not only refers to the constant reporting of disturbing news, but also often refers to the presence of sensationalism, hype and questionable news judgment, and the lack of feature stories, local news and 'soft' news."

Dashes convey ambiguous punctuation signals, representing opening parentheses, a comma, colons, pauses and even quotation marks. A reader encountering a dash does not know which of these uses that dash represents at that point in the sentence. The ambiguous signal throws readers and starts them wondering, and wondering readers become wandering readers, right into the next story written by someone else. Analyze the uses of the dash in this next sentence, and try to imagine the reader's confusion at any point in trying to anticipate what might come next:

Careless writers use dashes—represented by hypens in typing—instead of more precise punctuation marks—commas, colons, parentheses, even quotation marks—creating the worst effect in their readers—confusion.

So please observe this guideline for dashes:

AVOID THE DASH!

Well, one concession maybe, as this sentence demonstrates:

Dashes—especially a lot of them—create for the reader—sometimes without design—a feeling—or worse—an impression—of indecisiveness—even mental illness.

Perhaps we should allow neurotics expressing their neuroses to use dashes.

KEEPING STUFF TOGETHER

The second principle of sentence clarity flows from the first: Keep stuff together that belongs together. We've already described the steadying effect of sentences that start with subject and verb, an effect enhanced by keeping the subject and verb side by side. Read this sentence quickly and then cover it up with your hand:

> "The life of a fluffy orange kitten that was injured by a motorist on County Farm Road Wednesday afternoon ended in a brown plastic bag at the Strafford County animal shelter several hours later."

No peeking! What was the subject of the sentence? Most people say *kitten*, but now you see the subject was *life*. This sentence loses the reader, who cannot remember the subject because of the intervening junk. In the following sentence, notice how the parenthetical material between the dashes complicates the separated subject and verb:

> "Likewise, prosperity promised by project cargo—huge shipments dependent on individual overseas projects, such as the construction of King Khalid City in Saudi Arabia—fades like a mirage."

I asked the author what that sentence meant, and he had to study it to understand it himself!

The principle of keeping stuff together prevents *dangling modifiers*, phrases assigned to the wrong word, usually with unintended comic results. Try to read this sentence with a straight face:

> The Palestinians released the passengers, who had held them for several weeks.

The same principle applies to verb modifiers. Consider how this sentence might rudely surprise the reader at the end:

QUALITIES OF GOOD WRITING

The children visited their grandmother's house in the lovely countryside near Lexington almost never.

Or how this one might stun the Secret Service:

"President Reagan lecturod the Iranians last week on not threatening American travelers on the White House lawn."

TWO BASIC PRINCIPLES

Many other writing tricks help clarify sentences, but the two basic principles prevent most problems:
- Am I leading my reader at every point in every sentence?
- Is each item in each sentence next to the stuff it belongs with?

Remember: Write every sentence with readers in mind. They will not fail you if you do not fail them.

ROBERT GUNNING'S "TEN PRINCIPLES OF CLEAR WRITING"

Anyone interested in writing should read books such as these: "The Elements of Style," by William Strunk Jr. and E.B. White; "On Writing Well," by William Zinsser; "The Art of Readable Writing" and "A New Way to Better English," both by Rudolf Flesch; and "The Technique of Clear Writing," by Robert Gunning. There are others, but these form a solid nucleus.

Gunning, a former consultant to more than 100 daily newspapers including *The Wall Street Journal* and to United Press International, developed what he called the "Ten Principles of Clear Writing." The principles, which are examined in his book, are:

1. Keep sentences short, on the average
2. Prefer the simple to the complex
3. Prefer the familiar word
4. Avoid unnecessary words
5. Put action in your verbs
6. Write the way you talk
7. Use terms your reader can picture
8. Tie in with your reader's experience
9. Make full use of variety
10. Write to express not impress

These principles are straightforward. Examples and quotations from Gunning and other writing experts, however, bring them into even sharper focus.

KEEP SENTENCES SHORT, ON THE AVERAGE

Gunning wrote: "I know of no author addressing a general audience today who averages much more than 20 words per sentence and still succeeds in getting published." The key to that statement is the word *averages*. Gunning noted that "sentences must vary in length if the reader is to be saved from boredom." Indeed, don't hammer at the reader with a continuous flow of short, staccato sentences. A change of sentence length achieves variety and enhances readability.

Note the first five paragraphs of this article by Michael Allen. It was published in *The Arizona Republic* (the number of words in each sentence is in parenthesis):

ARMERO, Colombia—Five helicopters darted about like dragonflies over what had once been one of the most prosperous argicultural towns in Colombia. (20)

Viewed from several thousand feet in the air, it looked as if an immense cement mixer had spilled its load in the heart of the valley's rich, green field. (29)

Up close, it was a scene of unrelieved horror. (9)

Very little stuck out of the soupy, gray mud: the tops of a few trees, a church steeple, glimpses of a neighborhood near the old cemetery. (26)

And bodies. (2) Scores of blackened, putrefying corpses baking in the intense morning sun, a groping arm here, a blank, unseeing face there. (20)

Allen's sentences averaged 18 words. The sentences ranged, however, from 2 words to 29. The change of pace from long sentences to short ones helped to keep the story flowing.

PREFER THE SIMPLE TO THE COMPLEX

Gunning wrote that the emphasis in his second principle is on the word *prefer*. "The principle does not outlaw the use of complex form," he wrote. "You need both simple and complex forms for clear expression. At times the complex form is best. But if in your preferences, you use as good judgment as Mark Twain and other successful writers, you will give the simple forms more than an even break." Zinsser wrote: "Clutter is the disease of American writing. We are a society strangling in unnecessary words, circular constructions, pompous frills and meaningless jargon. . . . [T]he secret of good writing is to strip every sentence to its cleanest components."

Variety is achieved by blending some complex sentences with a staple of simple sentences. A *simple sentence* has but one *independent clause:* The council passed the resolution. A *complex sentence* has but one independent clause and at least one *dependent clause:* This is the council member who cast the deciding vote. (*This is the council member* is an independent clause because it is a complete sentence when left standing alone. *Who cast the deciding vote* is a dependent, or subordinate, clause; it is an adjective clause, modifying *member,* a noun.)

Greensboro (N.C.) *News & Record* reporter Greta Tilley, a journalism graduate of the University of South Carolina, won an American Society of Newspaper Editors Distinguished Writing Award for a six-part series on life at the Dorothea Dix Hospital, a state mental institution in Raleigh.

Tilley's writing was precise and vivid. Simple sentences were the staple of her writing. Through clear, well-paced writing, Tilley introduced readers to shock treatments:

RALEIGH—The clock above Anthony's head says 11 past eight.

It's morning. Anthony hasn't eaten or drunk since midnight.

He's strapped to a blue-sheeted hospital bed on wheels. Close by are two psychiatrists, two nurse anesthetists, one psychiatric nurse and two technicians.

"One-ten over 64," the psychiatric nurse says through the hiss of the blood pressure machine. She puts her fingers against Anthony's pulse.

"Sixty. After his treatment the last time he had a bit of a temp, so we need to watch that."

Anthony wears a medium Afro, a full mustache and a blue hospital gown. His tall, strong frame fills the skinny bed.

His bare feet, propped on a pillow, stick out from the end of the sheet covering his body. His eyes are half closed. A stethoscope rests on his stomach.

The technicians have just rolled him from the admissions ward, where he has lived for four months, to a small, clean room in the medical/surgery unit.

Thirty minutes before, he got an injection of atropine to dry his saliva.

In 17 minutes, 140 volts of electrical current will be shot into his brain.

This is Anthony's seventh treatment. He will have one more to go.

When the mental health center in his county sent him to Dorothea Dix Hospital, he couldn't talk, wouldn't eat and didn't respond. His chart described him as catatonic. Drugs didn't help.

Anthony's depression could be coming from a chemical abnormality or stress, or both.

The psychiatrist assigned to his case, Dr. Joe Mazzaglia, asked him to try electroshock therapy. He explained that an electrically induced grand mal seizure would release chemical substances in the brain that could jolt life back into his system.

Anthony gave a reluctant yes.

The writing in the remainder of the lengthy story was equally descriptive and powerful. The story illustrated that a careful blend of simple and complex sentences—with the emphasis on the former—is a solid formula for good writing.

PREFER THE FAMILIAR WORD

Gunning wrote: "Big words help you organize your thought. But in putting your message across you must relate your thoughts to the other fellow's experience. The short, easy words that are familiar to everyone do this job best." The authors of "The Elements of Style" wrote: "Avoid the elaborate, the pretentious, the coy, and the cute. Do not be tempted by a twenty-dollar word when there is a ten-center handy, ready and able."

A newspaper carried this wire-service lead paragraph on a national weather story published in mid-November:

> Tempestuous weather spanned the nation Tuesday as record snow and freezing temperatures swept out of the Rockies into the Plains.

Tempestuous? The Random House College Dictionary defines the adjective form as being "characterized by or subject to tempests." The dictionary defines *tempest* as: "an extensive current of wind rushing with great velocity and violence, esp. one attended with rain, hail, or snow; a violent storm." The dictionary defines span as "the full extent, stretch, or reach of anything."

The weather map, published on the same page as the story, clearly showed that at least one-third of the country had clear skies, although temperatures were cold. Obviously, "an extensive current of wind . . . attended with rain, hail, or snow" was not blowing across "the full extent" of America. The weather, indeed, was tempestuous in the Rockies and Plains, but the story would have been more accurate—and understandable—had it read:

> Winter-like weather spanned the nation Tuesday as record snow and
>
> freezing temperatures swept out of the Rockies into the Plains.

AVOID UNNECESSARY WORDS

"The greater part of all business and journalistic writing is watered down with words that do not count," Gunning wrote. "They tire the reader and dull his attention."

Note this sentence:

> One of the primary aims of the extremely new master's degree pro-
>
> gram, which will offer an innovative curriculum not now available to
>
> the area's population, will be to draw them back into post-graduate
>
> education to improve their communication skills.

That sentence can be cut from 40 words to 24 without changing its meaning:

QUALITIES OF GOOD WRITING

A primary aim of the new master's degree program, which will offer a curriculum currently unavailable to area residents, is to improve communication skills.

Every young reporter inevitably will hear the same thing: "Why did you write that it was 'very hot when the man was strangled to death?' There is no difference between hot and very hot, and to strangle is to kill."

Here are some frequently used redundancies, many of which were listed in an article in the *Oklahoma Publisher* written by Harry E. Heath Jr., a journalism professor at Oklahoma State University. Read these redundancies; never write them.

true facts	friend of mine
electrocuted to death	close in proximity
strangled to death	advance planning
totally destroyed	fully covered
totally unnecessary	open up
absolutely necessary	temporarily suspended
necessary requirement	redo again
very warm	refer back
canceled out	widow of the late
city of Dallas	consensus of opinions
university campus	fall down
still remain	close down
launch up	exactly identical
rise up	dead body
cooperate together	grand total
postpone until later	large in size
other alternative	first and foremost
continue on	each and every
totally engulfed	end result
last Tuesday	next Tuesday

Journalism major Greg Lamm of the University of Florida wasted few words as he placed his readers in the death chamber of the Florida State Prison. Lamm's article, which was published in the *Independent Florida Alligator* and which won an award in the annual William R. Hearst news writing competition, focused on the death by electrocution of convicted killer James Dupree Henry. In the following portion of Lamm's account, note how he made each word, each sentence, contribute to the story:

Before Henry died, he winked and grinned nervously several times to about 30 witnesses who packed a tiny viewing room a few feet—and a picture window—away from the electric chair.

Dressed in his burial clothes, a short-sleeved white shirt and navy blue pants, Henry nodded and licked his lips as the prison electrician and an assistant strapped down his arms and legs.

His mouth was muffled with a wide leather strap that also held his head in place. A metal cap with a sponge soaked in a saline solution was then placed over Henry's freshly shaven head before his face was covered with a black hood.

After that, the two workers connected an electrode to the cap and attached another that would take the current from Henry's body through his right leg.

Whether you wanted to be in the death chamber or not, Lamm's uncluttered, precise, descriptive writing pulled you there. His words made you experience the scene at the prison.

PUT ACTION IN YOUR VERBS

"Strong-flavored, active verbs give writing bounce and hold a reader's attention," Gunning wrote. Use of the active voice (subject acting upon object) rather than passive voice (subject acted upon) is considered more direct and vigorous. The passive voice: The avalanche was caused by an explosion. The active voice: An explosion triggered the avalanche.

Note the strength of the verbs in this paragraph by *Omaha* (Neb.) *World-Herald* sportswriter Terry Henion:

Under a slate-gray sky, the 28-degree temperature and a 23-mph north wind combined to plummet the wind chill to minus 5 degrees. The Husker defense chilled the Cyclones, too, holding Iowa State to 137 total yards. Nebraska's offense churned out 573 total yards, including 538 on the ground.

Note the following paragraph about sprinter Houston McTear:

His raw speed compensated for his lack of form. His stride was brute strength. He was aggressive in his races.

That paragraph describes McTear, but it lacks precision and strong verbs. The best writers search diligently for the right combination of words and the most powerful verbs. Tim Povtak of *The Orlando* (Fla.) *Sentinel* hit on that combination:

His raw speed obliterated the many flaws in his form. His stride was brute strength. He attacked a race and left only scorch marks behind.

QUALITIES OF GOOD WRITING   45

WRITE THE WAY YOU TALK

Reporters should work to avoid formal, stilted language in leads. Readers will appreciate it. When the Arizona Department of Public Safety raided a home brewery, *Tempe* (Ariz.) *Daily News Tribune* reporter Emil Venere could have written:

> Arizona Department of Public Safety officials, for the first time since 1923—four years after prohibition began—on Monday closed down a moonshine still near Gila Bend that was capable of producing 500 gallons of the tequila-like liquid a week.

Instead, Venere wrote:

> In a throwback to the days of bootleggers and speak-easies, Arizona officials raided a pig farm near Gila Bend Monday and dismantled what they claim is the biggest moonshine still ever found in the state.

Be specific. Summarize the thrust of the story in the lead paragraph. But don't bog readers down with alphabet-soup acronyms and bulging details.

USE TERMS YOUR READER CAN PICTURE

Gunning warned reporters to avoid "foggy" writing. The sports reporter who has played the game of basketball and covered it for years will know, for instance, what a "box and chaser" defense is. But the reporter should not assume that all his readers will. If such a term is to be used, it should be explained so readers can understand it: "Metropolitan State will play a box and chaser defense against City College. In this defense, four men will play a zone—they will cover a specific area of the floor, rather than guarding a particular man—while the fifth player will guard, or chase, City College's star no matter where he goes."

Such explanations also often are needed on the business pages. Almost every day, newspapers publish stories containing references to the gross national product—the GNP. Such a term might be familiar, but it's not meaningful to many readers. It needs to be put in perspective so readers can picture what it means:

> The Commerce Department said the gross national product—the total output of goods and services—grew at the fastest rate since a 7.1 percent increase in the second quarter of 1986.

TIE IN WITH YOUR READER'S EXPERIENCE

"A statement cut off from context is a 'figure' that simply floats about," Gunning wrote. "There must be another point of reference, a 'ground' to give it stability and meaning. And you can't count on the reader's going farther than the end of his nose to construct that ground."

What does it mean to the reader if the city budget is increased by $25 million? Not much. Most readers cannot fathom $25 million. But they can understand the tax consequences that a $25 million increase will have on them as homeowners. Break the $25 million down. Tell the reader how much taxes will increase on a house valued at $50,000, on a house valued at $75,000 and so forth.

After a preliminary census count, officials of one Arizona city thought they had been shortchanged. The lead paragraph in the *Tempe Daily News Tribune* read:

> Tempe stands to lose up to $3 million if a preliminary census count of 130,000 holds up, according to city officials.

Most readers cannot relate to the impact of $3 million on an entire city, so reporter Dave Downey used the next paragraph to help put the figure in perspective. And, to borrow Gunning's phrase, Downey saw to it that readers didn't have to go farther than the ends of their noses to comprehend the impact:

> City Manager Jim Alexander said the city could lose about $200 annually for each person not counted in the special mid-decade census being conducted in Maricopa County this fall.

When a volcano erupted in Colombia, it was difficult for most readers who had not experienced such an occurrence to imagine the devastation. Michael Allen, in the *Arizona Republic* article excerpted earlier, painted a word picture most readers could understand:

> Viewed from several thousand feet in the air, it looked as if an immense cement mixer had spilled its load in the heart of the valley's rich, green field.

MAKE FULL USE OF VARIETY

The authors of "The Elements of Style" wrote: "Every writer, by the way he uses the language, reveals something of his spirit, his habits, his capacities, his bias. This is inevitable as well as enjoyable. All writing is communication; creative writing is communication through revelation—it is the Self escaping into the open. No writer long remains incognito."

Indeed, all of us put our personal brand on our writing. We work toward and nurture a style we find comfortable. Gunning wrote that style must be developed—that one "cannot be satisfied with imitation and do any job of writing well." He continued: "You must be able to size up each new situation, see how it is different, and fit the different words to it that do the job best. To do this, you need a wide knowledge of the flexibility and variety of the language."

Zinsser noted that it is important for writers to believe in their own identities and opinions. "Proceed with confidence, generating it, if necessary, by pure will power," he wrote. "Writing is an act of ego and you might as well admit it. Use its energy to keep yourself going."

Readers could feel Tim Povtak's energy flowing through his article on sprinter Houston McTear. Writing as if he were sitting in a living room telling his best friend about McTear, *The Orlando Sentinel*'s Povtak began his story:

It took only nine seconds for Houston McTear to make history in 1975. It took nearly 10 years for him to cope with what he had done. His sudden rise to fame was so pure and innocent. The following fall, though, was so adulterated and complex.

He was once the "world's fastest human." He later would become the world's most misguided athlete.

McTear is alive and well today, quietly plotting his grand comeback that very few really believe is possible anymore. Too many years have passed, too many other "I'm back" claims have disintegrated, for people to take him seriously.

Ten years ago, on May 9, 1975, in Winter Park, Fla., McTear ran 100 yards in 9.0 seconds during an afternoon preliminary heat in the Class AA Florida boys track meet. It stunned the track and field establishment. He tied the world record.

He had an incredible gift—the ability to run faster than anyone else—yet the care-and-maintenance instruction packet got lost in the mail. The blessing became a curse.

Track and field experts across the country lost interest in McTear long ago. They grew weary of his unkept promises. They don't know, or even care to know, about him now.

Yet things are different now, McTear says. Things have changed, he says. This one's for real, he says. "I used to be the 'world's fastest human,'" McTear says. "I can do it again. I can prove that America didn't waste time on Houston McTear."

The article went on to detail McTear's overnight burst into the national spotlight a decade earlier, to quote his high school track coach, to describe his record-setting performance, to quote one of the timers at that meet, to tell of McTear's early-career lax training habits and to describe a drug habit that had plagued the sprinter. It was a difficult story to write; it told of developments that spanned a decade. But Povtak's style, his personal stamp on the facts, made the story flow.

WRITE TO EXPRESS NOT IMPRESS

Gunning said it succinctly: "The chance of striking awe by means of big words is about run out in the United States." Sports broadcaster Howard Cosell might say:

With his not-so-gallant gladiators finding themselves in the unenviable, precarious position of losing by six touchdowns, the sideline mentor, with unwavering resoluteness, dispatched his less-talented players into the fray.

But it would be better to write:

With his team losing by six touchdowns, the coach decided to let his substitutes play.

NEWSPAPER STYLE

Every news writer has an individual style, something that distinguishes one reporter from all the others. Newspapers also have individual styles; they try to be different from the others. This creativity and individuality is important in journalism.

There also is a style that reporters and newspapers must follow that keeps them consistent with others. This uniform style is important. It assures readers that a newspaper and its reporters are consistent in such things as spelling, grammar, punctuation, abbreviation, capitalization and the use of numerals. It helps a newspaper be accurate, precise, clear and credible.

WHO NEEDS A STYLEBOOK?

All reporters need to follow the uniform style and usage rules established at their newspapers. They must communicate with their audience in clear, concise sentences that are as free of clutter as possible and that follow established rules.

Most newspapers have a stylebook of rules that is to be followed by their reporters. Most of these rules are not dark secrets. They are based on dictionaries, grammar books and local customs and usage. The stylebooks are guides. They are not as comprehensive as the dictionary or grammar books, but they give reporters easy access to many of the common rules. For example, a reporter wants to know if *president* should be capitalized when it is not used with a person's name. Is the correct spelling *canceled* or *cancelled*? *Third Ave.* or *3rd Avenue*? *Percent* or *per cent*? The answers to these questions and many more can be found in a stylebook.

Many newspapers use the stylebook published by The Associated Press; some use a comparable book published by United Press International. Both books provide a uniform style that is used by newspapers and in university journalism programs throughout the country. A reporter well versed in AP or UPI style probably would be comfortable working at any newspaper in the country.

Other newspapers have developed their own stylebooks or style sheets, but most are based on the AP book or follow many of the same rules. They simply add their own local rules.

Some newspaper stylebooks are bound, and others are assembled in loose-leaf notebooks. At some newspapers, style rules are computerized. They are entered and stored in a file—it is called a *queue*—in the newsroom computer system.

Whatever the form, all stylebooks have the same goal. They help reporters be consistent, which helps readers understand what is being written. In the introduction of the *Los Angeles Times* Stylebook, reporters are told, "What the author has wrought here is not a revolution, however, but only a sensible accommodation to the ever-changing front of the language, a dressing of our scattered skirmish lines and a set of rules to be followed in the service of uniformity, clarity, grace, idiom and sense." The foreword to *The New York Times* Manual of Style and Usage says, " 'Style,' as it is used in the title, is not literary style; it is a set of rules or guides intended to assure consistency of spelling, capitalization, punctuation and abbreviation in printing the written word. . . . 'Usage' is something else. In this manual, it means the manner in which words are employed—or, most often, the preferred manner of using them when a choice can be made."

Of course, not all books are the same on every style or usage rule. For example, the AP and *Los Angeles Times* stylebooks say that *ensure* means to guarantee and *insure* means to take out an insurance policy. *The New York Times* book says to use *insure* in all cases. The *Chicago Tribune* Stylebook says to lowercase *southern Illinois;* the *Los Angeles Times* book says to make it *Southern Illinois.* The point is that, although stylebooks are the same on most rules, there are some things that make each stylebook distinctive and exclusive.

The most widely used style guide is The Associated Press Stylebook and Libel Manual. It has evolved from a handbook for AP staffers to a comprehensive book used by newspapers and journalism classes throughout the country. It continues to be similar to and written in conjunction with the stylebook used by United Press International.

Excerpts from the AP Stylebook are in Appendix B.

Summarizing the news often means observing it while it happens. Covering a dramatic rescue from a flooded river requires quick thinking. (Photo by Don B. Stevenson)

4 / Summary Leads

A summary lead gives readers the gist of a story in the first paragraph and invites them inside. It is terse, generally no more than 35 words in one sentence, and summarizes the major elements of a newsworthy event. Such leads usually are used on hard news stories so readers do not have to guess or wait to find out what is going on.

In this chapter you will be introduced to the following terms:

summary lead
inverted pyramid
five W's and H
multiple-element summary lead

clutter lead
buried lead
focal point
time element

Reporters are the eyes and ears of their audiences. When they cover a breaking news event, their first stories summarize what happened, to whom, where, when, why and how. More in-depth stories may be written later about people and things touched by the event, but initially, reporters are there to gather the essential facts and write their stories as quickly and as near their deadlines as possible.

Such hard news stories usually begin with a *summary lead*, a terse opening paragraph that provides the gist of the story and invites readers inside. Summary leads usually are used on news stories because they give the major points of the story immediately. That way, people do not have to guess or wait to find out the news. Most people do not have time to read a newspaper from cover to cover. Because they spend so little time with the news and often do not read articles from beginning to end, they demand the most important points high in the story.

TOPPING AN INVERTED PYRAMID

A summary lead generally tops a traditional writing form called an *inverted pyramid*, in which the news is stacked in paragraphs in order of descending importance. The lead summarizes the principal items of a news event. The second paragraph and each succeeding paragraph contain secondary or supporting details in order of decreasing importance. All the paragraphs in the story contain newsworthy information, but each paragraph is less vital than the one before it. This writing form puts the climax of a story at the beginning, in the lead, so it is different from the writing form used for novels, short stories, drama and some news features where an author begins with background and works to a climax.

Examples of the inverted pyramid form can be found in writing done before the mid-nineteenth century, but most journalism historians say that the concept was developed during the American Civil War. Newspaper correspondents in the field sent their dispatches by telegraph. Because they were afraid the system would malfunction or the enemy would cut the wires, the correspondents squeezed the most important information into the first few sentences. Wire services, which used telegraphers to transmit stories until computers were introduced in the early 1970s, have continued to use the inverted pyramid as their staple form of reporting. That enables the wire services to move stories quickly in small chunks and their customers to use the stories in whatever lengths they need.

Newspapers also adopted the inverted pyramid form because it capsulizes the news quickly. It gives readers the convenience of grasping the news of the day by simply skimming lead paragraphs. The form allows readers to decide if they want to continue reading the story or leave it after any one of the paragraphs. An inverted pyramid also can be trimmed from the bottom, which makes it easier to fit it in the tight news holes of a newspaper.

SUMMARY LEADS

THE FIVE W's AND H

A summary lead, generally in no more than 35 words, tells readers the most important of the six primary elements of an event, *the five W's and H*. They are:

- *Who* it happened to or who acted on whom.
- *What* happened or will happen.
- *Where* the action occurred.
- *When* it happened.
- *Why* the action took place; the reason behind it.
- *How* it happened or was solved.

Reporters look for these six elements whenever they cover a news event. It makes no difference how big or small the story is. Reporters gather the facts to answer who, what, where, when, why and how; they rate them for their importance; then they are ready to write a lead and news story.

The most important of the six elements go into a summary lead. The less important elements go into the second and succeeding paragraphs. In most cases it would take too many words to try to put all of the six elements into one lead paragraph; only the most important ones are used.

For example, here is what could occur at a press conference at City Hall. The name and situation are not real, but they are typical. In the press conference, the mayor—we will call her Mayor Kathy Riedy—announced that there will be no property tax increase this year, even though the city will lose more than $3 million in community development grants from the federal government. During her Monday press conference, the mayor said:

> There will be no property tax increase this year. We are not going to ask our residents to pay for the cuts they are suffering because of slashes in the federal budget. We had planned to spend $3 million in community development block grants to rebuild sidewalks that are crumbling in the downtown area. These sidewalks were built during the Depression, and we need to replace them. We will go ahead with the sidewalk project this year, but increased property taxes will not fund it. If we cannot find alternative federal funds, we will attempt to raise the city sales tax, at least for a year, to pay for this vital project.

RATING THE PRIMARY ELEMENTS

While taking notes, a reporter for the local newspaper decides *what* the mayor said about the sidewalk project was the most important point of the press conference; therefore, that will become the top of the inverted pyramid. Riedy covered several topics during the press conference, but she concentrated on the tax issue. Although the mayor said property taxes would not be increased, she said sales taxes may be. In a nice political way, Riedy said the city will not take any money out of one pocket; it will try to take it out of another.

While taking notes, the reporter highlights the five W's and H. That will make it easier to find them while the story is being written. The reporter marks:

- *Who:* Mayor Kathy Riedy.
- *What:* Downtown sidewalks will be rebuilt this year, without an increase in property taxes.
- *Where:* City Hall press conference.
- *When:* Monday.
- *Why:* Cuts in federal budget to cost city $3 million in community block grants.
- *How:* Look for alternative federal funds or increase sales tax.

After the five W's and H are identified, they must be rated according to their importance. That is not always easy for beginning reporters, but here are guidelines that will help:

- *Conduct research.* If possible, do not cover a news event without researching the subject and the people involved. That will make it easier to spot the freshest news, the key issues, elements that have been reported before and the embellishments.
- *Try to identify the five W's and H during the reporting process.* A news story is based on the six primary elements; look and listen for them. While taking notes, highlight them with an asterisk. Underline or put a double asterisk on those that are the most important.
- *Talk to editors.* They often will say what direction they want a story to take.

THE THOUGHT PROCESS BEHIND THE LEAD

Reporters all say the same thing about news writing: While they are interviewing a source, covering a speech or working the scene of a traffic accident, they are thinking about their leads and stories. This thought process begins even before they start taking notes and continues until their stories are completed. They often have their leads in their heads before they actually write their stories.

Several factors can influence how the reporter thinks about the story:

- *What has been reported in the past.* Reporters always are looking for something new. If Mayor Riedy has given six speeches this week in which she discussed exactly the same things about the sidewalk project, the reporter is likely to quit thinking about that as the best lead.
- *How the reporter feels about the subject.* Reporters take their prejudices and emotions into every story they cover. Reporters concerned about the city's sidewalks are more likely to concentrate on what the mayor says about them.
- *How readers feel about the subject.* If the sidewalk project has been an ongoing and controversial issue in the city, reporters should know that. They will want to keep their readers informed on the latest developments.

SUMMARY LEADS

- *Instructions from an editor.* If the boss says, "Get a lead on the sidewalks," the reporter is more likely to concentrate on that issue.

As the mayor talks, the reporter begins thinking about a lead, perhaps in this way:

> The mayor says no property tax increase this year. Sounds like rhetoric. What's she mean? She's going ahead with the sidewalk project. How is she going to pay for it? Bingo! No new property taxes, but she's willing to raise the sales tax. That means that ultimately the taxpayers are going to pay for it. Get as much as possible on that.

WRITING A SUMMARY LEAD

While at a newsroom video display terminal composing the lead, the reporter has to decide how many of the W's and H can be put into the lead while keeping it brief and easy to understand. The *who* is important because whenever the mayor speaks, it affects everyone in the city. *When* she spoke, *what* she said and the reason behind it also are critical to summarizing the story. *Where* she said it and her solution to the problem also are important, but the reporter decides they are not as vital to the summary and can be used in the second paragraph.

The first lead the reporter writes emphasizes the *what* and *why*:

> The city will not increase property taxes this year but still will rebuild downtown sidewalks, even if it loses $3 million in federal community development funds, Mayor Kathy Riedy said Monday.

The second paragraph provides the *how* and *where*:

> However, the mayor said the city sales tax may need to be increased to pay for the project. "If we cannot find alternative federal funds, we will attempt to raise the city sales tax, at least for a year," Riedy said in a City Hall press conference.

Like any journalist, the reporter looks over the initial lead. It is not wrong, but it should have emphasized both the property and sales taxes. By moving up the *how* and then putting the sidewalk project in the second paragraph, the reporter can make the lead stronger. The rewritten lead also begins with the *who*, rather than ending with it, to emphasize who is saying no new taxes here, but new taxes there.

The new lead:

Mayor Kathy Riedy said Monday that the city will not increase property taxes this year to pay for federal funding cuts, but it may have to increase sales taxes.

Second paragraph:

"We had planned to spend $3 million in community development block grants to rebuild sidewalks that are crumbling in the downtown area," Riedy said in a City Hall press conference. "We will go ahead with the sidewalk project this year, but increased property taxes will not fund it."

The reporter can write still other summary leads on the story that emphasize other W's or H. The lead can emphasize the *how:*

The city sales tax may be increased this year if the city cannot find alternative funding sources for a project to rebuild sidewalks, Mayor Kathy Riedy said Monday.

The *why* can be emphasized:

A $3 million cut in federal community block grants will not stop the city from rebuilding downtown sidewalks this year, Mayor Kathy Riedy said Monday.

The *what* and *where* can be emphasized:

Downtown sidewalks will be rebuilt this year without an increase in property taxes, Mayor Kathy Riedy said Monday during a City Hall press conference.

By giving the five W's and H in the beginning paragraphs, the reporter summarized the entire inverted pyramid. All of the key elements were reported in terse paragraphs; they were not crammed into one. Every paragraph in the story should be less important than the one before it,

SUMMARY LEADS

either giving additional details of Riedy's statements on taxes and the sidewalk project or reporting other things she said.

MULTIPLE-ELEMENT SUMMARY LEADS

The lead on Riedy that combined the property and sales taxes is an example of a *multiple-element*, or double-barreled, *summary lead*. Such a lead gives equal rating to two or more of the primary elements and informs an audience immediately that more than one major event is occurring.

Here is another example of a news story topped by a multiple-element summary lead. The story ran in the *Chicago Tribune*.

The lead:

> A 31-year-old motorist was killed and 900 customers in Hammond lost electrical power Thursday after a commuter train plowed into the motorist's car and the wreckage hit a power pole, police said.

This 34-word lead answered four of the W's and H:

- *Who*: A 31-year-old motorist (still unnamed) and 900 electricity customers.
- *What*: Was killed and lost electrical power.
- *Where*: Hammond.
- *When*: Thursday.
- *How*: The train hit the car, which then hit a power pole.

The lead summarized the news event. It also informed readers that two major events occurred: A motorist was killed, and 900 customers lost their power. It could have been shortened by moving the power outage information into the second paragraph, but because the reporter thought the motorist and the outage were equally important, he wrote a multiple-element summary lead.

Second paragraph:

> Killed was Ray Carey, of 749 118th St., Hammond, a steelworker, said Sgt. John Pohl of the traffic division of the Hammond Police Department.

Names usually are not used in the lead paragraph of a news story unless the person is widely known, as in the story about Mayor Riedy. That means it was necessary to put the name of the crash victim—and answer *who*—in the second paragraph. This paragraph also provided the victim's home address and the source of the information.

HOW MANY WORDS?

A summary lead should contain no more than 35 words. Of course, there will be times when more words are needed to summarize the story, but the longer the lead, the greater the risk that it will be difficult to read and/or understand. The general rule to follow when writing a summary lead is:

Use a single sentence of no more than 35 words to summarize the event. Use more words if needed, but make sure that the sentence is easy to understand.

Usually, a lead can be shortened by cutting out unnecessary adjectives. For example, here is a 44-word lead:

Two women were injured and part of Michigan Avenue was closed for nearly seven hours Saturday when a three-alarm fire at a high-rise construction site set off a series of explosions that sent metal and other debris flying across the Magnificent Mile. (*Chicago Tribune*)

This lead was long because it contained multiple elements and tried to get too much information into a single sentence. It reported that two people were injured and that explosions sent metal and other debris across Michigan Avenue, which is one of Chicago's busiest streets and which also is called the Magnificent Mile. Even with multiple elements, however, leads normally can be written in 35 words or fewer. Here is the lead again, with nine words in parentheses that could have been trimmed:

Two women were injured and part of Michigan Avenue was closed (for nearly seven hours) Saturday when a (three-alarm) fire at a high-rise construction site set off a series of explosions that sent (metal and other) debris flying across the Magnificent Mile.

Ten words could have been cut from the following 45-word lead by taking out adjectives and saving the name for the second paragraph. The words that could have been cut are in parentheses:

Two weeks after the Union Carbide gas leak in Bhopal, India, a wealthy Los Angeles property owner (named Surya Gupta) flew back to his native land to help (out) victims of the (industrial) disaster that killed 1,700 and injured (more than) 200,000 (late Dec. 2). (*Los Angeles Times*)

Here are two summary leads that in single, brief sentences summarized the news. The first one did it in 24 words; the second, in 29.

Williston moved into its fourth day of below-zero temperatures today, after a low temperature of 27 degrees

SUMMARY LEADS

below zero was recorded Sunday night. (*Williston, N.D., Daily Herald*)

CHICAGO (AP)—The Chicago Mercantile Exchange has expelled and levied a fine of $100,000 against a member who police believe was associated with a multimillion-dollar commodity scam in the Northwest.

MAKING THEM BETTER

Summary leads should do two things:

- *Summarize the story.*
- *Invite readers inside.*

Putting the most important of the W's and H into the opening paragraph will summarize the story. Using the strongest possible words will entice readers.

The trick to writing a summary lead that summarizes and entices, rather than one that simply wraps up the story, is to continue working on the lead until the best possible combination of words is used. That means:

- *Do not go with the first lead.* After writing an acceptable lead, rewrite it to improve it. Keep saying, "I can make this lead better."
- *Avoid superfluous words.*
- *Avoid redundancies.*
- *Write clearly and concisely.*
- *Use vivid verbs.*
- *Use colorful words.*

For example, this lead was written for a story about the traits women seek in their mates:

Women are likely to be disappointed in their choice for a permanent mate, a study shows.

The lead did summarize the story, but it was dull. It did not sing. Readers could have taken a look at it and said, "So what?"

The writer needed to work on the lead more, to use a better combination of words to better summarize the story.

Here was the rewritten version:

Women want permanent mates who are sensitive, self-assured and warm, but they usually come up cold, a sociologist's report shows.

The rewritten lead used five more words than the original lead, but it still was concise. It did a better job of telling the story. It used more colorful words, which meant readers could "see" the story better.

It also more clearly identified the source. *A study* means nothing to readers unless they know who conducted it. *A sociologist's report* gave the lead authority; it told readers that an expert in the field was the source.

Here is another lead that needed a boost:

Help has arrived for some of the students whose class times conflict

with their favorite soap operas.

This lead was not wrong; it just needed punch. It summarized the story (students could call a number in town to get a soap opera update), but it did not entice. With a little more work, the writer came up with:

Help has arrived for soap opera fans who choose to attend class

even though they would rather dote over daytime dramas.

Writers often can improve their leads if they read them out loud after writing them. This lead was written on a story about a new freeway in town:

Proposition 300 is a "dream list" of poorly researched proposals for

a freeway system that would not benefit taxpayers who are paying for

it but do not use it, a resident said Tuesday.

There are so many short words in this lead that readers would have tripped over them. They would have had to read the sentence two or three times to figure out what it was saying. And, who is this resident making such a profound statement?

The writer worked harder on the lead, coming up with:

Proposition 300 is a "dream list" of poorly researched proposals for

a freeway system that would not benefit the residents who pay for it,

an opponent of the measure said Tuesday.

AVOID CLUTTER LEADS

It's tough to try to cram the five W's and H into a single sentence, so why try? Doing so usually makes for an awkward and difficult-to-understand summary lead, which means lost readers and howling editors. The general rule to follow is:

Put the most important primary elements in the lead. Do not clutter it with all of them. Save the remaining elements for the second, third, fourth and, if needed, later paragraphs.

Following this rule will help avoid a *clutter lead* such as this one, which ran in a university daily:

> An 11-year-old boy who has less than a year to live is doing "remarkably well" after doctors implanted radioactive "seeds" on his cancerous brain tumor last week, the first time such a treatment has been used, a University Medical Center spokesman said.

The writer simply tried to cram too much into this 44-word, multiple-element lead. *The first time such a treatment has been used* should have been saved for the second paragraph. And, there was no reason to put the *last week* time element in the lead. Why tell readers a major element of the story is several days old? The time of the operation should have been used in the second or third paragraph.

AVOID BURIED LEADS

If the most important element of a news story is not in the summary lead, the writer probably *buried* it in another paragraph, which means readers have to hunt for the news. That is not good. A summary lead should provide the key point immediately; it should not keep readers guessing.

A beginning reporter handed this story to the city editor:

> Police Chief John Jones discussed the city's crime problem with interested townspeople at a meeting Monday night.
>
> Jones agreed to meet with residents who have grown increasingly concerned about the safety of their neighborhoods.
>
> The chief said there were more serious crimes reported here in the last 12 months than during any year in the city's history.

The editor scolded the reporter for "burying" the lead in the third paragraph. The most important element of this story obviously was that the police chief revealed that crime in the city was at its highest level ever, not that the chief discussed the problem. Citizens knew the topic of the meeting before it was held. The lead should have read:

> Police Chief John Jones said Monday night that there were more serious crimes reported here last year than during any 12 months in the city's history.

Here was the lead paragraph of a lengthy story about a university radio station:

Saturday marked the first anniversary of Pitt's radio station, WPTS-98.5 FM, and to celebrate, a party was held on the William Pitt Union lawn.

The story was not about the party, however. It was about the problem of running a professional radio station at a university. The fourth paragraph switched to the problems, and the rest of the story dealt with them.

The problems should have been in the lead. The party could have been mentioned in the second, third or fourth paragraph.

Here is another example of a lead that failed to report the news:

Faculty members and school administrators will have a chance to reflect on academic issues in an informal manner this weekend.

Reflect on academic issues and *in an informal manner* mean nothing to readers. The second paragraph told the news. It said the Academic Senate would hold a retreat at a downtown hotel to discuss its structure, purpose and future. *That* should have been the lead.

DETERMINE THE FOCAL POINT

A reporter directs the focus of a summary lead by choosing which of the W's and H to emphasize. If a widely known person is involved in the story, the *who* may be the most important element. In that case, *who* becomes the *focal point* of the lead, and the story probably would start with a name:

WASHINGTON—President Reagan will propose early next month a revolutionary change in farm policies, including a sharp reduction in price supports that have boosted farm income since the 1930s, Agriculture Secretary John Block said Tuesday. (*USA Today*)

or:

PARIS (AP)—Yves Saint Laurent was wired into some hot new colors in his summer ready-to-wear show Wednesday, winding up the Paris show week in which young-looking, short clothes won most kudos.

If a person who is not widely known does something newsworthy, the *what* element may be the focal point of the lead:

FORT WORTH—A firefighter was critically injured Sunday when a wall

SUMMARY LEADS

fell on him as he fought a poolhall blaze three blocks from the station where he had worked for 17 years. (*The Dallas Morning News*)

or:

Noblesville, Ind.—A 12-year-old Noblesville boy was killed Saturday morning when a rifle he took to his room after watching a horror movie accidentally discharged. (*The Indianapolis Star*)

If the *where, when, why* or *how* elements are the most important, one of them should be the focal point of the summary lead.

Where:

HARRISBURG—Ten state and federal investigators fanned out yesterday across south-central Pennsylvania searching poultry farms for signs that an outbreak of potentially devastating avian influenza in Maryland had come from or spread to this state. (*The Philadelphia Inquirer*)

When:

From December to February, the Earth's frigid underbelly, Antarctica, makes itself habitable. (*The Dallas Morning News*)

Why:

Faced with a potential windfall of $30 million in utility tax revenue over the next five years, Kansas City officials on Thursday outlined several spending options that also offer some of the most significant tax reductions in years. (*Kansas City Times*)

How:

Arson was blamed for a fire at the Flatbush Ave. station of the Long Island Rail Road yesterday that spread heavy smoke into nearby subway lines, delaying hundreds of thousands of commuters and straphangers. (*New York Daily News*)

Generally, the reporters covering a news event decide which of the elements are the most important. Sometimes most of the elements can be put into the lead; at other times only one or two may be appropriate.

NO TWO ARE THE SAME

Experienced reporters covering the same news event or interviewing the same people usually will come up with the same basic leads because they are able to pick which of the W's and H are the most important. That does not mean their leads will be worded the same. It means that the key elements of the story will be presented in one form or another in the opening paragraph.

For instance, here are two summary leads from two writers on the same event:

CHICAGO (UPI)—A grand jury indicted 18 people Thursday on charges they bilked homeowners, most of them elderly, out of more than $200,000 through home-repair schemes—including charging an elderly man $50,000 to unplug his toilet.

CHICAGO (AP)—A grand jury investigating home-repair schemes on Thursday indicted 18 people, including a contractor whose company charged an 84-year-old widow $50,000 to fix a leaky toilet.

Both leads emphasized the *what* of this story—grand jury indictments. The *who* was mentioned partially (18 people), but the names were listed later because none of those charged was widely known to most readers and 18 names would take up too much space in the lead. The *where* and *when* (Chicago Thursday) and the *why* (for charging people too much) were in the leads.

There were differences, too. The 35-word UPI lead told readers that the 18 indicted people allegedly bilked people out of more than $200,000, and one of those bilked was an elderly man. The 29-word AP lead contained fewer words and concentrated on another person who allegedly was bilked, an 84-year-old woman. It was more specific because it gave the woman's age and used "widow," a more colorful word than "man."

Of the two wire service leads, the shorter AP lead, which included an 84-year-old widow, was more inviting and probably enticed more readers to continue.

WHERE TO PUT THE TIME ELEMENT

The *time element*, the *when* of a story, is an important part of most summary leads because it conveys immediacy to the reader. It needs to be placed so that it does not disturb the flow of the sentence.

SUMMARY LEADS

AFTER THE VERB

Usually, the best position for the time element is immediately after the verb:

In a surprise shift that could clear the way for state officials to get pay raises, House Minority Leader Lee Daniels said Saturday that he would support "modest" increases. (*Chicago Tribune*)

or:

More than 400 people met Sunday to kick off a volunteer campaign in support of a $195.5 million bond election for the Dallas Independent School District, although officials said certain sections of town may not support the package. (*The Dallas Morning News*)

IN A "COMFORTABLE" SPOT

Sometimes, the time element cannot follow the verb directly because it reads awkwardly in that position. Therefore, it must be moved to a "comfortable" spot in the sentence:

The Reagan administration, responding to mounting criticism and growing nonviolent protests, yesterday described as "rubbish" claims that the president's policies toward South Africa help promote that country's segregationist system. (*The Washington Post*)

In this lead the time element was placed between the subject and verb, which most grammarians would say not to do. It would be awkward, however, to say that the administration "described yesterday." And the time element would not fit comfortably anywhere else in the sentence. Therefore, in this case, the subject and verb were split to make the sentence read more smoothly.

AT THE END

Sometimes the time element is put at the end of the sentence:

KINGMAN—A chair lift-type "aerial gondola" to convey people across the Colorado River between Bullhead City and Laughlin officially received the support of the Mohave County Supervisors Monday. (*Mohave Valley News*, Bullhead City, Ariz.)

AFTER THE OBJECT OF THE VERB

The time element may follow the object of the verb:

> The nation's investors surprised the pundits yesterday and voted with their pocketbooks, pushing the stock market up 14 points in heavy trading during the only Election Day action in the 193-year history of the New York Stock Exchange. (*Chicago Sun-Times*)

AFTER AN ADVERB OR PREPOSITIONAL PHRASE

The time element may follow an adverb or prepositional phrase:

> LONDON (AP)—The sagging British pound rose slightly today after Prime Minister Margaret Thatcher's decision to raise interest rates, but friends and foes of her government said the move was "too little, too late."

or:

> BEIRUT (AP)—Two French cease-fire observers were ambushed and killed in a hail of machine gun fire today as they drove a jeep through a Shiite Moslem area near Beirut's airport, a Christian-controlled radio stations reported.

WRITING IN ACTIVE VOICE

Whenever possible, write summary leads (or any other leads or paragraphs) in active voice rather than passive voice. In active voice the subject acts upon an object; in passive voice the subject is acted upon.

Editors consider active voice more direct and vigorous than passive voice. Here are examples:

> Like the biting Arctic wind that whips across Northwestern's campus, the onset of winter depression numbs many students. (*The Daily Northwestern*, Northwestern University)

or:

> NAPLES, Fla. (AP)—Three major fires and dozens of smaller ones, many of them set by arsonists, rampaged across Florida today after killing a rookie firefighter and devouring about 50,000 acres of woodland dried by cold weather. (Associated Press)

Passive voice should be used only when the person or thing receiving the action is more important than the person or thing doing the acting, as in:

SUMMARY LEADS

Five Northwestern students were arrested Thursday at Scott Hall as more than 70 people protested recruiting on campus by the CIA. (*The Daily Northwestern*, Northwestern University)

or:

Williston teachers were told at an informal forum Wednesday that they can pass or fail the four District 1 House candidates in the Nov. 6 general election. (*Williston*, [N.D.], *Daily Herald*)

In many cases, a lead written in passive voice should be rewritten into active voice. For example, here was the first lead written on a robbery story:

A downtown jewelry story was robbed on Saturday of $50,000 to $100,000 by a "well-dressed" gunman, police said.

It was rewritten to:

A "well-dressed" gunman stole $50,000 to $100,000 from a downtown jewelry store Saturday, police said.

Writing in the active voice does not mean that stories should be written in present tense. Because news stories generally describe events that already have occurred, the sentences should be written in past tense; voice and tense are different from each other and should not be confused.

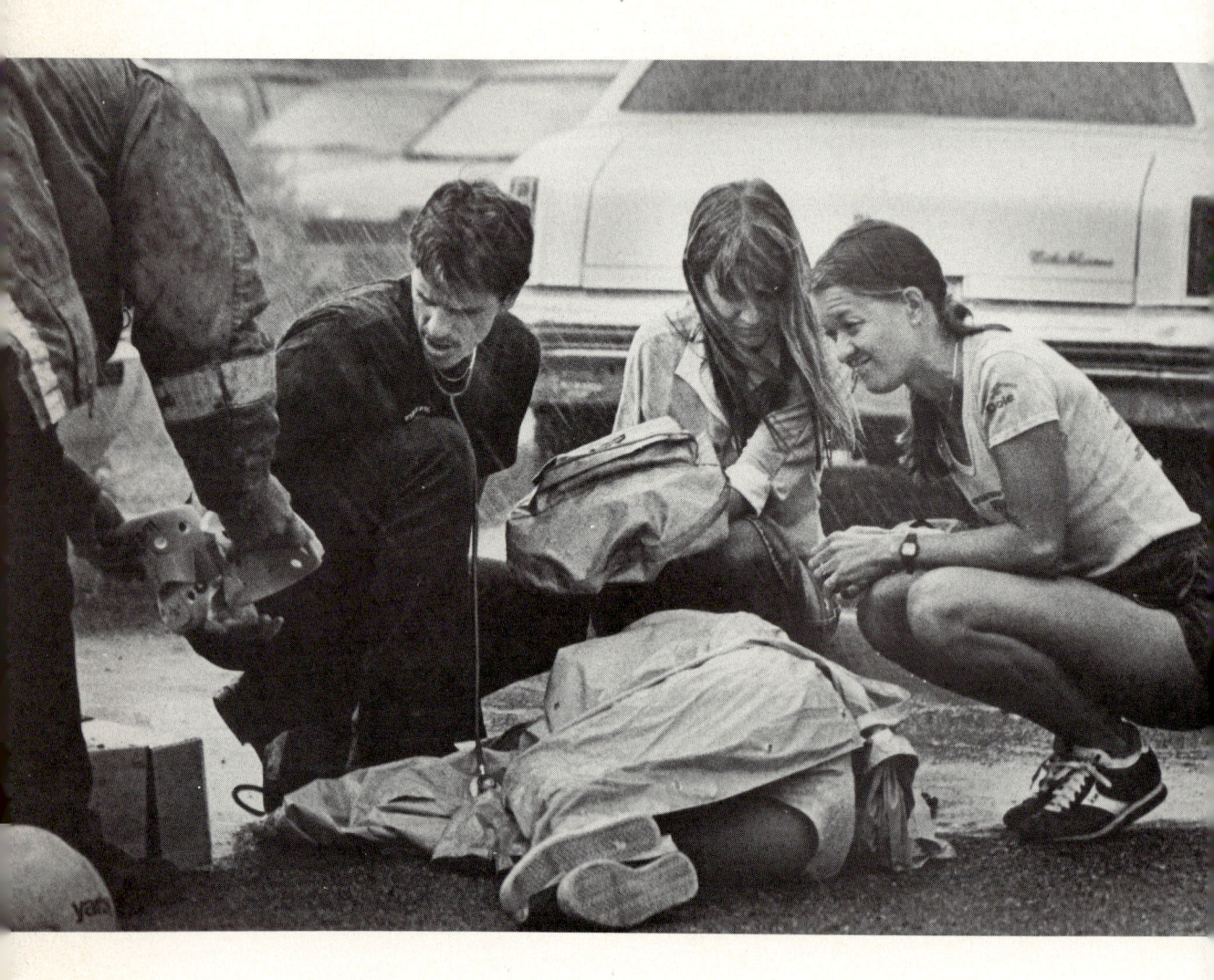

Witnesses to accidents can provide excellent quotes for news stories. (Photo by Ron Kuczek Jr.)

5 / Quotes and Attribution

Strong, vivid quotations can make a flat story bristle; they can supplement generalities with specifics; they can pull a reader emotionally into a story. Through quotes, sources can communicate directly with readers. To achieve maximum impact, quotes must be handled carefully and logically, and they must be attributed.

In this chapter you will be introduced to the following terms:

complete direct quote
partial quote
indirect quote (paraphrase)
"words-in-your-mouth" technique
rambling quote
fragmentary quote

objective verb of attribution
on the record
off the record
on background
on deep background

Quotations can be more than a string of words with punctuation marks surrounding them. They can generate emotion; they can provide vivid description, anecdotes and explanatory or exclusive material. Quotes can be the soul of a news story or feature. They can bring a dull story to life; they can make a good story even better.

Even ordinary statements, when placed in the context of a story, can send tingles down a back. Writing for the *Independent Florida Alligator*, University of Florida journalism major Greg Lamm quoted convicted killer James Dupree Henry, who was about to be put to death:

> "My final words are 'I am innocent,'" Henry said softly after he was strapped in the oak chair at 7:02 a.m., two minutes before he was jolted with 2,000 volts of deadly current. He was pronounced dead at 7:09 a.m.

Lamm went on to quote Florida's governor:

> Gov. Bob Graham, on the other end of an open telephone line, told prison Superintendent Richard Dugger at 7:03 that no stay would be granted. Graham ended the conversation by saying, "God bless us all."

The short direct quotes selected by Lamm enhance the narration. Lamm's description of the minutes leading up to the electrocution is vivid, but the quotation—"My final words are 'I am innocent' "—makes readers realize there is more to the death scene than a lethal electrical charge. A life is being taken, and that person is being given a last chance to reflect on his death. The human angle is further emphasized in the governor's quote: "God bless us all."

In a story published in *The Diamondback* at the University of Maryland, Alfred R. Hogan used direct quotes in an anecdote to move the reader into his story. The story was about Dr. Edward Brandt, a former acting surgeon general and assistant secretary for health in the federal Department of Health and Human Services. Brandt had just been named chancellor of the university's Baltimore campus. Hogan's story began:

> A New York cabbie once made the mistake of asking Dr. Edward Brandt for a smoke.
> "Do you realize you just asked the surgeon general of the United States for a cigarette?" Brandt's astonished aide broke in.
>
> "You mean the surgeon general's a real person? I thought that he was something like Betty Crocker," the cabbie quipped, before dropping Brandt off to make a speech.

QUOTES AND ATTRIBUTION

Quotes can make a reader want to continue with a story. The challenge is learning how and when to use them.

TYPES OF QUOTATIONS

Statements can be handled as:
- Complete direct quotes
- Partial quotes
- Indirect or paraphrased quotes

Assume that, during an interview, attorney John Jones said:

The U.S. Supreme Court will consider some of the most significant First Amendment cases of the decade during the upcoming term. Journalists have grown increasingly concerned about what they perceive to be the anti-press bias of the current court. Therefore, journalists will be watching the court with particular interest this term.

USING DIRECT QUOTES

The reporter could consider the three sentences to be so well stated, vivid and important that a *complete direct quote* (which provides readers with the precise language of the attorney) would be used. Attribution would be placed after the first sentence:

"The U.S. Supreme Court will consider some of the most significant First Amendment cases of the decade during the upcoming term," attorney John Jones said Monday. "Journalists have grown increasingly concerned about what they perceive to be the anti-press bias of the current court. Therefore, journalists will be watching the court with particular interest this term."

USING PARTIAL QUOTES

The reporter also could conclude that only portions of the three sentences are worthy of direct quotation. He could use *partial quotes*, altering the language—but not the meaning—of much of the statement while retaining specific parts of the original sentences. The reporter should make judicious use of partial quotes, striving not to overuse them in bunched parcels, which can be confusing to the reader, or to use them merely because he failed to get the complete quote. Under those circumstances, it generally is better to paraphrase. The reporter here could make good use of partial quotes by writing:

Attorney John Jones said Monday that the U.S. Supreme Court will hear "some of the most significant First Amendment cases of the decade" when it convenes for the upcoming term. Jones said journalists will be particularly interested in the court's actions because of "what they perceive to be the anti-press bias of the current court."

USING INDIRECT, OR PARAPHRASED, QUOTES

Finally, the reporter could conclude that the entire three-sentence quotation would be handled best as an *indirect quote*. He could *paraphrase* the attorney's statement. Being careful to provide attribution, the reporter could write:

Some of the decade's most important First Amendment cases will come before the U.S. Supreme Court this term, attorney John Jones said Monday. The cases will be of particular interest to journalists because many of them view the court as being biased against the media, Jones added.

Whether statements should be handled as direct quotes, as partial quotes or as indirect quotes depends on a number of factors.

WHEN TO USE QUOTES

Whether to quote or to paraphrase is a major consideration reporters face after conducting an interview or listening to a speech. Some reporters use direct quotations sparingly because they do not want to turn their stories completely over to their sources. Others use quotes as often as possible because only then can the speaker talk directly to the audience.

Quote marks around a sentence mean that the words are exactly—or nearly exactly—what the person said. Generally, most editors allow reporters to clean up grammar or to take out profanities in direct quotes. The AP Stylebook says: "Quotations normally should be corrected to avoid the errors in grammar and word usage that often occur unnoticed when someone is speaking but are embarrassing in print."

It is a good idea to sprinkle direct quotes throughout a story. Let the

QUOTES AND ATTRIBUTION 73

source talk to the readers, but make sure that the direct quotes are accurate. When in doubt, paraphrase what the source said. Remember, when paraphrasing what someone said, make sure to attribute it. Tell readers who is behind the statement.

Never make up quotes or paraphrases. This almost goes without saying, but some journalists have confessed to such a practice. Occasionally, however, reporters resort to a *"words-in-your-mouth" technique*, especially when a source never has been interviewed. Be careful here because this is when it becomes too easy to make up quotes. For instance, a reporter is interviewing an inarticulate person who seems to answer every question with a "yep." The reporter appreciates the terse responses and the easy note taking, but a story cannot be filled with "yeps." The reporter says to the person, "Did the pain feel like a sharp, blinding jab in your head?" The response is, "Yep, that is how it was." The reporter then paraphrases the source: Talmond said the pain felt like a sharp, blinding jab in the head. Use the technique when it is absolutely needed, but use it sparingly and never fake it and pass it off as a direct quote. "Yep" answers often are the result of bad questions. Reporters always should phrase questions in ways to elicit meaningful responses. (See Chapter 7 for a discussion of how to phrase questions when conducting interviews.)

GUIDELINES FOR THE USE OF DIRECT QUOTES

Here are some guidelines to consider when deciding whether to quote directly:

• **Use direct quotes on the most specific, vivid statements.** Do not waste a direct quote on a statement such as, "We will consider several important items at our next regularly scheduled council meeting." That statement should be paraphrased and attributed. Direct quotes should be saved for this type of statement: "Our next council meeting will be a blockbuster," Thornton said. "The zoning issue must—and will—be hammered out at that session."

Dan Prescher, writing for *The Gateway*, the campus newspaper at the University of Nebraska at Omaha, interviewed a clinical professor of pediatrics at the Creighton Medical School and a specialist in obstetrics and gynecology at the Women's Services Clinic in Omaha about their reactions to an anti-abortion film.

Prescher could have paraphrased a quote from Paul Byrne, the clinical professor of pediatrics, by writing: Byrne said all people have a right to life. But Prescher chose to quote directly:

"The basic right is the right to life," said Byrne. "The mother has a right to life. The baby has a right to life. Without life there are no other rights."

Byrne's direct quote has punch; it is strong and vivid. Prescher was correct in using the professor's precise words.

The *Gateway* reporter also chose a vivid quote from G.W. Orr, the specialist in obstetrics and gynecology. Again, Prescher could have used a paraphrase. For example: Orr said the question of where life begins can be answered only by individuals. He said people should have the opportunity to decide for themselves. But the reporter chose to use the direct quote:

"What people need is the truth. In the area of when human life begins . . . it'll be answered by individuals in view of their own moral and religious viewpoints. Hopefully [it] will not be answered by people who try to intimidate and coerce everyone to do what they believe."

• **Use direct quotes on particularly descriptive statements.** John Conway focused on Sen. Jesse Helms, R–N.C., in an article he wrote for the University of North Carolina's *Daily Tar Heel*. Conway chose the following direct quote from Helms to describe the senator's feelings about his father:

"My father had a fifth-grade education. Never made over $7,500 in any year of his life. He was a soul of honor," Helms says, grinning pleasantly at the thought. "If I had my one wish, I wish I could be as decent a human being as he was."

Later in the story, Conway quoted Helms' reactions to a legislative bill the senator voted against:

"But it [the bill] had nothing to do with voting rights," Helms counters. "That was already established. It was instead a wolf in sheep's clothing.

"It had a good title, but the guts of it were bad."

That quote, too, enables readers to hear Helms, vividly in his own words, describe his feelings about the proposed legislation.

• **Use direct quotes to describe the innermost feelings of a source.** Michelle Perron, in an article published in *The Daily Reveille* at Louisiana State University, quoted a gay student:

"They [his friends who found out he was gay] didn't have any cause to be afraid of me. . . . I myself was afraid to walk into a gay bar the first time I did," he said. "I had no idea what to expect. I was afraid there would be some wild orgy going on or something. But instead what I found out was that there were a lot of normal people there just like me. That's when I first realized I could still be a normal person and be gay."

QUOTES AND ATTRIBUTION

Quotes packed with such feeling do not come along in every story. When they do, make the most of them.

• **Use direct quotes to help paint a verbal picture of a source's personality.** Kelly Frankeny wrote a story about Dr. "Red" Duke, a native of Texas and professor of surgery at the University of Texas' medical school in Houston who offers medical expertise free in televised news health reports. Note the third paragraph of Frankeny's story, which was published in *The Daily Texan*:

He's Dr. "Red" Duke.
A television star?
"Shit no. I have a hard time with that," says the 56-year-old doctor who's taken to the airwaves to promote "wellness." "I call myself an over-exposed old man."

The story went on to say that Duke wanted to pass along health information to his viewers like an "old country school teacher." The quotes help to paint a picture of Duke's personality. (See Observing Taste in Quotations, on page 78, for a discussion on the use of profanities in direct quotations.)

• **Use direct quotes to supplement a statement of fact.** In a story about Monte Johnson, athletic director at Kansas University, Matt DeGalan wrote in the *Daily Kansan* that Johnson said firing basketball coach Ted Owens and football coach Don Fambrough was difficult. But, the reporter knew that such a statement should not stand by itself. DeGalan followed that observation with these direct quotes from Johnson:

"In my case it was extremely painful, because I cared about those people just like I would about one of my friends," he said. "I think the only thing that probably allows you to survive something like that is that you have to believe what you are doing is right.
"There's still emotion involved in it. There's still frustration involved in it and there's still mixed reaction to it, but I just have to go ahead and put my head on the pillow at night and say I made the most conscientious decision I could make with the facts I had available, and nobody will give you total credit for that."

• **Use direct quotes to capture exchanges in dialogue.** In a personality profile on television investigative reporter John Camp, Donna Moss of Louisiana State University's *Daily Reveille* used dialogue to illustrate how Camp got into the business. Moss recounted an early career exchange between Camp and the manager of a small radio station:

"Camp, you ever done any news?"
"Nope," he quickly shot back.
"You ever want to do any news?"
"Nope."
"Well, you're going to do the news."
"Okay."

- **Use direct quotes to avoid having to use attribution before or after every sentence.** Assume, for example, that Kareem Abdul-Jabbar of the Los Angeles Lakers, the leading scorer in National Basketball Association history, said this after a Laker victory over the Boston Celtics in a championship series game:

> I am uncomfortable with the threatening talk by players from both teams, with the escalation of rugged play in the games and the possibility of a brawl at any time. I think basketball is to be played as a game of beauty, not as an exhibition of brawn. But if someone brings a tire iron to the game, I am forced to respond in kind.

If Jabbar's statement is handled as a direct three-sentence quotation, it would read like this (with attribution following only the first sentence):

"I am uncomfortable with the threatening talk by players from both teams, with the escalation of rugged play in the games and the possibility of a brawl at any time," Kareem Abdul-Jabbar said. "I think basketball is to be played as a game of beauty, not as an exhibition of brawn. But if someone brings a tire iron to the game, I am forced to respond in kind."

If Jabbar's statement is used as an indirect quote, attribution would have to be provided for every sentence. This could get cumbersome. It does help, however, to vary the writing by alternating the placement of the attribution. For example:

Kareem Abdul-Jabbar said he is not comfortable with the talk, the escalation of rugged play and the promise of a brawl. Basketball is a game of beauty, not brawn, he said. But if tire iron tactics are used by the opposition, he said he will respond in kind.

QUOTATION PITFALLS TO AVOID

Reporters easily can fall into traps when quoting sources. Here are some guidelines to consider:

- **Beware of inaccuracies in quotes.** Reporters should verify quotations that sound suspect. If, for example, there is a bad connection or background noise when interviewing by telephone, always verify the quote. That will reduce the chance of error. It is easy to simply say: "I was distracted by

QUOTES AND ATTRIBUTION   77

the noise on the line. Could you repeat that for me, please?" Or: "Let me make sure I have that quote right. Could I read it back to you?"

Reporters should check further if the quote the source verifies still sounds suspect. For example, the manager of a local factory said: "My company employs 250 people—more than any firm in town." The reporter asks for verification; the manager confirms the quote. However, Chamber of Commerce figures show that his firm employs 200 workers—and there are 12 companies in town that employ more.

If follow-ups reveal that the quote is inaccurate, the reporter could call the source back to ask if there is an explanation for the discrepancy, or the quote could be left out. If the original source insists that his information is correct, that source can be quoted along with the conflicting information from a different source.

• **Beware of rambling quotes.** Some sources love to hear themselves talk. If their long, drawn out *rambling quotes* bore the reporter, chances are they also will bore readers. Assume a judge said:

> Because of the sensationalism surrounding the trial, I want to make sure the accused receives a fair hearing. Now, of course, I understand that the press will want to extensively cover the trial. And, according to *Richmond Newspapers* v. *Virginia*, the press has a right to attend public trials, absent overriding considerations. Now, good members of the press, you won't find a more fervent defender of First Amendment rights than I am, but, as a judge sworn to perform my duties fairly, let me tell you that I will do everything in my power to see to it that the accused receives a fair trail, for he, too, has basic Sixth Amendment rights that guarantee him as much.

The judge might have said it—and the reporter dutifully might have written it down. But getting accurate, direct quotes does not carry with it a license to bore readers unnecessarily. Under these circumstances, paraphrase the statement and possibly supplement it with some partial quotes.

• **Beware of "hard-to-understand" direct quotes.** When reporters interview lawyers, physicians, engineers or research scientists, chances are some of the quotations gathered will not be understandable to lay readers. In these instances, reporters must work diligently to paraphrase the quotation into understandable terms, to get the source to rephrase it or to supplement it with an explanatory paragraph.

Journalism Professor Edward Sylvester of Arizona State University, the author of two books based on science research and extensive interviews with scientists, said: "Science writing may be one of the few areas of reporting in which writers frequently show long quotes and even whole stories to sources before publication. The reason is that the material is often so complex and shades of meaning can change intention so much that even a close associate might put a statement in a way the source would consider quite wrong. On the other hand, as a popular writer/reporter, you cannot quote technical material in the precise yet dense language of the science specialty. The result of these two demands—for precision yet simplicity—is often a 'negotiated settlement,' in which the writer attempts to translate a difficult quote on the spot: 'Could we say that . . . ?' Or, 'In other words, you've found that . . .' Often as not, the answer is no, with an attempt to elucidate by the scientist and a reattempt to interpret by the reporter.

"This process is all the more important when you consider how often the words 'breakthrough,' or 'major discovery' or, most value-loaded of all, 'cure' appear in the press. It is extremely important to the public's interest and its perception of science that such words be used with the greatest care. To further complicate matters, the journalist who has just completed such a task may in the future be in a standard adversarial relationship to a source, rightly unwilling to reveal all information in hand until publication."

• **Beware of reconstructing quotes.** Do not add things to a quotation to make it better or to cover up your failure to get the entire quote. Use it merely as a partial quote or as an indirect quote. Do not take a partial quote (an incomplete sentence) and add your words to make it a complete sentence.

• **Beware of fragmentary quotes.** *Fragmentary quotes*—quotes used in extremely small parcels that are spread throughout a paragraph—serve no purpose. When set in type, they look confusing:

Sen. Johnson said he wanted to take care of the problem "immediately." He said that it was a "pressing issue" that should not be put "on hold." According to the senator, the issue will "come before the legislature" before the week "is half over." He said he is "anxious" to go about "settling" the matter.

Best advice on the use of fragmentary quotes: Don't.

• **Beware of ungrammatical quotes.** Assume a source said: "I intend to pursue this matter with all the energy I can summon." Do not write: Sen. Johnson said he will "pursue this matter with all the energy he can summon." Instead, write: Sen. Johnson said, "I intend to pursue this matter with all the energy I can summon." Or: "I intend to pursue this matter with all the energy I can summon," Sen. Johnson said. Remember: Quote marks mean you are using the precise words of the speaker. The speaker would not have referred to himself as "he" in a direct quote.

OBSERVING TASTE IN QUOTATIONS

The Associated Press Stylebook addresses the use of obscenities, profanities and vulgarities: "Do not use them in stories unless they are part of direct quotations and there is a compelling reason for them."

QUOTES AND ATTRIBUTION

HANDLING OFFENSIVE LANGUAGE

The AP always alerts editors to stories that contain profanities, indicating that the language might be offensive to some readers. Editors then can decide whether to leave it in or delete it. The AP also tries to limit the offensive language to paragraphs that can be deleted easily.

The AP Stylebook further notes:

> In reporting profanity that normally would use the words *damn* or *god*, lowercase *god* and use the following forms: *damn, damn it, goddamn it*. Do not, however, change the offending words to euphemisms. Do not, for example, change *damn it* to *darn it*.
>
> If a full quote that contains profanity, obscenity or vulgarity cannot be dropped but there is no compelling reason for the offensive language, replace letters of an offensive word with a hyphen. The word *damn*, for example, would become d--- or ----.

The Washington Post's Deskbook on Style notes that the test of whether to use an obscenity should be " 'why use it?' rather than 'why not use it?' " The *Post*'s stylebook urges reporters to check individual cases with appropriate editors. The *Post* advocates, when a profanity must be used, the "s--- form, which serves the purpose of communicating without jarring sensibilities any more than necessary."

Policies on the use of profanity can vary among media outlets. Always check with a supervising editor if you are unsure of how to handle a quote.

USE OF DIALECT

Use of dialect also can be a matter of taste; dialect often appears to ridicule the subject in condescending fashion. The AP Stylebook points out that dialect—"the form of language peculiar to a region or a group, usually in matters of pronunciation or syntax"—should not be used "unless it is clearly pertinent to a story."

The New York Times Manual of Style and Usage advises: "Unless a reporter has a sharp ear and accurate notes he would do well to avoid trying to render dialect."

ATTRIBUTION

Attribution tells readers the source of information. Not every piece of information, however, requires attribution. In the following lead paragraphs, a reliable source—either an individual or a government entity—provided the factual information, and the reporters knew beyond reasonable doubt that what they were writing was true:

> Evansville will earmark $750,000 or more for resurfacing and repairing city streets this year, several times the amount spent last year. (*The Evansville* [Ind.] *Press*)

> Secretary of State George Schultz returned home Wednesday without setting a time or place for a U.S.–Soviet summit meeting or erasing an impasse in arms-control negotiations. (Associated Press)

Attribution for some factual information would be ludicrous:

> Omaha Burke blasted Lincoln High 81–54 in a non-conference high school basketball game Friday night, according to the team's statistician.

Attribution is needed, however, when opinions or other information subject to change or controversy are cited. For example:

> The Trans Alaska Pipeline may have to be shut down temporarily so that a sagging section of pipe under the Dietrich River can be bypassed, according to the line's operators. (*Fairbanks* [Alaska] *Daily News-Miner*)

VERBS OF ATTRIBUTION

Because *said* is a neutral verb, it nearly always should be used in the attribution for news stories. *Added* also can be used because it, too, is an *objective verb of attribution*. Susan Sheehan, writing in *The New York Times Magazine*, noted that syndicated columnist Jack Anderson often allowed subjective perception to dictate his choice of verbs of attribution. She wrote: "Anderson's characters rarely have something to say, state or comment upon; they whine, huff, snort, grump, mutter, bare their fangs, or worse." Such a style might be appropriate for opinion columnists such as Anderson or in some features stories, but it is not appropriate for reporters who write straight news stories.

Using *said* as the verb of attribution might seem repetitive and unimaginative, but reporters do not have to bombard readers with it after every

QUOTES AND ATTRIBUTION

sentence. Some newspapers continue to follow the practice that loose-hanging quotes (quotes without an attributive tag) are unacceptable. Other newspapers allow them, however, if a source is quoted in two or more consecutive paragraphs. Here, attribution at the end of the first paragraph effectively tells readers who the speaker is:

"I think the budget will be approved at our next meeting," council member Susan Long said.

"I am sure the special interest groups will be out in force. We'll have to weigh both sides carefully.

"I'm confident we'll arrive at the correct decision."

Long added that she thought this year's budget was the most explosive issue the council had dealt with in four years.

Verbs of Attribution to Avoid

Here are some verbs of attribution that generally should be avoided:

- asserted
- bellowed
- claimed
- contended
- cried
- declared
- demanded
- emphasized
- hinted
- harangued
- maintained
- opined
- stated
- stammered
- stressed

Because verbs of attribution refer to speech and not to conduct or action, they should *not* be used in ways that suggest physical impossibilities:

"This is the best day of my life," Jones smiled.

"It will be a difficult task," Johnson grimaced.

The reporter should write:

"This is the best day of my life," Jones said with a smile.

"It will be a difficult task," Johnson said with a grimace.

Use of Verbs of Attribution

Verbs of attribution can be found in most stories. A portion of an article by Emil Venere, published in the *Tempe* (Ariz.) *Daily News Tribune*, is reprinted below. The verbs of attribution are italicized.

Democratic gubernatorial hopeful Bill Schulz *told* a group of supporters Saturday that inferior education for poor people and prison overcrowding are tied together and must be solved by first improving inner-city school programs.

Schulz, 54, also *said* the state has failed to provide care for chronically depressed people, another factor associated with the failure to rehabilitate jail inmates and help indigent children on the road to success.

The as yet unofficial Democratic candidate for governor spoke to about 75 members of the East Valley Democratic Breakfast Club during a regular 8 a.m. meeting in Mesa. The founder and former president of WRS Investments, an apartment-management firm in Arizona, *said* he intends to formally announce his candidacy in September.

Schulz has toured eight states, speaking to governors and officials about pressing economic problems, he *said*, and expects to visit two more by the end of this year.

"How can one person be really equipped to deal with all of them (issues)?" he *asked*.

By studying the ways in which other states have dealt with the same kinds of problems, he *answered*.

"We have got nothing in this state that can't be fixed," he *said*.

Calling high costs for prison operation and inmate overcrowding a horrendous problem, he *said*, "We're going to have to raise taxes just to operate our prisons."

Arizona is spending roughly $140 million, including special appropriations, to run its prisons this fiscal year. Next year, including all legislative appropriations, that figure will be closer to $167 million, he *said*.

"We're getting a lousy return," he *said*. At an average annual cost of $18,000 an inmate, prisoners who are not rehabilitated are a constant drag on the state's economy, while many students from indigent families are likely to become dropouts and end up in jail because of Phoenix's poor inner-city school programs.

"They're going to be tax users rather than tax producers," he *said*. "The people who need the education the most are getting the worst education."

IDENTIFICATION IN ATTRIBUTION

Seldom is a person so well known that his or her name will stand by itself in a lead. Thus, attribution usually identifies the source by title and name. For example:

Parking fees at the Fairbanks International Airport are scheduled to become a reality by early summer, according to airport manager Doyle Ruff. (*Fairbanks* [Alaska] *Daily News-Miner*)

Measures ordered Monday by a federal judge to prevent suicide at the El Paso County Jail were already being taken or were being planned, Sheriff Bernard Berry said Thursday. (*Colorado Springs Gazette Telegraph*)

First and last names are used on first reference, but only last names should be used in subsequent attribution.

Sometimes, to streamline the writing, only the title of the person is used in the lead. The person's name is used in a subsequent paragraph. For example:

A mining company in the Circle Mining District was fined and forced to shut down its operation last summer not because it violated regulations any more than other miners, but because it dared to point it out, according to their Fairbanks attorney.

Lynette and Dexter Clark were forced by the Environmental Protection Agency to shut down work at their mine last August after they refused to apply for a discharge permit. The EPA and the Clarks' attorney, William Satterberg, settled the dispute in December, but Satterberg said he is dissatisfied with the outcome. (*Fairbanks* [Alaska] *Daily News-Miner*)

Titles also should be used for attribution in leads when the opinion has been expressed by more than one person. Note also that when attributing statements to more than one person, direct quotes are not used:

Steps have been taken to improve leadership, morale and communications within the Colorado Springs Police Department in the past year, but internal problems have not disappeared, five City Council members said Monday. (*Colorado Springs Gazette Telegraph*)

Attribution in leads can lack specificity if a spokesperson is repeating an official position:

President Reagan has decided to postpone introduction of his tax-simplification package until May 28 because congressional leaders fear that it might interfere with debate over the budget, the White House said Wednesday. (Associated Press)

In paragraphs that follow the lead, first-reference attribution should contain the person's name and title or other means of identification. For example:

"I didn't know her well, but I thought she was a wonderful person,"

said a neighbor, Helen Johnson.

"She was one of the finest students I ever taught," said Gerald

Sylvester, a geography professor at State University.

Reporters also need to be aware of what some editors call "hearsay attribution." This is when a statement is made to sound as though it came from one source but actually came from another. For example: "Smith said he knocked one mugger down and then chased the other man two blocks before bringing him to the ground with a driving tackle." Actually, the reporter never talked to Smith. Instead, he relied on a police report. It is dangerous, as well as misleading, to write a sentence that merely implies attribution. If it sounds like a good angle, check with the source. In this case, the reporter should give Smith a call.

PLACEMENT OF ATTRIBUTION

Attribution usually *follows* the information because what is said normally is more important than who said it. For example:

Soviet armored units killed more than 1,000 men, women and children in attacks on a dozen villages in Afghanistan suspected of helping guerrillas fighting the communist government, Western diplomats said Tuesday. (Associated Press)

What appears to be an important advance in developing an X-ray-laser space weapon powered by a nuclear bomb has been made by scientists at the Lawrence Livermore National Laboratory, federal scientists said Tuesday. (*The New York Times*)

Sometimes, however, the attribution can be of such significance or relevance that it *precedes* the information. For example:

President Reagan announced Tuesday that he will nominate Lewis Arthur Tambs to become ambassador to Costa Rica after the diplomat leaves a similar post in Bogota, Colombia, because of reported death threats. (*The Arizona Republic*)

Financial experts believe Beaumont city officials ignored some standard practices that might have saved the city's investment when a securities firm through which it invested collapsed. (*Beaumont* [Texas] *Enterprise*)

GUIDELINES FOR HANDLING ATTRIBUTION

The following guidelines should be considered when handling attribution for direct quotations:

• **When quoting single sentences directly, attribution usually follows the quote:**

"The prices will continue to escalate," he said.

It is permissible, however, to introduce the sentence with its attribution:

He said, "The prices will continue to escalate."

• **When quoting multiple sentences directly, attribution normally follows the first sentence.** The reader should not have to meander through two or more complete sentences before being told who the speaker is. Note how confusing the following is:

"The proposal to change school district boundaries needs to be put into operation immediately. This change is necessary to distribute stu-

QUOTES AND ATTRIBUTION

dents evenly throughout the various schools in our system," superintendent Henry Smith said.

"School district boundary lines do not have to be changed. Many of the building principals merely are afraid their teachers will have to work harder if enrollments at their schools increase. The whole proposal is the self-serving idea of a handful of principals," said school board member Ben Johnson.

• **When speakers change, new attribution should be placed before the first quoted sentence.** Note the confusion in the following example:

"The Nuggets keyed on Kareem," said Lakers coach Pat Riley. "Some call it good defense, and others call it karate."

"The Lakers were the ones throwing the elbows and tackling us," said Denver coach Doug Moe.

The change of speakers should have been noted immediately. For example:

"The Nuggets keyed on Kareem," said Lakers coach Pat Riley. "Some call it good defense, and others call it karate."

Denver coach Doug Moe said, "The Lakers were the ones throwing the elbows and tackling us."

Often, though, a transition sentence is the most effective way to let readers know when speakers change:

"The Nuggets keyed on Kareem," said Lakers coach Pat Riley. "Some call it good defense, and others call it karate."

Denver coach Doug Moe saw it differently.

"The Lakers were the ones throwing the elbows and tackling us," he said.

• **Attribution can precede a multiple-sentence direct quotation (though many editors prefer that attribution always follow the first sentence).** When this occurs, the attribution should be followed by a colon:

Council member John P. Jones said: "We expect to ratify the new budget at our next meeting. We think we have worked out all the problems. It has been a difficult four weeks."

• **Attribution to the same speaker should not be used more than once in a quote, even if the quote continues for several paragraphs.** This construction should be avoided:

"We expect to ratify the next budget at our next meeting," council member John P. Jones said. "We think we have worked out all the problems," he noted. "It has been a difficult four weeks," he observed.

• **If a partial quote is followed by a complete direct quote, use attribution between them:**

No decision has been made on whether Israel will attack "with all we have," Eitan said. "We are sitting and waiting."

PUNCTUATION FOR QUOTES AND ATTRIBUTION

Punctuation often plagues reporters who deal with quotations and attribution. Here are some guidelines:

• **When introducing a direct quotation with attribution, place a comma after the verb and before the opening quotation marks:**

Jones said, "We will be there tomorrow."

• **When introducing an indirect quote with attribution, do not place a comma after the verb:**

Jones said he would be there Wednesday.

• **When following an indirect quote with its attribution, place a comma before the attribution:**

He will be there Wednesday, Jones said.

• **Always place commas and periods inside closing quotation marks.** Do not, for example, write:

QUOTES AND ATTRIBUTION

"All of our transcontinental flights are full", she said.

Instead, write:

"All of our transcontinental flights are full," she said.

Do not write:

She said, "All of our transcontinental flights are full".

Instead, write:

She said, "All of our transcontinental flights are full."

• **Always place colons and semicolons outside the closing quotation marks:**

Coach Jones said it was his "dumbest mistake": deciding to start an untested freshman at quarterback.

And:

Coach Jones said it was his "dumbest mistake"; he should not have started an untested freshman at quarterback.

• **Placement of a question mark depends on whether it belongs to the quotation or to the surrounding sentence.** Because the question mark belongs to the quoted passage—and not to the surrounding sentence—the following example is incorrect:

Coach Jones asked his team, "Can we win this game"?

It should be punctuated like this:

Coach Jones asked his team, "Can we win this game?"

Because the question mark belongs to the surrounding sentence—and not to the quotation—the following example is incorrect:

Did coach say, "We'll have to wait and see?"

It should be punctuated like this:

Did coach say, "We'll have to wait and see"?

Because the question mark belongs to the quoted passage—and not to the surrounding sentence—the following example is incorrect:

"Will we continue to win"? asked the coach.

It should be punctuated like this:

"Will we continue to win?" asked the coach.

Because the question mark belongs to the surrounding sentence—and not to the quoted passage—the following example is incorrect:

Why does every coach say "we're going to win this game?"

It should be punctuated like this:

Why does every coach say "we're going to win this game"?

Remember: If the quoted passage itself asks the question, the question mark should appear *inside* the quote marks; if the surrounding sentence asks the question, the question mark should appear *outside* the quote marks.

• **A quotation within a quotation should be set off in single quotation marks.** The following example is incorrect:

"Johnson's plea to "win this game for the community" really fired us up," Smith said.

It should be punctuated like this:

"Johnson's plea to 'win this game for the community' really fired us up," Smith said.

Or like this:

QUOTES AND ATTRIBUTION 89

"Johnson made a plea to 'win this game for the community,'" Smith said.

If you use a quotation within a quotation that quotes a third party, that quote should be in double marks. For example:

"I was shocked," the parent added, "when coach Johnson screamed, 'As my predecessor said, "Let's kill 'em."'"

• **Remember to insert closing quotation marks.** When working on deadline, it is easy to forget to provide closing quote marks. Note the following:

"We're so enthused about this project we can't stop thinking about it, Jones said.

It should be punctuated like this:

"We're so enthused about this project we can't stop thinking about it," Jones said.

• **Closing quotation marks are not needed at the end of a paragraph if the same speaker continues directly to the next paragraph.** The following is incorrect:

"We're so enthused about this project we can't stop thinking about it," Jones said. "We look forward to getting council approval."
"We hope that will come at the next meeting," Jones added.

It should be punctuated like this:

"We're so enthused about this project we can't stop thinking about it," Jones said. "We look forward to getting council approval.

"We hope that will come at the next meeting."

• **When a quotation is interrupted with its attribution, remember to insert additional marks.** Note the following incorrect example:

"Get in there now," the coach said, before I make you run extra laps."

It should be punctuated like this:

"Get in there now," the coach said, "before I make you run extra laps."

• **When reporting dialogue, start a new paragraph with each change of speaker.** For example:

"I think it is wise to lengthen the school year," Smith said.

"It would be ludicrous to do so," Johnson said.

"I think the only ludicrous thing around here is you," Smith said.

"Let's keep this discussion on a higher plateau," Johnson said.

Do not run the dialogue into a paragraph such as this:

"I think it is wise to lengthen the school year," Smith said. "It would be ludicrous to do so," Johnson said. "I think the only ludicrous thing around here is you," Smith said. "Let's keep this discussion on a higher plateau," Johnson said.

ANONYMOUS SOURCES

Each time reporters conduct interviews, they face the risk that their sources will request anonymity. Therefore, reporters in any size market must learn how to deal with people who are willing to provide information as long as their names are not used in the story. There are no hard and fast rules on dealing with requests for anonymity because every story is different, but there are general guidelines to follow.

GUIDELINES TO OBSERVE

Be up front with the source. Establish rules for the interview *before* it begins. That way, there should be no misunderstanding about how the material can be used. Never assume that sources, particularly those who

QUOTES AND ATTRIBUTION

are not accustomed to working with the media, understand established conventions that deal with the use of material.

These conventions are:

- *On the record.* All material can be used, complete with the name of the source and identification. For example: "We expect a quick settlement of the strike," said John P. Johnson, secretary of labor.
- *Off the record.* The material cannot be used. Period. Reporters must decide whether the information they potentially could gain under these circumstances is worth it. Often, reporters refuse to accept information off the record, choosing instead to try to ferret it from another source.
- *On background.* The material can be used, but attribution by name cannot be provided. For example: "We expect a quick settlement of the strike," a high-ranking Labor Department official said.
- *On deep background.* The material can be used, but not in direct quotations. Also, the material cannot be attributed to the source. For example: A quick settlement of the strike is expected. Reporters can, however, seek verification from other sources and possibly get them to agree to being quoted. If no verification can be found, the reporter must decide whether to take a chance on using the material. Editors should be consulted in these circumstances. If the material proves false or incorrect, the reporter and the newspaper are left holding the bag.

It is a good practice to tell the source immediately, "I am a reporter working for the *River City News.*" Then it is the source's responsibility to practice self-control because he or she should know that everything that is said is on the record, unless other arrangements have been worked out prior to the interview.

MAKING DECISIONS ON A CASE-BY-CASE BASIS

Some sources know that they are talking to a reporter and still ask for anonymity after they have talked too long and too much. When that happens—and it does quite often—reporters must decide whether to use the name anyway or to respect the source's wishes.

In making this decision, reporters must consider the importance of the story, the value of the source and the editorial policies of their employers.

For example, a prosecuting attorney in a murder case calls to tell you that the defendant has agreed to plead guilty to a charge of killing a 22-year-old woman. The attorney gives you the information, but then says, "The judge has told us not to discuss this, so don't use my name—this is on deep background."

You could say, "Look, you've worked with reporters before; you can't establish a non-attribution ground rule after you've given me the information." Or, you could reason that you will need the attorney again as a source. It is just as easy to make a few more calls to confirm the information as it is to use the attorney's name in the story and risk getting her in trouble or losing her as a source. Once the material is checked with other reliable sources, your lead can say (without attribution):

```
A Brookfield man has agreed to plead guilty to a charge of killing a
22-year-old woman.
```

Or you can use this construction:

```
A Brookfield man has agreed to plead guilty to a charge of killing a
22-year-old woman, according to sources close to the case.
```

Developing a strong network of reliable sources is the key to being an effective reporter, which means you sometimes will have to acquiesce when a source requests anonymity.

Sometimes anonymous sources are government or corporate officials who do not want their names used because they believe that their bosses or the institutions for which they work should have credit for the statement. For instance, "City Hall said today" may be the mayor's top aide discussing the police department's negotiations with City Hall for additional funding. The reporters know who said it, but they use the nameless attribution because that was the condition for the interview.

Anonymous sources also are valuable because they can lead you to other sources; do not turn them off simply because they do not want their names used. Explain to them newspaper policies regarding the use of anonymous sources and the importance of their being identified in the story. Often people can be convinced to go on the record if they realize how vital the story is and that without an identified source it may never be printed. If nothing works, look for other sources, using the unnamed source for guidance.

Quill published a story by John Doe, a person the magazine said wanted "to remain anonymous, mostly because his bosses don't approve of anonymous sources, and he'd like to preserve his job." The magazine said Doe covered stories of "national and international importance."

Doe wrote: "In these days of the credibility gap, decent, clean-living reporters are supposed to abhor...nameless sources. But if they never quoted one, their copy would lose much of its value."

Doe said reporters for large media outlets, in order to gain access to and publish certain information, routinely use anonymous sources. "Refusal to do so would deprive the public of much information it needs to form opinions about national and world affairs," he wrote. Doe emphasized, however, that "a conscientious reporter has to judge the reliability of the source, the facts that the source is professing to give and especially whether or not the source has a motive to distort the facts for a cause or for personal gain."

SOME POLICIES ON ANONYMOUS SOURCES

"Reporters must name the source of information in every story whenever possible," the *Denver Post*'s policy regarding sources states. "Exceptions must be thoroughly discussed with editors and house counsel." The paper also tells its reporters to avoid using unnamed sources if possible and when confronted with them to seek alternative sources and documentation.

The *Bangor* (Maine) *Daily News* instructs its reporters: "If reporter and editor see clear need for confidentiality, the reason for anonymity should be explained in the story as fully as possible short of identification. If the reason isn't good, scrap the source and the quote." Also, "Information from an anonymous source should be used only if at least one source substantiates the information."

Reporters must work hard to organize their stories so they flow smoothly from beginning to end. This editor at the *Detroit Free Press* evaluates a story to make sure it is organized logically. (Photo by Ellis Herwig/The Picture Cube)

6 / Organizing a News Story

Organizing a news story effectively is important. If the lead draws readers into the story, what follows must hold them to the end. To do this, reporters must write in a clear style that flows from paragraph to paragraph.

In this chapter you will be introduced to the following terms:

body   background
criss-cross directory   transition
bullets   hourglass style

When the call came in, it seemed almost unbelievable. At about the time extra police and fire units were being summoned over the police radio, which is monitored in the newsroom, a hysterical woman telephoned the city desk to say a person was dangling upside down outside a window of a high-rise apartment building.

Within seconds, reporters and photographers were in action. If a person were indeed dangling out of a high-rise, it could be a major news story, either of a man or woman falling to his or her death or of a dramatic rescue by firefighters and police officers. Reporters never know what they will find when they are sent to the scene of an emergency, where news is breaking, but here is where they must be their best. Every second will be critical.

In this case there indeed was a person dangling out of the window, 16 floors above a busy street. She was a 49-year-old woman who reportedly had swallowed sleeping pills and ammonia and slit her throat before diving out the window. However, somehow her heavy pullover robe had snagged the window, which slammed shut, leaving her dangling upside down. As about 100 onlookers and scores of firefighters and police gathered beneath her, she kicked frantically to free the robe so she could complete her ghastly attempt at suicide.

Two of the reporters assigned to the story were Lauren Silverman and Mark Eissman of the *Chicago Tribune*. While Silverman raced to the scene, Eissman worked the phones from the newsroom. It also was Eissman's job to write the story.

Because activity at the scene was over within minutes, most of the work of gathering information for the story had to be done over the phone. "All we really knew was that some woman apparently was attempting to commit suicide and somehow dangled out the window for about 10 minutes before being rescued," Eissman said.

AN INVERTED PYRAMID

When reporters cover news, they always are thinking of the stories they must write. They usually write their leads first, often composing them mentally while interviewing or checking records. When they write their stories, they must present the news in a clear style that flows from paragraph to paragraph.

Most breaking news stories are written in inverted pyramid style, in which the most important of the five W's and H are in the lead. What comes after the lead also is important. The lead should interest readers; the *body*, or middle, of the story should hold them until the conclusion.

The story that Eissman wrote on the woman dangling upside down from the high-rise illustrates a typical inverted pyramid with a beginning, middle and conclusion. The who, what, where, when, why and how of the event were high in the story, which could have been trimmed from the bottom. Along with the hard news facts, transitions and quotes were used to keep the story flowing and readers reading. And it ended with news, albeit the least important, which was an effective way to conclude the story without saying "the end." There even were a couple of things the writers should have avoided, which will be discussed as the story is analyzed paragraph by paragraph.

SHOULD A SUICIDE BE COVERED?

Despite a policy at the *Tribune* not to run stories of suicides or attempts, Eissman said his editors wanted to print this story because of the drama of the attempt and rescue. However, they decided not to reveal the woman's name or address.

The *Tribune*'s policy on suicide or suicide-attempt stories is not unusual. Most newspapers choose not to run such stories because of a sensitivity toward families or survivors. Most follow the same general guideline: They do not report a suicide or an attempt unless it is unusual or involves a widely known person.

"After we finished, I thought one last time about our decisions to write the story the way we did," said Eissman, who has a law degree. "I thought the work of the fire department should be highlighted. I was comfortable about our decision to say as little about the woman as was possible."

WORKING THE PHONES

To cover the story adequately, Eissman had to call as many people as possible before his deadline, and he ran into the same obstacles that all reporters face. "I called the head of the fire department battalion that had responded to the call and was told he'd call me back shortly," Eissman said. "I tried to reach a relative of the woman, but there was no answer."

He was able to talk to a spokesman at the hospital where the woman was taken, who gave him her age and told him she was in fair condition. Next he checked a *Haines Criss-Cross Directory*, which reporters use to find names and phone numbers when they know only addresses. A criss-cross directory is a big help in covering breaking news because reporters often know only where something is happening. By looking up an address in the directory, they can find the identity and phone number of the person at the address.

Eissman wanted to find the names and phone numbers of the woman's neighbors so he could try to find people who knew the woman and perhaps provide insight into why she was trying to kill herself.

"Most said they didn't know the woman," the reporter said. "Finally one of the neighbors said she knew quite a bit about the woman, but said she didn't really want to talk about it. I asked her why not, and she said she did not like to talk about her neighbor's business. I asked her if she would talk to me if I didn't use her name, and she said yes."

Eissman said he had no problem speaking to a woman off the record because the story was more about the rescue attempt than the woman herself. He was trying to find out what would make this woman want to kill herself.

"The neighbor said the woman had been despondent over the recent breakup of her second marriage and was suffering from a life-threatening disease," Eissman said. "I called back the hospital spokesman to try to confirm what the neighbor had told me. He said he was aware that the woman had been suffering from a life-threatening disease. The information about the disease and recently failed marriage was later confirmed by another neighbor and the woman's relatives."

Finally, the battalion chief who directed the rescue returned Eissman's call. The reporter said:

"He told me the rescue attempt was the most dramatic he'd ever seen. I asked him every question I could think about the incident. I asked him how the department was alerted to the call, and he said he wasn't sure but that he would check. He then told me the woman had ingested ammonia and sleeping pills, slit her wrists and had jumped out the window.

"He said her robe snagged on the bottom part of the window, and the window slammed shut, leaving her dangling in midair."

BREAKING DOWN THE STORY

The Lead

Eissman wrote a summary lead for the story, which carried his and Silverman's byline. It emphasized the *what* and *how:*

For 10 heart-stopping minutes Saturday morning, a 49-year-old woman dangled upside down outside the 16th-floor window of her Lake Shore Drive apartment, saved from falling only by a heavy pullover robe that had snagged on a window part.

The lead also told readers *when* (Saturday morning), *who* (a 49-year-old woman) and *where* (Lake Shore Drive apartment). It was strong because it contained vivid description and verbs:

- For 10 heart-stopping minutes
- Heavy pullover robe
- Dangled
- Saved
- Snagged

The lead was not as crisp as it could have been, though. It would have been stronger if the writer and his editors had pared it to 35 or fewer words and eliminated the introductory phrase. They could have retained the W's and the vivid descriptions and verbs by writing:

A 49-year-old woman dangled upside down outside the 16th floor of her Lake Shore Drive apartment for 10 minutes Saturday, saved from falling by a pullover robe that snagged on a window part.

ORGANIZING A NEWS STORY

The Body

After the lead—from the second to the final paragraph—an inverted pyramid story is structured to present the news in order of descending importance. It usually is not built chronologically. The most important of the W's and H are put in the lead. The second most important are in the second paragraph, the third most important in the third paragraph and so on. Each paragraph further explains or complements the ones before it.

In their second paragraph, Eissman and Silverman answered the *why* of the story. By combining information that Eissman gathered over the phone with Silverman's observations at the scene, the paragraph told readers the woman wanted to commit suicide. That information was kept out of the lead because the writers and their editors wanted to stress that this story was about how the woman was saved, not that she wanted to die.

The woman, who reportedly had swallowed sleeping pills and ammonia and slit her throat and wrists before diving out the window, kicked frantically to free the robe and complete the suicide attempt while more than 100 onlookers gathered and firefighters broke down seven doors in trying to find her apartment.

"As we wrote the story, additional questions about details of the incident came to mind," Eissman said. "The chief called back to tell me that a 9-year-old boy called from a nearby building and alerted firefighters about the suicide attempt."

Eissman said that even while his editors were reading the story, he called the fire department back to get additional details.

"I asked what kind of robe was she wearing," Eissman said. "Hughes (the battalion chief) had to ask others involved in the rescue before he could answer. I asked him why he picked the firefighter he did to rescue the woman by tying a safety belt around her leg and pulling her in through the window. He said, 'That guy was skinny enough to fit through the opening of the window.'

"I confirmed other details we were using in the story. I covered many elements of the story again to be sure they were accurate. I questioned Hughes about every part of the window until I could figure out how the woman's robe got caught."

Hughes was introduced in the third paragraph. He was the source for most of the story; therefore, he needed to be introduced early. As in most inverted pyramids, the opening paragraphs provided the W's and H and enticed readers into the story. Now it was time to introduce the main sources and further explain the primary elements:

"Her body was entirely, totally out of the window," said 1st Battalion Chief Michael Hughes, who directed the rescue from the ground. "Her head stretched down to the 15th floor."

In the fourth through seventh paragraphs, Hughes was allowed to tell the story through a series of direct quotes, which tell readers precisely what a source said, and paraphrases, which provide the essence of what a source said. Writers should avoid a long string of direct quotes to keep their stories from reading like speeches.

The bottom of the woman's full-length, red velvet robe was knotted on an 8-inch metal opening mechanism of a transom-type window, Hughes said. The floor-level window had snapped up as the woman jumped off it, catching the robe, he said.

"My heart was pounding," he said. "She could have gone at any second. It was a miracle. I've been on the job for 31 years, and this was the most dramatic rescue I've ever seen."

Firefighters were called to the 29-story condominium on North Lake Shore Drive at about 9 a.m. by a boy in a nearby building, Hughes said.

"When we got there, the hardest part was telling what floor she was on. At first we thought she was on the 24th. We had about 27 guys search and search until we found the right apartment."

During the telephone interview, Hughes gave Eissman the names of the firefighters who pulled the woman to safety. The reporter talked to one of them briefly, and now he wanted to introduce the man. To do that, Eissman had to write a transitional paragraph, which told readers that the story was passing from one area to another. By beginning the eighth paragraph with a transition—"Once inside the apartment"—the story moved readers from outside the building to inside the apartment, where firefighters rescued the woman:

Once inside the apartment, Hughes said, firefighters slid a safety belt through an 18-inch opening between the window and the frame and lassoed the woman's leg as she resisted fiercely.

"If we opened the window (any farther), she would have fallen," said firefighter Rory O'Shea, who did the lassoing. Firefighter George Beary helped pull the woman in.

O'Shea, 40, who is 5 feet 7 inches tall and weighs 145 pounds, was selected for the task "because he was skinny enough to fit through the opening of the window," Hughes said.

Now, through another transition, readers are moved from inside the apartment to the street below:

Below, 4 civilians joined 11 firefighters in holding out a 16-foot circular safety net.

"Right there I had to give them a crash course on how to hold it," Hughes said. "I was yelling for them to keep their feet forward and their arms away from their bodies so they wouldn't break their ribs if she fell."

Hughes said firefighters had tried to reach the woman with a hydraulic ladder that was too short, so they had to resort to the lasso maneuver.

As the woman was pulled to safety, applause erupted from the street and other battalion units where firefighters were listening to the ordeal, Hughes said.

The Conclusion

Writers do not conclude news stories by telling readers "the end." They simply quit writing after they have reported all the pertinent information they can get into the space they have been allocated. They often conclude their stories with a direct quote, letting a source talk directly to readers. The quote should tie readers emotionally to the story, reminding them that the writing has ended but the story and people involved in it have not. For example, a story on a town hit by a tornado could end with a local homeowner saying, "We won't let this drive us out. We will rebuild."

The final paragraph also can report additional facts, which remind readers that the writing, not the story, is ending. That is how Eissman and Silverman's story ended. The last paragraph described the woman further and updated her condition, which reminded readers that this person's story was not over. If this story had been about a woman attempting suicide, the information in the last paragraph would have been much higher. Instead, the story was about a heroic rescue; therefore, the description of the woman and her condition were used at the end:

> The woman, described by relatives and neighbors as despondent over a failed second marriage and a life-threatening disease, was listed in fair condition Saturday evening in Rush-Presbyterian Hospital.

REORGANIZING AND IMPROVING A BLAND STORY

Not every story is as exciting to cover and write as that of a woman dangling upside down from a high-rise apartment. Many of the stories reporters cover deal with more routine occurrences, such as traffic accidents, speeches by politicians and actions by governmental bodies. To keep their audiences interested in these stories, reporters must avoid bland and disorganized writing. They must write crisply and vividly.

THE INITIAL VERSION

Here is a story written for a university daily. It is used to illustrate the process that a reporter often goes through to come up with a story that is well written and organized. The story is real, but some of the writing is changed to avoid using the name of the school and sources.

> A $151 million state appropriations request may be cut due to monetary demands from other state programs, the chairman of the state Senate's education committee said Saturday.

Sen. William Delgado, D-Mainsville, said the budget proposal, which represents a $13 million increase over last year's request, may be limited due to demands on lawmakers to fund new programs for the chronically mentally ill.

The state appropriations request, which was approved unanimously by the Board of Regents Friday, totals $151,298,342. Last year's request was $138,298,356.

"It's kind of like a kid asking for an allowance," Delgado said, adding that the Legislature will have to determine how much money is available before approving the budget requests.

"There is just so much money to go around," Delgado said. "First of all we have to take a look and see what we have extra. I feel we may not have enough."

Delgado said the governor has been pushing for programs for the mentally ill, and the Legislature may have to consider funding those programs before allocating funds to the university.

The Legislature will begin discussion on the budgets in January, when its regular session reconvenes.

In other matters, the university will lose 22 faculty positions next year because of a decline in its full-time student equivalent counts.

The regents made the announcement at their meeting on campus Friday because they said FTE decreased by 499 this year.

The Legislature provides one faculty member for every 22 FTE.

Jim Horan, associate director of university budgets, said the decline in enrollments may be attributed to increasing enrollments at state community colleges.

The regents also approved new policies for the training of graduate teaching assistants at the university.

The new policies, which were prompted by complaints from students, require that foreign teaching assistants be required to pass a proficiency test of written and spoken English before teaching.

ORGANIZING A NEWS STORY

WHAT'S WRONG WITH IT?

The initial version of the story missed the boat for several reasons:

- The lead was wrong.
- The writing was dull and loose.
- It was not organized effectively. There are three major elements in the story—the appropriations request, the loss of faculty and the testing of foreign teaching assistants—yet two of them are buried at the end.

First, the lead. In the initial story, readers were told the legislature may cut the university's budget request. That is not news. Budget requests are wish lists. It would be news if a budget were approved exactly as proposed.

The lead also reported that something *may* happen. Avoid writing *may* leads. They are hypothetical. The action they are reporting may or may not happen. An audience wants something definite.

The lead of this story should have been that the university is going to lose faculty members next year because of declining enrollment. Twenty-two people are going to lose their jobs, or departments that were hoping for new faculty are not going to get them.

Next, the writing. Throughout the initial story, the writing was dull and loose. It needed tightening and sharpening.

For example, in the second paragraph the writer said the budget proposal "may be limited due to demands on lawmakers to fund new programs for the chronically mentally ill." The writing could have been crisper:

```
The budget proposal may be pared because lawmakers are being
pushed to fund new programs for the chronically mentally ill.
```

The sixth paragraph reported that the governor has been pushing for the new programs and the legislature "may have to consider funding those programs before allocating funds to the university."

Why not:

```
The Legislature will yield to the governor's demands for the men-
tally ill before it funds the university, Delgado said.
```

Finally, the organization. The story should be topped with the 22 cuts in the faculty. The new tests for foreign teaching assistants and the threat of budget cuts also should be mentioned high in the story. Then each can be explained later.

There are several holes in the story. FTEs need to be explained better, as do the reasons for the new tests for foreign teaching assistants. Readers also need to be told in what areas the faculty positions would be lost.

THE REWRITE

The rewritten story read:

The university will lose 22 faculty positions next year because of declining enrollments.

Funding for the positions is based on full-time equivalent counts, FTEs, which decreased by 499 this year. The Board of Regents announced the decrease during its meeting on campus Friday.

FTEs are the total number of hours being taken by all students divided by 12, a normal full-time load.

At their meeting, the regents also:

- Approved new policies for the training of foreign-born graduate teaching assistants at the university.
- Approved a $151 million budget request for next year, an increase of $13 million over last year.

Jim Horan, associate director of university budgets, blamed the decline in students here on the increasing enrollments at state community colleges.

"We cannot compete with them for underclassmen," Horan said. "They're easier to get into, smaller and half the price."

The Legislature uses a ratio of one faculty to every 22 full-time equivalents, or FTEs, when it appropriates salaries.

University officials said they will try to avoid laying off any faculty members. Instead, the 22 positions will be made up by attrition, they added.

The issue of training foreign graduate students came up after students in the math and history departments complained that they could not understand their instructors.

The new policies require that foreign teaching assistants pass a proficiency test of written and spoken English before they can teach.

ORGANIZING A NEWS STORY

The request for an increased budget was approved unanimously by the regents. It totals $151,298,342, an amount that Sen. William Delgado, D-Mainsville, called wishful thinking, "like a kid asking for an allowance."

Delgado, chairman of the state Senate's education committee, said the proposal may be pared because the governor is pushing lawmakers to fund new programs for the chronically mentally ill.

"There is just so much money to go around," Delgado said. "First we all have to take a look and see what we have extra."

The Legislature will begin debate on the budget in January, when its regular session reconvenes.

WHY IT'S BETTER

There are a number of reasons the rewritten and reorganized version of the regents story was better than the initial version:

- *The lead was stronger.* It reported substance rather than something that may or may not be. After reading the initial lead, someone was likely to say, "So what?" After the second lead, a reader was likely to say, "Wow! Who is going to be fired?"
- *The story was better organized.* By using *bullets*—bold dots that begin and highlight paragraphs—the writer introduced other major elements early in the story. After six paragraphs, readers knew what the article was about. In the initial version the three major elements were stacked on top of each other, which meant readers did not know all of them until the end. In the rewrite, the major elements were introduced right away, and the two least important ones were developed later.
- *The writing was tighter.* More vivid verbs were used.
- Holes were filled. FTEs were defined. Readers were told from where the 22 faculty positions would come, why community colleges are taking away students and which students complained about foreign-born teaching assistants.

STEPS TO FOLLOW IN ORGANIZING AN INVERTED PYRAMID

Every story is different, but there are some basic guidelines that generally should be followed in organizing an inverted pyramid.

WRITE A TERSE LEAD

Write a brief lead paragraph of no more than 35 words that gives the major news of the story. Write a second paragraph that provides major points of the news event that would not fit in the opening paragraph.

PROVIDE BACKGROUND

Use the third paragraph, and more if needed, to provide necessary *background*, which explains things for readers. Background can come from a source, who explains something technical, or from the reporter, to make a story clearer. Even breaking news stories need background paragraphs to explain what has happened before. For example, in a story on the first day of a murder trial, the writer may use the third, fourth and fifth paragraphs to give details of the crime.

If there is more than one major element, use background paragraphs high in the story to wrap up all of them. Then each one can be developed later.

HANDLING CHRONOLOGY

Continue reporting news of the story in paragraphs in order of descending importance. Inverted pyramids seldom are constructed chronologically. When reporters want to write a chronology, they often use another writing form, the hourglass, which will be explained in the next section.

SPRINKLE QUOTES THROUGHOUT

A good time to introduce direct quotes is after the audience has been given the major news and background information. Separate direct quotes by supplementary news and paraphrases. Sprinkle quotes throughout the story rather than stringing them together. Remember, quotes are useful because they let people in the news communicate directly with readers.

USE TRANSITION

A paraphrase, a background paragraph, a paragraph with additional news or even a direct quote can be used as *transition* to move readers smoothly from one paragraph to another. Transition alerts an audience that a shift or change is coming up.

Transition can be developed:

- *Numerically:* first, second, third, etc.
- *By time:* at 3 p.m., by noon, three hours later, etc.
- *Geographically:* in Tucson, outside the home, District 3 voters, etc.
- *With words:* also, but, once, meanwhile, therefore, in other action, however, below, above, etc.

AVOID "THE END"

Continue reporting news until the end. That helps readers know that even though the writing has stopped, the story has not. An effective way to conclude a news story is with a direct quote.

DO NOT EDITORIALIZE

Reporters are eyewitnesses to news. Their job is to tell readers what they saw and what other people said. They should not include their personal opinions. If they think something is rotten, they let the direct quotes from people involved in the story support, and rebut, their opinions.

AN ALTERNATIVE TO THE INVERTED PYRAMID

Most news stories are written in the traditional inverted pyramid, but there are alternatives. "When we are writing stories on deadline, we have to depend on strategies that have proven themselves," said Roy Peter Clark, associate director of the Poynter Institute for Media Studies in St. Petersburg, Fla. "We have to reach into our toolbox and pull out our handy gadgets that help us organize our thinking and communicate to readers. I think that the problem with some writers is that they have a single form that they go back to over and over again, and they don't have at their fingertips a variety of forms out of which they can find just the right one to tell a particular story."

Clark is an advocate of a writing form called the *hourglass style*, which often is used by reporters covering trials or police and fire news. In this form the writer provides the major news in the first few paragraphs of the story. The paragraphs are written in order of descending importance, just like in an inverted pyramid. Then the writer uses a turn, a transitional paragraph to introduce a chronology of the events of the story. Transitional paragraphs include: *Police gave the following account of the accident*, *The victim told the jury what happened*, or *Johnson said he was attacked shortly after he left work*. After the turn, the rest of the details of the story are told in chronological order.

ADVANTAGES OF THE HOURGLASS STYLE

Clark said the hourglass style offers these advantages:

- The important news is presented high in the story.
- The writer can take advantage of narrative.
- The most important information is repeated in the narrative so readers have a chance to absorb it.
- Unlike the top-heavy inverted pyramid, the hourglass has a balanced structure.

- It keeps readers in the story and leads up to a real conclusion.
- It discourages editors from slashing from the bottom.

"The hourglass is a natural way to tell a story," Clark said. "You blurt out the more important information right away, and then someone says, 'That was fascinating. How did it happen?' I've seen it on an interesting range of stories, including governmental meetings in which the writer tells the news at the top of the story and then how the events transpired in a chronological order. I think the hourglass opens up the reporter to a level of reporting that the pyramid sometimes discourages."

AN EXAMPLE

The news story from the *Philadelphia Inquirer* that follows was written by Reid Kanaley in the hourglass style. It was the story of a truck slamming into an office building and killing a man working at his desk.

The first six paragraphs of the story were written in typical inverted pyramid style, with the most important points first. The turn came in the seventh paragraph, where the story said, *Anderson gave the following account of the accident.* Then the narrative followed.

A Delaware County businessman died yesterday morning after a tractor trailer careened into a busy Chester County intersection and slammed through the office where he was sitting at his desk.

The truck driver was seriously injured in the 8:09 a.m. accident at Route 202 and Brinton's Bridge Road in Birmingham Township. There were no other injuries, officials said.

Police said the brakes of the tractor-trailer, a flatbed loaded with coiled steel, apparently had failed. The truck veered across lanes of oncoming traffic, hitting a van, plowing through the office building and into a parked van before coming to a stop, according to Birmingham Police Chief Wade L. Anderson.

The businessman, James E. Dever, 50, of Stonebridge Road, Thornton, died during emergency surgery at Chester County Hospital in West Chester about 10:30 a.m., hospital spokeswoman Donna Pennington said. She described Dever's injuries as "multiple trauma."

The truck driver, Steven Rowe, 26, of Chesapeake, Ohio, was taken to Chester County Hospital with multiple injuries. He was listed in satisfactory condition last night.

Dever was a salesman for the Logan Co., a conveyor manufacturer, according to his son, Thomas Dever, of West Chester.

Anderson gave the following account of the accident:

Rowe's tractor-trailer was northbound on Route 202. At Brinton's Bridge Road, the truck, apparently unable to stop for a red light, crossed the southbound lanes and struck the front end of a van making a left turn onto the road. The driver of the van, Joseph A. Koskoszka of New Castle, Del., was not injured.

The truck continued past the cross street and up a grade into the parking lot of the Birmingham Professional Building on the northwest corner of the intersection. Dever was the only person in the two-story building at the time. He was at his desk in a first-floor corner office when Rowe's truck crashed through the office and into a parked van owned by Anderson. The impact demolished two walls of Dever's office and pinned him under the debris.

The van rolled onto its side and

smashed the front window of the neighboring building, the Patterson Schwartz real estate office.

Anderson said he had just left his office in the basement of the Birmingham Professional Building and was sitting in a patrol car when Rowe's truck skidded by.

"I could see it was out of control, and the driver was making every attempt to miss anything," he said. "He did a fantastic job. He missed me; he missed the cars. He thought the lesser of the evils would be hitting the building, but, of course, it didn't work out that way."

Anderson estimated damages of $75,000. No charges have been filed, but the accident remains under investigation, Anderson said.

Besides his son Thomas, Dever is survived by his wife, Barbara; two daughters, and two other sons.

ORGANIZING AN HOURGLASS

The 30-word lead on Kanaley's story clearly summarized the event: A man was killed when a truck crashed into his office. In the second paragraph readers found out the time of the accident and that the truck driver was injured. Then in succeeding paragraphs (until the seventh) readers were told:

- *How* the accident occurred.
- *Who* was killed.
- *Who* was injured.
- *Where* the dead man worked.

This story could have been concluded after the sixth paragraph; instead, a transitional paragraph was written that invited the audience to read a blow-by-blow account of the accident. Readers had the option of stopping or continuing.

The second half of the hourglass should not repeat word for word the first half. Obviously, some facts will be repeated, but the second half of the story should make the succession of events clearer. For instance, the second paragraph of the truck crash story said the accident occurred at Route 202 and Brinton's Bridge Road. The eighth paragraph reported that the tractor-trailer was northbound on Route 202 and apparently was unable to stop for a red light at Brinton's Bridge Road. It repeated the location of the accident, but it provided additional details.

WHEN TO USE THE HOURGLASS

An hourglass cannot be used in every news story. It would be impractical, for example, when writing a personality profile, weather story, obituary or an advance on a holiday celebration. But in a story that has a succession of events, such as a trial, meeting or police or fire story, the hourglass style can be used effectively. "A story form does not have to be a straitjacket," Clark said. "It should be a liberating device. Reporters need to look for the best structure to tell the best possible story. I would call the hourglass a way of reconciling two essential values for the writer: (1) getting the news high up and not wasting the readers' time, and (2) telling a good story in a narrative style."

When Bishop Desmond Tutu came to the University of California, Davis, to speak out against apartheid in South Africa, radio, television and newspaper reporters were there to listen to him. (Photo by Cliff Polland, *The Reporter*, Vacaville, Calif.)

7 / Interviewing

An interview is the essence of a story. In any interview a reporter must ask the right questions with finesse at just the right time. That requires homework, confidence and the ability to listen, participate, observe and absorb.

In this chapter you will be introduced to the following terms:

morgue
closed-ended question
open-ended question
funnel interview
inverted-funnel interview

observation
color
follow-up question
hostile source

An interview is an exchange of information between a reporter and a source. When a reporter asks the right questions with finesse, a source becomes a window to the news. Conversely, a story can fail if the reporter asks the wrong or not enough questions, does not know how to ask them or gives up too early on a hostile or close-lipped source.

Interviewing requires patience, confidence and an uncanny ability to listen, participate, observe and absorb. Reporters must be able to ask a question and then listen to the entire response, all the time zeroing in on the key points. Reporters who are well prepared should be able to tell when a source is telling the truth, embellishing it or lying.

There are three stages in every interview:

1. The research
2. Setting up the interview
3. The questions and answers

Each stage requires careful attention and expertise. A shoddy job on any of the stages will show up in the final product. A thorough job on each stage will mean the best, most professional story possible.

THE RESEARCH

The key to a successful interview is establishing rapport with the source. To do so, reporters must do their homework so that they can go into an interview knowing both the background of the source and something about the subject of the story. Sources are more likely to relax and open up when they feel that they are talking to reporters who speak with knowledge and authority. Sources often volunteer little information when they think reporters are not asking intelligent questions or do not understand the subject.

USING THE MORGUE

Most newspapers have their own libraries—called *morgues*—in which clipping files are kept on sources and subjects. Reporters can do much of their research there. Stories generally are filed under subject and a reporter's bylines.

For a story on the trial of a suspect in a triple slaying more than a year ago, the reporter first would go to the morgue to read the earlier stories that were written on the slaying and on the arrest of the suspect. Some small newspapers do not have morgues. In these cases a reporter who did not cover the story originally and who does not have copies of the earlier stories would have to:

- Look through bound volumes of the paper at the time of the slayings.
- Hope that somewhere in the office there is a file on the case.
- Rely on police and court officials for necessary background.

INTERVIEWING

Newspapers that do have morgues would have the earlier stories clipped and filed in envelopes or would have the clippings stored in a computer. The stories should be filed under the subject—such as "slayings," the name of the suspect or the name of the victims—and the byline of the reporter who wrote the earlier stories.

Next the reporter would scour all of the earlier clips for background information, making sure facts such as spellings, dates and locations are consistent in each of the stories. If there are inconsistencies, the reporter would check with police or court officials for corrections.

The clips also would be used to identify potential sources and to formulate questions. The prosecuting and defense attorneys may need to be interviewed before the trial begins. A story could be written on the judge, the families of the victims and suspect or the last time there was a triple slaying in town.

Before the trial begins, the reporter should have culled from the clips all of the five W's and H of the case, the names of sources and any questions that need to be asked. Doing the homework takes time, but it will help ensure that the reporter will not be lost in court or baffled or spurned by a source. Sources are much more likely to answer a reporter when the questions are formulated by facts rather than guesses.

USING CAMPUS OR PUBLIC LIBRARIES

Some newspapers close their morgues to the public, which means student reporters may not be able to use them. Check on local policies. If the local morgue is closed, the newspaper may have an index of its articles, which will make it easier to find the correct microfilm or clips at public or campus libraries. (A more complete discussion of newsroom and library sources is found in Chapter 8.) Morgues and other libraries also have a wide selection of Who's Who, encyclopedias, city directories, other reference books and indexes to material in books, magazines and major newspapers. In addition, many have copies or microfilm of newspapers from other cities.

Library sources provide background information on sources and subjects, which means there is no reason to begin working on a story without being fully prepared. If nothing has been written on the source, thoroughly research the subject of the story. Look up the subject in books after checking the library's card catalog or in magazines after checking the Reader's Guide to Periodical Literature. Many people never have been interviewed, but there are few subjects on which nothing has been written.

OTHER SOURCES OF INFORMATION

If earlier stories have been written on a source, it is a good idea to talk to the reporters who wrote them. They can provide insight into a person's character and mannerisms. They will know if the person is easy or difficult to interview.

Some sources will be writers themselves. If they are, take a look at what they have written. A book or article does indeed reveal much about its author, and there is nothing like saying to a person, "I read your book" or "I read the article you wrote." Those few words can relax a source.

When preparing for an interview with someone who never has been interviewed, try to talk to some of the person's friends or professional acquaintances. Any bits of information that can be gathered before the interview will make the entire process easier; therefore, do not hesitate to call one person to ask questions about another.

SETTING UP THE INTERVIEW

Once the preliminary research has been completed, it is time to set up the interview. Here are some steps to follow:

- If the deadline is not tight, telephone or write the person in advance to request the interview.
- Identify yourself as a reporter and name the organization for which you work.
- Establish a time and place that are convenient for the person being interviewed.
- Tell the person the general type of information being sought. There is no need to reveal specific questions, but at least tell the source that you are doing a story on such and such and would like to ask him or her some questions.
- Tell the person approximately how long the interview will take.

MAKE AN APPOINTMENT IF POSSIBLE

In non-breaking news stories, for which the deadline is somewhat flexible, there usually is time to set up the interview in advance. In a breaking news story, however, reporters seldom have the time to call or write in advance to arrange interviews. In this situation, time is critical, and interviews are instantaneous. If there is an explosion at a refinery outside of town, and five people are killed and nine injured, reporters are on the scene almost as quickly as the fire trucks. Fire officials are interviewed. Questions are addressed to the survivors and families of people who died. Reporters ask the questions quickly, often speaking with anyone they can get to.

In stories with less deadline pressure, setting up an interview helps curb the adversary relationship that can exist between reporters and sources. It allows sources to prepare for the questions and to look their best. It allows reporters to be well prepared.

Phoning or writing in advance also helps reporters get past the secretaries, public relations people and others who are on a source's payroll and who may speak for the source. To get past these people, it may be necessary to keep calling, writing or hanging around a source's office until the ap-

INTERVIEWING 115

pointment is made. Explore every ethical avenue to arrange interviews with sources who are not interested in talking or who are well hidden from the press by other people.

IDENTIFY YOURSELF

Once sources are contacted, they should be told immediately that they are talking to a reporter. If the story is for class only, say so. When people know that they are being interviewed for publication, it becomes their responsibility to control what they say.

MAKE IT CONVENIENT FOR THE SOURCE

Since sources tend to be more talkative if they are on their own turf, let them decide on the time and place of the interview. Many times, they will ask, "When is it convenient for you?" If they do, then think of deadlines, dinner dates and growling editors. Otherwise, ride with them. Some of the best interviews take place in the middle of the night, at a gymnasium or on horseback. The point is, a reporter is stepping into someone else's world; therefore, an interview should be convenient for the source, not for the reporter.

Just be prepared for the interview before setting it up. That will avoid embarrassment when the source says, "I'll be busy later. Let's do it now."

DESCRIBE THE STORY

When setting up the interview, tell the source, in general terms, something about the story and how his or her information will fit into it. That will help relax the source before the questioning begins.

It also is important when setting up an interview to tell the person approximately how long the interview will take. Newsmakers usually are busy people who must budget their time, and so it is courteous to give them an idea of how much time is needed.

Ask for plenty of time. If the person will give only a few minutes, take it. That is better than nothing. The important thing is to get the interview, because once people start talking, they often keep going past the predetermined time limit.

DO NOT BE LATE

Once you make the appointment for the interview, keep it. If the interview is scheduled for 11 a.m., be there at 10:50. The only thing worse than coming to an interview unprepared is showing up late or out of breath. Getting to an interview early will show initiative and should impress the source. One other word of advice: Do not schedule one interview immediately after another. That way, the only person looking at a watch will be the source.

DRESS THE PART

There is no need to wear a coat and tie or high heels when covering a roundup on horseback. And do not wear a T-shirt, shorts and deck shoes or a sundress to interview the defense attorney in a murder trial. The best thing to do is dress at the same level as the person being interviewed.

ON THE INTERVIEW

During the interview, the reporter should pay particular attention to the ways in which questions are asked, the theme or purpose of the story, the structure of the interview, observations and personal and follow-up questions. The reporter also should become adept at handling hostile sources, using the telephone, taking notes and closing the meeting.

CLOSED-ENDED QUESTIONS

The timing and wording of questions during an interview can affect the source's response. Some interviews require only quick questions and short, specific answers. For these, it is best to ask *closed-ended questions,* which are structured to elicit precise answers. For instance, when one reporter questioned an irascible police chief about his department's investigation of the kidnapping and alleged rape of three teen-age girls, she asked such closed-ended questions as, "Do you agree with the county sheriff that the girls were raped before they were released by their kidnappers?" and "Is it true that your department did not respond to the parents' call for five hours because you believed the girls had run away and not been kidnapped?" By asking carefully worded questions such as these, the reporter forced the police chief to be precise.

OPEN-ENDED QUESTIONS

Open-ended questions are used when a short, precise answer is not immediately necessary. Because they allow a source more time to develop an answer, open-ended questions sound less intimidating. They are a good way to break the ice and establish rapport with a source. Examples of open-ended questions include: "How would you trace your rise from a clerk to president of the corporation?" or "In your opinion, what should the government do to reduce unemployment?" Open-ended questions give sources an opportunity to elaborate in considerably more detail than do closed-ended questions.

INTERVIEWING

Two factors determine whether a reporter should use open-ended or closed-ended questions:

- *How the subject seems to react to certain questions.* The reporter needs to gauge how the interview is going and then decide if specific, potentially threatening questions are necessary. Closed-ended questions should be reserved for the point in the interview when the source is relaxed and beginning to open up.
- *The length of the interview.* If an important source who is rushed for time is being interviewed, get to the heart of the interview right away. Chances are that sources such as these have been interviewed many times before and are used to specific questions.

FUNNEL INTERVIEW

Interviews follow one of two patterns that are determined by the subject matter and the type of person being interviewed. One is structured like a funnel; the other, like an inverted funnel.

The *funnel interview* is the most common and is the most relaxing for both the reporter and source because the toughest and most threatening questions are saved for near the end. These interviews begin with background talk, such as:

- How long have you been with this company?
- Where were you born?
- How old are you?
- Where did you get your experience?

The background questions are followed by open-ended questions, which are followed by closed-ended questions or adversary questions. Funnel interviews are most useful when:

- The source is not accustomed to being interviewed.
- The length of the interview is not important.
- Particularly touchy closed-ended questions need to be asked.

By beginning with general, easy-to-answer questions, the reporter has a good chance of establishing rapport with the source. Then, once the tough questioning begins, the source is more likely to respond candidly.

Art Geiselman, an investigative reporter for the *Albuquerque* (N.M.) *Journal*, calls this style of interviewing the "wolf-circling-the-sheep method." "It's the same style used by attorneys," said Geiselman, who has been an investigative reporter for newspapers and television stations for 35 years. "You start way out on the edges, establish rapport and get the person relaxed. Then you work toward the center of the interview.

"I think it works if you move in slowly. I don't let the source know exactly what I am interested in. Then, after the person is relaxed and talking, I hit him with the question I really want answered, something like, 'Did you misappropriate the funds?' "

INVERTED-FUNNEL INTERVIEW

In an *inverted-funnel interview*, the key questions are asked immediately. This style of interview is used with people, such as law enforcement or government officials, who are experienced in fielding closed-ended or adversary questions.

For example, when a U.S. senator voted for a controversial bill that would cost his state millions of dollars in lost federal aid, he was ready for the adversary questioning from reporters: "How could you do it?" "Don't you realize this vote might cost you your job?"

Inverted-funnel interviews also are used in breaking news stories when there is little time to ask questions.

MEMORIZING QUESTIONS

Before an interview, memorize or write down the important questions that need to be answered. Of course, the interview might take an unexpected turn and some of the questions might go unanswered, but still know in advance what should be covered. Here is where homework is important. Questions are formulated by reading earlier clips and conducting preliminary interviews.

Additional questions will pop up during the interview. Jot them down on a note pad, and ask them at the appropriate time. Try to avoid staring at or reading from the list. Do not check off questions one by one as they are answered. That could intimidate the source, who will begin talking to the note pad rather than the reporter. It could prevent the eye-to-eye contact that is important in an interview.

USING THE TELEPHONE

The telephone is a valuable aid to conducting interviews. When reporters are covering breaking news near deadline, when they need to talk to a source who is out of town or when they are interviewing one of their regular sources, they almost always use the phone.

However, in many interviews, particularly where the source does not know the reporter or there is no immediate deadline, eye contact is important. In these cases, telephone interviews are not suitable substitutes for going out into the field. Do not use the phone if:

- There is time for an eye-to-eye interview.
- The source is nervous.
- It is a breaking news story where many interviews are needed.
- Observations are important to the story.

"I don't like telephone interviewing because I like to see a person's eyes, hands and what he does with himself," Geiselman said. "It's hard for a source to hang up on you when you're right in front of him."

Guidelines

Here are some guidelines to follow when conducting interviews over the telephone:

- **Identify yourself carefully and fully.** This is especially important if you never have met the source. Remember, the person on the other end of the line cannot see you and will be hesitant to answer questions from a complete stranger.
- **Speak slowly and clearly.** You have to speak so you can be understood. Over the phone, you have only your voice to convince the source to talk to you.
- **Do things to put sources at ease.** For example, you might want to apologize for your tight deadline or the inability to be there in person. Sometimes, it even helps to apologize for the sound of the typewriter or video display terminal as you take your notes.
- **Ask brief questions.** It is easy for a source to forget a detailed question or not understand it fully when it is asked over the phone.
- **Put the telephone in a comfortable spot on your shoulder before the interview begins.** It is best to practice typing and talking at the same time before you actually interview someone for a story. That way you will not drop the phone or keep having to reposition it. Such fumbling may cause you to miss an important quote, and it could make the source worry about your abilities as a reporter.
- **Type your notes.** You soon will discover that, with practice, you can type much faster than you can write in longhand.
- **Do not worry about sloppy typing.** Go over your notes as soon as possible after the interview to correct mistakes.
- **Ask permission before you tape a telephone interview.** Many states have laws forbidding reporters from taping over the phone unless the other party gives permission. Be familiar with your state laws. Asking in advance also will let the source know you are not trying anything underhanded and will prevent you from being in an embarrassing position if you have to admit that you are indeed taping the interview.

FRAMING QUESTIONS TO FIT THE STORY'S PURPOSE

Reporters should know where they want their stories to go before they begin the interviewing process. Every story should have a theme or purpose. Once that purpose is determined, questions can be framed so that the interviews will help the reporter achieve it.

If a story's purpose is to show that a local politician is a crook, questions are designed so that the wrongdoing will be revealed by sources during the interviewing. Many of the questions likely will be adversarial.

If the purpose of the story is to show how a successful corporate president got to be where he is today, the questions are designed to bring out the best in the man. The questions likely will be easy to answer, seeking descriptions and anecdotes.

In news stories, sources generally are interviewed to support or criticize the peg of the article. Of course, news stories can be made from an interview with a single source, but generally the sources of a story are supplementary to the news event itself.

For example, the following inverted pyramid news story from *The Dallas Morning News* illustrates how interviews are used to supplement hard news stories.

Lead paragraph:

A World War II-vintage training plane crashed and burned in Abilene Monday, killing both people aboard.

This 17-word lead gave the *what* (fatal plane crash), *who* (two people), *where* (Abilene) and *when* (Monday) of the story. It provided readers with the most important news. The next two paragraphs gave additional key information:

Police said the plane belonged to a member of the Confederate Air Force, a flying group that owned a seaplane that crashed a month ago, killing seven people.

Abilene police identified the dead in Monday's crash as Jake Eustace Miller, 61, of Albany, and Kimberly Brooke Pardue, 19, of Breckenridge.

In the fourth paragraph, one of the people interviewed for the story was introduced:

Abilene police Lt. Ron Harris said he didn't know who was piloting the 1940s-era two-seat British Chipmunk when it crashed about 2:50 p.m. near Elmdale Airpark on the northeast outskirts of Abilene.

Now readers knew that at least one person was interviewed for the story. What Harris said was not important enough to put in the lead, but it added useful information to the story. The next paragraph also came from Harris:

The National Transportation Safety Board is expected to begin its investigation Tuesday, Harris said.

Later in the story, a witness to the crash—another person interviewed—was introduced:

Tye Lawrence, an Abilene high school junior who was working on a fence about a mile from where the British trainer crashed Monday, said it appeared that the pilot was in a downward spiral and couldn't level the biplane.

"At first, I thought he was just trying to do a spiral or something, then it looked like he just lost it," said Lawrence. "I just saw the plane kind of start tumbling and then it went into a nose dive and hit the ground."

As in any inverted pyramid story, this one could have been cut from the bottom and used without the quotes and paraphrases from the people interviewed. But by including those paragraphs, the writer provided additional information by named sources, which made the story more credible and readable. As in every news story, the reporter probably interviewed more people than showed up in print, but because of space and time limitations, the reporter had to choose only the best quotes and paraphrases that fit the story's purpose.

ESTABLISHING RAPPORT

Reporters must establish rapport with their sources as quickly as possible. That is the key to getting their questions answered. "You're like a door-to-door salesman selling yourself," said Jerry Guibor, a sports copy editor for the *Fresno* (Calif.) *Bee* who has been a news and sports writer in California, Oregon and Arizona. "You have to know the subject and not get bored with it. You have to know the person you are interviewing and ask intelligent questions. You have to have a good intro to stimulate the source."

Guibor said rapport should be established as quickly as possible during an interview because most sources will not answer questions candidly until they have "warmed up" to the reporter. "To establish rapport, you have to tell them who you are and what you are doing," he said. "And you have to thank them for their time."

Here are some additional guidelines:

• **Try to conduct the interview in person.** As discussed earlier, there are times when telephone interviews are necessary, but they make establishing rapport extremely difficult. Sources are more likely to warm up to someone they can see, particularly if they have never met the reporter before.

• **Begin with general, easy-to-answer questions, if possible.** Doing so will help relax the source. Hold the adversarial questions until the end of the interview, when the source is more likely to feel comfortable.

• **Do not ask vague questions.** Ask clear, concise questions that a source can understand quickly. A source is more likely to open up when the reporter is not confused or vague.

- **Do not pull any punches.** Do not beat around the bush. Ask questions straight out. Do not ask a related, non-adversarial question in the hopes that the source will respond in a certain way.

- **Avoid arguing.** Reporters have the last say when they write. "If the senior senator from your state tells you in a press conference or interview that the Earth is flat, he is to be quoted precisely," said Neil H. Mehler, a general assignment reporter for the *Chicago Tribune*. "Then, in the story or in a sidebar, it is mandatory that the reporter note that this is not the accepted belief."

- **Listen.** Let the person being interviewed feel that he or she is conversing with a friend rather than responding to a list of questions from a reporter. A reporter so wrapped up in the eloquence of his own questioning may ignore what the other person is saying.

- **Be open for any response.** Remember that responses to questions tend to be signals for additional questions, some that a reporter might not have thought of while preparing for the interview.

OBSERVATION

When reporters accurately write what a source has said, the readers can "hear." When they observe and then report the source's mannerisms and surroundings, the readers can "see." *Observations* add *color* to stories, which means they give readers a clearer picture of a person or an event.

During an interview, reporters should keep in mind the following:

- *What is unusual—or common—about this person or place?* If a photograph were made of the source, what would it show? How is the person dressed? new clothes? ragged clothes? latest fashions? How does the source look? wrinkled face? scars? bushy eyebrows? full beard? too much makeup? gold teeth? What are the person's mannerisms? nervous twitch? always winking? never smiling? How is the office decorated? western? paintings? posters? What is usual about the person's face, hair, mouth, eyes, ears, etc.?
- *Does the source articulate well?* Is the source "comfortable" discussing this subject? Are there any outside sounds that can be heard during the interview? Any pleasant or unpleasant smells? Is the source distracted?

Examples

Observations are vital to features, but they also can be effective in news stories. Here is a paragraph out of a news story in *The New York Times* about a $50 million libel case that pitted Ariel Sharon, former minister of defense for Israel, against the conglomerate that publishes *Time* magazine:

INTERVIEWING

> In the front row of the small, crowded courtroom, the stocky Mr. Sharon, who is 56 years old, sat with his arms folded across his chest as Judge Abraham D. Sofaer described the libel case to the jury.

The story would have read fine without the observations on Sharon, but they gave the hard news story just a bit of color, which can help keep readers' attention.

During an interview, reporters make notes of their observations. Then they decide during writing which ones are pertinent to the story. For instance, in a court trial one of the spectators may be wearing curlers in her hair and knitting during testimony. It is an interesting observation that is worth noting, even though it may not be used in the story. On the other hand, it could enhance a stark news story:

> Spectators packed the courtroom. One woman, with curlers in her hair, sat knitting while Parker admitted that he stole the words to the song.

Usually, observations are better than punctuation. There's no need to write:

> People could tell Johnson WANTED that fish to bite!!!!

Instead, use observations to let readers decide that Johnson did indeed want that fish to bite:

> Johnson stared at the water. He was so tense that veins in his neck were bulging. While the others joked in the boat and munched on pretzels, Johnson kept his eyes on the water, waiting, one hand on his reel, the other on the handle of his rod.

Observation is something only reporters can obtain. Editors can only ask or readers can only wonder, "How many gold teeth did he have?" or "What was she wearing?" Of course, if these observations are not made during the interview, they may be impossible to get later. That is why it is so important to make as many notes as possible about a source's looks, mannerisms and surroundings. None of these observations should get in the way of reporting the news; they are used to enhance the telling of the news, to make an audience feel more like it was there during the interview.

It is best to make more observations than ever will be needed in the story. Often, editors will ask for more color. Here is where observation is critical. Editors do not want a reporter to say a person is tall or old or big or young. They want the reporter to say how tall, how old, how big or how young. They may not want the story to say only that the police recruit jumped over the six-foot wall. They may want:

The recruit ran up to the six-foot portable orange wall that had been rolled onto the obstacle course. He jumped up and threw one leg over the top. He grunted, pushed and rolled the rest of his body over.

Sometimes, observations are the first things to be cut when there is a space problem. In cases such as these, a reporter will not be able to mention the woman in curlers or describe the portable wall over which police recruits jumped. That is the way daily journalism is. There simply never will be unlimited space to report a story.

PERSONAL QUESTIONS

Asking personal questions is, for some reporters, the toughest part of an interview. Even the most experienced reporters dread the times when they have to approach a grieving mother to ask how her son was killed or a government official to ask if the rumors of financial improprieties are true.

It is not easy asking such questions, but it is something all reporters must do. It also is the most difficult hurdle they have to clear in an interview. Usually, though, if a personal question is asked at the right time and with sensitivity, a source will respond passionately and candidly.

"I have more trouble asking personal questions when they involve interviewing people whose children died than when they involve government officials or people in the news," said Maren S. Bingham, education reporter for the *Mesa* (Ariz.) *Tribune*. "I really do feel like an intruder, like I don't have the right to intrude on someone's tragedy."

Bingham said that before she asks personal questions, she tries to show sources that she is a professional and will get the information correct. "I try to establish trust," she said. "I try to sit and talk to them, not take notes or turn on the tape recorder. I ask general questions to try to get to know them."

Marie Dillon, chief of the North Miami Valley Bureau of the *Dayton* (Ohio) *Journal Herald* and *Daily News*, agreed that the reporter must establish rapport with the source before asking personal questions.

Dillon recalled a story she wrote after a drunken driver slammed his car into another car and killed an entire family, except a 2-year-old boy. "I had to go interview the dead father's sister," she said. "I was worried how I was going to approach the subject. I did what I often do. I phoned first, and asked her if she had a photo of the boy we could use. That got me into her house. When I was there and she started to give me directions on where and when she wanted the photo returned, I got out my notebook to write them down. I never put it away."

For a story on teen-age suicides, Dillon had to interview the foster mother of a 13-year-old boy who shot and killed himself. Dillon said she was nervous about asking the woman for an interview because she would have to ask many personal questions about the boy, but once the interview began, she realized the woman was more than willing to talk. "She turned out to be a great interview," Dillon said. "She really opened up to me. She was by herself and really needed someone to talk to."

Mark Nykanen, a correspondent for NBC News who does investigative stories, continually has to ask personal questions. He said how he phrases a personal question depends on what he knows about the character of the person he is interviewing.

"If there is a history of mental instability, I would be more inclined to present the question in a general way," Nykanen said. "I might couch the question, offer a preface and say I'm sorry that I have to ask this difficult question. Then I would ask the question. If a person is not emotionally crippled in some way, such as a government official who raped his secretary, then I would ask the question very directly."

Nykanen said he also has to handle carefully people who have had a history of striking out violently when they are backed into a corner. "In these cases I would try to ask the questions in a public place where he has an out," Nykanen said. "My producer and I have that policy. We give them a physical avenue to escape to prevent problems for us and to prevent putting them in a position in which they would feel uncomfortable."

When Nykanen worked on a documentary on child pornography, he said he had no problem asking adults personal questions. "When talking to their victims, however, children, I had to be very tender and soft, not direct at all," he said. "I merely tried to provide a catalyst for the child to talk. Videotape is very cheap and I work on long-term projects. I don't work on things where people have to tell me something in five minutes. I try to spend some time with the source even before the camera is around. I try to open myself up, especially if it is a child who has been sexually abused. I try to let the child know that I'm genuinely interested. When the camera is on, I try to say, tell me what happened."

Art Geiselman of the *Albuquerque Journal* said, "If a question pertains to the story, I can ask it. I have found that people who are grieving often welcome the opportunity to talk to a reporter. They know that reporters are only doing their job."

Bingham said it is easier to ask personal questions of public officials or people in the limelight. Still, she said, personal questions have to be approached with a certain amount of forethought and finesse.

When she got a letter from a former high school student who claimed to have had sex with an assistant principal at a local school and planned to file charges against him, Bingham had to check out the letter by interviewing people on her beat whom she comes in contact with every day. If she was not careful, both in how she asked her questions and in what she wrote, she could have lost valuable sources for future stories.

"I work with these people all the time, and they think pretty highly of me," she said. "I had to talk to the superintendent and the assistant superintendent. I also knew the assistant principal pretty well. He was considered upstanding."

She said that before she confronted the man directly, she studied his background, called the police and checked with the man's supervisors. The police told her they believed the girl's story about the sexual encounter. After she talked to top school district officials, who said the charge was being investigated, Bingham knew it was time to call the assistant principal. She would tell him about the letter and her conversations with the police and school officials and give the man an opportunity to respond. Bingham said:

"It was difficult for me to ask him if he had had sex with the girl. Of course he said it was not true. I think he expected me to be sympathetic, but I wasn't. I asked the questions that needed to be asked. I called him in his office instead of at home and told him I had this letter. He said, 'I know about it.' I said, Would you feel more comfortable to talk about it in person？ He said, 'No let's talk about it now. It's not true.'"

Bingham gathered her facts and was prepared to write a story based upon all of her interviews, but the girl never filed charges against the assistant principal. Bingham's editors decided not to use the story.

Bingham and Dillon said their chief fear when asking personal questions is that sometime after the interview, sources will regret what they said and then ask that their quotes not be printed. "I find that most people do not mind answering personal questions, but they sometimes later regret it," Dillon said. She added that in cases like these she has to weigh the worth of the source to the current story and to future stories. Bingham said: "I usually very nicely say 'too bad.' I figure that they're responsible adults, and they knew they were talking to a reporter. But I also realize that I caught them at a bad time. I try to be sympathetic."

Guidelines

Bingham, Dillon, Nykanen and Geiselman offered the following guidelines for asking personal questions:

• **Do homework.** Know something about a source before trying to enter his or her personal life.

• **Try to interview the person face to face.** It is a lot easier for a person to respond to a personal question when looking at another person, rather than speaking to a strange voice on the telephone.

• **Interview in a casual setting.** If a source is relaxed, he or she is much more likely to respond candidly to personal questions.

• **Break the ice with general questions.** Sometimes it is best to begin an interview without taking notes or taping. Talk about the weather or the

INTERVIEWING

setting for the interview. Ask questions such as age or address. Humor helps, too. Making a source smile or laugh can work. There is no need to open with a joke, but smiling broadly and making a comforting comment should help put the source at ease.

- **Sometimes, it is easier to elicit a personal response by not asking a question at all.** Instead of asking, "How did your son die?" it might be easier to say, "Tell me about your son." Let the source talk about anything. Let the interview ramble for a while. Then later, if the source missed anything, ask more specific personal questions.

- **Preface the questions.** Sometimes, a source is more likely to answer a personal question if it is prefaced with something like "I'm sorry to bother you but I have to ask you this question," or "I know you are busy but I'd like to ask you this question."

- **Always be honest with people.** Never lie or misrepresent yourself under any circumstances. "If you mislead people, how can you report about other people who mislead?" Geiselman asked.

- **Be flexible.** You have to figure out how to handle people, sometimes in an instant. Everyone you interview is different; treat each person you interview as an individual.

FOLLOW-UP QUESTIONS

Anyone who has seen a televised news conference has seen reporters ask *follow-up questions*, in which they rearticulate their questions or ask a new question to elicit a new or more specific response from a source. The president may be asked, "How do you plan to cut taxes?" He responds, "We'll do whatever it takes to trim taxes, including an across-the-board 10 percent decrease, but I think it will be hard to get anything through Congress." The reporter follows up immediately with, "Do you think Congress is unwilling to go along with a tax cut because of the disastrous effects it would have on the already-huge federal deficit?"

The above scenario illustrates three things about the reporter who asked the two questions:

- He did his homework and asked an appropriate open-ended question.
- He listened intently to the response, realizing that the president was placing the blame on Congress, not himself, for high taxes.
- Because he knew his subject well, he was able to interpret the response quickly and follow it up with another appropriate question.

Of course, beginning reporters are not going to be interviewing the president on live television in front of millions of people. They are going to be talking to a variety of local sources, many of whom never have been interviewed. But just like the president, these sources are not always going to answer a question fully because:

- They do not understand it.
- They ramble too much and forget it.
- They are not qualified to answer it but try anyway.
- They do not want to.
- They answer another question instead.

It is up to the reporter to make certain that each question is intelligent, brief and easy to understand. That usually eliminates the problem of a source's not understanding. However, the other problems may be more difficult to solve. In these cases the reporter will need to ask follow-up questions.

"If a person doesn't understand the question, I immediately assume that that's my problem, and I won't let the person go on for too long in the fog that I have caused," Mark Nykanen of NBC News said. "I will say, 'No, no, no, I have done a terrible job of formulating my question. Let me rephrase it.' I never put the onus on the person by saying, 'You misunderstood me.'"

For people who clearly are trying to avoid the question or did not answer it completely, Nykanen said he either will break in and say firmly that the question is not being answered or wait until the person has finished and ask exactly the same question again. "That will let them know that their tactics didn't work," he said.

The key to asking follow-up questions is to go into an interview fully prepared and listen intently to the source, Nykanen said. "By the time I do an interview, I know the subject extremely well," he added. "I listen for inconsistencies and then I bore right in on the inconsistencies."

Nykanen said that before he interviewed an official of the U.S. Environmental Protection Agency, he had information that the EPA had done studies on the deadly pesticide EDB and knew it was in the flour used to make biscuits in school lunch programs throughout the country.

"I asked him whether the EPA had ever informed anyone publicly that it had this finding, that the majority of flour bound for school lunch programs contained this carcinogenic chemical," Nykanen said. "He said, 'We did extensive testing, we wrote down results.' He gave me a lot of the minutiae concerning the testing process and how complete it was. Of course, he never answered the question. I asked the same question again. I asked it several times before he finally said, 'No, we never did.' That brought up the follow-up question, 'Why didn't you tell parents their children were eating that carcinogen?' He finally ended up saying, 'I just don't know.' I asked, 'Do you think you should have.' He said, 'I don't know.' Within a few days of our broadcast, the EPA put an immediate ban on that chemical."

HANDLING HOSTILE SOURCES AND "NO COMMENT"

Not every source is cooperative, easy to talk to and ready to admit fault. Sources can be closed-lipped and say "no comment." They may talk only

INTERVIEWING

"off the record," which means they do not want anything they say to be printed. They may be *hostile*, especially if they are asked to reveal something they do not care to share with the public. In these cases, it becomes the reporter's responsibility to try to make the source open up.

If someone does not want to comment to the press, that is his or her right. No reporter can force a person to talk. Sometimes the reporter simply must give up on a source and look for another. In these cases, an audience must be told, for instance, "The mayor refused to comment."

If a source will talk only off the record, the reporter should take notes and try to convince the person to allow his or her information to be used. Sources cannot order a reporter to take information off the record. If they could, reporters would be at their mercy. Reporters violate no ethical principles of journalism if they ignore such a command, unless they have agreed before the interview to accept the information off the record. (For a further discussion of off-the-record reporting, see Chapter 5.)

Guidelines

Here are some ways to convince sources to open up, to go on the record or to keep them from becoming hostile:

- **Do not act like a prosecuting attorney.** Avoid hostile questions. Save the tough questions for the end of the interview.

- **Be sympathetic and understanding.** That does not mean a reporter has to be on the side of the source while writing the story.

- **Reason with the source.** Tell the source that using a name or comment will make the story better.

- **Genuinely try to understand the source's position.** Try to find a reasonable explanation for any charges against a source.

- **Repeat some of the damaging things that have been said about a source.** Often sources will open up to respond to charges against them.

- **Keep asking questions.** As long as the source does not end the interview, continue asking questions.

Mark Nykanen said: "When I get a 'no comment,' I always ask, 'Why not?' If you have done your homework and are pretty sure you know why they have no comment, you can ask something like, 'Is the reason you refuse to comment related to the fact that you did such and such?' or 'Do you mean to say you refuse to deny that such and such happened?'"

He agreed that there is no need to badger a source once it is obvious that the question will not be answered. "I think there is a point where you simply ease up," he said. "If you have other questions that need to be asked, you don't want to sit there and box the person about the head. He may quit the interview."

Art Geiselman said: "I'm basically a document man. If I have the records before the interview, I can go to the source with them. If you have the documents, it is hard for a source to deny something or say 'no comment.' Of course, I don't argue with a source. If he says 'no comment,' I will use that in the paper.

"I also don't like using unnamed sources. If a source is saying something detrimental about another person, the source's name should be used. If John Doe is calling the police chief a crook, John Doe's name should be used because the chief deserves to know who is calling him a crook. When the criticism is not aimed at someone specifically, then we have used unnamed sources."

Geiselman said that if a source wants to go off the record, the reporter should say, "It won't do me any good to know something that I can't put in the paper." He added: "You don't need to warn the source a second time. He cannot say something and then strike it off the record retroactively."

TAKING NOTES

During an interview, the reporter must understand and at the same time transcribe what the speaker is saying. To do that, it is necessary to write fast. Most reporters devise some system for shortening words. Many also use tape recorders, particularly in lengthy face-to-face interviews.

Tape Recorders

By using a tape recorder, the reporter can establish and maintain eye contact with the source and conduct the interview as if it were a conversation. Reporters who do use recorders usually take notes, too. Every experienced reporter probably has lost at least one interview because of a malfunctioning recorder, which is enough to make some reporters abandon the machines altogether. Tape recorders have two other disadvantages:

- Sometimes they intimidate and inhibit a source. Some people simply do not like talking into a machine that will record everything they say.
- They can waste time because the reporter has to go back and listen again and again to the recording until useful quotes are found. This problem can be eased if the reporter uses a footage meter with the recorder and makes notes of the location of pertinent quotes.

The great advantage of a tape recorder is that it provides a permanent and precise record of what is said, preventing the reporter from inadvertently misquoting. It is impossible to write down everything that is said, especially in in-depth interviews, and so the recorder is useful to back up the quotes. The reporter takes notes to remember key points of the interview; then, when it is over, the notes can be filled in by going over the tape.

A warning whenever using a tape recorder: Check the machine before the interview and take along extra batteries and tape.

"If I think the interview is going to be controversial or a source is going

INTERVIEWING

to come back later and question what I wrote, then I use a tape recorder," said Maren Bingham of the *Mesa* (Ariz.) *Tribune*. "But I do not use it routinely."

She said recording an interview is advantageous because sources generally choose their words more carefully, which can make for easier-to-understand quotes.

Bingham also listed disadvantages of taping:

- Because people choose their words more carefully, the interview may lack spontaneous quotes.
- When people are nervous about the tape recorder, they are more likely to clam up.

How Many Notes?

Take copious notes, more than will be needed to write the story. It is not unusual to write a two-page story from 15 pages of notes. It is better to have too many notes than not enough.

Still, there is no need to take notes on everything that is said. Listen carefully to the speaker, look for inconsistencies, formulate follow-up questions and write down only the pertinent information. And, most important, relax. Reporters run into trouble when they spend so much time frantically writing notes that they miss the meaning of what a source is saying. For example, a source might say, "Yes, I did break the law." But to get to that point, he says, "Well, all I can say is, what I mean is, gee this is difficult for me, but yes. I did break the law." A reporter so busy trying to write down the entire quote may miss the heart of it.

Write Faster

Even reporters using tape recorders take as many notes as they can. Some reporters learn shorthand or have their own list of abbreviations to make the job quicker. Another popular trick of taking notes is to leave the vowels out of most of the words. Of course, it is difficult to use this technique in the beginning, but its gets easier with practice. The source might say: "The black smoke looked like a mushroom cloud. I thought the area had been bombed." A reporter could write: Th blck smke lked lk a hg mshrm cld. i thght th ara hd bn bombd.

Whatever system they use, reporters go over their notes immediately after the interview to make sure they understand them. Many reporters will stay in a room after a press conference or sit in their cars for a while to review their notes. That is the time to insert the vowels in words or correct errors.

Where Does the Note Pad Go?

When conducting an in-person interview, put the note pad and tape recorder, if one is being used, in an inconspicuous place. The best spot for a note pad is on a reporter's lap. That makes eye contact easier and allows the person being interviewed to talk to the reporter rather than to the note pad. Eye contact is important in an interview. Neatness in taking notes is not.

Repeating a Quote

Do not be afraid to ask the source to repeat a quote. It is not rude or inappropriate to say: "Excuse me, but I did not get down everything you said. Can you repeat it?" It also is acceptable for a reporter to repeat a quote to make certain that it was transcribed correctly. After all, both the source and the reporter want to make sure a quote is accurate.

If the person being interviewed is using confusing terms, stop the interview. A reporter can say: "I'm sorry. I do not understand that. Can you explain it better?" Doing so will make the story better and will show the person being interviewed that the reporter is conscientious.

Use Symbols

Get in the habit of putting some type of symbol, such as a star, next to key phrases or quotes. That is a good way to identify possible leads or areas that need additional probing. Reporters facing a tight deadline often compose their stories mentally during an interview; then when it is over, they can head directly to a telephone to call in the story.

Reporters also should not forget where they obtain the information. People being interviewed give reporters their opinions; therefore, what they say should be attributed. Make sure everything that is not fact is attributed.

WHEN IT ENDS

The more a reporter and the source talk, the better the interview and resulting story; therefore, the reporter should try to keep the interview going as long as possible. Questions should be asked until the source halts the interview. And remember that key points for the story often are made at the end of the interview when the source has relaxed fully, so keep listening intently until the interview is indeed over.

At the end of the interview, thank the source and ask, "Where can I reach you by phone if I have additional questions while I am writing the story?" That will provide quick contact if more information is needed later and will show the source that you are trying to be accurate. It also forestalls a request from the source to see the story before it is printed.

Under no circumstances should a reporter agree to show a source the story once it is written. People almost always want to retract or edit their statements once they see them on paper. Reporters confused by something

INTERVIEWING

a source said should phone the person to ask for clarification or additional information. There is no reason to take the story to the source.

Notes should be reviewed immediately after the interview to make certain they are clear. Many reporters type their notes after interviews to help them fill in empty spots. If a tape recorder was used and it malfunctioned, call back the source immediately and set up another interview.

Reporters check library sources for background information before they interview sources. (Photo by David Petkiewicz)

8 / Gathering Information

Reporters can strengthen every story they write by consulting all available sources of information. Sometimes, however, they do not know where to look for information. It is important, therefore, to have a working knowledge of newsroom and library reference sources.

In this chapter you will be introduced to the following terms:

computer reference service   abstract

Information underlies good reporting and writing. But information must be gathered. It can be collected through interviews or observation. It can be harvested from public documents, private diaries, memos, letters, books, library statistical guides, magazines, newspapers, waste baskets or microfilm. Information can inundate reporters. It is essential, though, that reporters know where to find information.

"I came across a quote one time that said there's an answer to every question that a journalist has and his worth as a journalist is going to be determined by his ability to find the answer," journalism Professor Emeritus Harry W. Stonecipher of Southern Illinois University said. "All of this information is available someplace. You just have to find out how to locate it—and then make the effort to do so."

Stonecipher said there is a tendency for journalists and journalism students to underutilize sources available to them.

"I sometimes find seniors who are not aware of basic newsroom and library sources," Stonecipher said. He sees to it that students are introduced to these sources.

"I try to guide students to sources that should be available on the copy desk of most daily newspapers: Facts on File, Editorial Research Reports, Current Biography, Congressional Quarterly Weekly Report and so forth," Stonecipher said. "These sources are more authoritative than news magazines or opinion journals, upon which reporters often rely for background information. Journalists need to know their way around a library as well as a newspaper morgue."

STANDARD SOURCES

Information gathered from volumes on library shelves or from standard references that are found in most newspaper offices can be just as valuable as information gathered from public documents, public meetings or governmental sources.

The following list is not exhaustive, but it contains valuable references for working journalists.

NEWSROOM SOURCES

Stylebooks, atlases, almanacs and thesauri are common reference books that are found in nearly every newsroom or newspaper morgue. Reporters use them frequently. Another often-used book is the Guinness Book of World Records. It is used to provide information for stories and to answer questions that readers bombard newsrooms with at all hours of the day.

Other newsroom sources include:

• **Clippings.** If time permits, always check the newspaper library or morgue to see if there have been stories published on the topic or person you are assigned. Knowing the background of the person or topic will save you

GATHERING INFORMATION

time during the interviewing process. You could, of course, use the interview to confirm background information or to seek elaboration of it. If your editor tells you to interview a long time community resident about changes in city government but she neglects to tell you that this source was the mayor in the 1930s, save yourself the embarrassment of the source having to tell you.

- **Dictionaries.** Dictionaries can provide you with more information than correct spellings. They can, among other things, provide syllabification, parts of speech, inflected forms, cross references, abbreviations, etymologies, synonyms, antonyms and various usage notes. In addition, you can find such things as signs and symbols for astronomy, biology, chemistry, medicine, chess, music and mathematics. You also can find a directory of colleges and universities, and a basic manual of style that explains the use of the period, ellipsis, question mark, exclamation point, comma, semicolon, colon, apostrophe, quotation marks, parentheses, brackets, dashes and hyphens. Some dictionaries even include proofreading symbols.

- **Encyclopedias.** Encyclopedias provide information on most everything from *a*, the first letter in the alphabet, to Vladimir Kosma Zworykin, a Russian-born American physicist and electronics engineer, who lived from 1889 until 1982. Entries are arranged alphabetically and include cross references. The charts, maps and illustrations often provide excellent background. If you are assigned to do a story on drinking habits of students at your college or university, it would be a good idea to check an encyclopedia. You might be surprised at what you could learn about fermented beverages, Alcoholics Anonymous (A.A.), and alcoholism, its effects and treatment. And if you want to try to get a grip on how much beer the average student drinks, it wouldn't hurt to check the encyclopedia, where you will find such tidbits as the average yearly consumption of beer by people in the United States. (A recent World Book Encyclopedia entry says the average consumption is about 24 gallons per person per year.)

- **Telephone directories.** These sources can give you more than telephone numbers. They can, for example, provide you with such things as area postal ZIP codes, street indexes and city maps. The Yellow Pages can be particularly valuable when searching for sources. For instance, if you are assigned to do a story on local abortion agencies, a logical starting place to line up local interviews would be the Yellow Pages. In the Yellow Pages for the Phoenix metropolitan area, there is a main subheading for "Abortion Alternatives Information" (with nine cross references listed, including "Adoption Services" and "Birth Control Centers") and a main subheading for "Abortion Information" (with eight cross references listed, including "Marriage, Family, Child & Individual Counselors" and "Clinics"). A cursory glance at the Yellow Pages might provide you with sources you did not know existed.

- **City directories.** These volumes, which are published by private firms, include alphabetical lists of names, addresses and telephone numbers of adult residents. They also contain street address guides, telephone number directories, ZIP codes, elementary school districts for individual addresses and information on such things as population, average income per household, home value distribution, construction permits, utilities, news media, tax bases, airlines, buses, railroads, climate and industrial sites.

• **State directories.** Called "blue books" in many states, these volumes include information on the executive branch (official state rosters of elective and appointive officers, their salaries and so on), the legislative branch (rosters of officials, their districts and so forth) and the judicial branch (rosters of judges, circuits, maps and so on). These volumes also include information on things such as state schools and colleges, election returns and miscellaneous statistics.

• **Biographies.** Standard biographical reference volumes such as Current Biography, which is published monthly except in August, are available in many newsrooms. This service provides about 30 articles in each month's edition on newsworthy living persons. The annual volumes contain about 350 biographies. The Dictionary of American Biography, another common source, contains information on distinguished Americans who are dead.

Most small- and medium-circulation newspapers limit their biographical volumes to one or two major ones, but libraries have many from which to choose. These range from Who's Who in Switzerland to Who's Who in Communist China. Library shelves also include such specialized volumes as Who's Who in the United Nations, Current World Leaders, The International Who's Who, Who's Who in the World, *The New York Times* Biographical Edition, Obituaries on File, Biography Index and Biography.

• **Facts on File.** This reference, which is published weekly, summarizes, records and indexes the news. National and foreign news events are included along with information on deaths, science, sports, medicine, education, religion, crime, books, plays, films and people in the news. The index includes subjects (grain embargo, school prayer and so forth) and names of people, organizations and countries.

• **Editorial Research Reports.** Published four times a month, this reference deals with major contemporary news issues, presenting a balanced overview in about 6,000 words. This source is particularly valuable because of its objective approach and its footnotes, which can lead the reporter to additional sources.

LIBRARY SOURCES

Public or college libraries can provide scores of useful references for reporters seeking information that is not readily available in most newsrooms.

General Information

• **Computer reference services.** Many college and university libraries and some large public libraries now have *computer reference services*. A computer-assisted search for information is similar to a volume-by-volume search of a printed index. The computer will respond by spitting out a reference list on the topic—an almost-instant bibliography. Sometimes the citations include *abstracts* (brief summaries of the articles or books). Libraries are connected to computers by telephone; comprehensive systems in New York and California are "called" frequently. The librarian types questions into a terminal. The requested information then is returned electronically through telephone wires. Computer searches have advantages that can greatly benefit reporters working on major projects: speed (scores of references can be thoroughly searched in a matter of seconds), multiple-access points (the computer is not restricted to laborious checks limited to author, title and subject; it even can scan for title words) and currency (because of lag time in printing, computer lists are more current). Most libraries charge for the service. The fee generally is based on the time the library is connected to the computer.

• **Newspaper indexes.** *The New York Times, Los Angeles Times, The Washington Post* and *The Wall Street Journal*, among others, are newspapers that index news events. These indexes, which are published in bound volumes, usually contain subject and name indexes.

• **Miscellaneous indexes.** Reporters use specialized indexes when they are researching a particular topic. They include, but are not limited to, the Business Periodicals Index, the Reader's Guide to Periodical Literature, the Essay and General Literature Index and Indexed Periodicals (which is an alphabetically arranged listing of periodical and serial titles that are indexed in about 330 American, British and Canadian periodical indexes).

Reporters who seek book-length treatments of various subjects can consult the Subject Guide to Books in Print, which lists all in-print and forthcoming titles from publishers, or Books in Print, which lists books alphabetically by title and author. Overviews of various books can be found in Book Review Index, *The New York Times* Book Review Index and Book Review Digest.

• **American Statistics Index (ASI).** This volume lists, by subject, areas in which there are federal government statistics. A counterpart, Statistical Reference Index (SRI), covers statistics gathered by organizations, university research centers and state governments.

• **Monthly Catalog of U.S. Government Publications.** This volume can be helpful to the reporter who is not sure where to search for specific information. Subjects are derived from the Library of Congress Subject Headings and its supplements. The catalog consists of text and five indexes: author, title, subject, series/report number and stock number. Instructions for ordering publications listed also are included.

• **National Directory of Addresses and Telephone Numbers.** This book includes sections on business and finance, government, education, religious denominations, hospitals, associations and unions, transportation and hotels, communications media and culture and recreation. It also has an alphabetical list of all names included.

- **Statistical Abstract of the United States.** This book is a digest of U.S. statistical data that have been collected by the U.S. government and a variety of private agencies.

- **Gallup Opinion Index.** Published monthly, this index provides analytical as well as statistical data.

- **Editorials on File.** Published biweekly, this source contains editorial reprints from more than 130 American newspapers. There generally are 20 to 30 editorials on each subject. Indexes for subjects are found at the end of each binder.

In addition to the volumes discussed above, scores of other general reference sources are valuable to journalists who seek information. Freelance journalist Cynthia Scanlon, who also works at the Phoenix, Ariz., Public Library, said the following sources are helpful: Who's Who in American Politics, Facts About Presidents, Climates of the States and The Essential Guide to Prescription Drugs.

Scanlon listed these additional general reference sources (with descriptions of the contents of those that are not obvious):

- **The Address Book.** This book provides information on how to locate more than 3,000 celebrities, corporate executives and VIPs.

- **Yearbook of Higher Education.** This volume contains the names of the country's universities and colleges, listed by state, with an index in the back of the volume.

- **Johnson's World Wide Chamber of Commerce Directory.** This directory provides the addresses of Chambers of Commerce in cities in the 50 states and throughout the world; it also contains the addresses of the foreign embassies and consulates in the United States as well as those of the U.S. embassies and consulates throughout the world.

- **Directory of Medical Specialists.** This volume lists doctors by state or specialty.

- **Standard Directory of Advertisers.** This volume contains the names of the largest advertising agencies as well as a trademark index.

- **Dorlund's Illustrated Medical Dictionary and Taber's Cyclopedic Medical Dictionary.** These dictionaries define medical terms and provide an explanation of symptoms.

- **Reverse Acronyms, Initialisms and Abbreviations Dictionary.**

- **World Almanac.** This volume contains information about weather, sports, world facts, awards, U.N. ambassadors, measurements, officials of states and countries and so forth as well as a guide to the occurrence of full moons and a perpetual calendar. Scanlon said: "If our reference team were stranded on a desert island and could have only one reference book—this would be it. Just about anything you could imagine is probably contained in the World Almanac."

- **Standard and Poor's Register.** This volume contains the names, addresses, telephone numbers and names of all officers of major corporations.

GATHERING INFORMATION 141

• **Encyclopedia of Associations.** This book lists most associations, institutes, foundations and so forth; it gives the addresses, telephone numbers, and names of directors and a short paragraph about each organization.

• **IMS/Ayr Directory of Publications.** This volume contains the names of magazines, newspapers, journals and newsletters, listed by state; it includes circulations.

• **Standard Periodical Directory.** This directory contains the names, addresses, telephone numbers, circulation figures and subscription rates of most periodicals and newsletters in the United States.

• **Chase's Annual Events.** This volume lists a full year's calendar by month.

• **Who's Who in America, International Who's Who and Webster's Biographical Dictionary.** These books contain biographical information on individuals of national and international importance.

• **Places Rated Almanac.** This almanac contains ratings of cities according to their climate and terrain, housing, crime, health care, education, transportation, arts and recreation.

• **Christensen's Ultimate Movie, TV and Rock Directory.** This volume lists the addresses of famous people in the movie, television and rock industries.

• **The Official Museum Directory.** This directory contains the names of museums, listed by state and subject.

• **American Hospital Association Guide to the Health Care Field.** This volume lists the addresses of hospitals and clinics throughout the United States.

• **Encyclopedia of American Crime.** This source covers crime figures and crime events.

• **American Library Directory.** This volume contains the names of libraries throughout the United States, listed by subject or state.

• **Contemporary Authors.** This book contains the names, addresses and short biographies of contemporary authors.

• **Washington Information Directory.** This volume lists the addresses of almost every agency in Washington, D.C.

• **Symbols of America.** This volume contains information on America's trademarks and the products they symbolize; according to the cover, the information includes "their history, folklore and enduring mystique."

Information on States

• **Statistical abstracts for various states.** These volumes often will include information on such things as geography, climate, population, vital statistics (births and deaths), health, education, labor, employment, earnings, public lands, recreation, government, law enforcement, mining, construction, housing, manufacturing, transportation, energy, communications, utilities and real estate.

- **The Book of the States.** This volume provides information on the types of operating procedures, financing and activities of state governments. Scores of tables list all states and provide comparative information about such things as income taxes, campaign finance laws and voter turnout.

- **State Information Book.** This source presents basic information on aspects of all 50 states, such as officers; major services; legislatures; supreme courts; Washington, D.C., representation; and federal offices in each state.

Information on Congress and the Federal Government

- **Federal Register.** Administrative rules and regulations are published in this weekday service.

- **U.S. Government Organizational Manual.** This source describes the functions of departments and agencies in the executive branch. It includes a bibliography of publications prepared by each.

- **Congressional Information Service (CIS) Index.** This volume provides access to contents of congressional hearings, reports and documents. It contains testimony by expert witnesses. It is excellent for pro and con arguments.

- **Congressional Digest.** This source examines contemporary subjects being considered by Congress. It attempts to present all sides of an issue.

- **Congressional Directory.** This book contains short biographical sketches of all representatives (listed by state). It also lists the office and telephone numbers of members of Congress, along with the names of two principal staff members for each.

- **Congressional Quarterly Weekly Report.** Published weekly, this source contains voting records of congressmen, texts of presidential press conferences and major speeches.

- **Congressional Record.** This source contains verbatim reports of what is said on the House and Senate floors. Do not assume, however, that all statements in the Congressional Record were articulated on the floors. Senators and representatives also can enter materials into the Congressional Record that were not delivered on the floors of the respective Houses.

- **Congressional Staff Directory.** Reporters often find this source particularly valuable when gathering information on topical issues. It provides names of staff members of congressional committees and subcommittees along with nearly 3,000 staff biographies.

- **Guide to Congress.** The subject index of this source, published by Congressional Quarterly, includes a variety of topics on how Congress works. For example, reporters wondering about impeachment proceedings

GATHERING INFORMATION

could turn to this volume for a summary of the purpose of impeachment, its history, the procedures and a chart on federal officers who have been impeached by the House.

SOURCES ON LAW

Reporters who seek information on legal topics can consult the sources listed below.

- **Law dictionaries.** Reporters who have questions about legal terminology can consult law dictionaries. One of the most comprehensive is Black's Law Dictionary, which provides the meanings of legal terms and phrases found in statutes or judicial opinions. It also includes a guide to pronunciation.

- **Legal encyclopedias.** Corpus Juris Secundum and American Jurisprudence 2nd are excellent basic sources. Corpus Juris Secundum provides a look at American case law from the first reported case to the present. It also includes citations to such sources as treatises, form-books and law journal articles. American Jurisprudence provides overviews of various aspects of law arranged alphabetically by title. Some states, such as California, Florida, New York and Texas, have their own laws published in encyclopedias. General encyclopedias include, in addition to overviews of cases and statutory laws, definitions of words and phrases. Reporters who are exploring an area of the law for the first time will find encyclopedias to be excellent starting points.

- **Indexes.** The Index to Legal Periodicals is published monthly, except in September. Bound volumes by year can be found in law libraries and in many university libraries. The topical index is particularly helpful to reporters who would like a crash course in a specific area of the law. For example, reporters doing a series of articles on the fair trial–free press issue in America could consult the subheading "Freedom of the Press" in the Index to Legal Periodicals. Under that subheading would be a long list of articles dealing with press freedom. The reporters could pull from the list those articles that dealt with fair trial–free press issues. This volume provides the current index to more than 300 American legal journals and British periodicals.

- **Federal laws.** The United States Code and United States Code Annotated contain federal statutes. Sometimes journalists know the statute only by its popular name, such as the Smith Act or the Taft-Hartley Act. In these instances, Shepard's Federal and State Acts and Cases by Popular Names is helpful because it lists acts by their popular names and provides citations to the official acts.

- **State laws.** Each state publishes its codes. These generally are compiled under a title such as Arizona Revised Statutes or Ohio Revised Code. Reporters should familiarize themselves with the volumes of laws for their particular states.

- **Digests.** The American Digest System publishes all reported state and federal cases. The cases are arranged by subject. The U.S. Supreme Court Digest arranges high court decisions by subject.

- **Federal court decisions.** Opinions of the U.S. Supreme Court can be found in a variety of sources, including United States Reports (the official government edition), United States Supreme Court Reports (the Lawyer's Cooperative Publishing Co. edition), Supreme Court Reporter (West Publishing Co. edition) and United States Law Week (published by the Bureau of National Affairs). Opinions of the U.S. Courts of Appeal, the Court of Customs and Patent Appeals, and the Court of Claims can be found in the Federal Reporter series. Selected opinions of the U.S. District Courts and the U.S. Customs Court can be found in the Federal Supplement. These volumes are found in law library collections as well as in many university libraries.

- **State court decisions.** Some states publish volumes containing only their state court decisions; some do not. Selected state court decisions can be found in the National Reporter System's regional volumes. The North Western Reporter, for example, contains opinions from Iowa, Michigan, Minnesota, Nebraska, North Dakota, South Dakota and Wisconsin. Several regional reports are published.

Golfers, such as Nancy Lopez, receive considerable attention on the country's sports pages. Sportswriters must be versatile. They must be capable of writing about football and basketball games as well as everything from archery to yachting. (Photo by Steven E. Sutton/Duomo)

9 / Writing Basic Stories

Before reporters are assigned major stories, they generally have to prove their competence through basic writing assignments. At one time or another, most reporters write their share of obituaries, weather stories and sports articles.

In this chapter you will be introduced to the following terms:

death notice	year-end weather summary
hoax	sportswriting cliché
same-day obit	"gee whiz" school
second-day obit	"aw nuts" school
courtesy title	minor sports
meteorologist	box score
human angle	team statistics
state weather forecast	individual statistics
local weather forecast	play-by-play chart

147

Journalism school students often dream about what their first reporting jobs will be like. They envision themselves traveling around the world and reporting on the president, ducking machine-gun fire while covering civil insurrections in far-away places and writing Page One stories about sensational murder trials.

Those dreams may indeed be realized, but the students will write hundreds of basic stories first. Most, if not all, of today's White House correspondents have written their share of obituaries, weather pieces and even sports articles.

This chapter provides information on how to write these basic stories.

OBITUARIES

Reporters sometimes consider writing obituaries to be a chore worse than death, but the fact remains: Obits enjoy high reader interest.

Karen Swope, a reporter for *The Evansville* (Ind.) *Press*, has been writing obituaries—*death notices*—for more than a decade. She takes her responsibilities seriously. "It's an important job—as important as any other on the newspaper," she said.

Most editors agree.

The policy of *The Berkshire* (Mass.) *Eagle* possibly best summarizes the philosophy of many newspapers: "It is our policy to run obituaries and funeral notices involving deceased persons who have any connection at all with our circulation area. If John Jones fished here in 1937 and lived happily ever after in Tacoma, we use his obit because we deem it news, it creates good will (or at least it avoids creating bad will), and we try to be the paper of record for our area."

SELECTING OBITS TO PUBLISH

Most newspapers have an obit page. Depending on the circulation of the newspaper and the population of the area served, obituaries might fill a portion of the page or they might spill over to more than one page. Most newspapers publish obits—free—for every resident and former resident. Some larger-circulation newspapers obviously do not have sufficient space to publish obits of everyone who dies in their areas, but they do publish obits of as many people as they can. Some newspapers provide a list of the deceased with only basic facts, such as age and date of death. Still other newspapers publish complete obituary information in classified advertising space purchased by funeral homes or by families.

In addition to obits published regularly on their designated page, newspapers occasionally carry front page stories on the deaths of well-known people.

A national survey of 165 randomly selected daily newspaper managing editors, which was conducted in 1985, found that 94 percent of the country's dailies publish obits for all area residents and nearly 9 in 10 of the dailies publish them free of charge.

Many newspapers are so conscious of their responsibility to publish obits that they will print them several days after a death if word of the death has been delayed. This often happens in the case of individuals who had lived and worked in the community but retired to another area of the country. A week after the person's death, the newspaper might receive a letter with obit information. Then, after verifying it, many papers will publish an obit beginning something like this: Word has been received of the death of John P. Jones, 75, former Riverdale electrician, who died Oct. 25 at his home in Palm Springs, Calif.

BASIC INFORMATION IN OBITS

Obits should include basic information, such as:

- Name of the deceased
- Age
- Address
- Occupation
- Date of death
- Cause of death
- Time and date of services
- Accomplishments
- Names of survivors
- Visitation information
- Place of burial
- Memorial information

In addition to this basic information that generally is included in obituaries, some smaller-circulation newspapers carry follows to obits in which pallbearers are listed.

SOURCES FOR OBIT INFORMATION

Most information for obituaries is provided to the media by funeral homes (sometimes called mortuaries). However, the policy of the *New Haven* (Conn.) *Register* emphasizes the need to gather information beyond that provided by mortuaries: "In most situations the *Register* depends on funeral homes to submit obituaries. This does not mean, however, that the newspapers' position should be supine. If a prominent person or a person violently injured is known to be near death, the newspapers should check with the hospital, the public relations officer of the person's employer or a similar authority in order not to miss the news story. Information concerning funeral services may be put off until subsequent editions."

The *Register's* policy also emphasizes the importance of checking the newspaper library: "If anything in an obituary suggests the person may have been prominent in the New Haven area, reporters and desk editors should consider it mandatory to check the clippings in the library for background. Frequently a family, under stress, will provide inaccurate or incomplete information to a funeral home; checking the files can set this straight. If necessary, the funeral home should be called to confirm that the individual who died is the same person mentioned in the clippings."

After gathering additional information from clippings and possibly from interviews with law enforcement officials, hospital officials, employers, fellow workers and friends, calls to family members may be in order. This, of course, should be handled delicately.

IMPORTANCE OF ACCURACY

Accuracy is immensely important in any news story, but inaccurate information in an obit can cause severe pain to surviving family members. Thus, it is particularly important to confirm all information gathered for obits. Because most of the facts contained in obits come from telephone calls from the mortuary, reporters should be diligent in checking names, cities and addresses in available directories. It also is wise to compute the age of the person from his or her date of birth to verify the age supplied by the mortuary. Also, when taking calls from the mortuary, always ask the caller to repeat any words or spellings that sound unusual.

Editors or reporters at *The Kansas City Times* verify all information supplied by funeral homes by calling family members, according to managing editor Monroe Dodd. Additional information may be sought from or verified by police, coroners and other law enforcement officials. Occasionally, reporters at the *Times* will speak with business associates or close friends of the deceased if the family is vague or uncertain on some pertinent matters.

HOAXES

The *New Haven Register*'s policy warns reporters to confirm deaths in order to avoid *hoaxes*. "An obit called in by a funeral director with whom the reporter is not familiar should be confirmed by calling back. Get the number from the phone book or long-distance information; don't trust the number the caller may just have given you. If the obit is submitted by someone other than a funeral director, call the funeral home to confirm it. If the funeral home cannot be reached, the death should be confirmed with a reliable—that word should be emphasized—second source."

Some newspapers, such as *The Trentonian* in Trenton, N.J., verify calls from mortuaries by asking for the funeral director's obit code. "If he doesn't have one," the newspaper policy states, "verify that he's a funeral director by calling back the number listed in the telephone book, no matter where in the world it is. This will hopefully eliminate the dreaded hoax, the bane of all obit writers."

OBITUARY STYLES

Routine obits at the *Chicago Tribune* and scores of other newspapers normally follow one of two styles. The style adhered to by the *Tribune* city desk is this: If the obit is written on the day of the death—a *same-day*

WRITING BASIC STORIES

obit—the fact that the person died is the lead. If the obit is written one or more days after the death—a *second-day obit*—the time of services is the lead.

Same-Day Obit

An example of an obituary written on the day of the death follows:

John E. Jones, 72, Riverdale, died Wednesday in Samaritan Memorial Hospital after a short illness. Mr. Jones was an accountant and a partner in the firm of Smith and Jones, 2020 W. Main St., until his retirement seven years ago.

Mr. Jones was a board member of the Samaritan Memorial Hospital at the time of his death.

He is survived by his wife, Mildred; two sons, John Jr. and Michael, both of Riverdale; a daughter, Mary Smith of New York; four grandchildren; a great-grandchild; two brothers; and a sister.

Mass ["services" for Protestant churches] will be said ["held"] at 9 a.m. Saturday in Resurrection Catholic [Methodist, Lutheran, etc.] Church, 1136 Central Ave. [the chapel at 1244 Kansas St., Riverdale].

Second-Day Obit

An example of an obituary that is written one or more days after the death follows:

Mass ["services"] for John E. Jones, 72, Riverdale, will be said ["held"] at 9 a.m. Saturday in Resurrection Catholic [Methodist, Lutheran, etc.] Church, 1136 Central Ave. [the chapel at 1244 Kansas St., Riverdale].

Mr. Jones, who died Wednesday in Samaritan Memorial Hospital after a short illness, was an accountant and a partner in the firm of Smith and Jones, 2020 W. Main St., until his retirement seven years ago.

Mr. Jones was a board member of Samaritan Memorial Hospital at the time of his death.

He is survived by his wife, Mildred; two sons, John Jr. and Michael, both of Riverdale; a daughter, Mary Smith of New York; four grandchildren; a great-grandchild; two brothers; and a sister.

CAPTURING THE FLAVOR OF THE DECEDENT'S LIFE

Obits often fall into the standard, concise forms outlined above, but most newspapers strive to go beyond the mechanical restrictions. The policy of the *New Haven Register* makes this clear: "The obituary writer's job is not simply to report the fact of death, but also, so far as available information permits, to capture the flavor of the decedent's life. This means that, although obituary writing can be reduced to a formula, the formula never should become a straitjacket that prevents writing a better news story. A number of style rules [are set forth by the *Register*] but in any case where style and news judgment appear to conflict, news judgment should prevail."

Dave Downey, a reporter for the *Tempe* (Ariz.) *Daily News Tribune*, was assigned the task of writing an obit on Edith S. Getz, a longtime resident for whom a local school had been named.

Relying on Multiple Sources

Downey gathered information from the mortuary and from the newspaper's clip file. But he didn't stop there. He conducted interviews with:

- A former governor
- Three neighbors of the deceased
- A high school teacher
- The wife of a former mayor

This required extra time and effort, but, by conducting the interviews to supplement biographical information, Downey put together an obit that captured the flavor of the decedent's life.

Downey's first three paragraphs provided the essentials:

Edith S. Getz, 77, Arizona's second woman attorney and longtime Tempe philanthropist, died Tuesday at Friendship Village of Tempe. She had suffered a heart attack.

Getz, who lived in Tempe 53 years and ran the old Boston store, faced adversity much of her life.

Born in Hungary, she was raised in a poor family and had to work her way through college to get a law degree.

Painting a Word Picture

After providing these essential facts, Downey then painted a vivid word picture of Getz based on his interviews. The obit continued:

WRITING BASIC STORIES　　　　　　　　　　　　　　　　　　　　　　　　153

After moving to Arizona 55 years ago and obtaining her attorney's license, she endured the sneers of male attorneys, who didn't want women invading their profession.

In later years, she endured the painful loneliness brought about by the deaths of her daughter, Barbara, and husband, Charles. And, eventually, she had to endure the decline of her own health.

"It's been kind of a dreary existence for her because she hasn't been well," said former Arizona Gov. Howard Pyle. Getz had suffered from diabetes, breast cancer and high blood pressure.

Yet, through it all, she never gave up.

"She was never bitter . . . just very kind, very soft spoken and really neat," said Mary Stewart, a neighbor. "She always put other people first and herself second."

Betty Boles, who lived across the street from Getz, said, "She was forever, until she got sick, doing something for someone."

Boles' husband, Ray, said Getz, on numerous occasions, donated money and resources to people and organizations. He recalled one instance where she gave a family $1,000 because their child had cancer.

At the same time, "she was never one to brag about what she was doing," he said.

"She was just a wonderful person," said another neighbor, Mrs. Margaret Christiansen. "She's one of those special people that come along once or twice in a lifetime."

Christiansen recalled that Getz was especially fond of children.

"She was always aware when children were around, and they were never ignored," she said.

Jean Brill, a high school teacher in Tempe for 10 years, noted that Getz donated land to build Getz School in 1970. She also donated money to the Tempe school for the handicapped that bears her name. And she made it a point to attend special school activities.

The obit went on to quote other people, to provide a summary of the organizations she had belonged to, to list her survivors and to give information about graveside services and memorial contributions.

Downey's story clearly illustrates that it is worth the extra effort to dig through clippings and to seek out people who knew the deceased.

WRITING INTERESTING LEADS

Leads normally should contain the full name and age of the person, but other information can be added so all obits do not read the same way. The policy of the *News-Journal*, Daytona Beach, Fla., states: "Put any interesting fact of the deceased's life in the lead, even if it is only how many years he/she lived here. Since the number of years a person had lived here is overused, dig for something else. This means the funeral home must be questioned every time it gives an obit. Occasionally, you may have to ask the director to contact the family to get something more."

Using Anecdotes and Description

The New York Times is well known for its interesting, well-written obits. Reporters at the *Times* indeed dig deep for fascinating anecdotes and descriptive information that make their obits a pleasure to read. This is not to suggest that the media should exploit a person's death by writing eloquently about it. Rather, it should be noted that obituaries can effectively bring out the significance of the person and his or her death. That is good writing.

Note these leads of two obits published in the *Times*:

Margaret Hamilton, the actress whose role as the cackling Wicked Witch of the West in "The Wizard of Oz" unnerved generations of children, died yesterday, apparently of a heart attack, at a nursing home in Salisbury, Conn. She was 82 years old.

Colin Shaw Maclaren, a Scottish Highlander whose career took him from fighting Afghan tribesmen on British India's Northwest Frontier to 38 years as a reporter for The New York Times, died Wednesday at the Booth Memorial Medical Center in Flushing, Queens. He was 86 years old and lived in Flushing.

Not all obits, of course, are written about well-known people. But, if the reporter works hard, interesting facts can be found about nearly everyone. The information might not be earth-shattering, but it can help establish an identity for the deceased.

Here is an example of a lead with interesting information about the deceased:

John E. Jones, who had not missed a Riverdale High School home basketball game since 1947, died Wednesday in Samaritan Memorial Hospital after a short illness. He was 72.

Sometimes, if the circumstances merit, the name of the deceased can be delayed until the second paragraph:

For the first time in more than four decades, when the Riverdale High School basketball Broncos take to the floor next season, one of their biggest fans won't be in his 10th-row, midcourt seat.

John E. Jones, who had not missed a Riverdale High School home basketball game since 1947, died Wednesday in Samaritan Memorial Hospital after a short illness. He was 72.

Delayed leads on obits are the exception, rather than the rule, but occasionally they are acceptable.

Names and Nicknames

Newspapers generally use the first name, middle initial and last name of the deceased. Most do not use nicknames—particularly if they sound de-

WRITING BASIC STORIES   155

rogatory. If the deceased was known to most people by his nickname, however, some newspapers will use it. For example:

John E. "Booster" Jones, who had not missed a Riverdale High School home basketball game since 1947, died Wednesday in Samaritan Memorial Hospital after a short illness. He was 72.

Note that the nickname is set off on quotation marks; in obits, use of parentheses indicates a maiden name. Also, if the nickname would slow the cadence of the lead sentence, save it for later. For example:

John E. Jones, who had not missed a Riverdale High School home basketball game since 1947, died Wednesday in Samaritan Memorial Hospital after a short illness. Mr. Jones, who was known to his friends as "Booster," was 72.

Courtesy Titles

In the above examples, a *courtesy title* (Mr.) was used on second references. Few newspapers use courtesy titles (such as Mr., Mrs., Miss, Ms. or Dr.) on second references in news stories, but many do so in obits.

Ages and Addresses

Many newspaper policies mandate that the age and address of the deceased be printed. The *News-Journal* in Daytona Beach, Fla., has a policy that states: "Always include the age of deceased and address. If necessary (but only after having exhausted all avenues) fudge a bit and say 'in his/her 70s or 80s' or whatever. There MUST BE some indication of age."

The reader never should have to use arithmetic to figure out the age of the deceased (obit writers should not merely give the date and place of birth). Reporters must be careful when computing ages. Reporters and their sources often forget to take the date of birth into account. For example, a person is born Feb. 15, 1928, and dies Feb. 1, 1988. That person would be 59, not 60. A common blunder is to merely subtract 1928 from 1988 to come up with 60.

Ages can be handled a number of ways, including:

- John E. Jones, 72, died Wednesday in Riverdale.
- John E. Jones died Wednesday in Riverdale. He was 72.
- John E. Jones died Wednesday in Riverdale at the age of 72.
- John E. Jones died Wednesday in Riverdale at 72 years of age.

The first two examples are preferable to the last two. In the last two examples, the extra words make the language more stilted than necessary.

Practices vary on the use of addresses. Some newspapers use full addresses (2142 S. 168th Ave., Riverdale); others use only the town. The policy of *The Trentonian*, for example, states: "The family, usually through the funeral director, may sometimes ask that exact addresses not be used to avoid possible burglaries. We'll go along with this request, although we usually prefer using full addresses."

Cause of Death

Policies vary on stating the cause of death in obits. The national survey of 165 randomly selected daily newspaper managing editors cited earlier in this chapter showed that 9 percent of the papers always publish the cause of death in obituaries. Nearly 78 percent said they sometimes do; 13 percent said they never do.

The policy of the *New Haven Register* for example, states: "If relatives do not want information disclosed concerning a particular disease, 'a long illness' or similar phrase may be used. If death is violent, however—for example, in an auto accident or a shooting—that fact should not be disguised. Rule of thumb: If the funeral home does not volunteer a cause of death, ask. Too many times there have been attempts to slip obituaries through when the deaths were homicides or suspected homicides."

The policy of the *Fargo* (N.D.) *Forum* states: "Usually we do not specify the cause of death but we ask the question in case we might miss an accident or death under suspicious circumstances. If an accident is involved, notify the city desk so a news story can be prepared about the accident. Obituaries of accident victims should note 'she died of injuries received in an auto accident Friday.'"

The Trentonian's policy also provides flexibility: "We do not insist on using the cause of death unless it involves accidental or other unusual circumstances. Where the deceased is young, we always ask the funeral director the cause of death. Where the deceased is prominent, regardless of age, try to determine whether it was a long or short illness. We don't usually specify the type of illness unless the family requests it. Also, don't call it a 'lengthy' illness. It's short or long."

Most newspapers use the cause of death if the person was well known. Here are two examples taken from wire-service stories:

BEVERLY HILLS, Calif. (UPI)—Actor Rock Hudson, the square-jawed movie hero who played the role of the suave ladies' man for three decades, died Wednesday after a yearlong battle with AIDS—the first major celebrity known to have been felled by the disease....

In Washington, the House, acting hours after Hudson's death was announced, voted 322–107 to substantially boost the amount of federal money for the battle against AIDS. The measure provides $189.7 million for AIDS work, $70 million more than President Reagan requested and 90 percent more than is being spent this year.

WINSTON-SALEM, N.C. (AP)—Former Sen. Sam J. Ervin Jr., the self-styled "country lawyer" whose homespun humor, animated eyebrows and love of the constitution made him a folk hero when he presided over the Senate Watergate hearings, died of respiratory failure Tuesday. He was 88.

Ervin died at about 4:15 p.m. at Bowman Gray Medical Center at N.C. Baptist Hospital in Winston-Salem, according to Roger Rollman, a spokesman at the hospital.

"The cause of death was attributed by his doctors to respiratory failure which developed during the day," Rollman said. "The kidney failure for which Mr. Ervin was admitted to the center was a significant contributing factor in the death."

Suicides

One of the major dilemmas facing newspapers is how to handle obits or news stories when suicide is the cause of death. Again, policies vary. The *Bangor* (Maine) *Daily News*, for example, stopped including that information in its obits in the early 1970s. "We feel that the obit is a permanent record which families keep and neither they nor their descendants should have to be reminded of a suicide every time they take out the family album," said Kent H. Ward, associate managing editor. "Further, we do not run suicides as news stories unless they involve prominent people or the suicide was committed in public or in some spectacular manner. In other words, if Mr. Average Joe goes down in the privacy of his basement or out behind the barn and kills himself we do not give it a play. And his obit would probably state that he died unexpectedly."

The *Iowa City* (Iowa) *Press Citizen*'s policy states: "If someone commits suicide, it is generally handled as an obit. But calling someone's death a suicide requires confirmation from the medical examiner."

The *New Haven Register* labels deaths as suicides or apparent suicides only if "the person taking his or her life is a public figure or the suicide takes place in full view of other people. Any statement that a death is a suicide must be attributed."

The national survey of managing editors showed that 17 percent of the newspapers always use the word *suicide* in obits if it is determined to be the cause of death; 21 percent sometimes use it; 62 percent never use it.

PROVIDING ADDITIONAL INFORMATION

The most pertinent information—name, age, address, date of death, time of funeral and sometimes cause of death—is placed in the lead of an obit;

supplementary facts fill the remaining paragraphs. Newspaper policy and the importance of the deceased are primary factors in determining the length of obits. Generally, however, information on the following is provided:

- Background of deceased (place of birth, education, work experience and so forth)
- Memberships held
- Survivors (names of spouses, children and siblings; number of grandchildren and great grandchildren)
- Visitations (when friends and relatives may view the body at the mortuary)
- Details on memorials (newspaper policies on this vary, but most use a wording similar to this: The family suggests that memorials be made to the Heart Fund)

TERMINOLOGY AND OTHER OBIT HANGUPS

Editors often single out words, phrases and usages that should be considered when writing obits. A sample follows.

- **Terminology for death.** "People die—period! They don't die suddenly any more than they die slowly, although they may have died quickly after being struck in the heart with an MX missile."—Policy of *The Trentonian*.

"Nobody dies suddenly. We all die at the same speed. Some causes of death are quicker than others, but the speed of death itself is constant. A person dies of an ailment, not from it. A person is dead on arrival at a hospital, not 'to' it. You arrive at a place, not 'to' it. Also, people are 'taken' to hospitals. If we say they are 'transported,' it sounds like they are freight."—Policy of *The Findlay* (Ohio) *Courier*.

- **Place of birth.** "Funeral directors are fond of saying that John Jones was a 'former native' of some place. Native means the place of birth, so a person cannot be a former native."—Policy of the *Jamestown* (N.Y.) *Post-Journal*.

WEATHER

Many of the country's newspapers are expanding their coverage of weather. *USA Today*—Gannett's national newspaper—is among the pacesetters. It is no accident that *USA Today*'s weather package is highly praised and widely imitated; its coverage is colorful and comprehensive.

Jack Williams, a *USA Today* weather page editor, noted, however, that "at most newspapers, writing weather stories is looked upon as some terrible chore." Williams said this is merely a matter of attitude. "Newspapers seem to draw people who were afraid to take calculus in college," he added. "But, writing about the weather involves more than science. There's also the human side."

Williams functions as a translator when he talks to a meteorologist. According to The Random House College Dictionary, a *meteorologist* is versed in "the science dealing with the atmosphere and its phenomena, including weather and climate."

"I can use their jargon," Williams said. "But I always translate it for my readers. There are some weather concepts that are very difficult to understand. You can put them in ordinary terms that will not tell the whole story, but the story will be correct as far as it goes. Still, I worry a lot that we will oversimplify to the point that we will make the 10th grader who has been paying attention in his earth science class cringe."

The reporter of weather stories must convey technical information in accurate, understandable terms to lay readers.

Working closely with meteorologists, Williams puts together his own weather stories each day. "We also make an effort to try to get hold of people other than law enforcement officials and weather forecasters to quote in stories," Williams said. "We want to show how people are affected by the weather. I also try to show readers that weather, in a sense, is connected—that the storm on the East Coast is tied to the clear weather on the West Coast somehow. A lot of stories treat weather as if it popped up out of nowhere. As a national newspaper, we want to get a national perspective."

LOCAL WEATHER COVERAGE

Most television stations place strong emphasis on weather forecasting. It is not uncommon for stations to hire meteorologists to assemble and present weather forecasts and reports. People rely extensively on television, as well as on radio, for these forecasts.

Readers often turn to newspapers, however, when they want details of weather from across the country. While most television stations focus on weather forecasting, most newspapers place primary emphasis on weather coverage. Forecasts published in most newspapers are from the wire services and are based on information provided by the National Weather Service.

Naturally, most newspapers cannot devote the time and money to weather coverage that *USA Today* does. Nor can most newspapers match the sparkle and sophistication of electronic media weather forecasting. But most editors realize the importance of solid weather coverage.

Phyllis H. Thompson, managing editor of the *Statesboro* (Ga.) *Herald*, said: "We are a farming community and feel local weather coverage is important. But we have a small staff. UPI provides us with most of our weather coverage, but . . . it is not specific enough to help our farmers on a daily basis." Thus, the newspaper must supplement the national material from the wire services with local information.

Jim Haney, managing editor of *The Sumter* (S.C.) *Daily Item*, said reporters at his newspaper "are always on the alert for stories about severe weather or weather trends that affect agriculture."

James E. Hammer, editor of the *Daily Pioneer* in Bimidji, Minn., said "localizing statewide weather forecasts and special warnings are of prime importance" at his newspaper.

Editors and reporters of the *Fairbanks* (Alaska) *Daily News-Miner* are particularly aware of the importance of local coverage of weather. They live just 130 miles south of the Arctic Circle, and they often find themselves telling readers about local developments.

Impact of Weather on Readers

Local readers, like others around the country, want to know how the weather will affect them. It is not enough merely to give high and low temperatures and precipitation totals. Readers also want to know, for example:

- If it is safe to travel
- If schools will be open
- If the mail will be delivered
- If planes are on time at the airport
- If fog will make it difficult to see
- If it will be bitterly cold

Readers want to know these things—and more—because their lives are affected each day by the weather. People depend on the media for this information.

COVERAGE OF A SNOWSTORM IN FAIRBANKS

When a storm hits, weather coverage is particularly important at the *Daily News-Miner*, which has a circulation of about 18,000. Several reporters and editors play a role in gathering information when a weather story dominates the front page. This was the case when a snowstorm paralyzed Fairbanks. The headline in Monday's editions told the story: 17.2″—but don't stop counting!

Sources for Weather Information

The story was not routine; it went beyond providing statistical information. It contained facts, figures and direct quotations from a variety of sources, including:

- National Weather Service
- Alaska State Troopers
- Fairbanks International Airport
- State Department of Transportation
- Fairbanks Police Department
- Various weather forecasters
- Towing company owners
- Private citizens

Writing the Weather Story

The storm was a major story that required extensive interviews and the gathering of factual information. It was the type of story encountered regularly at newspapers all across America. The straightforward opening paragraphs on the Page One story by *Daily News-Miner* reporters John Creed and Kris Capps made it clear that the weather was wreaking havoc with travel and probably would continue to do so:

> The largest snowstorm in years is continuing to dump near-record amounts in much of Interior Alaska, causing slick roads and lots of accidents.
>
> Travel warnings are in effect, and the National Weather Service is predicting even more snow before the storm tapers off by noon Tuesday.
>
> "It ain't over yet," said weather service forecaster Paul Flatt this morning. "It's real tough to call, but we should pick up another six to 10 inches through Tuesday. This much snow is unusual in Fairbanks. It happens, but not very often."
>
> Weather officials at the airport tallied 17.2 inches of snowfall by 9 a.m. this morning—2.9 inches on Saturday, 11.5 inches Sunday, and 2.8 inches by 9 a.m. today.
>
> "And it is still falling like mad," said National Weather Service meteorological technician Wayne Nelson this morning.

This lead block of paragraphs certainly provided readers with the most pertinent information: The storm was a major one; it would continue to dump snow on Fairbanks; and the snow was approaching near-record amounts.

Had there been deaths as a result of the storm, major power outages or monetary estimates of damages, this information likely would have been included in the lead. However, in the relatively early stages of the storm, this information was not yet known.

After the lead block, the reporters focused on facts and quotations from sources in Fairbanks and outlying areas. The story continued with information crucial and interesting to area readers:

> Fairbanks International Airport remained open this morning, but traffic was slow due to snow clearing operations on the runways, said Nelson, who also does pilot briefing.
>
> "Operation is close to normal for the major airlines," Nelson said. "But for the little guys it's different. These bush pilots can't take off in this kind of stuff."
>
> Alaska State Troopers are urging people to stay home to avoid the nasty driving conditions.
>
> Over the weekend, both Troopers and Fairbanks city police kept busy with a string of accidents and stalled vehicles.

After the writers provided readers with information that most directly touched their daily lives, they went on to discuss the origins of the storm and to provide a summary of conditions in other area towns:

According to forecasters, the snow is the result of a raging storm that originated in the North Pacific and pounded the state's western shores with high winds, snow—even rain—much of last week.

"If people think it's rough here, it's rougher in Nome and Kotzebue," said Glen Glenzer, local deputy commissioner of the Department of Transportation. He said recent flooding in Nome did not cause excessive damage, but, now "It's still blowing, still drifting there. The airports were closed occasionally (over these past few days) for zero visibility."

In Fairbanks, road-clearing crews are working around the clock to stay ahead of the storm, Glenzer said.

The story concluded with quotes from area residents, a police officer, a state trooper and managers of local towing services, who reported doing a record business.

STEPS TO FOLLOW
WHEN WRITING ABOUT WEATHER

Comprehensive, complete weather stories, such as those published by the *Daily News-Miner,* are not developed simply by incorporating a few comments from local weather service officials into a wire service account. Reporters must diligently ferret out information from all available sources. Some suggestions to consider when writing stories about storms follow:

• **Keep in constant touch with the National Weather Service bureau nearest you.** Don't wait until a major storm hits to develop sources at the bureau. If possible, visit the bureau nearest you. Get to know the forecasters. Then, when a major storm hits and you want information from the bureau, you will not be just another voice on the telephone. Other media representatives will be in touch with the bureau on days of major storms; if you have taken the time to develop sources there on less hectic days, it will pay dividends for you.

• **Keep in constant touch with the state patrol.** The state patrol can provide you with information on accidents, road conditions and the like. As is the case when working with the National Weather Service, if you have maintained ties with the state patrol throughout the year, it will be easier to get information on days of inclement weather. It is only natural for sources to be more accommodating to those journalists who check in regularly. One way to cultivate sources such as the state patrol, the National Guard, the Army Reserve, the Coast Guard and the like is to do an occasional feature story on their training or on new equipment or facilities they might have. Such stories will be of interest to your readers and will help officials at the agencies remember you when you call on deadline and need some information from them.

• **Keep in touch with the state department of transportation or comparable agency for your area.** Officials there can keep you posted on road closings, on bridges that are out or on areas of the state where travel is not advised.

WRITING BASIC STORIES 163

• **Keep in touch with local enforcement agencies, such as the police and sheriff departments.**

• **Keep in touch with local agencies responsible for snow removal, storm cleanup and the like.** They can provide you with information on timetables for cleanups, how many workers are on the job, whether they are working shifts around the clock and estimated costs.

• **Interview area residents who have been caught out in the weather.** Do not limit weather stories to quotations from authorities; provide details and quotations from residents, too. Readers will appreciate and relate to the *human angle*.

• **Keep in touch with officials at local institutions, agencies and entities that are affected by the storm.** These include, but are not limited to:

- Schools (Will classes be held? Are buses running?)
- Utility companies (What effects did the storm have on electrical and gas usage?)
- Telephone companies (Did the storm down lines? Did use of telephones go up during the hours of the storm?)
- Civil Defense departments (Are shelters being provided for the homeless or stranded motorists?)
- National Guard, Coast Guard or Army Reserve units (Have these units been mobilized to aid residents or to help clear debris or snow? If so, how many men are involved? How long will the mobilization last?)
- Post office (Is the mail being delivered? If so, are deliveries running late?)
- Hospitals (Have any persons been hospitalized as a result of storm-related incidents? What is their condition?)
- Bus companies (Are they running on schedule?)
- Airport (Are planes arriving and departing? If so, are they on schedule?)
- Train depots (Are trains arriving and departing? Are they on schedule?)
- Taxi companies (Are they running?)

In addition to consulting with the sources listed above, reporters might want to check weather records kept by the newspaper or local observers. Also, academics at local colleges or universities might provide additional scientific information or background on the storm.

TYPES OF WEATHER STORIES

Several reporters and editors often are mobilized in newsrooms to help cover major storms, but on a day-to-day basis, one reporter generally assumes responsibility for routine weather coverage. It is common for new members of staffs to be assigned the task. Examples of various types of weather stories and advice on how to write them follow.

Weather Forecasts

The wire services routinely move *state weather forecasts*. Often, reporters will use information in the wire stories to help them localize the forecasts.

Generally, a call to the nearest National Weather Service station will provide sufficient information for a local angle. If a region has been hit with a storm, is in the middle of a drought or is trying to dry out from several days of rain, *local weather forecasts* are particularly pertinent to readers.

La Grande, Ore., after being hit with a "stinging combination of arctic cold, freezing rain, snow and massive power outages," looked for better days, according to *The Observer*, a 7,800-circulation daily. Brian White interviewed sources at three agencies before writing his forecast story: the National Weather Service; the county emergency services department; and the U.S. Soil and Conservation Service. The opening paragraphs emphasized the uncertainty of the weather:

Even though the skies have cleared and temperatures have risen, local officials are keeping a wary eye on the weather.

Early forecasts from the National Weather Service in Pendleton this morning called for warming temperatures locally on Saturday and Sunday. At first, forecasters thought the mercury might reach the 50s in some areas, but later they revised the predicted highs to about 40.

Sudden warming after the recent heavy snowfalls is a concern, said Rich Huggins, Union County emergency services director.

"As long as it freezes at night we'll be okay," Huggins said. "But flooding is something we're watching for."

The lead block of paragraphs was carefully written. Reporters who piece together forecast stories must be particularly careful to not overstate or understate the ramifications of the weather. The next two paragraphs of White's story provided additional specifics:

Huggins has contacted shelter managers to help prepare a contingency plan in case scattered flooding problems occur over the weekend.

"We're in pretty good shape because the snow is pretty dry, but it's hard for the Weather Service to forecast locally because there's a pocket of cold air that's settled over the valley," Huggins said.

These paragraphs make clear that flooding could occur, but the writer used good judgment in not overstating the potential dilemma. An overly dramatic lead could have read:

Local officials are busily preparing for scattered flooding problems

that could occur locally this weekend.

That lead, though not exactly inaccurate, would sensationalize the situation. It is important for reporters to proceed cautiously with weather forecast stories. Readers should be informed as completely as possible about potential weather problems, but if there is uncertainty, it is best to seek information from several sources before rushing to print with leads that overdramatize the weather. Conversely, if hazardous weather clearly is moving into an area, that should be emphasized in a story's lead.

Hard News

Regions that are hit particularly hard with adverse weather sometimes are declared disaster areas. When that happens, it almost always creates Page One news. Brian White of *The Observer* in La Grande was asked to write the story when his county was declared a disaster area. As he did when he put together the forecast story examined above, White called several sources in order to gather information to supplement the lead:

> Gov. Vic Atiyeh today declared Union County a disaster area as the region braced itself for its second week of brutal winter weather.

Stories such as this almost always are written in inverted-pyramid form:

Who: Gov. Vic Atiyeh
What: declared a disaster area
When: today
Where: Union County
Why: the area had been hard hit with a week of bad weather and there was no relief in sight
How: not applicable

Like any good reporter, White went on in subsequent paragraphs to develop his lead. He outlined weather conditions, he explained what the disaster status meant, he brought readers up to date on power outages and he gave road conditions.

Travel Conditions

Another basic weather story is one that deals with travel conditions. Again: readers constantly are on the roads; they need to know how safe the roads are. Quite often, if travel conditions are poor, schools and other institutions are closed. Therefore, it is common for newspapers to publish stories that provide information on road conditions.

Information for these stories usually comes from the National Weather Service, from state transportation officials and from local law-enforcement personnel.

Jeff Boone, a reporter for *The Gleaner*, Henderson, Ky., made use of these sources in a story that he wrote. The story led with road conditions:

> Henderson was included in a traveler's advisory on Thursday and is under a winter storm watch tonight and Saturday as the latest storm saw cold temperatures digging in and motorists digging out.

WRITING THE NEWS

Wednesday's snow-sleet-rain storm left a covering of slush on area roads that froze as hard as concrete on Thursday, and, combined with high winds and blowing snow, made travel dangerous.

Very cold arctic air on the surface and moist southwest air in the upper atmosphere are combining to bring a winter storm to the area this weekend, said Francis Burns, a forecaster with the National Weather Service.

Hazardous road conditions and a threat of 2 to 4 inches of snow Thursday night forced officials to cancel classes today, and the coming winter storm will not make conditions any better.

Seasonal and Year-End Weather Stories

Newspapers regularly publish seasonal stories on the first day of winter, Groundhog Day, the first day of spring and so forth. Most are reported, with new approaches, each year. Newspapers also often publish *year-end weather summaries*. Jan. 1 is traditionally a slow day for news. It is common for reporters to dig through the weather reports for the preceding 365 days and to base stories on the statistics. The statistical information, of course, is complemented with direct quotations from weather officials.

In his year-end summary Jeff Boone of *The Gleaner* in Henderson, Ky., provided the relevant numbers, but he also told how "many of the year's top news stories were weather-related."

Agriculture is important to Henderson. And, to an extent, farmers live and die economically as a result of the weather. Realizing this, Boone wrote:

It is only fitting that 1984, a year farmers will remember for precipitation, should end with nearly an inch of rain.

Local weather observer George Street said 60 inches of measurable precipitation fell in 1984, 16.27 inches more than normal. There were 141 days of measurable precipitation last year.

That included 28.8 inches of snow, he said. The average is 15.7 inches.

Too much spring rain kept area farmers "twiddling their thumbs" waiting to plant, and recording-breaking deluges in the fall kept them from harvesting crops that were planted too late, said Bill Hendrick, Henderson County extension agent.

Boone's story went on to detail other big stories that were weather related: An engineering firm was hired to design a proposed multimillion dollar flood abatement program, and rains delayed construction of a bypass highway and progress on a flood abatement project.

News reporters sometimes are assigned the task of writing these year-end weather stories. The assignment should not be looked upon as an unimportant busy-work assignment. Good reporters will go beyond the statistics and emphasize the human ramifications of the year's weather.

CONSULTING THE AP STYLEBOOK

The Associated Press Stylebook and Libel Manual has a comprehensive section on weather terms, ranging from *blizzard* to *flash flood* to *hurricane watch* to *travelers' advisory* to *wind chill index*. Check the stylebook if you have any questions about weather terms or their meanings.

SPORTS

Lee Barfknecht, an *Omaha* (Neb.) *World-Herald* sportswriter, feels just as comfortable prowling the sidelines at a high school football game as he does covering one of America's finest college teams from the press box atop Memorial Stadium at the University of Nebraska.

Barfknecht likely could handle most any journalistic assignment. A Phi Beta Kappa, he was graduated from the University of Nebraska with high distinction. He majored in journalism and minored in English, history and economics.

"I'm happy as a sportswriter," Barfknecht said. "I think our pages are as well read as most other sections of the newspaper and people often read them critically because many readers consider themselves to be sports experts."

Barfknecht had to study hard to live up to his Regents scholar status while at Nebraska, but he also found time to work two years for the *Daily Nebraskan*, the university's student newspaper, as a sportswriter and sports columnist. He earned a summer internship at the *World-Herald*. He returned to Lincoln for his final semester of school but continued to drive to Omaha (about 50 miles) each weekend to work the sports desk. *World-Herald* management liked him; he was offered a job upon graduation on the regional news desk, where he worked before moving to sports about two years later. Barfknecht enjoyed his time on the regional desk, but he jumped at the chance to return to his first love—sportswriting.

GETTING AWAY FROM CLICHÉS

Some writers still gush over such *sportswriting clichés* as "flashy freshmen," "sophomore sensations," "brilliant field generals," "lanky leapers" and "diminutive, sparkplug point guards," but today's sports pages are filled with better, more balanced writing than ever before.

It has been a while coming. Stanley Woodward, sports editor of the old *New York Herald Tribune*, may have been a bit optimistic when he wrote in his book, "Sports Page" (published in 1949), that the better sportswriters had started to turn the corner on hyperbole, profuse praise and strained similes. He wrote: "The horrendous clashes of fearsome Tigers and snarling Wolverines, which usually were concluded in purple sunsets, now are taboo in the better sports departments. The sports editor doesn't mind picturesque writing if the reporter can handle it, but he no longer wishes to see his vehicle smeared with wild and indiscriminate pigments."

Woodward wrote that sportswriters should strive for the middle ground; they should avoid the *"gee whiz"* school (where athletes perform nothing but heroic feats) just as they should avoid the *"aw nuts"* school (where gifted athletes and great games are treated with near disdain).

Scores of today's sportswriters are providing readers with the quality coverage and writing that Woodward strived for in 1949.

Indeed, writing styles have changed. During the first part of this century, flowery prose adorned sports pages. Stanley Woodward claimed that World War II helped to put sports in better perspective. Writers no longer routinely extended hero status to mere athletes. A more spartan, streamlined sportswriting style evolved after World War II. This style, with an emphasis on the five W's and H—and a horde of statistics—started to give way in the 1970s and 1980s to a more balanced approach. Some of today's best sportswriting certainly includes valuable statistical information and essential ingredients (who won, what the score was, who starred), but it is more literary than the bare-boned scores-and-statistics approach that held sway at many newspapers after World War II.

CONTEMPORARY SPORTS PAGES

An examination of today's sports pages shows that clichés and hyperbolic adjectives are not extinct, but they are found less frequently, and lavish praise is not as gushy as it once was. Soft news approaches are used more frequently on stories that once were topped only with summary leads. Even morning newspapers are providing more analytical writing than ever before.

The amount of space devoted to various sports, including women's, is undergoing increasing scrutiny by the nation's sports editors. Merely because some minor-league baseball franchises routinely received 20-inch game stories in 1960—when they played before relatively large crowds—does not necessarily mean that they still should be covered so extensively.

Despite attempts by sports editors to expand coverage of women's sports, in most instances, women's coverage still plays a weak second fiddle to competitive men's athletics.

More newspapers are providing coverage—particularly through features—of *minor sports* such as gymnastics, volleyball, tennis, wrestling and swimming, but football, basketball, track and baseball continue to command the most space.

Local coverage is being expanded, particularly at medium- and small-circulation dailies. Some professional sports coverage is being relegated to the agate page (a page in the sports section devoted to scores and statistical information). More space is being devoted to game and feature coverage of high school athletics, recreation sports and participation sports.

DECIPHERING THE STATISTICS

A city hall reporter must know how to read a budget, a court reporter must know how to interpret a legal brief and a sports reporter must be able to decipher statistics. Every sport has its own statistical language. Reporters do not necessarily have to be experts on each phase of every sport (though it certainly helps), but they must have a working knowledge of scoring procedures and significant statistics of the sports they cover.

WRITING BASIC STORIES

A portion of a basketball game *box score* follows:

ASU	Mn	FG	FT	Rb	At	PF	St	Tr	Pt
Deines f	22	2–7	0–1	7	0	5	0	0	4
Everett f	20	2–3	1–1	9	0	5	0	0	5
Taylor c	26	1–4	1–1	4	1	2	0	5	3
Thompson g	34	6–17	4–4	1	7	1	5	0	16
Beck g	35	4–10	5–6	7	3	4	1	2	13

The numerals listed above tell us a lot about what five players did in a basketball game. We know, for example, that these competitors play for Arizona State University. We also know how many minutes each of them played in the regulation 40-minute game, how many field goals they made (and attempted), how many free throws they made (and attempted), how many rebounds they grabbed, how many assists they had, how many personal fouls they accumulated, how many steals they made, how many turnovers they committed and the number of points they scored.

At a glance, we can tell that guards Bobby Thompson and Steve Beck were the leading scorers with 16 and 13 points, respectively. We also can tell that: Thompson and Beck played most of the game; center Jon Taylor had a rough night (he had more turnovers than he had points); forward Warren Everett led the team in rebounds; and Everett and forward Jim Deines both fouled out.

Team statistics are computed by adding numerals from the individuals. For example, after adding the *individual statistics* of the Arizona State substitutes to the statistics listed above, we find that in an 81–72 loss to the University of Oregon in a Pacific 10 Conference basketball game, ASU made 28 of 70 shots from the field (a frigid .400); made 16 of 20 free throws (a respectable .800); snared 44 rebounds (10 more than Oregon); had 14 assists (compared to 19 for Oregon); made 29 personal fouls (compared to 18 for Oregon); had 8 steals (compared to Oregon's 4); and committed 15 turnovers (the same as Oregon). These are significant statistics.

Sports reporters, of course, could delve deeper. They could, for example, determine how many points both teams scored within five feet of the basket (this might reveal which team was able to get the ball consistently deep inside the lane); they could determine which team had the most blocked shots; or they could determine how many times the lead changed hands.

Depending on available space, reader interest in the game or importance of the contest, the reporter would decide which statistics are worth mentioning in the story.

The key is this: Reporters covering basketball or any other sport must know which statistics are relevant and important. For instance, what are the magic numbers in football? For starters, there are scores by quarters, first downs, rushing yards, passing yards, return yards, passes attempted and completed, number of punts and average distances, number of fumbles and fumbles lost, number of penalties and yards penalized and time of possession. Many of these statistics are relevant for individuals also.

In gymnastics, it is important to know that judges score a routine or exercise by totaling points from four areas for a maximum of 10.0. Those four areas are execution; combination; difficulty; and risk, originality and virtuosity (known as ROV).

It is not the purpose of this section to provide a comprehensive summary of applicable statistics for all sports. It is imperative, however, for aspiring sports reporters to realize that they must understand the statistical undercurrents of the sports they cover. If they do not, they cannot report or write intelligently.

Suggestions for Working with Statistics

• **Provide readers with statistical information that is useful to understanding the contest or its trends.**

• **Avoid being a "statistics junkie."** There is a difference between providing readers with information necessary to understand what happened at the contest and inundating them with irrelevant strings of numerals that interrupt the flow of the story's narration.

• **Review team and individual statistics before a contest.** Preparation is a key ingredient to solid coverage of any sport. If you review team and individual statistics before a basketball game, when you write your story after the game you can note, for example, that a 22 points-per-game scorer was held to 11 points; that a team that normally makes 53 percent of its field goal attempts made a cold 37 percent; or that a team that averages 11 turnovers a game made 23. These statistical differences help put a victory or loss in perspective.

• **Review statistics after a game for trends and turning points.** It is standard to focus on individual and team totals, but running *play-by-play charts* can help the reporter piece together important sequences in the contest. Play-by-play charts provide a chronology of a basketball game. The chart notes who scored, on what kind of shot, who fouled, who turned the ball over and what the score was at the time of the play. For example, the play-by-play chart could tell a reporter if one team went 6 minutes and 23 seconds without scoring a field goal (while the other team was making 10 field goals) or whether one team made six consecutive field goals midway in the half without a miss. These factors probably will be worth mentioning in the game story.

WRITING SPORTS CONTEST STORIES

Reporters could be assigned to cover any of a dozen sports. The most common assignments, however, send reporters to football or basketball games. Essential information to include in these stories:

- The teams and the score
- Reference to whether it was a conference or non-conference game
- Site of the game
- When the game was played

WRITING BASIC STORIES

- Key plays (who made them, who was responsible for calling them and so forth)
- Scoring summary
- Reference to star players
- Key offensive statistics (for football: rushing and passing)
- Key defensive statistics (for football: tackles, interceptions and fumble recoveries)
- Direct quotes by players
- Direct quotes by coaches
- Injuries and condition updates
- Results of previous games between the teams (the series record or outcomes of most recent games, whichever is more relevant)
- Overall records
- Conference records
- Reference to rankings, if relevant
- Next games for both teams
- Historical significance, if any, of the game

For the most part, morning and afternoon newspapers cover the same athletic events played the night before, but the writing angles should be different. Reporters at morning (AM) newspapers face tight deadlines because their newspapers are printed late at night, oftentimes very close to the conclusion of the athletic event. Traditionally, morning newspapers have offered a straightforward account of the preceding night's game, but, as noted earlier, even these newspapers increasingly are opting for softer, analytical leads. Readers who open their morning newspapers might not know the score of the game they are interested in; thus, even when using a soft lead, writers for AM newspapers generally try to get the scores of games high in the stories. The reporter who covers the contest generally is rushed to make his deadline; the story must be complete, but quite often there is not sufficient time to conduct extensive interviews or to develop an extended feature lead.

By contrast, sports reporters working for afternoon (PM) newspapers have time to write comprehensive stories that encompass not only the essential ingredients (victor, score, team records, key statistics and so on) but also a unique angle or feature lead. They therefore lose the standard alibi given for a poorly written story—they cannot contend they were under extreme deadline pressure. These sports reporters should analyze the games they cover—probing deeply into the why and how of the events—for most of their readers know the score before they open their newspapers. They should combine a synopsis of the game, a statistical summary and an angle not covered in morning newspapers or by the electronic media. The afternoon account should not be primarily a play-by-play rehash.

Writing for Morning Newspapers

When the University of Oregon played host to Arizona State in basketball, the wire services moved a streamlined account for morning newspapers:

EUGENE, Ore.—Center Blair Rasmussen scored a season-high 30 points and grabbed nine rebounds Thursday night to power Oregon to an 81–72 Pacific 10 Conference basketball victory over Arizona State.

The Ducks sank 13 of 15 free throws, nine of them by the 7-foot Rasmussen, in the final two minutes to clinch the victory.

The Oregon victory left both teams at 2–4 in the Pac-10. The Ducks are 9–10 overall, while ASU dropped to 7–9.

The summary lead moved by the wire services provided key information in the opening paragraph:

Who: University of Oregon
What: Defeated Arizona State in basketball
When: Thursday night
Where: Eugene, Ore.
Why/How: Blair Rasmussen scored 30 points

Arizona's morning newspapers were nearly on deadline when the game ended (because of the time zone difference, it was 10:15 p.m.); thus, the wire services moved the straightforward account minutes after the contest.

Bob Cohn covered the game for the morning *Arizona Republic* in Phoenix. Cohn was operating under deadline pressure, too, but his newspaper had saved space for his story. He had extra minutes to write a longer, more complete story than was moved by the wire services immediately after the game. Cohn opened his story with analysis. Still, he provided the score in the second paragraph. Cohn wrote:

EUGENE, Ore.—Oregon went with three guards Thursday night and, in a way, so did Arizona State. But the Ducks have an inside game and there the resemblance ended.

Playing at home after four games on the road, Oregon broke open a close contest in the last seven minutes and beat the Sun Devils, 81–72, in front of 8,036 at McArthur Court.

The Ducks got 30 points from 7-foot center Blair Rasmussen, who made 14 of 16 free-throw attempts. Forward Greg Trapp scored another 16.

For the first time, Oregon coach Don Monson employed a three-guard lineup, starting senior Chris Harper and freshmen Anthony Taylor and Rick Osborn and using them for nearly the entire time. Of the Ducks' starting five, Taylor played the least, 36 minutes. Harper, who had arthroscopic knee surgery two weeks ago, played 38 minutes, scoring 14 points.

Monson's strategy seemed to work. The guards combined for 35 points and 13 assists.

Monson said he altered his lineup because "we hadn't been making crisp passes and getting the ball where we wanted to. Our turnover ratio was bad and we weren't getting many steals."

The story went on to quote Monson, to give a rundown on the best Arizona State performers, to discuss significant statistics and to conclude with several direct quotations from the ASU coach.

Cohn's story was written under deadline pressure, but he went beyond a bare-boned statistical account. He focused on how and why Oregon won.

Writing for Afternoon Newspapers

Doug McConnell, writing for the afternoon *Phoenix Gazette,* relied even more extensively on direct quotations and analysis in his story. Of his 18 paragraphs, nine contained direct quotations. McConnell, whose deadline was not until early the following morning, had much more time to write his story. He conducted several post-game interviews to put the trends and statistical accounts of the contest in better perspective. McConnell's first paragraphs focused on the outstanding performance by Oregon's center and on the lack of contributions by the Sun Devil post men:

EUGENE, Ore.—Blair Rasmussen overlooked his 30 points in 39 minutes and the fact that it was his highest output of the season and tied the 7-foot center's career best.

"I could have played better defense," Rasmussen said.

Arizona State got a total of 12 points from its starting front line in falling, 81–72, to Oregon in Pacific 10 Conference basketball Thursday night.

"If we have to count on our centers for our scoring we're in a lot of trouble because we haven't been able to do that," Sun Devil coach Bob Weinhauer said.

SOME SPORTSWRITING TIPS

Obviously, there is no magic formula for writing game stories. Writing approaches depend on the circumstances. Here, though, are some tips:

• **Go with a summary lead if warranted, but you are not wedded to it.** The wire services generally will provide summary leads, so many sportswriters strive for other approaches.

• **Avoid chronological game-story approaches.** Always lead with the most significant aspect of the contest. For example: "Chuck Johnson hit a 15-foot jump shot with three seconds left to give Grand Junction a 61–60 basketball victory over Wymore Friday night." The game story would not begin like this: "Chuck Johnson controlled the opening tip for Grand Junction, and his team went on to beat Wymore 61–60 in basketball Friday night."

• **Remember that good stories are a blend of facts, turning points, quotations, statistics and analysis.** Stories should be a careful, thoughtful blend tied together with effective transition.

• **Avoid clichés.** One-point victories, indeed, are "cliffhangers"; effective offensive line blocking often opens holes "big enough to drive the student body through"; and dominant teams often "take it to" the losers. Good writers, though, find more original descriptions.

• **Avoid "ridiculous" direct quotations.** "We whipped 'em good," has a down home ring to it, but it doesn't add much to the story.

• **Use vivid description when appropriate.** You could write: "John Jones caught the winning touchdown pass with 14 seconds left." But, it might be better to write: "John Jones swerved between two defenders, stretched high in the air, cradled the ball in his left hand and pulled it to his chest for the game-winning touchdown with 14 seconds left."

• **Double-check spellings.** Particularly at high school contests, spellings listed in the official score book and on the program can be different. Find out which one is correct.

• **Do your homework.** The more background information you take with you to a contest, the easier and faster it will be for you to write the story once the contest is over.

Reporters take notes during a New Hampshire presidential primary event. In order to gain background information about candidates, reporters often review press releases issued by the political hopefuls. (Photo by Arthur Grace/Sygma)

10 / Press Releases

Press releases are sent to newspapers for two reasons: The people who wrote them want to gain publicity for their organizations and to reach as many people as possible. It is up to the journalist opening the release to decide if it has any reader interest, if it has news value or if it is nothing more than an attempt to gain free publicity.

In this chapter you will be introduced to the following terms:

handout
news release
public relations people
immediate release

cut the fluff
free ad
local news value

Each day, anywhere from dozens to hundreds of press releases—they're also called *handouts* or *news releases*—are sent to newspapers. Some are worth printing; many are not. It is up to the journalist to:

- Decide which of the press releases have any local news value
- Present those with value in such a way that readers are given the most important news

Nearly every corporation, business, university, organization or political party—large or small—has one or more people whose job it is to gain media attention. Many of these *public relations people* are former journalists or were journalism majors who planned careers in public relations. They know that much, most or all of the support that their organizations receive is linked directly to the publicity that they receive from the news media, and they know how to get it.

Some of the firms and groups really do have news to release, and they help the media greatly by acting as news sources. Others merely are hoping to get their names in the newspaper without paying for an advertisement.

To get their message across, PR people telephone or visit newspapers to describe the "news," or they send press releases.

Some examples of press releases include:

- A "media alert" from the Tandy Corporation announcing a mock election by an estimated 1 million American students and parents from all 50 states and the District of Columbia
- A "press advisory" from Greenpeace, the international environmental organization, announcing that it will conduct a protest at the Japanese consulate to press for an end to Japan's efforts to continue hunting the endangered sperm whale
- A news bureau release from the state university, called "Worms and Your Pet," which discusses the dangers of internal parasites in dogs and cats
- A news release from the Office of Public Information from an out-of-state university telling local news media that a student from their area has enrolled in the school
- A press release announcing the arrival of 16 Lipizzaner stallions for the beginning of a U.S. tour
- A release from National Frozen Food Association Inc., a trade group representing the frozen food industry, announcing that an area plant has gained, for the second consecutive year, a certificate of excellence for a sanitation program sponsored by the association
- A pamphlet from a congressional candidate describing how the candidate plans to solve the problems created by public housing
- A handout from a firm "specializing in effective public relations" that announces the first anniversary celebration at an area restaurant
- An announcement from the local zoo that on Thanksgiving Day the turkeys will do some gobbling of their own
- A release from a company announcing the promotion of one of its executives

DETERMINING THEIR VALUE

There are several factors that determine whether a press release should be used or tossed in the wastebasket:

• *Does it have news value?* Is it of interest to local readers? Does it contain timely information? If the answer is yes, the press release should be edited and/or rewritten to conform to correct print style and to eliminate the overuse of the name of a person or company. Superfluous, overwritten and untimely information should be eliminated.

• *Is it trying to gain free publicity for a person, company or group?* If so, toss the release in the wastebasket or tell the PR person to check with the advertising department. Remember, though, that with careful rewriting to eliminate many of the adjectives and the overuse of the name of a person or company, there could be some news value in the handout.

• *Is it worth following up, perhaps as a photograph or a story at a later time?* Many press releases simply announce an upcoming event. Even if they are not used in the newspaper, they may provide a good tip for later coverage. For instance, the press release mentioned earlier on the protest by Greenpeace could be turned into a photo assignment or a feature story on the latest movements by the activist group.

• *Can it be trusted?* Always be leery of press releases because they may have been written by a person with little or no journalism training or by someone who does not have the same standards as a professional journalist. Remember, the purpose of a press release is to get information in print. It is up to the journalist handling the release to make certain that the information is accurate and fair. For example, the pamphlet from the congressional candidate makes some serious charges, including accusations that federal housing officials are guilty of waste and deceit. Before such allegations are printed, they should be verified, and the housing officials should be given an opportunity to respond to the candidate's charges. The release also should be checked for any missing information that, had it been included, would have changed the thrust of the release.

WHICH RELEASES MAKE IT?

Every person looking at a press release has different ideas on what is newsworthy and what is not. That is why some press releases are used and others are thrown away.

Some newspapers—particularly the large ones—simply frown on using press releases. They may use them as ideas for future stories or photographs, but they seldom run them the way they are sent in. Many editors believe that all public relations people really are selling ads and should pay for advertising space rather than be given news space.

There is only so much news space—the *editorial news hole*—each day, and even though a press release may be of some value, there never is enough space to run all of the press releases that are received. At metropolitan newspapers, the news space is taken up by staff-produced stories; there is no room for handouts. In smaller markets, however, editors may depend heavily on press releases to help fill their news space.

NO STRICT RULES

There are no strict rules to follow in deciding which press releases to use and which to throw out. Much depends on the journalists looking at them. Usually, editors run press releases that they believe their readers will find interesting or that they find interesting themselves. For example, an editor who likes animals may give the handout from the zoo to a reporter to rewrite into a story; another editor may toss it in the garbage. A reporter whose aunt works for the county health department may think a press release from that agency is important while another reporter may not.

Most press releases sent to newspapers probably contain some news value, especially if the person writing them has had any dealings with the media in the past. PR people with journalism training usually have a solid understanding of news and features stories, which means they can produce usable copy. They know what editors and reporters like and dislike.

It is up to the journalist at the receiving end to pick the most timely and important handouts that have the most interest to local readers. Then, based on the amount of time and space available, these top handouts can be converted into news stories or used as foundations for future stories.

BOILING DOWN A HANDOUT

Here is the press release from the zoo, announcing that turkeys are going to do some gobbling of their own. Assume that a newspaper city editor has asked for a two-paragraph story on it.

As in any press release, at the top is the name of the person to contact if there are additional questions. The words *for immediate release* tell the media that this information can be used as soon as it is received. All handouts give the release date. Most are "immediate," but some request a future release date.

News Release

Contact: Sandy Rodman
      Public Relations Representative
      485-0263

                For Immediate Release

PRESS RELEASES

THANKSGIVING DAY WITH THE ANIMALS

Instead of being gobbled, the turkeys at Chicago's Brookfield Zoo will do some gobbling of their own during Thanksgiving Day with the animals at 12:30 p.m. in the Children's Zoo.

Special food pans will be prepared to tantalize the palates of the guests of honor: the turkeys, ducks, and geese. Children's Zoo visitors will be invited to help serve the holiday feast in this Thanksgiving Day celebration to be thankful for our animal friends.

Children's Zoo admission is $1 for adults, 50 cents for children (ages 3–11), and 75 cents for senior citizens and juniors (ages 12–17).

Brookfield Zoo is open from 10 a.m. to 5 p.m. Admission is free Thanksgiving Day through December 31. Located at 31st Street and First Avenue in Brookfield, the Zoo is accessible from the Stevenson and Eisenhower expressways and Interstate 294.

FINDING THE LEAD

The first thing to do is to find the lead, the most important point of the story. In only two paragraphs, it is impossible to be as cute as the person who wrote this press release. Look for the *who, what, where, why, when* and *how*, and then build a story around them. Every press release may not contain all of the five W's or the H, but a news story can be constructed around the ones that are included.

Who: Visitors to the Children's Zoo.
What: They'll be able to feed the turkeys, ducks and geese.
Where: Brookfield Zoo.
Why: To be thankful for the animals.
When: 12:30 p.m., Thanksgiving Day.
How: With special food pans.

Once the five W's and H have been identified, the next step is to put them into a news story, in this case two paragraphs. The more space, the more information that can be put in; however, in only two paragraphs, all that can be included are the essential ingredients—the five W's and the H.

THE RESULT

Here is an example of a two-paragraph story based on the zoo's press release:

Visitors to Brookfield Zoo's Children's Zoo Thanksgiving Day will be able to help feed the turkeys, ducks and geese beginning at 12:30 p.m.

Zoo officials said special pans of food will be prepared for the animals to show that people are thankful for their feathered friends.

With more space, such things as the zoo's hours and the admission charges could have been included. A call to the zoo could provide a quote or two as well as information on what will be on those special plates. But with only two paragraphs, readers will have to call the zoo—or the newspaper—if they want additional information.

ELIMINATE THE FLUFF

Not all press releases are one page long and easy to boil down to two paragraphs. The handout from the university news bureau on "Worms and Your Pet" is three pages long. It clearly seeks publicity for the veterinarians in the university's teaching hospital, but it also offers helpful tips. The trick is to *cut the fluff* and concentrate on the tips.

Some press releases already are boiled down when they are sent in because the people writing them know that a release that reads like a news or feature story has a better chance of being used. For example, the following press release from Ithaca Industries Inc. of Wilkesboro, N.C., announces a promotion of one of its executives and is written by a public relations firm. It is one of the most common types of releases sent to the news media.

News Release

For Release: Immediately

Contact: Mr. Jim Waller, Ithaca Industries Inc.

(919) 667–5231

WILKESBORO, N.C.—Nicholas Wehrmann, president and chief operating officer of Ithaca Industries Inc., has been elected to the additional offices of Chairman of the Board of Directors and Chief Executive Offi-

PRESS RELEASES

cer, replacing Gregory B. Abbott, who resigned to pursue other business interests.

Ithaca is a leading manufacturer of hosiery, underwear and sportswear.

The release gives only the basic facts. If journalists want more they will have to call Jim Waller. Here is a rewrite of the handout, cutting the bulky 40-word lead to a more readable 24 words:

Nicholas Wehrmann, president and chief operating officer of Ithaca Industries Inc., has been elected chairman of the board of directors and chief executive officer.

The remaining facts can be given in the second paragraph:

Wehrmann replaces Gregory B. Abbott, who resigned to pursue other business interests. Ithaca manufactures hosiery, underwear and sportswear.

HOW TO AVOID FREE ADS

The following press release—on the first anniversary celebration at an area restaurant—is a good example of one that probably would not show up in print or on the air. Even though it is written by a firm that "specializes in effective public relations," it is nothing more than a *free ad* masked as a news release.

For Release: October 12

Please Contact: Bruce Smith Media Communications Inc.
Specializing in Effective Public Relations
(312) 337-3352

AT THE WINNETKA GRILL: A FIRST ANNIVERSARY CELEBRATION

Henry Markwood and John Stoltzmann, owners of The Winnetka Grill, 64 Green Bay Road, Winnetka, are pleased to announce a festive celebration of their restaurant's first birthday. The festivities last from November 9 (the actual birthday) through November 18. Key to the celebration is The Winnetka Grill's highly imaginative anniversary menu created, in dialog with the owners, by Chef de Cuisine John Draz. The full menu is available at dinner, while select items will be offered on the luncheon menu as daily specials.

The Winnetka Grill Anniversary Menu

Cold Appetizers:

   Grilled salmon with walnut oil

   Belon oysters with malt vinegar & black pepper sauce

   Country paté with apple relish

Hot Appetizers:

   Batter fried acorn squash with orange butter

   Duck fois gras with wild onions

   Wild mushrooms stewed with gamay and garlic

Entrees:

   Grilled ribeye with shallots and thyme

   Grilled pheasant with gamay and red grapes

   Blackened redfish prudhomme

   Grilled rockfish with gamay sauce

   The Winnetka Grill's First Anniversary Wine is the Charles F. Shaw

Noveau Gamay Beaujolais, first released on the market on November 9.

   This handout has the same elements that would be in a typical press release: The firm's name is mentioned more than once, the address is given, the names of the owners are listed and there is even a special wine that will be released. There is only one thing missing: news value.

   Remember: Just because a press release is sent to newspapers does not mean that it has news value. Many releases are merely seeking free publicity for a person, business or organization.

HANDOUTS WITH LOCAL NEWS VALUE

   A few of the press releases mentioned earlier in this chapter could be interpreted as free ads: The Tandy Corp. handout is seeking publicity for

PRESS RELEASES

its computers, and the National Frozen Foods Association is trying to get its name in print.

Big newspapers probably would not touch them, but community newspapers and radio stations may find value in them because they could contain news of local interest. Local people may be participating in the mock election sponsored by the Tandy Corp.; the local firm being honored by the frozen foods group may indeed be worthy of a story.

What lands in the wastebasket in one newsroom may be a candidate for a story in another simply because of *local news value*. The news release from the out-of-state university announcing that a student from a small town in Iowa has enrolled is probably of no value to any news operation in the country, except those in the small town in Iowa. To them, it may be worth a one-paragraph filler, a photograph or a story and picture. While one editor is cursing the university for wasting postage to send in the release, another editor may be thanking the school for the valuable information.

AN EXAMPLE

Here is the press release announcing the arrival of the Lipizzaner horses. It was sent to newspapers in Chicago because it clearly had value only in their area. Try to pick out the fluff and publicity information that can be cut easily. Also look for a local news angle.

Sixteen white Lipizzaner horses arrived here Wednesday via trans-Atlantic jumbo jet for a rare U.S. tour that starts next week at the Rosemont Horizon.

Austrian Consul General Hans Sabaditsch and his family greeted the spirited horses upon their 2:44 p.m. arrival at O'Hare International Airport after the 8 hour and 40 minute Lufthansa flight from Frankfurt, West Germany.

The occasion marked the first Chicago visit of the Lipizzaners in more than 20 years, and their fourth American tour, according to publicist Janine McLachlan. The most recent U.S. performance was in 1982.

The horses, finely bred and trained for specialty display and dressage, traveled in specially constructed stalls stacked two high in the cargo area of a 747 jet. Five grooms stayed with the Lipizzaners in the chilly compartment to feed and water them, and to calm them down.

The horses were not drugged in any way, McLachlan added.

Spanish Riding School Brigadier Kurt Albrecht also arrived on the flight.

After touching down, the horses were inspected by veterinarian Dr. Ridge Scott and whisked away to Arlington Park racetrack for a 25-hour quarantine.

Another dozen horses are scheduled to arrive Thursday afternoon, at 2:44 p.m. at O'Hare. The horses will stay at Arlington Park until after their performance at the Rosemont Horizon, 6920 Mannheim Rd., on Nov. 15 to 18.

Later they will be driven to St. Louis, flown to San Francisco, driven to Los Angeles and flown back to Europe on Dec. 9 or 10 at the conclusion of the four-week tour.

The Lipizzaner breed, regarded as an Austrian national treasure, was developed by crossbreeding Spanish, Danish, Italian and Arab stock at the Austrian Imperial Stud.

What is the news and what is fluff in this handout? A reporter assigned to write a three-paragraph story on the release will need to know. Certainly, much of the publicity for the four-day performance is better left to the advertising department. However, there is news value in that the show is coming to town and that the horses flew safely to Chicago and will be performing in the area for the first time in 20 years. That is not saying that every newsroom in Chicago will run an item on this release; some certainly will not. Assume that one newsroom does decide to run a three-paragraph story. Here are the steps that can be followed in writing it and an example of the story:

Who: Not applicable.
What: The arrival of 16 white Lipizzaner horses.
Where: O'Hare International Airport.
Why: For a U.S. tour, which begins next week with a four-day performance at the Rosemont Horizon. It is their first performance in Chicago in 20 years. After Chicago, they will perform in St. Louis, San Francisco and Los Angeles.
When: At 2:44 p.m. Wednesday.
How: Aboard a 747 jet from Frankfurt, West Germany; in specially constructed stalls stacked two high in the cargo area.

PRESS RELEASES

Sixteen white Lipizzaner horses arrived safely in Chicago Wednesday afternoon from Frankfurt, West Germany, for their first performance here in 20 years.

Another 12 of the show horses will arrive Thursday. The horses are in the United States for a four-city tour, which begins Nov. 15–18 at the Rosemont Horizon.

The Lipizzaners traveled in specially constructed stalls in the cargo area of the jet during the 8-hour, 40-minute flight. They are staying at Arlington Park racetrack while they are in Chicago.

ON THE JOB IN EVANSVILLE

One reporter who rewrites press releases as part of his daily routine is Mark Massa, chief of the Warrick County bureau for *The Evansville* (Ind.) *Press*. Massa, a graduate of Indiana University, had summer internships at the *Milwaukee Sentinel* and the *South Bend* (Ind.) *Tribune* before landing the job in Evansville upon graduation. Besides working for the daily, Massa and his staff produce the *Warrick County Press*, a weekly that is inserted into the main paper.

He said most of the press releases he handles are for the weekly. "We have been trying to get more hard-hitting news in the weekly, but it also is a vehicle to carry things we wouldn't put in the daily, such as announcements from churches, schools, service organizations and athletic booster clubs," Massa said.

He said church notices are the most common press releases that cross his desk. "Most of the churches out here show films or have in evangelists, and they want to get the word out that they are showing the film or having a visitor," the reporter said. "The press releases always talk about how fulfilling the night will be and how much fun there will be. I usually take the basic information out of it—such as the title of a film, who the star is and where and when it will be shown. I go through the release and try to find the newsworthiness in it.

"You can always tell if the people writing press releases know how newspapers operate. They are the ones that are pretty straightforward. But sometimes you get press releases that say a great time is promised for all. Things like that we naturally take out."

STEPS TO FOLLOW

Massa suggested that reporters who handle press releases follow these steps:

- *First, look for any advertising copy that might be in the release.* People who do not know the difference between an ad and a news story often issue a press release.
- *Second, do not use press releases verbatim.* They almost always need tightening.
- *Third, stick to the basic facts that are in the release.* Tell what is happening, when, where and what time.

"For us, press releases are another source of news," Massa said. "There is no way you can know everything that is going on in the area you cover. You have to depend on people calling you or writing you. Out here in the bureau, we are faced with space problems some days in that we need copy to fill extra pages. That's when the press releases come in handy, either in planting an idea in our minds or providing a public service announcement."

REWRITING A TYPICAL HANDOUT

Here is a press release that Massa received and then decided to use. It is from a civic group, refers to youngsters from his area and is typical of the handouts he likes to use.

Immediate News Release

KIWANIS CLUBS GIVE ATHLETIC MENTAL ATTITUDE AWARDS

The Newburgh and Chandler Kiwanis Clubs held a special Athletic Mental Attitude Awards Banquet last Tuesday at the Homestead and awarded seven Castle High School youth the Kiwanis Mental Attitude Award in the athletic sports during the first semester of this school year. The award is given upon the positive spirit of competition and fairness in performing the particular athletic endeavor. The young person is chosen by his or her colleagues and teammates.

Those who received the awards were Steve Whitehead, tennis; Tony Mooney, football; David Hatchett, cross country; Julie Nichols, cross country; Kristy Ashby, diving and swimming; Melody Huff, volleyball; and Anita Horn, golf. The coaches present for the banquet were John Lidy, Steve Edwardson, Ginger Lutterman, Beth Watson and Jess

Shelby. The coordinator for the evening and banquet arrangements was Noble Katter, the past President of the Newburgh Kiwanis Club.

The program of the evening was a special presentation to all of the youth, coaches, the members and their wives by Dr. Roy France, a dentist from Boonville. Dr. France spoke on the many values we have as citizens of this nation of which we should be thankful. These values, which cannot be bought for any amount of money in the world, are for each of us as persons of faith and Americans to cultivate in our own lives and to pass on to future generations. The Lt. Governor of the Lincoland Division of Kiwanis International, Robert Rideout, and his wife, Pat, were special guests of the evening. Larry Washington, President of the Newburgh Kiwanis Club, presided over the meeting and evening.

The "news" of this press release is who won what, Massa said. "What was said at the banquet isn't really important to anyone else who wasn't there," he added. "Most of us feel lucky to be Americans. We don't need to read it in a 3-inch story."

To write the story, Massa first read the release carefully and made notes to himself on what was newsworthy and what was not. In the margin next to the third paragraph, he wrote, "Very valid words, but not necessarily newsworthy." Next he found the key element for the lead paragraph: Seven high school athletes have been honored. Then he made mental notes to himself on which parts of the release he could cut. Here is how the rewritten handout appeared in the weekly *Warrick County Press*:

7 Castle High Students Get Kiwanis Awards

NEWBURGH—Seven Castle High School athletes have received the Kiwanis Mental Attitude award from the Newburgh and Chandler Kiwanis clubs.

The award is given each winter and spring to athletes who display a positive spirit of competition. The winners, chosen by their teammates, were:

Steve Whitehead, tennis; Tony Mooney, football; David Hatchett, cross country; Julie Nichols, cross country; Kristy Ashby, swimming and diving; Melody Huff, volleyball; and Anita Horn, golf.

Like the handout itself, the finished product was only three paragraphs long. But the story that Massa wrote was tighter. It contained a terse, newsworthy lead and the editorializing was cut. Massa did what any journalist attempts to do to a press release: He culled the newsworthy facts from a verbose handout and molded them into a news story of interest to readers in his area.

Lawyer F. Lee Bailey conducts a press conference before his speech. (Photo by Rick Wiley)

11 / Press Conferences and Speeches

Press conferences and speeches are not the same as one-on-one interviews where a reporter has an opportunity to question and challenge a source. People holding press conferences or giving speeches usually say just enough to get their message across to as many reporters as possible. It is up to reporters covering them to go beyond the public event to find additional newsworthy items.

In this chapter you will be introduced to the following terms:

gang interview
media event
advance

second-day lead
advance text

11:50 a.m. The speech is to begin in 10 minutes. The hall is filling quickly. Reporters already are busy.

Two reporters set up microphones and tape recorders on the lectern from where flamboyant and world-famous trial lawyer F. Lee Bailey will make his speech.

11:58 a.m. Another reporter sets up a microphone and tape recorder. A photographer makes readings with his light meter. Two other photographers sit in front of the lectern. Nearly all of the 1,100 seats are full.

12:08 p.m. Bailey and two others walk up to the lectern. He is introduced, quickly. The audience applauds.

12:10 p.m. Bailey begins his speech.

The reporters responsible for covering Bailey's speech were ready long before he began. They knew the steps they had to follow to cover his speech adequately. Some of the reporters also had attended the press conference Bailey held 30 minutes before his speech.

PRESS CONFERENCES

Candidates, officials and other people hold press conferences for one or all of the following reasons:

- They feel an obligation to make information public.
- They want to get a message across to as many people as possible.
- They would like to be seen in the newspaper and on newscasts.

A press conference is a *gang interview*, which means that every reporter present is going to get the same information. People who hold them also usually know in advance what they want to say. They will get their message across and will not say much more, especially if they are experienced at fielding adversary questions from reporters.

MEDIA EVENTS

Press conferences often make good TV, which means that even on the local level they have become *media events* where both the interviewee and the reporters are in the limelight.

The granddaddy of press conferences is the one with the U.S. president. It has become a major media event, staged in prime time and featuring the nation's top reporters challenging the president. It is a big show for both sides; millions of people watch every move and listen to every statement.

The presidential news conference began during Theodore Roosevelt's administration. Reporters simply gathered around the president's desk for a chat. When Herbert Hoover walked into his first meeting with the 30-member Washington press corps in his office on March 5, 1929, he reportedly said, "It seems that the whole press of the United States has given me the honor of a call this morning."

PRESS CONFERENCES AND SPEECHES

By Harry Truman's presidency, the press conference drew big crowds; 322 reporters attended his last one on Dec. 31, 1952.

Television and radio coverage of presidential press conferences began during Dwight Eisenhower's first term. In the early days of his presidency, portions of film and sound track were released for broadcast hours after the conference, which gave Eisenhower's staff time to delete questions and answers they felt were potentially sensitive or embarrassing. After several months, however, the entire transcript was released for broadcast and newsreels. Eisenhower also started the practice of having reporters identify themselves and their connections before asking questions.

Today, the presidential press conference lasts about 30 minutes and draws about 300 reporters. The president is well coached and rehearsed on the questions most likely to come from the handful of reporters who actually are allowed to ask a question.

"You're not trying to be tough or obnoxious" when you're questioning the president during a press conference, said Helen Thomas, who covers the White House for United Press International. In a speech at the annual convention of the Society of Professional Journalists, Sigma Delta Chi, Thomas added: "You have to know what you want to get and you have to ask the questions that you think are relevant. We're not trying to be liked or disliked. We're trying to do our job, and I think that's the perspective you keep, even with presidents."

Thomas, who has worked in the nation's capital since the 1940s, is the senior wire-service reporter covering the president. Her seniority ensures her the first or second question at a presidential press conference and the right to say, "Thank you, Mr. President," at its end.

"I think that presidents should respect the press," Thomas said. "They know we're very important to the whole operation of democracy. There couldn't be democracy without us. We in the press know that we must live up to the high standards that we set for others. We are guided by one ethical goal: to pursue the truth wherever it leads us."

BEFORE IT BEGINS

Before a press conference begins, reporters should research the subject and speaker thoroughly. Because they may have a chance to speak only once, they want to make sure their questions are on target. Being prepared helps them pick the key information from all the rhetoric.

To prepare for a press conference, reporters:

• *Read press releases announcing the conference.* Some type of press release usually is issued by an agency, organization or news bureau before a person speaks. It should give the time, date and place of the conference; provide some background information on the speaker; and tell reporters whom they can call for more information.

• *Read as many clippings as possible about the person holding the conference and its subject.* Research should be conducted in the newsroom morgue as well as public or university libraries.

- *Read articles or books that the interviewee has written.* Writings reveal much about their authors. People also warm up much quicker to reporters who tell them they have read their work.
- *Talk to editors.* They often will give reporters specific questions that they want answered.
- *Talk to other reporters.* This is particularly important for reporters who never before have covered the person holding the press conference. Reporters who have can offer helpful advice about mannerisms or the types of questions the person will or will not answer.

Advance Press Releases

Days before the F. Lee Bailey press conference and speech, a press release was issued by the news bureau at the university where the attorney was speaking. It said:

PRESS PREVIEW

One of the nation's top defense lawyers, F. Lee Bailey, will speak at Arizona State University on Tuesday, November 5, at noon in the Arizona Room of the ASU Memorial Union.

Bailey will discuss the problems and inadequacies in our criminal justice system. He also will talk about some of his most famous cases and his writing.

Some of Bailey's more well-known clients include kidnapped heiress Patricia Hearst, the Boston Strangler (Albert DeSalvo) and U.S. Army Captain Ernest Medina, who was charged with the mass murder of civilians at My Lai, Vietnam.

Bailey is also the author of the best selling novel "Secrets," which tells the story of a lawyer charged with murder.

The lecture is sponsored by the Associated Students of Arizona State University Lecture Series in conjunction with the Liberal Arts College Council and the Student Bar Association.

This is the fourth lecture in the "Celebration of Diversity" series sponsored by the student association.

For more information, contact Brad Golich at the Lecture Series Office, 965-3161. Or call the News Bureau and ask for Keith Jennings.

Under no circumstances should a reporter rely solely on an advance press release for background information on a speaker. That is because a release seldom gives enough information, and what it does give should be double-checked. For instance, the release on Bailey does not mention other books he has written, it provides only sketchy information on clients and it does not give his age.

The Advance Story

A release often is used to write an *advance*, a brief story announcing an upcoming event. In this case the advance would inform people that Bailey would be speaking. It could read:

> F. Lee Bailey, one of the nation's top defense attorneys, will speak at noon Tuesday in the Arizona Room of Arizona State University's Memorial Union.
>
> Bailey will discuss his most famous clients, including newspaper heiress Patricia Hearst and the Boston Strangler. He also will discuss the problems of the U.S. justice system.
>
> Bailey's lecture, the fourth in the "Celebration of Diversity" series, is being sponsored by the Associated Students of ASU, the Liberal Arts College Council and the Student Bar Association.

Checking the Clips

Much more background information on Bailey than that contained in the press release was available in the university library. For example, the microfiche catalog, a computerized version of a card catalog, listed Bailey's books and an audiotape interview of him by CBS. The attorney also was listed in the Biography Index, Contemporary Authors, Current Biography, *The New York Times* Index and the Readers' Guide to Periodical Literature. (Chapter 8 discusses additional sources that contain biographical information.)

Here is a set of notes gathered on Bailey during the library research. The material is from Current Biography and Contemporary Authors.

> 1950 completed college preparatory training at Kimball Union Academy in New Hampshire. Entered Harvard University on a scholarship, intending to specialize in English. Left school at the end of his sophomore year to join the Naval flight training program and after 18 months transferred to the Marines as a jet pilot.
>
> While in military service, volunteered to join 3-member legal staff at Cherry Point Marine Corps Air Station in North Carolina.

52 years old.

Quoted in Saturday Evening Post, Nov. 6, 1966: "You can learn enough to practice criminal law without ever going to law school."

His experience in defending accused servicemen along with reading Lloyd Paul Stryke's "The Art of Advocacy: A Plea for the Renaissance of the Trial Lawyer" led him to pursue law as a career.

Returned to Harvard but shortly afterward transferred to Boston University Law School, which waived its requirement of three years of college because of his experience in the Marines.

Took bar exam June 1960 and was admitted to practice the following November.

Insists upon spending as much money as he feels is necessary for meticulous investigation. In his opinion, his skills in finding and analyzing facts are more than anything else responsible for his success.

Attended Chicago's Keeler Polygraph Institute.

Cases:
Pied Piper of Tucson (Charles Schmid Jr.), a loner found guilty of murdering two teen-age girls.
T. Eugene Thompson, a Minnesota attorney charged with killing his wife for $1 million in insurance benefits.
Mark Fein, serving 30 years for killing a bookie.
Dr. Sam Sheppard, a Cleveland osteopath accused of killing his wife.
The Boston Strangler (Albert DeSalvo), charged with killing 13 women.
Patricia Hearst.
Punk-rock star Sid Vicious, accused of murdering his girlfriend. Vicious committed suicide before the trial began.
Working on case of chemical leak in Bhopal, India, that killed and injured thousands. It's Bailey against Union Carbide.

Established the Professional Air Traffic Controllers Organization and served as its first director.

Owns two helicopters and two airplanes. He has a remote chateau in the Bahamas. Drives flashy cars. Often called flamboyant outside the courtroom, but he never is inside.

Lives on an 80-acre estate in Marshfield, a Boston suburb, with his wife and former secretary, Froma Vicki Bailey. They have a son, Scott. Bailey also has two sons from an earlier marriage, which ended in divorce.

Obviously, not all of the information gathered in the library research will be used in the final story. But it can be used to help formulate questions. It also gives the reporter insight, the ability to go into the press conference and speech with a clear vision of who F. Lee Bailey is.

PRESS CONFERENCES AND SPEECHES

During the library research, a tentative list of questions to ask Bailey was assembled. This step is important because, in the heat of the press conference, it is too easy to forget the specific questions or issues. Here are the questions:

- You are sharply critical of the American legal system. What are the current problems?
- What solutions to these problems do you propose?
- What makes you a better trial lawyer than others in your profession?
- What special skills do you have that make you more successful?
- You once said in an article that "You can learn enough to practice criminal law without ever going to law school." Do you still believe that today?
- What do you look for in a good lawyer?
- Was the Patty Hearst case an unpleasant memory for you?
- You once said in an article that the "press is the only effective policy force on government." Can you comment on that?
- You established PATCO. Why did you establish the organization? How did you feel when President Reagan ordered the air traffic controllers back to work during the 1981 strike?

These questions are a reporter's wish list. If there is not enough time or the interviewee concentrates on several questions or topics, much of the list will have to be abandoned.

THE QUESTIONS AND ANSWERS

All reporters are at a press conference for the same reason: They want to ask questions that will elicit newsworthy responses. Those who have done their homework the best, and those who actually are able to ask questions, will be the most successful.

Television reporters have an advantage over print reporters during a press conference because the speaker usually wants to be seen as well as heard. Hence, television reporters are more likely to control the questioning, which usually is limited in time.

Print reporters must make themselves visible and heard. First, they should arrive at the location of the press conference early enough to get a front-row seat. That will help the speaker spot them easier. Print reporters also must sometimes be the most vocal in the group to make certain that the speaker calls on them. That is particularly important at a large press conference where there are many reporters and the interviewee cannot answer every question. At a local press conference attended by only several reporters, an official, candidate or newsmaker usually will try to answer all of the questions.

Because of time or space limitations, reporters often attend press conferences only to obtain answers to specific questions. Their job is to challenge the speaker to provide something more than rhetoric. They all know that they cannot report everything that is said. Still, they should listen to the other questions and the answers just in case something unexpected pops up.

Attorney Bailey agreed to hold a press conference a half-hour before his speech. Here is a transcript of the questions by various reporters and Bailey's responses.

Q. What are you here to speak about?

A. Primarily, it's directed to the law students. Litigation segment of the practice, which many are quite normally interested in today.

Q. I read an article in which you sharply criticized the legal system. Are you going to talk about that?

A. Uh huh. Drawbacks. I think the two primary shortcomings are cost and delays. Most civil cases take so long that by the time the remedy comes around, if it does, it's either too late or it's not needed.

Q. What suggestions do you have for that?

A. I think there needs to be a lot of alternatives to litigation. Much greater use could be made of arbitration, mediation and conciliation. I think there is some evil in the conflict between the plaintiff's and defendant's fee structures. The tendency is to string out litigation.

Q. Is that what you did when you became a litigator?

A. No. The evil is on the other side. It's the fellow being paid by the hour who likes the delays and the case going on and on and on.

Q. What solutions do you offer?

A. Well, I don't have a quick answer to that dichotomy in fees, but I think it needs to be addressed. We need to pay more attention to people getting skunked unnecessarily much of the time. In as much as the plaintiff system is structured on incentive, probably that needs to be part of the defense lawyer's motivation as well. Right now he has no incentive to get rid of the case early if it is one that deserves to be resolved. He's simply cutting down his gross fees.

Q. How do you feel about lawyers advertising on television and in newspapers?

A. I think within limits it's helpful to the public. It gives the public a better understanding of the mystique of legal fees and gives a choice. Like anything else, it can be abused. There are some silly ads running around and some that are offensive. By and large, I think the principle is sound.

Q. Do you think the public needs to be aware of how much a divorce is going to cost?

A. Sure.

Q. Sort of like comparative shopping?

A. That's right. Competition is the only thing that keeps the price in line.

Q. What do you think of the direction that the law is taking now? More conservative?

A. With the Arizona crowd in the Supreme Court, I would say there's a lot of pressure to try to be very conservative. Coming from the White House, all of the judicial appointments now are being heavily screened for a stereotyped kind of judge.

Q. With that kind of emphasis in the federal government and with some pretty important Supreme Court cases coming up, what do you think is the role of state government?

A. Well, that has a trickle-down effect. Every state judge who wants to be a federal judge knows he won't make it if his decisions are liberal. Not with this administration. So the state judges are motivated to be more conservative so they can qualify if they manage to get suggested as a candidate to the federal bench, which in most states is more desirable than the state bench.

Q. How do you feel about your career so far?

A. There isn't much I'd change.

Q. Have you been happy with it?

A. Oh, I'd say decidedly yes within the limits of practicing what I call trouble-shooting law; that is, criminal cases and difficult civil cases. There's a lot of agony in any litigation.

Q. Concerning your most notorious trials, any comments on the Patty Hearst trial?

A. I don't think she got a fair shot, but on the other hand I don't think it made any difference because if she hadn't been hooked there she was gonna be hooked in Los Angeles and we pretty well knew we were going to lose that one. Our main objective was to get her out of the murder indictment and we did that.

Q. What role do you think the press has on a trial like that, when you are trying to separate a free press from a fair trial?

A. Normally, except under special circumstances, I feel that we can handle the press and get rid of the prejudice. In the Hearst case I can't say that we did that. The press really whipped up the public on the grounds that she was going to get away with something because she was rich. The truth is, if she hadn't have been rich, she would have never been caught up in it.

Q. I understand that when you went to Harvard that you were going to major in English.

A. I did all the way.

Q. What made you go into law?

A. Military experience. But even when I got out of the military with plans to go to law school, I still went back to Harvard and majored in English. Not many lawyers do.

Q. Why did you go into English and not law?

A. Well, originally, I wanted to be a writer. When I got back, I stayed with the English courses because the most effective advocates I bumped into in four years of watching court cases had a good command of the king's English and that seemed to be a fading phenomenon among lawyers.

Q. Do you recommend that to lawyers today?

A. Very strongly if they want to be trial lawyers.

PICKING OUT THE NEWS

Once a press conference is over, reporters whose deadlines are near must head directly to telephones. They need to know their leads and how they will organize their stories even before the gang interview has ended.

Reporters who phone in their news stories do not have a video display terminal or typewriter in front of them on which to compose a story, erase mistakes and rewrite if necessary. They must dictate a story that makes sense the first time. It also helps to have a good rewrite person on the other end of the phone to polish the rough edges, shuffle paragraphs if necessary and look up additional information.

PRESS CONFERENCES AND SPEECHES

The closer the deadline, the quicker a reporter must pick out the news and compose the story. Most reporters, even those not under a tight deadline, begin to construct their stories during the press conference, while they are asking questions, listening and taking notes. They continually ask themselves:

- Which questions are the best?
- Is the speaker answering candidly?
- What is new and what has been said before?
- Is the speaker skirting any issues?
- What is the best lead?
- How should the story be organized?

The story's lead and organization are determined by several factors:

- *What is the most newsworthy response during the press conference?* Are the responses good enough and complete enough to be developed into a lead paragraph?
- *What are the other key points of the conference?* Would any of them make better leads? The major points covered during the conference should be rated for importance.
- *What are the editors looking for?* Do they want a specific lead or angle to the story?
- *Is a second-day lead required?* Reporters from evening newspapers who are covering a morning press conference are most likely to use a first-day summary lead. Those from morning papers with an evening deadline may use a *second-day lead* to avoid repeating the earlier stories. A second-day lead reports something fresh or "featurizes" the earlier news.

Seldom will all of the reporters covering a press conference agree on the same lead, unless the interviewee uttered something completely unexpected. They may agree on the importance of certain issues, but that does not mean their stories will begin the same way. Five reporters at the same press conference may write five different leads because each was interested only in his or her own questions and the responses to them.

Rating the Key Points

Much of what Bailey said during his press conference was a rehash of what he had said before. That is not newsworthy. He did, however, talk about state judges' motivations to be conservative and the "Arizona crowd" in the Supreme Court, which probably would be of some interest to local readers. Of course, he gave a speech after his press conference, which meant reporters still had more information to gather before composing their stories. Based solely on the press conference, however, here is how Bailey's comments could have been rated:

No. 1: State judges motivated to be conservative if they have ambitions to be federal judges.

No. 2: "Arizona crowd" on Supreme Court illustrates how White House screens judicial appointments carefully to pick out conservatives.

No. 3: Two primary shortcomings in U.S. legal system and possible solutions.
No. 4: Advertising by lawyers.
No. 5: Comments on Hearst.

It is possible that one or more of these five points would be dropped from the final story, either because of space limitations or, more important, because Bailey said something more newsworthy during his speech.

SPEECHES

Like press conferences, speeches are used by people to get a message across to an audience. Reporters cover a speech a little differently, though, because they have no control over what the speaker says.

Reporters attend a press conference to elicit responses to specific questions. They are on a hunting trip. Reporters who attend speeches are there to be the eyes and ears of people who cannot attend. If they cannot get to the speaker before or after the speech, they merely digest what was said, mix it up and feed back to their audience that which was newsworthy. Because no interviewing is involved and reporters cannot challenge the speaker, many of the story leads are likely to be on the same point.

Speeches usually are not organized like news stories. They often build up to a major point rather than putting it at the beginning. Reporters recognize this difference. As they are listening to a speech, they are editing it, anticipating its main points and cutting out all the unnecessary information.

Reporters realize that a 30-minute speech would take up considerable space in the daily news hole if it were printed in its entirety. Metropolitan newspapers occasionally print complete speeches by the president or other important officials, but usually they rely on their reporters to pick apart speeches and report only *the new, the important or the unusual*.

Clever speakers realize the reporter's function, which means they will make every attempt to say something new, important or unusual.

THE PREPARATION

As in preparing for a press conference, it is important for reporters to do their homework *before* covering a speech. Only under the most unusual circumstances, such as an extremely tight deadline, would they cover a speech without first researching the subject and the speaker. Even if the assignment is given only a short time before the speech, it is easy to go to the library or newspaper clipping file to find out what has been written previously on the speaker or the topic of the speech. Here are some tips on how to prepare for covering a speech:

• *Do homework.* Check news clippings and resource books in libraries.

PRESS CONFERENCES AND SPEECHES

Interview friends of the speaker as well as fellow reporters for background information. Go into research asking, "Who is this person?" Come out with the answer.

• *Prepare questions.* Know in advance the questions that the speaker needs to answer during the speech. If they are not answered, interview the speaker in person immediately after the speech or over the phone as soon as possible.

• *Catch the speaker early.* Every reporter covering a speech will hear the same thing; if possible, break away from the pack beforehand to obtain exclusive information. Interview the speaker over the telephone or make arrangements to see him or her just before the speech. If that is not possible, find out where the speaker will enter the room and wait there. It sometimes is possible to get in a few questions while the speaker is being introduced and before he or she walks to the podium.

Advance Texts

Advance texts of the speech are useful because they provide most of the what the speaker will say. They also make the research phase easier.

Copies usually are available from the speaker or his or her agents before the speech. A well-known person who speaks often probably will have plenty of copies to hand out. A lesser-known person probably will not, which means reporters may have to ask if they can look at the speech or make copies of it.

A warning, though: Never write a story based solely on the advance text. Speakers often wander from their prepared texts, adding some things and omitting others. Occasionally, they abandon the texts altogether and speak off the cuff. Reporters who do not attend the speech and write stories from an advance text may end up looking foolish.

Use the advance text as a guide for doing the research and covering the speech. Follow the text during the speech, making changes in quotes and adding and deleting necessary phrases and sentences.

Tape Recorders

A tape recorder will ensure that any quotes used in a news story will be precise. Just make certain that it is working properly. Keep extra batteries and tapes on hand.

Also take notes. A tape recorder is a useful backup tool for making sure that quotes are exact. Most reporters do not use it exclusively because it takes too much time to play back the tape, take notes and then write the story. (Chapter 7 lists additional guidelines on using tape recorders.)

COVERING A SPEECH

Once the speech begins, there are certain steps reporters must follow.

Take Copious Notes

Even reporters who use tape recorders take as many notes as possible. It is impossible to transcribe the entire speech, but reporters usually take a lot more notes than they ever would need to write a story. Nearly every reporter uses shorthand or a self-devised system of speed writing.

The key here is to listen carefully for information and quotes that can be used in the story and write them in a notebook as quickly as possible. A tape recorder can be used as a backup for incomplete quotes.

If the speaker says something that is hard to understand, put some type of symbol in the notebook next to the confusing statement. After the speech, try to have it clarified.

When writing a direct quote, put quote marks around it in the notebook so that it will not be confused with a paraphrase.

Experienced reporters also try to stay calm when taking notes. They know that they often will be scribbling one quote when the speaker starts to say something else important. They merely quit writing the first sentence and begin the second. People always are going to speak faster than reporters can write. All a reporter can do is write down the key points and quotes.

Make Observations

Note the speaker's clothing and mannerisms. If the speaker smokes or laughs continually or shouts at someone in the audience, make a note of it. These observations can add color to the story.

Estimate the number of people in the room. Count small crowds. For larger crowds count the number of chairs in each row and multiply by the number of rows. Or ask a security officer for an estimate or ask a custodian how many chairs were set up.

Listen for the New, Important or Unusual

Remember, an audience does not care about old news. There has to be a reason for each story.

If the speaker says something that could make a lead or needs further development, put a star next to it in the notebook so that it can be found easily. If there is time for questioning after the speech, ask for clarification of confusing points.

Never be afraid to ask a speaker to repeat a quote, explain an unclear statement or expand on any topics of the speech. Speakers usually will answer questions when they have completed talking. They know that reporters can get mixed up, and they do not want to be misquoted.

Listen for Summaries

A speaker usually will summarize the speech, either at the beginning or the end. Many times, that will make the lead for a news story. Of course, reporters might disagree on what is the best lead, but they still need to know what the speaker considered the main point.

PRESS CONFERENCES AND SPEECHES

In most cases, the speaker clearly tells the audience. "I am here to talk about . . ." or "In summary, let me say . . ." Other times, summaries are masked. Listen for changes in the speaker's voice or points repeated several times.

Also listen for topic sentences, numbered points and transitional words. These will signal major points and could be potential leads. Good speakers are clear in the points they want to make because they want their audiences to understand what they are saying.

Keep Asking Questions

When the speech has ended, it is time to ask the questions that should have been covered but were not. Try to get the speaker alone after the other reporters have left. If there is time, follow-up phone calls to the speaker may be helpful, too.

EXAMINING A REPORTER'S NOTEBOOK

Here are the notes taken during F. Lee Bailey's speech. Some of the sentences will be incomplete; others will make no sense at all. However, these notes are real, and they are typical of what a reporter covering a speech would come up with.

Dark gray suit.
No vest.
Red tie.
Hair shorter than photos.

"How many in the audience are presently law students?"
Lots of hands.
"How many expect to become law students?"
Lots of hands.
"How many are concerned there are too many lawyers?"
Lots of hands. Laughs.
There is one area where there is no difficulty in finding work. "It is greatly understaffed. That is the litigation branch." The people there aren't very good.
"The reason is because when law schools took over from the apprentice system, they improved on almost every area except one. That was litigation."
"The things that were learned from carrying a bag and being in court have pretty much been abandoned and indeed many cannot be taught in academic circles."
No good course for masters in advocacy in the U.S. Will be next year at the National University Law School in San Diego. Bailey helping develop the program.
"Many litigation lawyers are not equipped to do battle with someone who is specially trained in that field." Most law students come to law school ill equipped for litigation.
"The reason is that in undergraduate work they have been diverted

into specialties such as political science, economics, accounting, government, judicial administration, police administration. This curriculum overlooks two important tools that every litigator has got to have if he'll ever be top rank:"

1. Consummate command of the English language. "The ability to speak and communicate persuasively in an interesting fashion so the jurors don't fall asleep and the judge doesn't fall asleep." Should be able to communicate "without resorting to notes, outlines or other crutches."

2. Deep grounding in psychology generally, which is utilized every day in dealing with clients, opponents, witnesses, jurors, judges and so forth.

"Included in these must be courses on memory expansion. You must condition yourself to develop capacity of memory to its peak."

Not telling the truth corrupts 90% of all litigation in the U.S. simply because the lawyers are not equipped in the art of cross examination to confront liars and expose them. To do that, one has to be able to deal without constantly diverting attention to written crutches."

Bailey is doing this lecture without notes. Practicing what he preaches?

"It is up to the trial lawyer to pick up deception, to go for the jugular and to get it. That requires a lot of homework."

"If you are not a person who enjoys doing homework and being prepared to the hilt, don't engage in litigation as a specialty. Unless you enjoy being in a pressure cooker, find a more sedentary specialty."

"Perry Mason is not a good image of a lawyer." Basically a coward.

"He's afraid of jurors and what they will do to him. He arranges in some corrupt fashion to have witnesses who are the true guilty parties and will confess in open court. This is a handy way to win lawsuits. It spares the agony of jury selection."

"I would gladly take a case without a fee if I . . ." missed the quote here.

Future bright for litigators. Computers with a search and find capability. Now necessary to take a deposition, read cases, go look for witnesses. "Data bases will make other things a flick of a switch rather than long, hard work by a paralegal summarizing long documents. Now those aids are not present, so what is needed is hard work and teamwork."

Trial lawyers can become folk heroes.

Income in later years much higher than average lawyers.

High-risk business. Often don't get a dime for years of hard work. Sometimes get a windfall, particularly in injury and wrongful death cases.

Often the impact of outcome on the litigants is enormous. "In a criminal case the defense is a born loser. If you are innocent to begin with, and you prevail at the trial, you still are statistically guilty. When you walk out, you're much poorer and probably broke." Half your constituency will assume you are guilty and "shyster got 'em off on a technicality."

PRESS CONFERENCES AND SPEECHES

"Due process is a process that must swell or shrink with the times in which it is found. We have so . . ."

Greatest disgraces in our legal system:

Abuse of the writ. "If you are licensed to practice law, you can sue anyone who doesn't have absolute immunity and make his life miserable." The costs, particularly in civil cases, will be enormous if the litigation . . . Many cannot afford it.

Delays. Average delay of 3–5 years before client ever sees courtroom. Contingency cases motivate litigator "to get our one-third or one-fourth of recovery anytime it's available." Defense is being paid by the hour, which means in no hurry to settle the case. "A defense lawyer who knows his client is liable and that the case should be settled for the plaintiff has two reasons to refuse to do that. No. 1 is if he settles it, his meter stops running. And when you're paid by the hour, a running meter is a symphony.

"Secondly, if he uses the greater financial clout of his client, normally an insurance company, he may wear the plaintiff out and run him out of money and settle the case for a smaller figure." "These conflicts have to be rooted out of our system. They daily plague . . ."

A key factor when defending anything is speed. You must have speed. For that you need memory. "You need to stuff memory. If you are used to cramming for exams, you have the ingredients." Practice. Have 500 telephone numbers at your command. Give yourself a means to recognize.

There are knocks in this business. "If you are a bad loser, stay out." Statisticallly, trial lawyers lose half their cases. You perform a function. You demonstrated to the world your client was wrong even though you tried. That's a service, too.

English justice system is superior. Solicitor evaluates claim. Writes brief for barrister. If he accepts the brief, you're in court. If not, you can try another solicitor. If he doesn't accept it, you're out. People in Britain understand the court system better than those in the U.S. "British courts are an elegant function." They expect a tremendous ethical standard in court and they get it. "I've never heard of a case of a corrupt British barrister or judge." 3,000 barristers responsible for all litigation for a country of 50 million. "In England, judges have the last say. They have ultimate control over the press, something I'm not ready to advocate yet in this country."

To be an effective trial lawyer, one has to enjoy shouldering the responsibility others cannot shoulder themselves.

"No one is going to make a magician out of you. You can apprentice with the 10 best trial lawyers, and you're still just a lawyer. Perhaps a good one. If you walk into a case well prepared, you're still going to lose some cases. You have to be able to walk away from it."

If you spoke good English when you arrived here, the law will destroy it. "You have to fight that. You'll be so full of jargon. Get out of the jargon and get back on your feet. If you want to try cases you have to be streetwise."

If you defend a lot of cases plan on getting indicted, especially if you beat a lot of prosecutors. That antagonizes them.

"To be a trial lawyer, you have to keep your skirts clean. You'll be under a microscope much of the time."

"The best that justice can do is treat you as badly as your neighbor. Justice is not nice; it's consistent."

Be prepared to take it on the chin or get out.

"I learned early if I wanted to try cases, I wasn't going to learn about it in the classroom."

He spoke about an hour.

Q&A after speech:

Man asks about plea bargaining. "Plea bargaining is absolutely necessary just as settlements are necessary in the civil side. By and large the give and take of plea bargaining is necessary and appropriate. To shoot down plea bargaining is to shoot yourself in the foot. It's unavoidable, it works and it can be corrupt. Without plea bargaining, the court system in every major city would break down in 30 days.

Woman asks, "How do we get 5 minutes of your time to discuss a case?" Bailey says his number is listed in the Boston phone book.

Man asks about military courts. Bailey says they are much better. "I was weaned in a cocoon. I got out and went to a civilian court and I was shocked by the corruption. If I had to stand trial for a crime I didn't commit, I would pick a military trial every time."

Didn't have time to answer more questions.

About 1,140 people at the speech.

WRITING THE STORY

Before writing the story, the reporter must answer several questions:

• *What is the key point?* The answer to this question becomes the lead to the story.

• *What are the other major points?* All of them should be rated.

• *Which quotes are the best?* The reporter must look for quotes that best illustrate the speaker's points and also make the story readable.

• *Is any of this news?* Reporters who have done their homework will know if the speaker has given the same speech before.

• *When is the deadline?* If there is time, the reporter can ask more questions. Or, if the speaker has made charges, the reporter can obtain an opinion from the other side. In most speech stories, reporters simply write a brief story on what the speaker said. If there is time to interview the other side, the reporter must start the research again to find the best possible rebuttal.

Bailey made several key points during his speech. Obviously, his theme was that there are not enough good trial lawyers. He illustrated his point with some excellent quotes. He also gave advice to law students, telling them that good litigators need a consummate command of English, grounding in psychology, a good memory and the ability to go for the jugular.

He said the greatest disgraces in the U.S. legal system are that too many lawsuits are being filed and there are too many delays. He also warned students, "If you're a bad loser, stay out."

After his speech, Bailey praised plea bargaining and military courts.

There was little new in what Bailey said during his speech. He has been criticizing the lack of training of trial lawyers for years. He did make some important points and uttered some unusual quotes, however, both of which could be the basis of a story. The people who attended the speech, as well as those who wish they could have, would be interested in reading a story on Bailey's appearance.

Reporters who attended the press conference before the speech would have additional information from which to pick. Bailey's comments on the growing conservatism in American courts still would be good lead material.

ORGANIZING THE INFORMATION

Most press conference and speech stories follow the same pattern. They are written as inverted pyramid news stories. They begin with a terse lead paragraph that summarizes the key points of the press conference and/or speech. If the *what* is more important than the *who*, the lead will present the key point first and the attribution will follow. If the speaker is well known, a name is used in the lead. Otherwise, a title is put in the lead to give it authority, and the speaker's name is used in the second paragraph.

If a university professor told a reporter that freeway construction is needed on the west side of town, the lead of the story likely would say:

Freeway construction must precede development on the west side of

town, a university transportation expert said Monday.

In this story the professor's name was not used in the lead because she was not well known. Instead, the reporter used her title to give the lead authority. If the mayor of the city said the same thing, the lead likely would say:

Freeway construction must precede development on the west side of

town, Mayor Donald Stevens said Monday.

In this lead the *who* was as important as the *what*. The lead just as easily could have started, "Mayor Donald Stevens said Monday . . ."

After the lead, paragraphs are written in order of descending importance, but each one should contain vital information. Here is how a typical story would be organized after the lead:

• *Second paragraph.* Back up the lead with a strong quote or paraphrase. Name the speaker if the name was not used in the lead. Give the speaker

additional authority. Tell where the press conference or speech occurred and who sponsored it. Give the speaker's age.
- *Third paragraph.* Continue developing the points made in the lead or write a transitional paragraph moving into another key point. A transitional paragraph also can introduce a set of bullets highlighting all of the speaker's important points. Background the speaker more. Introduce observations. Tell how many people attended the speech.
- *Fourth paragraph or the one after the bullets.* Continue developing the lead or begin developing the bulleted items one by one. If possible, use a strong quote to illustrate one of the key points.
- *The rest of the story.* Follow up with quotes and paraphrases. Continue to sprinkle in observations.
- *The final paragraph.* Try to end with a direct quote, the speaker in direct communication with the reader. That will help avoid an abrupt ending and make the reader feel that the dialogue continues even though the story has ended. Do not use an attribution such as "he concluded" in the last paragraph. Make sure all of the key points are fully developed.

THE RESULT

Here is one newspaper story that could have been written after Bailey's press conference and speech. This story's 27-word lead summarized Bailey's concern about growing conservatism in the courts.

The growing conservatism of the U.S. Supreme Court has trickled down to state courts, criminal lawyer and author F. Lee Bailey said Tuesday at Arizona State University.

The second, third and fourth paragraphs followed with direct quotes and background. They backed up the lead:

"Every state judge who wants to be a federal judge knows he won't make it if his decisions are liberal," the 52-year-old lawyer told reporters before his speech sponsored by three student groups. "The state judges are motivated to be more conservative so they can qualify if they manage to get suggested as a candidate to the federal bench, which is more desirable than the state bench."

Bailey's clients have included newspaper heiress Patricia Hearst and the Boston Strangler. He also has written books on the legal profession as well as a best-selling novel, "Secrets," which tells the story of a lawyer charged with murder.

PRESS CONFERENCES AND SPEECHES

Bailey blamed the Reagan administration for the growing judicial conservatism. "Coming from the White House, all of the judicial appointments now are being heavily screened for a stereotyped kind of judge," he said. "With the Arizona crowd on the Supreme Court, I would say there is a lot of pressure to be very conservative."

The fifth paragraph clarified Bailey's fourth-paragraph reference to the "Arizona crowd." During his press conference, he did not identify the people he was talking about. Their names needed to be in the story, however, because readers may wonder who they are. Such explanatory paragraphs are common to news stories:

Bailey was referring to William Rehnquist and Sandra Day O'Connor, two court members with Arizona ties. O'Connor was sitting on the Arizona court of appeals when President Reagan nominated her to replace a moderate, Potter Stewart.

In the sixth paragraph, the story shifted gears. A transitional phrase moved the reader from the press conference to the speech. This paragraph was a paraphrase. A direct quote was used in the seventh paragraph to back it up. Observations also were used for the first time.

In the eighth and ninth paragraphs, Bailey defended his statements and offered a solution. The story let him develop his thoughts further in the 10th and 11th paragraphs. By ending with a direct quote, the writer let Bailey communicate directly with readers and avoided wrapping up the story.

During his speech before approximately 1,140 people, Bailey warned that there is a shortage of qualified trial lawyers in the United States.

"The things that were learned from carrying a bag and being in court have pretty much been abandoned and indeed many cannot be taught in academic circles," he said. "Many litigation lawyers are not equipped to do battle with someone who is specially trained in that field."

Bailey said law students are not prepared for litigation because their curriculum overlooks two important tools: a command of English and deep grounding in psychology.

Lawyers need "the ability to speak and communicate persuasively in an interesting fashion so the jurors don't fall asleep and the judge doesn't fall asleep," he said.

Bailey, who spoke without notes, added that trial lawyers also must be able to communicate "without resorting to notes, outlines and other crutches."

A good trial lawyer must "pick up deception, go for the jugular and get it," Bailey said. "That requires a lot of homework. If you are not a person who enjoys doing homework and being prepared to a hilt, don't engage in litigation as a specialty."

The reporter could have developed the story further by writing a transitional paragraph and introducing another one of Bailey's topics, but in this case an 11-paragraph story probably was adequate to summarize the press conference and speech.

SAME EVENT, DIFFERENT STORIES

It is possible that every reporter who covered Bailey will have a different lead and story. Those who attended the press conference could have different stories than those who attended the speech only, and vice versa. Reporters who caught Bailey alone likely would have exclusive stories.

The point is, no two reporters are the same. Most of the reporters who attended the speech wrote leads that had Bailey criticizing the U.S. legal system, but they did not have to. The above story, with a lead on the growing conservatism of the courts, illustrates that.

Here is how reporter Simon Fisher of the *Tempe Daily News Tribune*, the community newspaper in the city where Arizona State University is located, approached the story:

There may be an abundance of attorneys in the United States, but there are few excellent trial lawyers who have polished their craft to perfection, one of the nation's foremost lawyers said Tuesday.

"Young lawyers will have no difficulty finding work in the litigation branch," F. Lee Bailey said. "There are people out there, but they are not very good."

Bailey, attorney for such notables as Patricia Hearst and the Boston Strangler and author of several books on defense law, urged the law students in the audience of about 500 at Arizona State University not to enter the litigation aspect of the profession unless they function well under pressure.

"One has to enjoy the responsibility others cannot handle."

PRESS CONFERENCES AND SPEECHES

The story continued for another 14 paragraphs, weaving together quotes and paraphrases. It ended with a quote from Bailey, warning budding lawyers not to become corrupt:

> "The worst is to wind up at age 50 and find out you won nothing but the money."

The story in the *State Press,* the daily student newspaper at Arizona State University, also concentrated on Bailey's comments on trial lawyers, but it differed from the other stories. Reporter Andrea Han wrote the story. She began:

> Trial lawyers today lack the basic training they need to confront liars on the witness stand, criminal lawyer F. Lee Bailey said Tuesday.
>
> Bailey, defense attorney for Patty Hearst, "Boston Strangler" Albert DeSalvo and other famous clients, said the profession needs good lawyers who are better trained to litigate.
>
> "Lawyers are not equipped to confront and expose liars because they have a lack of training in the science and art of cross-examination," he said.
>
> Bailey, who spoke to a crowd of about 300 students, faculty and staff, said lawyers are "ill-equipped" to litigate because their specialties are diverted elsewhere.

This story contained another 21 paragraphs. It followed the same pattern as the other two, but probably gave Bailey's press conference and speech too much space. Clearly, his comments on and criticisms of the judicial system could have been summarized in a dozen or so paragraphs.

Han ended her story with a direct quote from Bailey's press conference, in which he responded to Han's question about Patricia Hearst:

> "I don't think she got a fair shot, but our main objective was to get her out of a murder indictment, and we did that," he said.

That the three stories on Bailey differed so much does not mean that the three reporters attended different functions. All of them got the same information. They simply approached the story differently.

Obviously, their systems for estimating the size of an audience are different. The first reporter counted the number of seats in the hall (rows times the number of chairs in one row) when he first entered the hall. Midway through the speech, he looked over his shoulder and noticed that the hall was filled. The other two reporters probably did not use that technique.

Adrianne Flynn covers City Hall for the *Tempe* (Ariz.) *Daily News Tribune*. (Photo by Paul O'Neill)

12 / Beat Reporting

Many of the stories published in newspapers are written by beat reporters. These reporters must master the structures of the institutions and agencies that they cover, learn the terminology and write stories in understandable language.

In this chapter you will be introduced to the following terms:

organizational structures
police log
fire report
unrestricted access
mayor-council government
council-manager government
commission government
story budget
agenda
executive session
federal judicial system
state judicial system
misdemeanor
criminal case
civil case
indictment
information
warrant
arraignment
initial appearance

plea bargaining
preliminary hearing
grand jury
defendant
true bill
no bill
felony
brief
docket
filing
plaintiff
complaint
petition
damages
summons
pleading
deposition
settlement
tort

Beat reporters cover breaking news and features in specific geographic and subject areas. Whether they are covering police and fire, city government or the courts, these reporters make daily stops at or telephone calls to their sources.

Newspapers depend heavily on beat reporters; these journalists must monitor their domains. They are responsible for covering all the news that breaks on their beats, for cultivating sources and for developing ideas for stories.

COVERING POLICE AND FIRE

Scenes from old movies perpetuate the stereotype of police and fire reporters: They are booze-guzzling, cigar-chomping hacks who have difficulty stringing together complete sentences. They are devious, unscrupulous (but usually likable) people who gather facts, call their newsrooms, ask for rewrite and feverishly tell their stories of crime.

For the most part, this late-night television image is disappearing. Today's police and fire reporters do know how to write. During an eight-hour shift, they often read dozens of record forms, interview several people, make small talk with scores more and still find time to write hundreds of words. That's on a routine day. If a major story breaks, they also handle it.

Roger Aeschliman, a law enforcement reporter for the *Topeka* (Kan.) *Capital-Journal*, is typical of today's police and fire reporters. Aeschliman, a graduate of Kansas State University, majored in journalism and political science. He took a variety of mass communication classes, including radio and television, and worked on the campus newspaper: the *Kansas State Collegian*. He served as a staff writer, the arts and entertainment editor and, eventually, the managing editor.

He was a midterm graduate, so he spent the fall semester pestering Rick Dalton, managing editor of the *Capital-Journal*. "I think he decided to hire me just to get me off his back," Aeschliman said.

Aeschliman was offered a job as a staff writer two days before graduation. It was a great gift. After six months, he started filling in on the weekend police beat. He was named one of the two *Capital-Journal* law enforcement reporters as he started his second year on the job.

STAFFING THE BEAT

The size of a newspaper usually determines how its reporters cover police and fire news. At newspapers with less than 20,000 circulation, one person might juggle coverage of police and fire news while reporting on all other city and county institutions (such as the mayor's office, the engineer's office, the civil defense office, the assessor's office and the clerk's office). At newspapers with larger circulations, a reporter might be responsible only for coverage of law enforcement agencies and the fire department.

Large-circulation newspapers generally have more than one reporter covering the police and fire departments.

Regardless of the newspaper's circulation or the population of the community, police and fire reporters cover similar stories. Routine crime news, however, often is played down at the major metros. Small-circulation dailies and weeklies generally report on all minor crime stories and accidents. Sometimes they are given play on the front page.

At the *Capital-Journal,* a morning newspaper with a circulation of 70,000, there are two law enforcement reporters: Steve Fry, who works from 6 a.m. until 2:30 p.m., and Aeschliman, who works from 2:30 p.m. until 11 p.m. Both reporters work out of the *Capital-Journal*'s newsroom. At some metro papers police reporters work out of pressrooms at the stations and are connected to their newsrooms by telephones and/or video display terminals. The *Capital-Journal* publishes two editions: The 3 a.m. press run is distributed statewide; the 5 a.m. press run is distributed to Topeka residents and to residents of the immediate surrounding counties.

"I enjoy my job," Aeschliman said. "It is very exciting. Every day is different. Some days, though, can be depressing: All you see happening are bad things. That's the only drawback as I see it."

Aeschliman's days pass quickly; he spends much of his time away from the office reviewing records and talking with sources. During the late afternoon and evening hours, he routinely types into his video display terminal 50 one- or two-line items that come from police, fire or court records. These are published in the newspaper's daily record section. He also writes four or five short stories (three to 12 paragraphs) on events that merit elaboration and a longer story on a significant breaking news event or feature.

COVERAGE OF DEPARTMENTS

Aeschliman's primary responsibilities are coverage of the Topeka Police Department (Topeka, a city of 110,000, is the state capital); the Shawnee County Sheriff's Department; the Kansas Highway Patrol (northeast Kansas); the Kansas Turnpike Authority (which has highway patrol-type duties for northeast Kansas); the Topeka Fire Department; four Shawnee County township fire departments; and Medevac MidAmerica (Shawnee County area ambulance).

His secondary responsibilities are the police, sheriffs' and fire departments and ambulances of seven surrounding counties. Tertiary responsibilities include police and fire developments for the state of Kansas on weekends and evenings if the state desk or The Associated Press does not get the story.

DEVELOPING SOURCES

After reporters have a working understanding of the *organizational structures* of the agencies and departments they cover, sources must be developed and cultivated. Some of Aeschliman's primary sources within the Topeka Police Department, for example, are detectives, patrol and traffic officers, record keepers and high-ranking captains and majors.

In Topeka, detectives work two rotating shifts: They work mornings for two weeks and evenings for two weeks. Aeschliman figures "two or three" detectives on each shift are his best sources. He does not try to gain their trust overnight. "I start slowly in cultivating them," he said. "I use their names in feature articles or in routine stories to put them in a favorable light. After this, they often are more willing to help me with stories that are not routine."

Getting to Know Sources

Aeschliman always tries to determine whether sources like to see their names in print. "If I perceive they like to see their names used, I will use them," he said. "Some sources like to provide information, but do not like to see their names in print. If that is the case, I do not overuse their names. It all depends on the person and the circumstances."

Aeschliman relies extensively on patrol and traffic officers. "They know exactly what is happening because they are close to the action," Aeschliman said. He estimated that of the 75 officers on the shift he covers, about 20 "would tell me most anything," another 20 "would be friendly and generally helpful" and the remainder would not be as cooperative (they are the "I'm kind-of-busy types, so please don't bother me"). "Since more than one officer usually works a case, I am not bothered much by those who don't want to be helpful. If I am at the scene of a crime or accident and one officer tells me to stay back and don't bother him, I'll go to another officer who might be helpful."

Some of Aeschliman's best sources are the keepers of records at the department. "These sources are the hardest to get, though, because they operate under strict legal requirements," Aeschliman said. "Occasionally, I try to buy them a cup of coffee or a soft drink. If you work at it long enough, you can earn their trust. After several months, I was on a first-name basis with many of them. Now, I get some good tips from them. It is always off the record, and I respect their wishes."

Aeschliman relies on upper-echelon officers—majors and captains—for information for some stories. "I find that these officers always are looking to be placed in the best possible light," he said. "I never go out of my way to write fluff pieces about them, but it is good to use their names as favorably as possible in routine stories. That way, when you are writing an unfavorable story about the department, they might be more willing to talk to you about it. If they remember you only for the bad stories, they will provide little information to you."

The reporter does not have the time to cultivate sources within other departments on his beat, particularly the fire department, to the extent he does at police headquarters.

"Not as many stories come out of the fire department," he said. "But I try to write a couple of nice fire prevention stories now and then. I quote the fire officials. Then, they are more willing to talk when I am covering breaking news stories."

BEAT REPORTING

Aeschliman realizes that coverage of hard news is his main responsibility. But he added that "writing soft features about the departments, their activities and their officers plays a big part in cultivating sources for the hard-news stories."

Treating Sources with Honesty and Fairness

Naturally, many of the stories police reporters write are not favorable to the department. Sometimes, the timing of a story may conflict with a police investigation. At other times, the reporter must criticize law enforcement officials for abuse of power or other questionable activities. These stories obviously do nothing to solidify relations between the department and the reporter. Reporters, though, must overcome these obstacles. The best way is to be as fair, professional and diplomatically aggressive as possible. Officers often will respect you for handling stories fairly, even if it puts them in a bad light.

"I never try to snow my sources," Aeschliman said. "If I make a mistake, I admit it and I try to recover my credibility as best I can."

The next section provides an overview of a typical day on the job with Aeschliman. A composite day is presented to best illustrate Aeschliman's thought processes and writing strategies on a variety of stories common to the police and fire beats. It is realistic in the sense that one major story dominates the day while several smaller ones need to be written and routine work still needs to be accomplished.

A DAY ON THE BEAT WITH ROGER AESCHLIMAN

About noon the telephone rings at Aeschliman's house. Steve Fry, the *Capital-Journal*'s morning shift police reporter says: "It's going to be a big day, Rog. Can you come in an hour early? I'm all tied up with the sheriff's contract negotiations, and there's been a fatal fire."

Aeschliman reports to the office at 1:30 p.m., instead of his usual 2:30. The notes and requests to return calls piled on his desk indicate he probably will not be going home at the normal 11 p.m.

Fry has wrapped up coverage of the contract negotiations for the day; he fills Aeschliman in on the session. The deputies approved the contract; the county did not. A factfinder is coming in.

Fry then tells Aeschliman two children were killed and their father was injured in a mobile home fire this morning. "That's big news anywhere," Aeschliman said.

Fry normally would have been at the scene, but he was locked up in the contract meeting, and no one on the skeleton morning staff heard the call go out on the police scanner.

Fry also relates that there was a burglary suspect arrested at a Topeka high school early in the morning. Fry did not have time to write the story, so that falls to Aeschliman.

Aeschliman goes to the city desk to talk with his boss, the city editor. Today, Don Marker says only: "Do a good job on that fire story."

"On another day, he might have a news tip, or a feature story idea for me," Aeschliman said. "In any case, a check-in at the city desk is vital. All the reporters clear through the city editor and if there is something happening, he's probably going to know about it.

"Back at my desk I start calling around. I make routine checks to find out what's happening. Included are calls to the highway patrol, police traffic, patrol and detectives, the ambulance service, our sheriff, the sheriffs from the surrounding counties and the fire department."

Covering a Major Fire Story

On this day the big news comes from the fire department. The preliminary report from the inspector is fragmentary: "A mobile home fire at 245 E. 29th, was reported at 10:11 a.m. The fire destroyed the structure doing an estimated $10,000 damage. Two children, ages 3 and 1, were killed. A man was severely burned."

"That's all I am going to get from them for the rest of the day," Aeschliman said. "It's up to me. This is the kind of story that can't wait until later. Firefighters and police change shifts soon, and witnesses have a way of disappearing. I'm going to the scene; the boss agrees."

The area still is cordoned off, and the fire chief is shuffling through the debris. He comes out to make a statement for the television crews. Again, he uses no names. The cause and origin of the fire are unknown. But he does give some details of the fire and some good quotes.

"I can use the quotes," Aeschliman said. "A door-to-door canvass is next on my list. Do you know who lived there, sir? Do you know the names of the children? Where was the mother?

"A half hour of that and I've got the names of the injured man, and his wife, and found that they moved recently from a small town north of Topeka. I've also got the name and address of a man who restrained the father from going back into the blaze to try to rescue the girls. Next stop: the witness.

"He is a shy man with children of his own. He just happened to be shopping across the street when the fire broke out. He didn't know any of the victims, but he saw what happened and he tells about it vividly. I can sure use him.

"It feels like the day is half gone, but it's only 3:30 p.m. I check back in at the office. Nothing new. Time to follow up on some leads. I call the victims' hometown sheriff and ask if he's heard of the deaths. 'Sure, sure, it's the talk of the town,' he says. I tell him the names of the mother and father and he confirms them."

The sheriff also provides the names of the girls: Shena and Kimberly.

"Now I've got the story no one else has: the victims' names and an eyewitness account of the disaster. I tell the boss and he sends a photographer out to work up some kind of photo from the scene."

Making the Rounds

After Aeschliman has gathered most of the information for the fire story, he must make his regular stops on the beat. There still is a lot of day left; he will write the major fire story later.

• **Checking the Logs and Dockets.** The *Capital-Journal* publishes a *police log* (a daily report of activity involving the department), *fire reports* and court dockets in small print. That job, tedious as it is, falls to the police reporters. Fry gets the night shift reports, and Aeschliman picks up the morning shift reports when he makes afternoon rounds. That means checking in at the sheriff's office for traffic and offense reports. Then he goes to the police department for the same type of information. Aeschliman summarizes each report in one or two lines.

A typical item from the police blotter might read: Fleet Service and Equipment, 1534 N. Tyler, burglary of business and theft of tools. A typical item from the fire department log might read: 7:53 p.m. Wednesday—3700 W. 29th, fire started in water heater caused by short in wiring, burned wiring and water heater, $50 loss.

"Even if the paper did not run the small print, I'd still be looking through the reports," he said. "There are important stories hidden in the pile and you've got to find them."

On this day, he finds two he regards as worthy of more than a mention in small print: burglary and arson at a church and the arrest of a person accused of purse snatching. Also, there is the arrest of the burglary suspect Fry talked about earlier in the day.

• **Ferreting Out Additional Details.** "Before leaving, I talk to detectives about the three cases," Aeschliman said. "They fill me in with enough details to make each story interesting, though short. The purse snatch arrest happened after I came on duty and from what the detectives say it is worth getting a few quotes from the officers involved. A couple of them are at the headquarters writing reports. They are friendly enough and receptive so we talk about it. They're both natural and open and give me good material.

"Often, the detectives try to be so precise that they sound like a boring report. That's why I like witnesses; the closer you get to the event the more accurate and more colorful the information becomes."

Aeschliman returns to his office and calls the fire department again. This time, he asks for the entire list of fire reports. He enters them quickly on his video display terminal and sends them, along with the rest of the short items for the small print, to the city desk.

It is 6:35—five minutes past deadline. "Because of the time I spent on the fire story, no one yells at me for missing the deadline," Aeschliman said.

The reporter has nearly an hour for a dinner break. He does not eat but he does spend the time lifting weights at the YMCA. Now, back in the office, he is ready to write.

Planning to Meet Deadlines

Gathering the information is only half the job. A beat reporter must organize his or her time to meet deadlines. Aeschliman's next deadline is 10:15 p.m. All copy should be in, but some minor local stories do not have to be rushed. It is 7:30 p.m. Aeschliman figures two hours and 45 minutes should be enough time to get everything written—that is, if nothing else happens.

"In addition to writing for deadline, I've got to monitor the scanners to keep on top of any breaking news," he said. "If everything breaks loose, some of my stories could be reassigned to another reporter or dumped entirely if something more important happens.

"For now, the boss decides each story—the fire, the church arson, the burglary arrest and the purse snatch—should be written. I go to work."

Writing the Fire Story

Aeschliman always sets priorities when writing on deadline. He turns initially to his major story; on this day, it is the mobile home fire. His first task is to develop a strong, concise, accurate lead. It takes thought.

- **Thinking About and Developing the Lead.** "The fire deaths go first," Aeschliman said. "Everything is secondary to that. It would be good to identify the girls in the first paragraph because I know who they are and no one else does. I play around with that idea a bit, but every lead comes out extremely long. The boss suggests a simple lead: 'Two young girls were killed when a fire destroyed their mobile home Saturday.'

"That is a nice starting place, but I know I can do better," Aeschliman said. "I look through my notes and decide to go with a little extra about the injured father trying to get back in." Aeschliman writes:

> Two Topeka girls, 3 and 1 years old, died Friday in a mobile home fire, and their critically burned father had to be restrained from re-entering the inferno to try to rescue them.

"That tells the story," Aeschliman said. "The lead may be a tad long, but I like it."

- **Constructing the Entire Story.** Stories about fires should answer several basic questions. First: Was anyone killed? Beyond that, fire stories obviously should provide additional information. Aeschliman tries to work in most of the following details:

- Identification of the dead
- Cause of death (for example, smoke inhalation, burns and so forth)
- Results of or status of autopsies
- Location of the fire
- Cause and origin of the fire
- If arson is suspected, details on leads or arrests
- Identification of the injured
- Description of the scene
- Details of treatment to the injured at the scene
- Details of where the injured were taken
- Current condition of the injured (generally obtained from hospitals)
- Time of the fire
- When the fire was reported and by whom

BEAT REPORTING

- Response time of firefighters
- Length of time to get the fire under control
- Length of time firefighters spent on scene
- Heroics by firefighters
- Extent of property damage (including damage to adjacent buildings)
- Estimated damage in dollars
- Insurance details
- Quotations from police and fire officials, witnesses, neighbors and so forth

"I like to use good quotes high in the story; they attract attention and keep the reader interested," Aeschliman said. "In this case, using quotes from the witness in the first paragraph would be confusing. I have to tell the readers generally about the fire, so that the quotes can be read in context. But I don't have to overdo it, and the quotes can be used about halfway through the body. The witness has a story to tell, so I just let him. I've done rearranging to make more sense of it, and I've paraphrased when he wasn't very clear, but I try to use as much of what he said exactly the way he said it."

Aeschliman's story continues:

> The girls, Shena and Kimberly Bryan, were killed in the fire at their mobile home, 245 E. 29th, lot 1, at the Crest Mobile Home Park, a fire department spokesman said.
>
> Kenneth Bryan, father of the girls, was burned over most of his body and was taken to St. Francis Hospital and Medical Center before being transferred to the burn center of the Kansas University Medical Center in Kansas City.
>
> He was in critical condition late Friday, but hospital officials would not release further information.
>
> His wife was not at home when the fire broke out, fire department officials said.

- **Importance of Attribution.** Note that Aeschliman is careful to attribute factual information to reliable sources. Reporters always should tell readers the source of information.

Aeschliman obtained information for the first paragraphs by:

- Ingenuity (scouring the neighborhood for witnesses and to get background information on the family)
- A telephone call to the sheriff who served the nearby small community where the family used to live (to verify and to get names)
- Routine reporting work (talking with fire department officials at the scene and, back at the office, calling the hospital for a condition report)

- **Describing the Scene.** Aeschliman's next paragraphs provide additional details from the scene of the fire—details that the reporter would not have been able to relay to readers had he not gone to the site:

> The mobile home was destroyed with only the skeleton of charred 2-by-2 timbers still standing after the fire. The aluminum siding was mostly melted away, the strips remaining dangling and pockmarked from the heat.
>
> The body of one girl was found in a

rear bedroom, the area that had the least fire damage. Officials at the scene said she was not severely burned and probably died from smoke inhalation. The other girl was found in the front living area and was burned beyond recognition, a spokesman said.

"You had to move debris before you saw the body, and even then it was hard to tell what it was," he said.

Autopsies are pending.

Both the cause and origin of the fire are under investigation. No details as to how or where the fire began were available late Friday.

The fire was reported at 10:11 a.m. by neighbors, but Jerry Fitzgerald, 25, 2834 Topeka Ave., the first person to arrive on the scene, said the fire was burning about 15 minutes before anyone called for help.

Aeschliman strengthened his story—and earned an advantage over his competition from other newspapers and the electronic media—by locating and interviewing Fitzgerald. His description of the scene was indeed vivid. Aeschliman's story continues:

He [Fitzgerald] said he was shopping across the street when he saw a single cloud of smoke billow skyward. Fitzgerald said he drove over right away, and when he arrived he saw Bryan run out of the front door and saw the interior of the residence explode into flames behind Bryan.

Fitzgerald tried to help Bryan, who was covered with burns. But Bryan broke away and ran around to the rear of the trailer where he wrenched open a second door in an attempt to get inside. But flames roared out at him, and Fitzgerald restrained him.

Aeschliman then incorporates some vivid direct quotations into the story:

"He tried to get back inside, so I grabbed him and another man grabbed him and pulled him back and sat him down," Fitzgerald said.

"He just kept saying that his girl was in there and for somebody to go in and get her out. I just said no way, the heat was ungodly."

The smoke pouring out was so thick "it was like you could reach out and hold it in your hand," he said.

Aeschliman then quotes Fitzgerald on how the police and fire were summoned and when the ambulance arrived.

• **A Question of Taste.** Aeschliman's city editor objects to a vivid, gruesome quote the reporter uses near the end of his story which reads:

"You could tell he [Bryan] was realizing what had happened to him. He was looking at his hands and they were bleeding, and he had shoes on and there was blood coming from the shoes. His skin was peeling off like wallpaper. And he still wanted to go into the house," he said.

"The quote graphically details the man's injuries and his feelings at the time," Aeschliman said. "I believe it has value in demonstrating the horror of a fire. It is not just sensationalism; it may scare people, but we might save a life because of the morbid paragraph."

The reporter convinces the city editor to let the quote run. A lot of newspaper editors and reporters, however, undoubtedly would have deleted the quotation as being too gruesome. They would have reasoned that the survivors already had suffered enough and that the vivid description was not necessary to tell the story. Matters of taste often crop up. It is the reporter's job to consider carefully his position in printing material that could be offensive to some readers and to discuss it with an editor.

As Aeschliman closes his story with more details from fire department officials, a couple of fire alarms go out, but they both turn into false calls. "We don't waste manpower by running out on every alarm," Aeschliman said. "Fire trucks are almost always at the scene in three minutes or less, and they immediately report the extent of the fire upon arrival. We can wait three minutes to decide."

Writing an Arrest Story

After completing the major fire story, Aeschliman is ready to write a short story about the purse-snatch arrest. He always tries to work most of the following information into his arrest stories:

- Name of the suspect arrested
- Identification (for example, address and/or occupation)
- Site and time of the arrest
- Name and/or identification of the victim of the alleged crime
- Time of the alleged crime
- Details of the alleged crime
- Details of the capture and arrest of the suspect
- Details of the booking and charges
- Details of bail
- Quotes from police officials, the victim and the suspect

One officer used the words *cornered* and *flushed out* when he was interviewed by Aeschliman. The reporter's lead reads:

A man who police think took a purse from a woman Friday was cornered in a nearby alley and arrested when a police dog flushed him out.

Aeschliman uses direct quotes in the second and third paragraphs:

Police in the area closed in on the alleged purse snatcher and cordoned off the area of 7th and Jewell, while the police helicopter circled overhead. He was in custody "before he knew what hit him," an officer at the scene said.

The arrest was "one of those things when everybody was at the right place at the right time," one officer said. "It was very satisfying."

"The story can be told without repeated reference by name to the suspect, so I can identify the arrested person early in the copy block but later in the story refer merely to a man," Aeschliman said. "Officers and I never say, for example, that "John Smyth took the purse and then hid" or anything close to that. I have to be especially careful when writing my stories to avoid convicting the suspect in print. Libel is always on my mind." (See "Covering the Courts" later in this chapter and Chapter 15, on law and ethics, for further details.)

Aeschliman's story continues:

> The suspect, John C. Smyth [not his real name], 19, of Wichita, was arrested in an alley behind 704 Lindenwood and booked into Shawnee County Jail in connection with burglary and theft, officer Mike Casey said.

Note that Aeschliman says Smyth was booked *in connection with* burglary and theft. Aeschliman is careful not to write that Smyth was booked *for* burglary and theft. Use of the word *for* would imply guilt and could be libelous.

Aeschliman goes on to provide additional details on the booking of the suspect and to use direct quotations from officers:

> Smyth remained in jail late Friday in lieu of $5,000 bond with surety.
>
> Casey said the theft happened at 2:48 p.m. An 81-year-old woman had just gotten out of her car near 6th and Franklin when a man leaped past her, into the car, grabbed her handbag and ran away.
>
> The woman and a witness tried to chase the suspect but stopped and phoned police. The victim was not injured.
>
> Officer J.W. Harper was patrolling a few blocks away and on a hunch circled to 7th Street where he saw a man walking down the middle of the street. Harper said he drove to within 100 feet of the suspect before the man looked up and sprinted away down an alley.
>
> "He pulled a vanishing act," Harper said. "I was only seconds behind him and couldn't see him, so I figured he was holed up in a garage or something."

Aeschliman then went on to describe the arrival of a police helicopter, additional officers and a police dog. He quoted Harper again: "We put so much coverage in there so fast that he (the suspect) just froze up." Aeschliman also quoted Detective Greg Halford who said the suspect had been interrogated and that the woman's purse and money were recovered.

- **Importance of Follow-up Interviews.** Again, it is clear that reporters can add considerable spice and detail to their coverage of relatively routine events by interviewing the officers involved. Also, one sentence in this story could have alerted reporters to a follow article: It is not every day that an 81-year-old woman chases a 19-year-old burglary suspect.

Aeschliman emphasized that he likes to have officers tell of their participation in an event. "Detective Halford has always been good to me," he

BEAT REPORTING

said. "He really didn't do much in the arrest, but it never hurts to stroke a few egos by putting a name in print."

WRITING STORIES FROM DEPARTMENT RECORDS

Reporters write many of their stories about fires, crimes, accidents, arrests and bookings after examining reports that are on file at various departments. Many times, reporters will follow up information from official reports by interviewing officials. The types of reports and the level of legal access to them varies. It is imperative that reporters fully understand reports and records that are available to them in the states and cities in which they work.

Aeschliman, for example, has complete, *unrestricted access* to Topeka Police Department accident forms. He also has access to Kansas Department of Revenue Motor Vehicle Accident Report forms.

Writing an Accident Story

Most small-circulation dailies and weeklies publish stories about all accidents reported to the police—no matter how minor. The *Capital-Journal*, a larger-circulation daily, does not publish stories about insignificant fender benders, but it does publish daily agate listings of all injury accidents. Each short item contains information about the location of the accident, names of injured parties and condition reports from hospitals.

"Any injury reported by the police in their forms is listed as an injury in the paper," Aeschliman said. "We contact the hospital to see if the injured were seen, admitted or treated and released. In the event the police say a person was injured but no hospital has a record of the person, we write 'Police reported John Smith was possibly injured but no record of hospital treatment was found.'"

For a story to graduate from the agate listings in the *Capital-Journal* to a regular article, the victim must have been injured severely or killed, or the accident must have an interesting feature, such as a 10-car pileup in the fog or semitrucks jackknifing across the highway.

The *Capital-Journal* reporter said stories about people who are injured seriously usually rate five to six inches near the classified ad pages. Stories about life-threatening injuries often are played on Page 2. "Fatalities or some spectacular accident merit Page 1 treatment," Aeschliman said. "Topeka, for example, sees only five to 10 fatal wrecks a year. When they occur in a city of 110,000, many readers know the victims or someone who knew the victim, so it's news. We're also big on follow-ups. We report the victims' conditions until they are out of the hospital. Occasionally, we do a feature story a year after of the 'how life has been since' type."

Basic Information on Forms

The use of forms to get information for accident stories is crucial. Accident reports vary, but information found on the Kansas Department of Revenue Motor Vehicle Accident Report forms is representative:

- Location of accident
- Name of investigating officer
- Owner of vehicle
- Driver of vehicle
- Age and occupation of driver
- Names of passengers and witnesses
- Severity of injuries to parties involved
- License number of vehicle
- Owner's liability insurance company
- Year, make, model and type of vehicle
- Damage (fixed objects, such as utility poles, as well as animals, pedestrians and so on)
- Damage to vehicle (windshield, trunk, hood and so on)
- Severity of damage to vehicle (disabling, functional and so on)
- Time authorities notified
- Time authorities arrived at scene
- Time emergency medical service notified
- Time emergency medical service arrived at scene
- Hospital to which injured parties were removed and by whom
- Narrative that contains the drivers' and investigating officers' opinions of what occurred
- Principal contributing circumstances (driver condition, vehicle, human behavior and so on)
- Driver and pedestrian condition prior to accident (ill, fatigued, apparently asleep, apparently normal, taking prescription drugs, taking illegal drugs, consuming alcohol and so on)
- Chemical test results
- Road surface (dry, wet, slippery and so on)
- Weather
- Light conditions
- Vehicle defects (turn lights, worn tires and so on)
- Visibility (vision not obscured, rain, snow, fog and so on)
- Diagram of what happened (drawing of the scene as observed; vehicles, drivers and pedestrians normally are referred to by numbers assigned in the report). The diagram includes an outline of the street and access point paths of units before and after impact, skid marks and point of impact; location of signs, traffic controls and reference points; location of other property hit or damaged; special features at the location (bridge, overpass, culvert and such); location of temporary highway conditions; and all measurements to locate the accident relative to a specific, fixed, uniquely identifiable and locatable point.

Key Elements to Consider

Aeschliman glances through dozens of accident reports each day. Because stories will not be written about all of them, here are some of the key items he looks for to determine which are newsworthy:

- **Time and location of accident.** "The location helps to give me an idea of how many people might have seen the accident," Aeschliman said. "A minor injury accident at 8 a.m. on the freeway may be more newsworthy than a more severe injury accident at 2 a.m. on a rural gravel road."

• **Names of those involved.** "The names are necessary to obtain condition information from hospitals," Aeschliman said. "It is important also not to overlook the names of passengers who may have been injured worse than the drivers. I always check the names of the vehicle owners as well. You might find that the son or daughter of a respected citizen was out joyriding. The owner's name also gives you another person to contact for more information."

• **Severity of injuries.** The Kansas form that Aeschliman works with is coded: 0 means no injury; 1 is a death; 2 is an ambulance injury; 3 is obvious injuries but not ambulance worthy; and 4 is possible injuries. "Of all the numbers in a report, this one throws up the red flag for a reporter," Aeschliman said. "If the number indicates an injury, the form deserves further attention. If no injury is listed, I usually only glance at the report to see if the mayor was in an accident while driving drunk, or something like that."

• **Chemical test results.** Any number that appears in this box on the Kansas form shows alcohol consumption. In that state, any number more than .1 indicates that the person was legally drunk. "If the number indicates consumption, I check into it," Aeschliman said.

• **Ambulance service.** The Kansas form indicates which ambulance service arrived at the scene. "Finding out which ambulance was involved saves me time trying to find out where the injured were taken," Aeschliman said.

• **Diagram section.** "This is an important section because it gives you a quick once over of the wreck and how it occurred," Aeschliman said. "The diagram allows you to understand the wreck and to then ask intelligent questions of the officers or the people involved."

• **Statements made by drivers.** "I often quote people involved in an accident," Aeschliman said. "But I am always careful to note that the statement was attributed to the people by the police in their report."

• **"Nuts and bolts" section that provides information on road conditions, light conditions, visibility, use of seat belts and so on.** "If properly read, this section allows you to write a story as if you were there when the crash occurred," Aeschliman said. "For example, you might write: 'The car's tires were bald and the road was slick with spilled oil, the police report said.' Also, at the *Capital-Journal*, at the risk of sounding preachy, we often use information about seat belts, such as 'police said Jones might not have been injured if he had been wearing a seat belt.'"

An Accident Story

Aeschliman worked much essential information from the police report into the first three paragraphs of an accident story published in the *Capital-Journal*. He also called a hospital for a condition report. Here are his first three paragraphs:

A Grantville man was thrown from his car and died instantly in a three-car collision Friday, and the driver of another car was seriously injured.

Police said the man, Richard Bigham, 55, was westbound in the 800 block of US-24 when he lost control of his car and slid across the median broadside and into the eastbound lanes where his car was struck by two other vehicles.

Marcella Conklin, 19, Shawnee, the driver of one of the eastbound cars, was admitted to St. Francis Hospital and Medical Center for treatment of broken ribs, a broken kneecap, and cuts and bruises, a hospital spokesman said. She was in serious but stable condition late Friday in the intensive care unit, a spokesman said.

The story then provided condition reports on a passenger in one of the cars and on two firefighters who had been sprayed in the eyes with hydraulic fluid while pulling people from the vehicles. Then, by attributing information to a police accident investigator, Aeschliman provided additional details on the collision:

The traffic accident happened at 3:28 p.m. at 851 E. US-24, said police accident investigator Lyndon Weddle. Bigham was westbound in the left lane when another vehicle turned west onto US-24 from Goldwater Road in front of Bigham, Weddle said.

Apparently, Bigham swerved to avoid that car, and in doing so dropped his two left side tires off the road onto the shoulder, Weddle said.

When Bigham tried to steer his car back onto the road it went out of control on the snowy shoulder and spun broadside into the median ditch, she said.

Bigham's car slid on into the eastbound lanes of US-24, facing south, directly in front of Conklin, eastbound in the interior lane, and a third car in the exterior lane, driven by John Stein, 54, Valley Falls, Weddle said.

The story continued with additional details about the accident, a preliminary autopsy report and information about how rush-hour traffic was routed around the accident.

Aeschliman's story showed that reports can provide an abundance of details that, if gathered carefully, can be woven into a complete, understandable story.

TIPS FOR POLICE AND FIRE REPORTERS

There is no foolproof formula to ensure competent police and fire beat reporting, but some suggestions are:

• **Develop and cultivate sources.** Get to know sources as persons—not merely as officials. Hang out at the departments as much as possible. "I don't stay in the newspaper office any longer than I have to," said Aeschliman. "You can't cultivate sources sitting in the newsroom."

• **Learn how to handle hostile sources.** Reporters on the scene of investigations run the risk of being perceived as interfering with official business. Some front-line police officers and firefighters dislike talking to reporters under these circumstances. If reporters persist, they run the risk of being arrested. Officers do not have to cooperate with reporters. In these cases, begging or shouting usually does not do much good. It is best to go to fire or police supervisors, who should provide information or instruct those under them to provide it. (See Chapter 7 for additional details on how to deal with hostile sources.)

• **Know the job responsibilities of sources.** Titles can be deceiving. Know what their jobs entail.

• **Don't deceive sources.** If reporters make an error, they should admit it.

• **If a big story comes along—one that places the department in a bad light—go after it aggressively.** Work hard on the story, even if it costs you some sources. Make sure, though, that the story is important enough to justify the loss of several major sources. If it is a piddly story, think twice about whether it is worth losing valuable sources.

• **Know the territory.** Spend time driving around; get to know the streets and alleys in the community. Know where the major crime areas are. That will make it easier to write stories when the *where* element is important.

• **Learn the terminology.** Police might say they are *interrogating an individual* who is in custody. Report, however, that police are *questioning a suspect*. Learn the terminology and jargon, but always write understandable English for readers.

• **Be aware of the special vocabulary of an agency.** In turn, explain terms to readers. For example, one-alarm, two-alarm, three-alarm and four-alarm fires can have different meanings, depending on the community. In general, more men and equipment are dispatched to two-alarm fires than to one-alarm fires. More still are sent to three-alarm and four-alarm fires. The number of men and equipment sent to fight the blaze, however, depends on the size of the community and the size of the fire department. Don't assume readers understand these terms.

• **Double-check spellings of names and streets mentioned on law enforcement department reports.** Police officers are not trained journalists. Always verify information.

• **After reading a police report in which injuries are mentioned, always check with the hospital or the morgue to update or verify the information.** If the new information conflicts, another story angle might materialize.

• **Be particularly careful when reporting arrests.** Remember: Always write, for example, John Jones was arrested *in connection with* (or *in the investigation of*) a burglary at 1122 E. Norwood. *Don't write* Jones was arrested *for* a burglary at 1122 E. Norwood. That implies guilt.

• **Don't confuse an arrest with the filing of a charge.** A lot of suspects who are arrested are subsequently released and never charged with a crime. Also, if someone is arrested and you report it, write a follow-up story when the person is charged or released.

- **Be leery of libel.** Journalists have a privilege to report most information from public records, but they must do so fairly and accurately. And, during interviews, merely because a police officer utters a potentially libelous statement about a suspect does not give reporters the right or the legal privilege to reiterate it to readers.

- **Be sure to know an organization's policy on the use of names of minors.** Some newspapers have a policy against using the names of juveniles who are involved in misdemeanors. Also, be familiar with the laws of the state that govern coverage of juvenile proceedings.

COVERING CITY GOVERNMENT

Most newspapers take pride in their coverage of city government. Readers are interested in issues that affect the roads they drive on, the parks they play in, the water they drink, the police protection they depend on and the taxes they pay.

Coverage of city government often is one of the first assignments young reporters receive—particularly if they go to work for small- or medium-size newspapers or broadcast outlets, where extensive coverage of local government is a primary goal. A typical example is the *Tempe* (Ariz.) *Daily News Tribune*, a 10,000-circulation morning daily.

The *Daily News Tribune* is published in a university community of 150,000 that is in a metropolitan area of nearly two million. Tens of thousands of Tempe residents also subscribe to the morning *Arizona Republic* (circulation: 300,000-plus) or to the afternoon *Phoenix Gazette* (circulation: 100,000-plus). The *Republic* and *Gazette* provide detailed coverage of state government and devote some space to Tempe's local affairs, but like any community newspaper, the *Daily News Tribune* is able to provide a more comprehensive package of local government news than can the metropolitan newspapers that serve a large area.

Adrianne Flynn, a journalism graduate of Arizona State University, covers city government for the *Daily News Tribune*. She worked on the copy desk at the *Mesa Tribune* and *Chandler Arizonan*, two other newspapers owned by Cox Arizona Publications Inc., before she took the reporting job.

Flynn's primary responsibility is coverage of local government. She does her share of city council stories, planning board stories and budget stories, but she has earned good play with enterprise pieces such as these:

- The city, as seen through the eyes of garbage collectors. "I spent the day in a garbage truck, bouncing through alleys," Flynn said. "It was fun to see the backside of the city—the side no one ever wants to see."
- Cemetery space—or the lack of it—in the city. Flynn found that Tempe did not have enough cemetery space to last beyond a calendar year.

Flynn pursued these stories—and dozens like them—after picking up on off-the-cuff remarks made by various city officials as she made her daily rounds and as she sat through various meetings.

Good city beat reporters obviously do not limit their coverage of the community to daily government developments, but contact with elected and appointed officials does provide the foundation—the building blocks—for effective reporting.

LEARNING THE SYSTEM

When she took over the city beat, Flynn realized she had to learn the structure of government and the officials who had power and influence. Forms of government vary from city to city. Nicholas L. Henry wrote in "Governing at the Grassroots" that municipalities use two primary types of government: the "weak executive" model and the "strong executive" model. Forms of municipal governments within these categories are: mayor-council, council-manager and commission.

Forms of Municipal Governments

In *mayor-council* systems, the mayor can be categorized as "weak" or "strong," depending on the powers assigned to the position. In a "strong" mayor system, the mayor has the power to form budgets and to make and administer policy. This system, according to Henry, exists in six of the nation's 10 largest cities as well as in other communities. Under this system the mayor is a primary source of news, for he or she is attuned to all city government activity. In a "weak" mayor-council system the mayor is, in essence, the chairperson of the city council; most managerial functions are divided among other elected officials and the council.

In *council-manager* systems, the city manager, according to Henry, "controls the administrative apparatus of the city." The manager possesses significant power, but the council retains the authority to hire and fire this person. Henry noted that the council-manager plan is used by more than one-third of all cities with more than 2,500 people and by more than one-half the cities with more than 25,000 population. As more cities moved to a council-manager form of government in the 1960s, 1970s and 1980s, the mayor became more of a figurehead. The main source of city government expertise became the city manager, a trained professional adept at administering a community's affairs.

In *commission* systems, which are used by about 5 percent of the nation's municipalities, a committee of city leaders assumes both executive and legislative functions.

Labels can be placed on various systems, but it is important to remember that there are variations within the systems. Tempe, for example, has a council-manager form of government. The city has a mayor, but his vote counts the same as others on the council. The mayor is elected every two years, the council every four in staggered terms. Elections are non-partisan. The mayor chairs the council; he conducts the meetings. He also has authority to appoint short-term boards and commissions. The council approves all action in the city and sets policy to be carried out by the city manager. Figure 12.1 diagrams the government structure of Tempe.

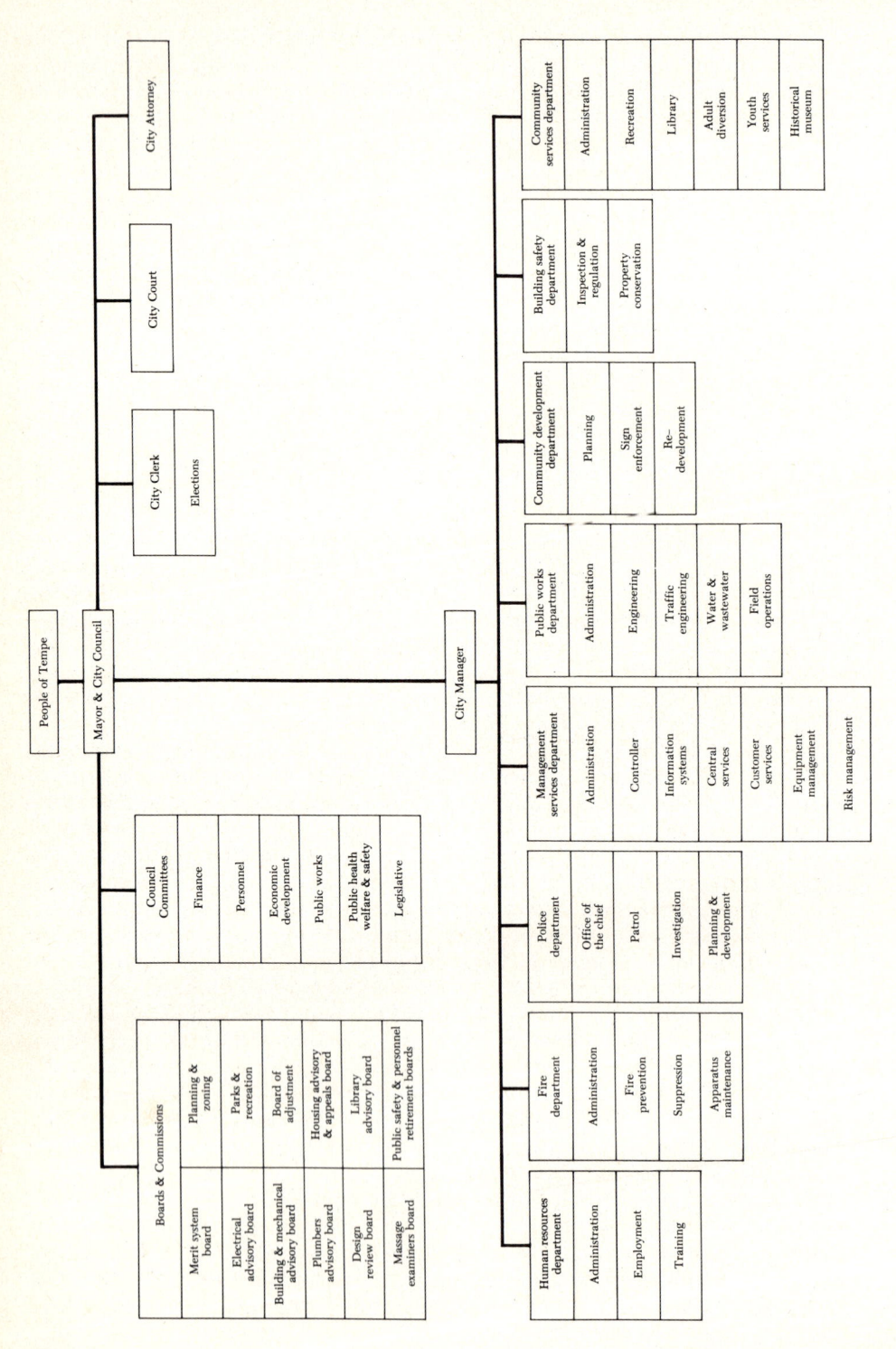

Figure 12.1 Government Structure of Tempe, Arizona

A DAY ON THE CITY BEAT WITH ADRIANNE FLYNN

Flynn said there is no typical day when covering city government. "The smaller the paper, the more your beat crosses over into others because there just aren't enough reporters to go around," she said. "I cover some police issues, do a smattering of features, cover awards ceremonies, plus all the boards and commissions. I also cover Tempe's state legislators and Tempe's U.S. congressman. I also occasionally cover a fire, a traffic accident or a hazardous waste spill."

Flynn's hours vary, depending on the meetings she has to cover. But she's usually in the office by 9 a.m. "The first thing I do is read our paper," she said. "I get all my gripes about how my stories were treated out of the way, read the editorials in case someone asks me about them and find out what's going on in other people's beats in case I have to cover for them.

"Next, I read the competition. If I have been beaten on anything, I hustle to catch up. Fortunately, because all we cover is Tempe, we rarely get beat on the day-to-day stuff. On some of the bigger stories, we get shelled because we don't have the resources in Washington, D.C., or Costa Rica or even the state capital."

Flynn then checks her *story budget*—a list of articles she is to work on—and her date book. "I probably do 70 percent of my work by telephone, so I get on the horn and call the sources for my stories and ask them all kinds of stupid questions until I understand what they're talking about."

She likes to deal with her primary City Hall sources face to face. "It is harder for people to lie to you when you're sitting across from them," she said. "I always get better and more information in a face-to-face interview than I do on the phone."

Flynn checks in at City Hall at least twice each day—even if she has absolutely nothing to talk about. "This is a terrific way to get story ideas," she said. "It also keeps you informed of ongoing issues and lets the people know you are around."

While at City Hall, Flynn reads the agendas for posted meetings to see which ones she might sit in on and possibly write about. She usually is back in the office by midafternoon, where she writes her stories for the following day's paper. "The *Daily News Tribune* likes us to keep our stories short, so my stories average about 12–15 inches," Flynn said. "Unless it is a really big issue, I never write more than 20 inches."

After she writes her stories, Flynn checks her date book for the next day's schedule and assigns art to accompany stories she is working on, particularly features. She then writes her next day's budget. Occasionally, she is home by 6 p.m. Usually, however, she is still in the office, reworking a story, rewriting or localizing wire copy and eating dinner while waiting to go to a meeting.

The Tempe City Council meets every Thursday night. The Planning and Zoning Commission meets Tuesdays, Design Review meets Wednesdays and other boards compete for attention on remaining nights. Most of the meetings do not end until 9:30 or 10 o'clock. By the time Flynn gets back to the office and writes her story for the next morning's newspaper it usually is 11 o'clock.

"I love it, though," Flynn said. "The variety of stories is stimulating. Working for a small newspaper keeps you busy constantly and even dull meetings seem interesting when you know what goes on behind the scenes."

COVERAGE OF CITY COUNCIL MEETINGS

One of Flynn's primary assignments is coverage of the Tempe City Council. The *agenda*—an outline of matters to be considered—for the Thursday night council meetings is available to Flynn after 5 p.m. on Tuesdays. Reporters who cover city council meetings always should pick up a copy of the agenda *before* the meetings.

A Look at the Agenda

Here is an agenda for a Tempe City Council meeting that Flynn covered:

7:00—1. STUDIES AND SURVEYS—Mobile Home Parks—Committee Report

7:20—2. PLANNED DEVELOPMENT—Warner Ranch Village—Plan Modification UDC, SE & SWC Warner Rd/Warner Ranch Rd

7:40—3. STUDIES AND SURVEYS—Aircraft Noise, Michael Brandman Report

8:00—4. PARKS—Tempe Soccer Club—Request for use of Diablo Stadium for Thanksgiving Tournament (Please bring booklets delivered to you)

8:15—5. ADMINISTRATION AND POLICY MANAGEMENT—Real Estate Signs, Police Enforcement

8:30—6. COMMUNITY SERVICES FACILITIES/ACTIVITIES—Latchkey Program, Mary Lou Burem

8:45—7. PARKS—Rolling Hills

9:00—8. ZONING AMENDMENT—Mixed-Use Parking Formula

9:20—9. REAL PROPERTY MANAGEMENT—Use of Parking Garage

9:30—10. ENVIRONMENT—Noise Ordinance Proposed Modification

9:40—11. PUBLIC SAFETY—FIRE TRUCK BID

9:45—12. STREETS—Street Name Change

9:55— Adjourn

Writing the Pre-Meeting Story

Flynn usually reads the agenda Tuesday night and writes a pre-meeting story on Wednesday. Because she regularly covers the council, seldom does she find an agenda item that surprises or confuses her. When this occurs, however, she calls appropriate city officials for background. Her pre-meeting stories are published in Thursday's edition.

Flynn's pre-meeting stories normally focus on what she projects to be the most important item on the agenda. After discussing this issue in the first few paragraphs of her story, Flynn uses bullets (●) to precede a synopsis of other agenda items. Her pre-meeting story this time led with the fact that a consultant would report the results of a study concerning airplane noise over Tempe.

The noise issue had been a long-running news story. Articles had been written when the consulting firm was commissioned to study the problem. Thus, it was logical that the report would be of interest to readers.

Writing the Meeting Story

Occasionally, items will surface at council meetings that turn out to be more important than the projected primary topic. That was not the case this time, however. Flynn wrote her council story in an inverted pyramid, with a summary lead that focused on the report:

> Tempe is getting most of the noise pollution and too little of the benefits from Phoenix Sky Harbor International Airport, a consultant told the City Council Thursday.
>
> "It seems to me you deserve to have the noise levels reduced," said Sam Lane, a consultant with Michael Brandman Associates. "They are dumping their noise garbage all over you, and you're having to clean up the garbage, and you're not getting paid for it."

After Flynn presented readers with the thrust of the report and a vivid direct quotation in the first two paragraphs, she provided background:

> Lane's company was hired by Tempe to study the airport noise problem and to recommend technical solutions. A second consultant, Stewart Udall, is considering political solutions and will submit his report to the city within a month.

After this background paragraph, Flynn continued with more new facts from the report:

> Lane said Tempe derives about 10 percent of the economic benefits from Sky Harbor while receiving about 75 percent of its noise. He said the situation will not improve without city action.
>
> Lane said predictions made 10 years ago are far short. Sky Harbor's daily departures are now almost twice those estimates.

He said city and citizen action will "break the monopoly" that the airport and the Federal Aviation Administration have on information. He also said Sky Harbor has insulated itself and is "beholden to the airline industry, not to the general public, even though federal money has been used by them in the past."

"The cost and the benefits are not equitable," Lane said. He recommended Tempe focus on what he considered immediate solutions.

Among those solutions are to send more flights to the west over Phoenix, to require aircraft to follow the river bottom longer before turning and to reduce low-altitude approaches over Tempe.

The council will study the proposals while waiting for Udall's report. It also will wait for analysis by Tempe's Airport Noise Abatement Committee, which will consider Lane's report April 9. ANACOM will meet at 7:30 p.m. in Pyle Adult Recreation Center, 655 E. Southern.

Using Transition

Flynn devoted nearly half of her main council story to the airport noise issue. This is common when one topic is of overriding importance. Because none of the remaining items considered by the council merited expanded treatment, Flynn employed a writing device that many reporters use when covering meetings where multiple issues are discussed. Flynn wrote:

In other action, the council:

Those transitional words opened the door for a brief discussion of other council issues. Flynn used bullets to precede each separate item, thus providing a concise, summary overview of how the council treated them. Here is part of the remainder of Flynn's story to illustrate this common, punchy style:

• Reviewed the final report of the Ad Hoc Commission on Mobile Home Parks. The group was formed to give mobile home park tenants more rights through recommended changes in state and local law. It asked for more time to read the report and will make recommendations at a future meeting.

• Gave informal approval to a proposal by Universal Development Corporation to change plans for Warner Ranch Village condominiums. The company wants to make the units smaller and wants to bypass Planning and Zoning Commission approval for the change.

• Gave informal approval to a request by the community development department that confiscated illegal signs be considered non-returnable abandoned property. The signs now are locked in a city maintenance yard.

• Reviewed a proposal by the Community Services Department to run a program for latchkey children—kids that are left alone after school until their parents return from work. The report was for the council's information only.

Note that Flynn was careful to write grammatical bulleted items. Because she included the subject (council) in her introductory phrase ("In other action, the council:"), she started each bulleted entry with a verb.

IMPORTANCE OF PREPARATION

City council meetings often are a study in chaos and confusion. To write a good story, reporters must follow up with lots of questions; double-checking of facts is essential. For example, sometimes a vote count is in doubt and must be checked with the meeting recorder.

Reporters should go to city council meetings as prepared as possible. Adrianne Flynn always does. "Most of the issues already have been discussed at study sessions (the Tempe council meets for one hour before regular meetings)," Flynn said. "Because reporters can attend the study sessions, most of us have ample background on the issues before they formally are considered at the regular meetings."

Reporters are not, however, allowed to attend *executive sessions* (meetings at which no official action can be taken and at which members of the press and public are excluded) of the council. State laws specify the types of items that can be considered in executive sessions. Many times, when a council goes into executive session, it is to discuss personnel matters or financial matters such as the purchase of property.

Reporters often can find sources who will tell them what occurred at executive sessions on the condition that it cannot be printed or that it can be printed but not attributed. "I have a couple of good sources who trust me," Flynn said. "I can usually get them to tell me what happened during the session. If it is not of earth-shattering importance, I hold off on it until it comes up at a regular meeting. But by finding out about it ahead of time, I can be better prepared to deal with it when it does come before the public."

Preparation is essential before covering a city council meeting. To prepare for a meeting, reporters should review the agenda and talk to council members and other city officials about any "hidden" issues that may surface. Complete, understandable council stories can be written only after diligent preparation and after industrious, painstaking checking of facts after the meeting.

TIPS FOR COVERING CITY GOVERNMENT

• **Learn the system.** Check the newspaper morgue to see if stories about the hierarchy of the local government (city and/or county) have been done. If they have, they should provide good background. If they have not, consider writing such a series as one of your first major undertakings.

A textbook can do no more than generalize about a local government system. Each is unique. Reporters must immerse themselves totally to become familiar with the local government structure of the city and county in which they work. This requires diligence, patience and concentration. This familiarization must be accomplished quickly; reporters cannot adequately report on local government unless they thoroughly understand its structure.

• **Get to know the personalities.** It is one thing to master a local government organizational chart; it is another to pick out who among those occupying positions listed on the chart is truly significant. Once this determination has been made, reporters should get to know these persons as well as possible. If the city attorney is a Boston Celtics fan, the reporter should learn about the Boston Celtics and mention the team to the official. It might help the reporter get a local government story sometime.

- **Develop reliable sources.** Many local government stories are obtained directly from persons who occupy elected or appointed positions. Reporters obviously should build a network of sources from within these ranks. It is just as important, however, for reporters to develop a subnetwork of sources. Administrative assistants, secretaries and other staff members can be important sources. Reporters should choose them wisely, cultivate them and build a bond. But they should never take advantage of them.

"Be honest with your sources," Adrianne Flynn advised. "Let your sources know you will print all the facts on both sides of an issue no matter what, but you're not out to do a scandal sheet on every issue. Find two or three really well-informed folks on your beat that you can find out most anything from and cultivate them as sources. Don't butter them up, just be forthright and get to know them as people. Be interested in their personal as well as professional lives."

Flynn said that reporters, when they first start a beat, should do some "nuts and bolts features on how things operate." She suggested that they ride along with the garbage collectors or follow the city manager around for a day and write a feature. "They love it and you get to know them and their department," she said.

- **Be persistent.** "You catch more flies with honey than with vinegar, but if one method does not work, use the other with gusto," Flynn said. "If you want a story you must be persistent. Call every day. Every hour, if need be. Make your source so sick of you he will have to talk to you just to get you off his back. I got a great story once by waiting in a developer's office for three hours when he wouldn't return my phone calls. But I finally got to talk to him."

- **Never let friendship interfere with the job.** Reporters who cover specific beats sometimes spend as much time with officials—their sources—as they do with their personal circle of friends. It is not surprising, then, that reporters and news sources sometimes become friends. Reporters must handle this situation with care—always striving to be fair in their handling of news stories.

- **Always be prepared.** To succeed, local government reporters must know more about city government than their competition. They must have more sources, do more homework on the issues and work longer hours. Good reporters never skim an agenda casually and write a meeting off as unimportant. Instead, they work harder to find something of value in an otherwise routine meeting.

"It is important to know about the issues in advance," Flynn said. "Ask smart, informed questions. Know how the place operates and who can provide you with facts and figures on any given assignment."

- **Make note of story possibilities.** Many good local government stories do not evolve from coverage of meetings. Rather, they evolve from in-depth follow-ups of news tidbits tossed out at meetings or in informal conversations with local government sources. Even if reporters are working on another story at the time and do not have time to develop the new angle, the idea should be noted and carefully filed away for future reference.

• **Read other newspapers and listen to radio and television news.** Reporters should not operate in a vacuum, smugly assured that their sources will keep them informed of all possible stories. Other media should be surveyed constantly. Some of the best story ideas arise from less-than-satisfactory handling of stories by other reporters.

• **Write to inform, not impress, readers.** Develop local government stories from the standpoint of what the issue means to readers. For example, if a city intends to raise an additional $14 million in property taxes during the next fiscal year, reporters should explain what this increase means to readers as homeowners. What will the increase do to taxes on a house assessed at $50,000, at $75,000 or at $100,000? That is what is relevant to readers.

• **Use your brain.** "If you think you're so smart you can conquer the world, you're wrong," Flynn said. "Some of the littlest facts can hang you up. When they do, think your way out of it.

"I tried once to find out when a local congressman [John McCain, who had been a prisoner of war in Vietnam and who, a decade later, had visited the country] was returning from a trip to Vietnam. I hoped to scoop the competition by meeting him at the airport. It turned out he arrived too late for our deadline, but I found out, despite the fact that his staff was sworn to secrecy.

"I tried the airlines and narrowed down the flights to about five possible that he could be on. I called the congressman's aide, but he would not tell me which flight it was. I called his wife and said, 'He's going to be on this plane at this time,' but she would not confirm it.

"Then I called his travel agency and almost had it because a new girl in the office was going to give it to me when she suddenly had a guilt attack and checked with her supervisor.

"Finally, I called The Associated Press in New York, who relayed me to the AP bureau in Bangkok and someone there called McCain and asked him when he was returning. He told the AP correspondent and the correspondent told me. Because we belong to the AP, we can get all kinds of help from them. Don't be afraid to use the wire service, even when working on a local issue."

• **Do not be afraid to ask questions.** If you want to know something, ask. It is better than seeing your mistakes in print or seeing the competition get the jump on you.

COVERING THE COURTS

Reporters covering the courts must master judicial structures, learn the terminology and write stories in understandable language. The stakes are high: reporting errors can ruin lives and lead to additional lawsuits. Court reporting requires persistence, diligence and an eye for detail.

Mike Padgett, court reporter for the *Mesa* (Ariz.) *Tribune,* vividly pointed out the perils of the job: "If you make one screwup, at the very least, you lose some credibility. At the most, you libel somebody and end up in court yourself."

Padgett has worked at the 40,000-circulation daily for a decade. He started as a general assignment reporter, moved to the police and fire beat and then to the county government and court beats.

The reporter follows nearly two dozen cases regularly. He tracks them through the various steps in the judicial process. "It can be slow and cumbersome," he said. "But it is important to carefully keep up with cases as they move through the system."

Unlike some court reporters, Padgett is not an attorney. His college degree is in journalism, and he earned a minor in political science. He also has worked for The Associated Press and as an investigator for the Task Force on Organized Crime for the Arizona House of Representatives before he started work at the *Tribune.*

Coverage of the courts is one of the most demanding assignments a reporter can receive. During one day of testimony in a criminal trial, enough words can be spoken to fill 200 manuscript pages. From the testimony the reporter must extract the significant points and construct a readable, concise newspaper account of perhaps fewer than 500 words. Broadcast reporters face even more stifling word restrictions.

"The biggest challenge in court reporting is getting a grasp of the system" said Robert Rawitch, suburban editor of the *Los Angeles Times* who covered the federal courts in that city for more than four years. "It is difficult to develop an understanding of legal procedures and jargon. You must strive diligently not to exaggerate or underplay the importance of any happening."

Metropolitan dailies generally have more than one reporter assigned to the courts. For example, one reporter might be assigned to the federal courts, one to the state criminal courts and another to the state civil courts. In addition, some metro dailies have legal affairs reporters who are not responsible for daily developments in the various court systems but who write on broader issues, such as the workings of grand juries, civil rights prosecutions of police officers, sentencing patterns of judges, unaccredited law schools and the trend toward national law firms. The largest-circulation dailies also assign a reporter to cover the U.S. Supreme Court full time in Washington, D.C.

At the *Mesa Tribune,* as at most dailies with circulations under 100,000, one person has primary responsibility for coverage of the local and state courts. The newspaper relies on the wire services for coverage of the federal courts.

THE JUDICIAL SYSTEM

Reporters need to have a basic understanding of the judicial system, on both the federal and state levels. Aspiring court reporters should take appropriate college courses such as law and society, public law, American national government and constitutional law to help develop that understanding. The following overview serves as a starting point.

The Federal Judicial System

The U.S. Supreme Court is the nation's highest court. The wire services, the largest newspapers and the networks assign reporters to cover the high court regularly. The term of the court begins the first Monday in October and usually lasts until late June or early July. It is divided between sittings and recesses. During sittings, cases are heard and opinions announced. During recesses, the nine justices consider the business before the court and write opinions. Sittings and recesses alternate at approximately two-week intervals.

Reporters who cover the Supreme Court must have a solid understanding of the law and legal procedures in addition to being capable journalists. Complex legal language filling scores of pages must be deciphered when the written opinions are distributed. The facts of the case and the significance of the holding must be grasped. Reporters often select pertinent direct quotations from the majority, concurring or dissenting opinions. For background, law school professors or practicing attorneys sometimes are consulted for an interpretation of the significance of the case or for direct quotations.

Below the Supreme Court, at the intermediate level in the *federal judicial system,* are various circuits of the U.S. Court of Appeals. At the next level are U.S. District Courts, where trials in the federal system generally are held. There are nearly 100 such courts. Each state has at least one; the more heavily populated states have more than one.

The federal system also includes several specialized courts such as the Court of Customs and Patent Appeals, the Customs Court and the Court of Claims.

State Judicial Systems

There are about as many types of state court systems as there are states. Usually, a *state judicial system* has three layers:

- Trial courts, where proceedings are initiated
- Intermediate courts, where appeals are first heard
- Supreme courts, which are panels of final resort

The names assigned to the courts at each of these levels vary, but generally the highest is called the state supreme court. The intermediate level (used by about half the states) is called an appellate court. Trial-level bodies, often called superior courts, are the highest trial courts with general jurisdiction in most states. Sometimes they are given other names; for instance, in New York the trial-level body is called the Supreme Court.

Several other courts complete the various state systems. According to a West Publishing Co. chart, these include probate courts (which handle wills, administration of estates and guardianship of minors and incompetents); county courts (which have limited jurisdiction in civil and criminal cases); municipal courts (where cases involving less serious crimes, generally called *misdemeanors*, are heard by municipal justices or municipal magistrates); and, in some jurisdictions, justice of the peace and police magistrate courts (which have very limited jurisdiction and are the lowest courts in the judicial hierarchy). Justice courts in Arizona, for example, hear matters that involve less than $500.

TYPES OF COURT CASES

Court cases can be lumped in two divisions: criminal and civil. *Criminal cases* involve the enforcement of criminal statutes. Suits are brought by the state or federal government against an individual charged with committing a crime such as murder or armed robbery.

Civil cases involve arriving at specific solutions to legal strife between individuals, businesses, state or local governments or agencies of government. Civil cases commonly include suits for damages arising from automobile accidents, suits for breach of contract or even suits for libel.

CRIMINAL CASES

As noted, criminal cases involve the enforcement of criminal statutes. In his book "The Reporter and the Law," Lyle Denniston, veteran U.S. Supreme Court reporter, wrote: "Crime is the main staple of legal reporting. Of course, crime alone does not make all the news on the court beat. But it does dominate the beat."

Denniston continued: "Criminal law is simply more 'newsworthy' than civil law. More often, a criminal case will have in it the ingredients of human interest, public policy and clear-cut controversy that make news. At a more fundamental level, criminal law provides the most vivid test of a community's sense of justice and morality."

The Basic Process

Criminal charges may be brought against an individual through an indictment or through the filing of an information. According to Black's Law Dictionary, an *indictment* is "an accusation in writing found and presented by a grand jury . . . charging that a person has done some act or been guilty of some omission which by law is a public offense." An *information*, according to the dictionary, differs from an indictment in that it is "presented by a competent public officer [such as a prosecuting attorney] on his oath of office, instead of a grand jury on their oath."

According to "Law and the Courts," published by the American Bar Association, the steps that occur after an indictment has been returned or an information filed basically are as follows (naturally, these steps and the names assigned to them can vary slightly among jurisdictions; reporters need to understand the process in jurisdictions in which they work):

- The clerk of the court issues a *warrant* for the arrest of the person charged (if the person has not been arrested already). According to Black's Law Dictionary, a warrant is "a written order issued and signed by [an appropriate official], directed to a peace officer or some other person specially named, and commanding him to arrest the body of a person named in it, who is accused of an offense."
- An *arraignment*, where the charge is read to the accused, is held. The arraignment often is held in a lower court. Typically, a plea is entered. In some states, this step is referred to as an *initial appearance*.
- *Plea bargaining*, when the prosecutor negotiates with the defense lawyers over the kind of plea the suspect might enter on a specific charge, can take place at any juncture. Often it takes place after the arraignment but before the preliminary hearing. At this time, the prosecutor might propose that, in exchange for a plea of guilty, the state will bring a lesser charge against the suspect. The prosecutor might propose, for example, that the state bring a charge of assault instead of a charge of aggravated assault, a more serious crime that carries a more stringent penalty. In return, the defendant would plead guilty as charged and the state would be spared the time and expense of further proceedings. Plea bargaining, which helps unclog the courts, is a common practice. According to Denniston's "The Reporter and the Law," the "terms of a plea bargain ordinarily will have to be disclosed in open court, and usually will be subject to some inquiry by the judge as to the advisability of the bargain." Denniston wrote that the purpose of plea bargaining "is to determine whether a trial might be avoided, and a just result reached, by encouraging a person whose guilt is not in serious doubt to plead guilty or 'no contest.'" Criminal cases often conclude through plea bargaining.
- A *preliminary hearing* is held at which the state must present evidence to convince the presiding judge that there is probable cause to believe the defendant committed the crime that he or she is being charged with. If the judge agrees that there is probable cause, he or she will order the defendant bound over for trial.
- In some states, in lieu of a preliminary hearing, a *grand jury* is convened to determine if there is probable cause that a crime has been committed and if there is probable cause that the person charged with the crime committed it. A finding of probable cause is not, however, the same as a finding of guilt. That is determined at a trial. A grand jury is so labeled because it has more members than a trial jury. The number of people who serve on a grand jury varies among jurisdictions. In Arizona, for example, 16 people are impaneled. Nine are needed for a quorum.
- A date for another arraignment is set. The second arraignment is held in a court that has jurisdiction over the case.
- The *defendant* appears at the arraignment, where the judge reads the charge and explains the defendant's rights.
- The defendant then pleads guilty or not guilty. If the defendant pleads not guilty, a trial date is set. If the defendant pleads guilty, the judge sets a date for sentencing.

- For those defendants who plead not guilty, a jury is selected.
- Once the trial is under way, opening statements by the prosecuting attorney and the defense attorney are made (presentation of evidence by the state is always given first).
- The defense attorney then presents evidence.
- Final motions and closing arguments are heard.
- The judge then reads instructions to the jury.
- The jury deliberates and returns with a verdict.
- The judge enters a judgment upon the verdict.
- If the defendant is found guilty, the judge sets a date for sentencing.
- After a presentence hearing, the judge will pronounce sentence.
- The defendant, if unhappy with the verdict, may appeal to a higher court. In most states, death penalties are appealed automatically.

All these steps are potentially newsworthy. Reporters must of course be extremely careful to attribute statements to legal documents or to individuals who make them in court. Accurate reporting based on legal documents or statements made in court is virtually libel-proof. (See Chapter 15 for a discussion of libel defenses that include the privilege of reporting.) The source of the information should be clear to the reader. It always is sound practice to attribute information, but it is particularly important when covering litigation.

For a complete discussion of steps in a criminal case and the role of the journalist in the process, Denniston's "The Reporter and the Law" is an excellent source.

Reporting Criminal Cases

As stated earlier, steps in criminal proceedings can vary. To illustrate general reporting procedures, however, this section will trace selected junctures in the *Mesa Tribune*'s coverage of a criminal case. Coverage started in May with a story about a missing 13-year-old girl. More than 13 months and 100 stories later, a man was convicted of murdering and raping the teen-ager.

- **The Arrest.** Police reporter Tonia Twichell carefully crafted a summary lead when an arrest was made. The first part of her story naturally focused on:

    - The fact an arrest had been made
    - Details on charges that were being requested
    - Subsequent steps in the judicial process

The story began:

The 29-year-old maintenance man who found the body of 13-year-old newspaper carrier Christy Fornoff on May 11 was arrested Monday in connection with her death.

After 10 days of undercover police surveillance, Don Edward Beaty was taken to the Tempe City Jail, where he is awaiting an initial appearance today in Tempe Justice Court.

First-degree murder, robbery and sexual abuse charges are being requested by the Maricopa County Attorney's Office and Tempe police.

Beaty, who refused to talk to police and asked for a lawyer, could be released on his own recognizance after the court appearance, but probably will be ordered held on bail in the Maricopa County Jail in Phoenix.

Beaty was arrested at 4:15 p.m. in the manager's office of Rock Point Apartments, 2045 S. McClintock Drive, where he worked until Friday.

Police Chief Arthur Fairbanks refused to say what led to the Monday arrest, but other police officers said the department had been awaiting test results from the Department of Public Safety crime laboratory.

• **Writing carefully.** Twichell was careful to write that Beaty had been arrested *in connection with* the death of the teen-ager (some newspapers prefer to use *in suspicion of* or *in the investigation of*). Twichell did not write that Beaty was arrested *for* the death; doing so would imply guilt and could lead to a libel suit. Also note that the story said the arrest was made in connection with the *death*—not the *murder*. The AP Stylebook emphasizes that reporters should not write that a victim was murdered until someone is convicted of murder. The stylebook advises that reporters should use the words *killed* or *slain*.

• **The Lower-Court Arraignment.** The *Tribune* followed with a story about the lower-court arraignment, which is termed an initial appearance in Arizona. In most states, an arraignment in a lower court (designations of these courts vary but they include *police courts, municipal courts, magistrate courts* or *justice courts*) generally takes place within a specified short period after the arrest. At the arraignment the charge is read to the accused, who then enters a plea. The plea normally becomes the story's lead. For the first time, the *Tribune* used in the lead paragraph the name of the accused, who by now was well known to readers.

Donald Edward Beaty pleaded innocent to charges of first-degree murder and child molesting in the death of 13-year-old Christy Fornoff Tuesday in a heavily guarded courtroom.

After receiving phone calls threatening the 29-year-old Beaty's life, police switched courtrooms for the hearing, beefed up security and searched everyone who came to his initial appearance.

Beaty, looking disheveled after a night in Tempe City Jail, was ordered held under $685,000 bail in Maricopa County Jail in Phoenix.

Tempe Justice of the Peace Fred Ackel read Beaty the charges—which included robbery—and ordered him to appear May 31 for a preliminary hearing.

Beaty is accused of killing Fornoff after she disappeared May 9 while collecting for her *Phoenix Gazette* paper route at Rock Point Apartments, 2045 S. McClintock Drive. Beaty, who worked as a maintenance man at the apartments until Friday, found Christy's body May 11 in the complex behind a trash dumpster.

The story went on to provide attributed, documented details on Beaty's prior criminal record.

• **The Preliminary Hearing/Grand Jury Proceeding.** At a preliminary hearing, the judge must decide if the state's case is adequate to bring the accused to trial. The state, often without revealing all the information it has, nevertheless must present sufficient evidence to convince the judge that there is probable cause to believe the defendant committed the crime. The preliminary hearing story often includes specifics on testimony of law-enforcement officers or other officials. Their testimony probably will be pivotal in deciding whether there is sufficient reason for the accused to stand trial.

As noted earlier, the procedure in some states is to bypass a preliminary hearing by referring the case to a grand jury that will determine if there is probable cause that the person charged with the crime committed it. If the grand jury determines there is sufficient evidence, it will return an indictment known as a *true bill*. If the grand jury decides that a sufficient probability does not exist that the accused committed the crime, it will return a *no bill*.

In Arizona, a preliminary hearing sometimes will be held; at other times the case is referred to a grand jury. Both procedures are used. The prosecutor can exercise either option. The Beaty case was referred to a grand jury.

The *Mesa Tribune* police and general assignment reporters had been covering the Beaty story to this point. Once the case went to the grand jury, however, court reporter Mike Padgett took over. Grand jury proceedings are held behind closed doors. Details are given to the press if a true bill is returned. Padgett's first paragraphs were punchy and to the point:

> A Maricopa County grand jury has indicted Donald Edward Beaty on charges of sexual assault and first-degree murder in the death of 13-year-old Christy Ann Fornoff of Tempe.
>
> And a county official said Thursday tighter security will surround Beaty's arraignment next week.
>
> Beaty, 29, was indicted by the grand jury late Wednesday. News of the indictment was not released to reporters until Thursday after Beaty received his copy, said Jane Bradley, spokeswoman for the county attorney's office.
>
> Beaty's bond remains at $685,000. His scheduled arraignment is at 8:45 a.m. Wednesday before Maricopa County Superior Court Judge John H. Seidel.
>
> Bradley said Seidel's courtroom is the smallest in Superior Court and easier to guard.

• **The Superior Court Arraignment.** If the judge at the preliminary hearing decides the evidence is sufficient (or if a grand jury returns a true bill), the accused is arraigned in a court that has jurisdiction. In Arizona, felony cases are heard in Superior Court. A *felony*, according to the American Bar Association's "Law and the Courts" is "a crime of a graver nature than a misdemeanor [and generally is] an offense punishable by death or imprisonment in a penitentiary." The same source defines a *misdemeanor* as generally those offenses "punishable by fine or imprisonment otherwise than in penitentiaries."

Padgett always makes an effort to sit in on the arraignment, even though most only last a few minutes. "You never know when someone—usually one of the attorneys—will come up with something newsworthy," he said. Generally, however, most arraignment stories lead with how the accused pleads to the charge. The *Tribune* story began:

Donald Edward Beaty pleaded innocent Wednesday to charges of first-degree murder and sexual assault in the slaying of Tempe newspaper carrier Christy Ann Fornoff.

At Beaty's arraignment, Superior Court Judge John Seidel scheduled a July 5 pretrial conference and a July 25 trial before Judge Rufus C. Coulter.

Both court dates are expected to be postponed by defense and prosecution motions.

Beaty, 29, remained in the Maricopa County Jail Wednesday in lieu of posting $685,000 bail.

Seidel accepted Beaty's pleas of innocent from a public defender, Mary Wisdom, who was appointed to defend Beaty.

Note that the story said Beaty pleaded *innocent*. Actually, a defendant would plead *not guilty*. But newspapers long ago adopted the style of using the word *innocent* instead of the words *not guilty* to alleviate the possibility that the word *not* would be inadvertently dropped from the story and thus render it inaccurate.

• **Importance of Background.** Note also that Padgett's Superior Court arraignment story contains background on the circumstances that led to the arraignment. Reporters always should provide background. Background information can be developed by reviewing clippings of previous stories written about the case and by interviewing attorneys and others close to the case. Even when reports of judicial proceedings are in the news for an extended time, journalists must assume that most readers do not know the background of the case.

• **The Trial.** Reporters provide gavel-to-gavel coverage of only the most important trials. Certainly the Beaty trial fell into that category for the *Mesa Tribune* and Padgett. "I try never to miss the opening day of a trial," Padgett said. "On that day, most prosecuting attorneys are going to say 'that guy did it and we have the evidence to back up the charge.' Once they are finished, the defense attorneys will say something like 'the evidence is not there. My client did not do it.' They will try to shoot holes in the opening statement of the prosecutor. You want to get the opening statements down for the readers. I often use a tape recorder because I want to get as much color as possible. I also take notes. I have found, however, that tape recorders allow me to be more productive and more accurate."

Relatively minor cases might go to the jury within a day or so. Major trials, however, run much longer. The first Beaty trial lasted seven weeks (and then six more weeks for a second trial after the first one ended in a mistrial).

Reporters must diligently follow the testimony in long-running major trials. "You have to spend several hours each day in the courtroom," Padgett said. "It does not do much good to drop in for an hour or so because you have no way of predicting what will happen. One hour is not enough. You simply must sit and listen. Sometimes it gets really tedious. There were days at the Beaty trial when it would be 4 p.m. and I still did not have a strong lead for the day. On several days, key testimony the last 30 minutes of the session gave me my lead. If you are not there for the duration, you risk missing the most significant angle."

- **Closing Arguments.** Padgett was in court for the closing arguments. "Just like I never want to miss opening statements, I never want to miss the closing arguments," Padgett said. After the closing arguments, the case goes to the jury. If the closing occurs late in the afternoon, the judge generally will instruct the jury members to return the next morning to begin deliberations.

"I always try to stay in the courtroom when the jury is locked in its room deliberating," Padgett said. "I want to be there when the jury comes out."

- **The Verdict.** The climax to a criminal trial is the verdict. There is no sacrosanct formula for writing verdict stories, but they should contain this basic information:

  - Outcome (Was the accused found guilty or innocent?)
  - The precise charge (for example, murder)
  - Length of jury deliberations
  - Date of sentencing
  - Range of penalties established by law
  - Reactions of the defendant, his family and attorneys
  - Reactions of the victim or the victim's family
  - Reaction of attorneys for the prosecution
  - Background of the case
  - Review of key testimony throughout the trial
  - Possibility of appeal

Here are the first six paragraphs of Padgett's story (note how he worked many of the key ingredients into the first part of his story):

A Maricopa County Superior Court jury deliberated less than 10 minutes Thursday before finding Donald Edward Beaty guilty of murdering and raping 13-year-old Christy Ann Fornoff of Tempe.

Beaty, 30, is scheduled to be sentenced July 22. He could face the death sentence for first-degree murder.

Defense attorney Michael Miller said he probably would appeal.

Reaction to the verdict ranged from relief by the girl's family to anger from a woman who sat behind Beaty in court and who had taken charge of having his clothes cleaned and pressed.

The victim's parents, Roger and Carol Fornoff, were not in court Thursday morning because they hadn't expected a decision so quickly. After the verdict was announced, they met with reporters in the county attorney's office.

"It's a relief for us, knowing this man has been convicted," Carol Fornoff said. "We know he won't be on the streets. He won't be doing it again."

Note that the word *murdering* is used after the conviction. The lead often practically writes itself in a verdict story, but the reporter must work hard to assemble the remainder of the account.

- **The Sentencing.** Padgett was well prepared to write the story of the sentencing. He had been covering the Beaty trial for months; he had background information at his fingertips; he understood the nuances of the case. His lead was straightforward:

Donald Edward Beaty, convicted last month of the first-degree murder of 13-year-old Christy Ann Fornoff, Monday was sentenced to die in the gas chamber.

Maricopa County Superior Court Judge Rufus Coulter Jr. told Beaty he had "committed the offense in an especially heinous, cruel and depraved manner."

The death penalty will be appealed automatically.

Coulter also sentenced Beaty, 30, to the maximum term of 28 years in prison for sexually assaulting the girl.

Beaty, who has maintained his innocence, stood before the judge handcuffed and dressed in blue jail fatigues and soiled red tennis shoes. Almost imperceptibly, he began trembling after he was sentenced to death.

Coverage of the Beaty case by the *Mesa Tribune* illustrates that there are several newsworthy points as a case makes its way through the judicial system. The coverage often extends beyond courthouse drama. Analysis pieces and feature articles often accompany coverage of litigation.

STEPS TO FOLLOW WHEN COVERING THE COURTS

• **Learn the judicial system.** Reporters need to master the intricacies of the court systems in their jurisdictions. All state systems vary. Do not be afraid to ask questions. It is imperative to grasp the workings of the system.

• **Learn the record-keeping system.** Once the procedural and structural aspects of the court system are mastered, reporters need to know how to ferret out information. A knowledge of the record-keeping system is essential.

• **Provide sufficient background for the reader.** For example, even though the Beaty case was in the news for more than a year, Padgett never failed to provide a background paragraph in each story that explained how the case started.

• **Double-check facts.** Names, ages, addresses and the specific charges always should be verified. The stakes are high. Reporters never want to make errors, but there is a monumental difference between saying that John Jones was the leading scorer for his basketball team (when he really was only the second-leading scorer) and saying that John Jones was charged with driving while intoxicated (when he really was charged with running a stop sign).

• **Use complete names and addresses or occupations.** To avoid confusion—and head off potential lawsuits—list full names and middle initials, ages and addresses or occupations of persons charged with crimes.

• **Attribute all statements.** Never use hearsay in a court story. Carefully explain to the reader the source of the information. Information in official court documents is privileged. That is, reporters have a legal right to report their contents accurately. The privilege however, does not extend to erroneous reporting of court documents. (See Chapter 15 for a discussion of libel defenses, including privilege of reporting.)

- **Report all relevant facts.** Search for all relevant news angles. For example, when a man is on trial for murder, a reporter could provide details on the minimum and maximum penalties as established by law, the number of murder trials in the same court during the past year and the circumstances of the arrest.

- **Don't be afraid of the terminology.** You will encounter new legal terms regularly as you cover the courts. Rely on court personnel to give you information to supplement definitions in a source such as Black's Law Dictionary. A comprehensive dictionary of legal terms is indeed a valuable reference.

- **Write simply.** Strive to translate "legalese" into lay terms whenever possible. Reporters need an understanding of the law, but they should not forget to communicate as informed laypersons—not as lawyers.

- **Take careful notes.** Be extremely careful to take accurate notes during proceedings. When tape recorders are allowed, they provide a good backup. If notes are not clear, or if the tape recorder malfunctions, check with the official court reporter who records verbatim the transcript of the proceedings.

- **Be alert for testimony that contradicts previous testimony or evidence.** Develop your own system for emphasizing such occurrences in your notes. As you listen to a full day of testimony, place asterisks beside such occurrences to jar your memory when you begin to write.

- **Watch for reactions (including facial expressions) of trial participants.** You should not play the role of amateur psychiatrist; but it sometimes is worth reporting when witnesses break down on the stand, attorneys raise their voices and spectators orally react to testimony.

- **Remember that stories can develop away from the witness stand.** Be alert for feature pieces by observing spectators and other persons associated with the proceedings.

- **Be fair.** Strive to report as objectively as possible. Remember: People involved in litigation are undergoing a traumatic experience. Do not allow prejudicial reporting to interfere with the rights of the accused. Report aggressively, but stay within ethical and legal bounds.

CIVIL CASES

Often, dozens of *briefs* (written reports in which lawyers set forth facts that support their positions) are filed in civil suits. Reporters must periodically check court *dockets* that record progress in specific cases. All complaints filed, motions made and other developments in a case are recorded chronologically on a docket. In Superior Court for Los Angeles, the average civil suit is in the system—from time of *filing* until trial or settlement—approximately four years. It is not unusual for cases to extend six or seven years. Metropolitan court systems often are short on personnel for civil cases, and legal requirements force them to give priority to criminal cases. The normal criminal cases in Superior Court for Los Angeles generally will conclude from two to four months after the arrest.

Understanding record-keeping systems is a critical element in good court coverage. Reporters in small cities do not face the crunch of cases that metropolitan reporters do, but regardless of the case load, reporters must watch dockets and calendars closely. In Superior Court for Los Angeles, the civil courts reporter for the *Los Angeles Times* usually is following the progress of more than 500 pending suits. "It is a bookkeeping nightmare," suburban editor Robert Rawitch said.

The filing system in Los Angeles' civil division of Superior Court is efficient and detailed, but the *Times* reporter must spend more than an hour each day checking case numbers listed on the court calendar.

The Basic Process

Steps taken in a civil suit vary. Procedural maneuverings can be complex and time-consuming. According to "Law and the Courts," here is the basic process:

- The *plaintiff* (the party bringing the suit) selects the proper jurisdiction (federal or state system, and the appropriate court thereof).
- The plaintiff files a *complaint* (sometimes called a *petition*) against a party (called the *defendant*). The complaint usually contains a precise set of arguments that include the damages sought. *Damages* are the estimated monetary value for the injury allegedly sustained. Of course, the filing of a complaint does not ensure that the plaintiff has a cause of action.
- The defendant is served with a *summons,* a writ informing him that he must answer the complaint.
- After a specified period, the defendant is required to file his *pleading,* or answer, to the plaintiff's charges.
- *Depositions* (out-of-court statements made by witnesses under oath) are taken.
- After all the pleadings have been filed, attorneys for both parties appear before a judge at a pretrial conference to agree on the undisputed facts of the case. (Often a *settlement* is reached at this point without trial.)
- If no settlement is reached the case is scheduled for trial.
- Testimony as to the dispute is presented and arguments are heard at the trial.
- After the arguments, the judge instructs the jury (unless the defendant has waived his right to a jury proceeding) on legal considerations.
- The jury goes to its room for deliberations.
- The jury returns with a verdict.
- The verdict is announced, and the judge enters a judgment upon the verdict.
- If either party is unhappy, an appeal can be made.

Reporting Civil Cases

Scores of civil suits are filed each day in metropolitan jurisdictions. Certainly not all of them are newsworthy. Reporters must decide which suits are important and then constantly check court dockets for developments.

A story written about the filing in a civil suit should contain the following information:

- It should tell who is bringing the suit (the plaintiff).
- It should tell who is being sued (the defendant).
- It should tell when the suit was filed.
- It should identify the parties as fully as possible.
- It should provide background on the circumstances that brought about the suit.
- It should give specifics on the damages sought.
- It should give the defendants' response to the complaint.
- It should fully attribute all information. When appropriate, it should make absolutely clear to the readers that the information came from court records.

As mentioned earlier in this chapter, reporters and their newspapers can defend themselves against libel charges by quoting accurately from official court documents. (See Chapter 15 for a discussion of libel defenses.)

If they are on deadline, reporters sometimes will report the filing of a complaint based on information supplied by attorneys in the case or from the clerk of the court, but the safest, soundest journalistic procedure is to write the story from a copy of the complaint. Comments from attorneys can be used to further explain the filing.

Most of the essential information about civil-suit stories can be found in the first two paragraphs of an article by Sally Bedell published in *The New York Times:*

> Gen. William C. Westmoreland, former commander of United States military forces in Vietnam, filed a libel suit yesterday against CBS Inc. for its portrayal of him in January in a documentary, "The Uncounted Enemy: A Vietnam Deception." The documentary said he was the head of "a conspiracy at the highest levels of American military intelligence, to suppress and alter critical intelligence on the enemy" during the Vietnam War.
>
> The suit asks for $120 million in compensatory and punitive damages. General Westmoreland said that if he were to win, he would donate the money to charity.

The 19-paragraph story went on to provide details on where the suit was filed; it named the other defendants in addition to CBS; it quoted an attorney who specializes in First Amendment cases; it quoted one of the defendants in the suit; it quoted the lawyer for Westmoreland; and it gave a synopsis of the current state of American libel law.

- **Selecting Civil Suits to Cover.** The majority of civil suits do not involve high-ranking officials or major networks. According to Tom Spratt, courthouse reporter for *The Phoenix Gazette,* many civil suits merely "fade away" after an initial filing. More than 90 percent never make it to trial.

Still, if a story has been written about the filing, a reporter must be diligent in following the case to its conclusion. It is important to report dismissals, settlements or judgments. Many civil suits make headlines when they are filed, but as they become tangled in the shuffle of paperwork and forgotten in the passage of time, they are not followed up by reporters. This, of course, is unfair to the parties involved. If a newspaper reports that a malpractice suit seeking $15 million in damages was filed against Dr. John Jones, the newspaper owes it to its readers and to the parties in the suit to report how the case ultimately is decided.

No magic formula determines if a civil suit is newsworthy. Spratt, however, tries to examine systematically all civil complaints. He glances at the general headings listed at the tops of the complaints: contract; tort motor vehicles (a *tort,* according to "Law and the Courts," is "an injury or wrong committed, either with or without force, to the person or property of another"); tort non-motor vehicles (this category includes personal wrongs and often is newsworthy); and non-classified (which includes an assortment of cases that do not fit under common headings).

Spratt also looks at damages sought. Because a party seeks more than $1 million does not necessarily make the complaint newsworthy. "After the reporter is on the courthouse beat for a while, he or she will begin to recognize which lawyers consistently file suits seeking huge damages, but which never get very far in the judicial process," Spratt said.

After Spratt isolates cases of potential interest by reading the headings and determining the damages sought, he reads the complaints in their entirety to see if they seem to be particularly important, interesting or significant.

Once a civil suit has been filed and Spratt decides it deserves coverage, he often calls the attorney who filed it for a further explanation. "I make an effort to talk to attorneys for both parties, whenever possible," Spratt said. "This is particularly important in civil cases where filings and rulings are very complicated." Sometimes, to get additional background, he also calls attorneys who are not involved in the suit but who are experts in the area being litigated.

Newspapers do not cover most civil suits at every step in the judicial process. Often, a short story is written when a suit is filed and another story is written when the suit is dismissed or settled or when there is a judgment.

THE CHALLENGE OF COVERING THE COURTS

Rawitch of the *Los Angeles Times* estimated that it takes a reporter six months to a year to become attuned to covering courts in a metropolitan setting. Naturally, it does not take as long to gain a grasp of the judicial system in a non-metropolitan setting. But the job of reporters for big-city dailies and for community dailies or weeklies is the same: They must accurately, in understandable language, inform readers.

"The role of the court reporter is to break through the legal jargon—to translate the special role of the court to the everyday role of the reader," Rawitch said. "But just like the specialist on any beat, the court reporter must be careful—once he or she begins to feel comfortable with the system—not to lose sight of what is important to the reader."

Covering the courts involves more than reporting on procedural filings in civil suits and on spectacular criminal trials. Many good court-related stories are the result of a reporter's persistently searching for information that can lead to in-depth stories on the workings of the judicial system or on the interaction among those involved in the system.

It is a news event for the Japanese media when one of its baseball teams comes to the United States for spring training. The presence of one of the teams also would make an interesting feature or news story for American dailies. Such a story could be topped by any of several special leads. (Photo by Don B. Stevenson)

13 / Special Leads

A brief summary lead is the best for breaking hard news stories. However, today's reporters do not cover only breaking stories. Their daily reports include non-breaking news and feature stories on a myriad of topics. These stories go beyond merely reporting the who, what, where, when, why and how of an event; for them, leads are written to tease, to entice.

In this chapter you will be introduced to the following terms:

narrative lead	staccato lead
lead block	direct address lead
nut graph	question lead
news peg	quote lead
contrast lead	follow-up story
turn word	

Reporters do not cover only breaking news. Newspapers use non-breaking stories such as the year's forecast for farm prices or the way one neighborhood is fighting crime. They use personality profiles that describe interesting people in or out of the news, and "how-to" stories, such as repairing household appliances or cooking Thanksgiving turkeys. There are interpretive and analytical pieces that detail the weaknesses in this year's legislature or explore the way the city might go about developing park land. There are sports, business, consumer, travel, fashion, entertainment and other special-interest stories.

Because many of these stories are not reporting the news firsthand, it may not be necessary to begin them with a summary lead. Instead, the lead may entice or invite readers. It may put them in the middle of the action, talk directly to them, ask them a question or set them up for a climax.

This chapter will discuss alternatives to the summary lead. Although the best lead on a breaking news story continues to be a one-paragraph, terse summary, on some news stories and on most features, writers may choose one of the following leads:

- *Narrative*
- *Contrast*
- *Staccato*
- *Direct address*
- *Question*
- *Quote*
- *None of the above*

NARRATIVE

A *narrative lead* is the most popular lead on features and non-breaking news stories. It draws people into a story by putting them, suddenly, in the middle of the action. It should entice a person to continue reading.

Although a narrative lead can be written in a single paragraph, it usually is written in a *lead block*, two or more paragraphs that build up to the major point of the story. Like any journalistic writing, it is constructed with terse sentences.

Because a narrative lead often involves a person, it is acceptable to use that person's name in the opening paragraph. That usually is not done in a summary lead, unless the person is widely known, but using a name right away in a narrative allows an audience to identify more quickly with a major player in the story.

Here is a two-paragraph narrative lead block from *The Daily Northwestern*, the campus paper at Northwestern University. The story was about an annual contest sponsored by a sorority. In the first paragraph, the writer, Sarah Okeson, introduced a young man, allowing readers to feel some emotional attachment to him and, Okeson hoped, to the story. The opening paragraph also began in the middle of action:

SPECIAL LEADS 263

> Peter Spears swiveled his hips to the tune of "Neutron Dance," turned his back to the audience and ripped off his jacket, revealing a shirt opened to the waist.

The second paragraph continued the narrative. It painted a picture, drawing readers deeper into the story:

> Spears strutted to the beat and slowly tossed off his shirt and pants. Still wearing a black bow tie and black bikini swimsuit, he dove into the Patten Gymnasium pool.

By now, the writing should have caught the readers' interest. Okeson used vivid words—*swiveled, ripped, revealing, strutted, tossed off, black bikini*—to paint a colorful picture. By the end of the second paragraph, readers should have felt as if they were in the action, emotionally tied somehow to Peter Spears.

A summary lead could have been written on the story, saying:

> A freshman Sigma Nu member won the Mr. Splash title Sunday in the fourth annual contest sponsored by Delta Gamma sorority.

But the narrative worked better. The contest was not a hard news event. Readers might not have been interested in how sorority and fraternity members spent this Sunday. The narrative was used to entice them.

THE NUT GRAPH

After two or three paragraphs of narrative, it is time to use a *"so-what" paragraph*, telling readers precisely what the story is about. (Narrative is used to entice readers; it should not dominate the story.) The common name for the explanatory paragraph that follows the introductory narrative is *nut graph*. It explains the significance of a story or gives its *news peg*, which links the story to previously reported news. The nut graph should be placed fairly high in the story—the third, fourth or fifth paragraph.

Here is Okeson's nut graph, which was the third paragraph of the story:

> Spears, a CAS (College of Arts and Sciences) freshman and Sigma Nu member, won the Mr. Anchor Splash title Sunday in the fourth annual competition sponsored by Delta Gamma sorority.

USING OBSERVATION

The key to writing an effective narrative lead is to write it around observation, what a reporter sees, hears, smells, tastes or touches while working on a story. When interviewing people, it is critical to make notes on:

- How they move.
- What they are doing during the interview.
- What they are wearing and the color of their clothes.
- How loudly or softly they speak.
- How long it takes them to answer a question.
- The smells and sights around them.
- Anything that makes them unusual.

These observations are extremely important in stories; they are vital to a narrative lead. Okeson would not have been able to write her narrative on the Mr. Splash contest if she had not observed the action herself.

An observation often is used to begin a narrative, as in this lead from the *Montrose* (Calif.) *Ledger*:

> Anderson L. Brooks was about to leave home for another day at work. He adjusted his black, narrow necktie the way he had for 40 years. He slipped on his favorite brown hat, the one with a sweat ring showing through the band. He lit a cigarette and left for downtown Los Angeles.

In another narrative lead, Barbara Brotman of the *Chicago Tribune* used observation to paint a vivid picture of a Romanian immigrant who drives a taxicab in Chicago. In the first two paragraphs, Brotman put readers inside the cab, just as the driver was taking a call. In the third paragraph, her nut graph, she told readers, this is the story of a cab driver who put a mobile telephone in his car. Readers could not help but want to know more about the cabbie after reading the opening paragraphs:

> The phone rings in Constantin Gogu's office, which he has pulled over to a curb on North Michigan Avenue. Gogu picks it up.
>
> "Hello," he says. "To pick you up in 20 minutes?" The office is open for business, and business has been so good that it must seem to this Romanian immigrant that the Statue of Liberty is lifting her lamp beside the door of Checker Cab No. 4468.
>
> Gogu's place of business is the 1983 Chevrolet Impala taxicab he owns. One month ago, Gogu spent nearly $2,000 to install a mobile telephone in the taxi.

KEEPING IT GOING

Additional observations and narrative should be used later and throughout the story, not only about the person in the lead but about other characters. That should keep readers so emotionally attached to the main players that they would want to read the entire story, no matter how long.

SPECIAL LEADS

For example, in the story on Constantin Gogu, Brotman used this paragraph in the middle of the story to introduce three paragraphs on Gogu's first year in the United States:

> It is a wonderful job, it is a marvelous country. Gogu, whose nickname is George, pulls out a wad of his morning's take—about $130—buys coffee in a downtown McDonald's and explains.

DEVELOPING RAW MATERIAL INTO A NARRATIVE LEAD

Tom Blodgett, a reporter for the *State Press*, the daily at Arizona State University, had plenty of material from which to work when he was ready to write his story about Valentina Vega, an ASU volleyball player and a single parent. He had interviewed the woman extensively. He had talked with her teammates and coach. He also watched her interact with her 6-month-old son during a study hall session in the arena where the team competes.

Because he had so much information, deciding on the lead was not easy. He wanted to make certain that the beginning paragraphs set the stage for the entire story. There was no need for a summary; this story was not breaking news. Many earlier stories had reported that the woman had to miss a year of play because she was pregnant.

This story would update readers, telling them how an unmarried mother is coping with school, her baby and her attempt to once again be a star volleyball player.

Blodgett's first lead was:

> Every collegiate athlete faces the challenge of balancing school and sport.
>
> All single mothers know what it is like to juggle a career and parenting.
>
> Perhaps only ASU volleyball player Valentina Vega knows what it is like when the two divergent lives are fused together through circumstances.

Dull, isn't it? The three paragraphs use some important buzz words—*balancing school and sport, juggle career and parenting, divergent lives are fused* (fused together is a redundancy)—but they do not project an image, they do not paint a picture that will draw readers into the story.

After three paragraphs, readers still have little idea what the story is about, nor do they feel they are part of any action.

Blodgett went back to work, looking over his notes in search of a better lead. One of the things he remembered was the study hall session. In his observations he had made a note on Vega, sitting at a table studying math with her son at her side, propped up against a chair in the arena.

What better way to show readers sports, school, mom and child? That single observation became the basis of Blodgett's new lead, a narrative that put readers in the middle of the action:

> Valentina Vega sat in the Activity Center studying math with her teammates on the ASU volleyball team.
>
> At her side, propped against a chair, was her newest teammate, the one who changed the way she thinks about sports, school and her life.
>
> Vega, a 21-year-old junior, redshirted last season when she learned she was pregnant. In April, she gave birth to a boy, Brandon Michael Vega. She has remained single.

The rewrite was a typical narrative lead block. It was simple and easy to understand. It painted a picture in the first two paragraphs so that readers could see the young mother and volleyball player studying with her son at her side. The third paragraph was the nut graph, which told readers the reason for the story.

CONTRAST

A *contrast lead* compares or contrasts one person or thing with another, or several people or things with each other. These "old and new," "short and tall" or "yesterday and today" leads tell an audience the way something was and now is. They can be used on any type of news or feature story. Here is an example from the *Williston (N.D.) Daily Herald*:

> When Buster Jones took over the little bar on Main Street in Williston, his hair was the color sometimes referred to as "fire in the woodshed."

The opening paragraph told readers that this story would be about Buster Jones, who opened a bar on Main Street when he was a young man. The second paragraph brought them up to date:

SPECIAL LEADS

Now there's "snow on the rooftop," and next January Buster will celebrate his 40th year in business at the same little bar. He took a little time Wednesday to reflect on some of the changes in Buster's Old Inn since Jan. 1, 1946, when he went into business for himself.

KEEP IT BRIEF

Most contrast leads are written in two-paragraph blocks. The first paragraph sets the stage, explaining a past event or perception. The second paragraph brings the audience up to date. There is no reason to keep bouncing readers back and forth before giving them the news peg. It even may be possible to write the contrast lead in a single paragraph, as in this example from the *Milwaukee Sentinel*:

A baby who was so small at birth that, if she had died, she would have been considered a miscarriage, this week reached 4 pounds and is thriving at St. Joseph's Hospital, physicians and nurses said.

GOOD AND BAD EXAMPLES

Here is a two-paragraph contrast lead from the *Chicago Sun-Times*:

When Gloria Jean Wilson was arrested on murder charges last April, police were only able to piece together the first name of the deaf mute woman, so they nicknamed her "Gloria Swanson" in honor of the legendary actress.

Yesterday, following months of language training so she could tell her story in court, Gloria was found not guilty in the April 25 murder of Wilbert Taylor by Criminal Court Judge Earl Strayhorn. Gloria was convicted of involuntary manslaughter and sentenced to one year probation.

Although this lead was wordy (both the first and second paragraphs could have been tightened), look how it compared with another contrast lead on the same story, this one from the *Chicago Tribune*:

She is a deaf mute, and she survives by collecting aluminum cans on the Near West Side.

She lives by her wits and knows only a crude sign language of the streets. When she was arrested and charged with fatally stabbing a transient in April, she refused to give police her last name and, for a month, she sat in jail.

Her name is Gloria, and, somewhere along the line, prosecutors began referring to her as Gloria Swanson. Although they were trying her for murder, they admired her work ethic.

"Gloria is one of those people that slipped through the cracks," said Assistant State's Atty. Thomas Roche. "She has some education, but she mainly walks the streets. We had no choice but to charge her."

On Wednesday, with the help of an interpreter, Gloria Wilson, who is 24 and lives at 2710 W. Cortez St., told her story for the first time.

After a short hearing, in which she testified that the man she stabbed sought to rape her, Criminal Court Judge Earl Strayhorn found her guilty of involuntary manslaughter and sentenced her to 12 months' probation.

Finally, in the sixth paragraph, readers are given the news peg. As in the first story, the writer attempted to contrast Gloria as she was then to as she is now, but readers were left hanging too long. They should have been told in the second paragraph—as they were in the *Sun-Times* lead—that Gloria was cleared of murder charges but found guilty of involuntary manslaughter. Most of the material in the second, third, fourth and fifth paragraphs of the *Tribune* story should have been used later, after readers were told the news.

THE NEED FOR OBSERVATION

As in a narrative lead, observation can make a contrast lead crackle. It can help convince an audience to stay with a story until the end. Here is a three-paragraph contrast lead from the *Los Angeles Times* that used observations in the first two paragraphs:

One of the things that strikes motorists about the Santa Ana Freeway in downtown Los Angeles is the sharp turn it makes just east of the Civic Center to swing around a big, bulky building emblazoned with the words *Home of Brew 102*.

Each day, thousands of motorists in the freeway's eastbound lanes pass within a few feet of the landmark plant, which was around long before the freeway was built in the mid-1950s.

The old Maier Brewery building, reportedly unused for 13 years, was a formidable obstacle when the freeway was laid out. Now, 30 years later, state highway planners are preparing to bypass it again, as they prepare to build a downtown extension of the San Bernardino Freeway busway along the freeway's north side, next to Union Station.

STRONG "TURN WORDS"

Strong *turn words* should be used to introduce the second half of the contrast. The most common turn words are *but*, *now*, *today* and *yesterday*. However, there is plenty of opportunity to be creative. For instance, in the above lead on the Los Angeles freeway, the turn word in the third paragraph was *now*. It did not have to be. Instead, the writer could have left out the word and simply started the sentence with *Thirty years later*. Or, the paragraph could have started: *Highway planners are hoping the*

SPECIAL LEADS

beer plant won't brew trouble again as they prepare to build a downtown extension . . .

Just a little bit of creativity, often a single word, may mean a larger audience. There's no need to be overly cute; it is just better to avoid the standard words, to avoid being trite. Here is an example from *The News-Sun* in Waukegan, Ill.:

> Anton Kolb, the 51-year-old Libertyville chauffeur who is the state's newest Lotto millionaire, hasn't had a vacation in 12 years.
> He may take a few days off now.

ON A HARD NEWS STORY

Because a contrast lead often reports breaking news, it is an effective alternative to a summary lead on a hard news story. As in the above examples, contrasts can be used on news stories about babies who beat the odds and survive, court cases and new construction on freeways. Here are two more examples of hard news stories topped by contrast leads, the first from the *San Jose Mercury News*, the second from the *Chicago Tribune*:

> It now takes an hour to drive from San Jose to Palo Alto when commuter traffic clogs Highway 101.
> By the end of this century, it could take twice that long, and Santa Clara County transportation planners are trying to head off that commuter's nightmare.

> Fans of Lawrence "Mr. T" Tero, the tough-talking heavyweight known for his Mohawk hair style and gold jewelry, are used to seeing him dispose of a new crop of challengers each week on television. But in a court drama that began Tuesday, the fearsome-looking star has a more familiar challenger: his brother.

STACCATO

A *staccato lead* is made up of a short burst of phrases that carries an audience into a story by dangling some of its key elements in front of them. It is meant to tease readers and set the mood for the story, as in:

> Friday. The night the music stopped.

> The first day of his prison term. 3,649 to go.

The staccato lead can be used on newspaper news and feature stories, but it most commonly is used in television news stories. For example, on a story about a reunion of Vietnam War veterans, an Independent News Network story began with tape of a veteran saying:

"THIS IS BEAUTIFUL. THIS IS GREAT."

Then, the reporter told viewers:

IT WAS A HAPPY REUNION FOR VIETNAM WAR VETERANS.

On the same day, *The New York Times,* using a summary news lead for the same event, reported on Page One:

Vietnam veterans accepted New
York City's thanks yesterday at a bit-
tersweet tickertape parade through
the canyons of lower Manhattan.

GET THE NEWS PEG HIGH

After the short phrase or burst of phrases, a sentence or paragraph must tell readers the news peg of the story. Readers should not have to wait to find out what the story is about. An *Orlando Sentinel* story on color schemes for apartments began with a staccato lead:

Off-white or beige walls. Brown or
gray carpet. Beige vinyl kitchen
floors.

The phrases should have brought readers into the story quickly. In the second paragraph they were told the reason for the story, which was about using something other than natural colors in decorating an apartment:

These are the staples of apartment
decor. Which is fine if you are into
earth tones and neutrals. But what if
you have a brighter color scheme in
mind and the rules forbid any change?

The *Orlando Sentinel* also used a staccato lead in a story about a new play that would be performed on the roof of a downtown parking garage. It began:

SPECIAL LEADS   271

Sixth floor, Orlando City Parking Garage, 53 W. Central Blvd., downtown Orlando.

In the second paragraph readers were told:

Things are happening on the roof of the city parking garage, but not what the place's builders had in mind—there are hardly any cars in sight. In their place are a unicyclist, a roller skater, a rock band, a handful of parents and some three dozen kids, putting in one of their last rehearsals for the original young people's musical "Stack 'Em in the Streets."

DIRECT ADDRESS

In a *direct address lead,* the news or feature writer communicates directly with readers by using the word *you* in the lead. These leads give writers an opportunity to reach out to their readers, to include them as individuals in a story. Instead of telling how experts say spark plugs should be changed, a writer tells an individual reader: This is how you should change your spark plugs. The direct address lead can be effective because it works like a recruiting poster, telling readers "we want you" to take the time to complete this story.

A direct address lead is usually one paragraph long. The second paragraph of the story provides the news peg, as in this example for the *Santa Ana* (Calif.) *Register*:

MIAMI—Your corner gas station—and the entire U.S. oil industry—is about to change more dramatically than ever in the 100-year history of the car, experts say.

Gas prices, which have been creeping up, are on the way to a nearly 20-cent jump, a leading oil analyst said. A sizable number of oil refineries face extinction, according to the federal government. Spot gas shortages are likely. And some motorists will start hearing their engines knock annoyingly.

A direct address lead also can string readers along for two or three paragraphs before the nut graph is written. Here is an example from the *Mohave Valley News* in Bullhead City, Ariz.:

Imagine you're in Lake Havasu High School basketball coach Chuck Taylor's place.

Your team is rated No. 3 in the Arizona Republic's Class AA top five poll; it's off to a rocketing 7–2 start and it has won the Parker Christmas Tournament for the first time ever.

You're opening AA-Conference action tonight—but not against No. 4-ranked Kingman High. Your team is playing in Bullhead City against 2–8

Mohave High, a team long on hard luck, short on experience and short on height. What do you tell your players before they take the floor at 7 p.m.?

"We're looking at the game like we're going against Kingman," said Taylor. "It's a conference game. It's an important game and I expect a lot of intensity from the kids. We aren't taking Mohave lightly."

This lead on a sports story was effective because it put readers in Coach Taylor's place. Then it let him talk directly to readers and also give the news peg of the story. Along with involving readers in the story, the first three paragraphs also provided the following essential information:

- Lake Havasu's record and rating
- Conference play is opening
- Mohave's record and weaknesses
- The time the game starts

USE IT SPARINGLY

Direct address is not for every story. It is not appropriate on breaking news, where it is necessary to give a brief summary of the event without becoming personally involved with an audience. If there is a fire and three people are killed, the lead probably would say:

Three people were killed today in a fire on West 35th Street.

It would not say:

Imagine what you would have seen if you were walking down West 35th Street today.

As the sports lead from the *Mohave Valley News* illustrates, however, writers can weave the news into direct address leads.

BE PREPARED TO REWRITE

Some editors dislike direct address leads because they believe reporters never should talk directly to readers. Editors also argue that direct address leads often are aimed at a narrow segment of the readership or generalize in a way that would anger readers, as in:

You wouldn't think this city could come up with such a creative plan, but...

SPECIAL LEADS

If a direct address lead is the best for the story, discuss it with an editor and defend it if necessary. Editors who say they do not like direct address leads often can be talked into running them if the writer makes a good enough case. Otherwise, be prepared to rewrite.

The next leads to be discussed—question, quote and none of the above—are the toughest ones to get into print. The reason: Editors want the news high in the story. They do not want their writers to flimflam the audience.

QUESTION

Some editors would say that *question leads*—which begin a story by asking an audience a question or a series of questions—are never acceptable because they rarely work, are overused or force people to look for answers that should have been in the opening paragraph. Also, editors contend that writers sometimes rely on question leads as crutches, using them when they cannot decide what the key point is. Despite the obstacles, questions can be used effectively to begin stories. Just use them sparingly and appropriately.

The key to writing a question lead is to answer the question as quickly as possible. It is best to answer it in the first paragraph; it must be answered in the second. Do not leave an audience hanging, trying to figure out what the story is about.

For example, here is a question lead by UPI writer Iris Krasnow that worked. Notice how she answered her staccato-brief questions immediately, rather than asking them all before giving the answers:

WASHINGTON (UPI)—Waltzing? It's in. Bedhopping? Out. Miss Manners etiquette? In. Raunchy locker room talk? Out.

Marriage? In. Non-commitment? It's sweet history.

Seems all that is left to the torrid sexual revolution is the faint smoke of candlelit romance, one on one. Even rocker Linda Ronstadt has turned to vintage torch songs—what's going on?

In this question lead from *The Wall Street Journal*, writer Christopher Conte waited until the second paragraph to give his readers answers:

FAIRFAX COUNTY, Va.—Every weekday morning, Gretchen Davis drives down Fairfax Farms Road on the way to work at the Ayr Hill Country Store in nearby Vienna. Sounds pastoral, doesn't it?

But a short way down the road, Mrs. Davis reaches Route 50, a major arterial highway through this Washington, D.C., suburb. There, a river of cars roars through the suburban calm. "Sometimes you have to wait 20 minutes just for a gap in the traffic big enough to get out—and even then you have to take a chance," the shopkeeper says. For Mrs. Davis, stop-and-go traffic often stretches what used to be a pleasant 20-minute commute into a nerve-wracking hour.

TEASING AN AUDIENCE

Conte's question lead was effective because it teased readers, telling them to read the next paragraph to find the answer. The story began in the peaceful setting of the suburbs, but told readers quickly that suburbia has grown so quickly that it is facing the same traffic nightmares as big cities. Although it could have started with a summary lead telling readers that years of explosive and unplanned growth have flooded the suburbs with too many cars, it used a question to move readers from peaceful image to stark reality.

COMBINING QUESTION WITH DIRECT ADDRESS

Question leads can use direct address to ask readers, individually, a question. For example, when *The Daily Northwestern* at Northwestern University ran a story on demands by women to be paid the same as men for comparable jobs, it began:

Okay, you're the boss. Who's worth more to you—your secretaries or your truck drivers? Your librarians or your electricians? Your carpenters or your nurses?

QUOTE

A *quote lead* allows a central character to begin a news or feature story by talking directly to the audience. The quote may be the most powerful one in the story, or it may set the tone for what is to follow.

Use this lead sparingly. Most newspaper editors ban quote leads on breaking news stories because quotes may not provide the major points of the story.

When writing a quote lead, put the attribution in the first paragraph. That way, readers do not have to wait to find out who is speaking. Do not write a long quote in the opening paragraph and then begin the second paragraph with *Those were the words of* . . .

Also try to incorporate some elements of news with the quote in the first paragraph. If that is not possible, put some news in the second paragraph.

Avoid carrying a quote lead for more than a paragraph or two. There is no need to keep an audience hanging before attributing a quote and giving the news peg. Use more quotes after the news is reported.

Here are two examples of quote leads. The first one is from the *College Heights Herald* of Western Kentucky University, with the attribution at the end, and the second is from the *Mohave Valley News* in Bullhead City, Ariz., with the attribution in the middle:

SPECIAL LEADS

> "Dumb jocks are not being born, they are being systematically created," Dr. Harry Edwards said at a lecture Tuesday night in Garrett Auditorium.

> "It was bedlam," smiled George Burden. "It really was. My teammates told me I looked a little white in the face and that I should sit down."

DO NOT MISREPRESENT

Before writing a quote lead, make sure it is powerful enough to draw in an audience or significant enough to set the tone of the story. Also be careful that the quote, if used out of context, does not misrepresent the point of the speaker.

For example, the mayor might say: "I'm the boss. I'm the person who ultimately has to decide if we are going to spend all that money on the downtown renewal project. Of course, the voters can change my mind." In this case, a reporter would be misrepresenting the mayor's point if a news story began:

```
"I'm the boss," the mayor said today.
```

BEWARE OF LIBEL

Before using a quote, screen it carefully for libel. (See Chapter 15 for a discussion of libel and ethics.) Just because someone said something does not allow a writer to use it worry-free. In this story from the *Kenosha* (Wis.) *News*, a potentially damaging quote was used in the lead:

> "I'm glad he's in custody so he can stop killing people," said Vernita Wheat's brother, Anthony, 18, when he was told Friday the man accused of killing his sister had been taken into custody.

The suspect later was found guilty, and the chances were slim that he would take action against the paper, but the writer should have been more careful. Reporters do not have license to use anything uttered by a source.

NONE OF THE ABOVE

Sometimes, a lead is *none of the above*. It simply will not fit into one of the above categories. It may be a combination of several of the categories, or it may be what some editors call a "freak lead," which defies definition. It may be lines from a published poem or song that introduce a news or feature story. It may be a poem or song that the writer makes up, as in:

> Today is Tuesday.
> A day to sail.
> Tomorrow is Wednesday.
> Beware of a gale.

This example points out the fundamental problems with none-of-the-above leads: they may be too cute; they may be difficult to understand; they may turn off readers.

Still, if they are used sparingly and appropriately, these leads can work, as in this story from the *Milwaukee Sentinel*:

> Dear God,
> Things are rather confused here at the State Senate in Madison.
> On Monday morning, Senate President Fred Risser (D-Madison) was quoted as saying senators had abandoned their formal opening prayer at the beginning of each session.

COMBINING SEVERAL LEADS

None-of-the-above leads probably work best when they are a combination of several categories of leads, rather than a poem, song or some other type of strange beginning. Here is a lead from the *New York Daily News* on a story about an 18.6-mile walk to raise money for the March of Dimes and a 36-mile bicycle tour. It is a summary; it's an anecdote; it also has a touch of music in it.

> Over hills, over dales, 40,000 people hit the city trails yesterday for charity and fun.

THE NEED FOR STRONG, VIVID VERBS

Reporters must write sentences that are concise, accurate and easy to understand. A strong, colorful verb in each of those sentences will make the writing even better. This is particularly important in special leads, which may not provide the main news of the story right away. In these cases, the words, rather than the news, draw an audience inside.

SPECIAL LEADS

A vivid verb can animate a sentence, as in, "The hostages snaked their way along the dusty road to freedom." Words can paint a picture. Sentences can so accurately describe a snowstorm, a riot, a trial or a parade that an audience can see the event.

EXAMPLES

Here is a narrative lead on a story that appeared in the *Des Moines Sunday Register*. By using vivid verbs in his narrative, writer Bob Shaw effectively drew his readers into the story.

MESQUAKIE SETTLEMENT, IA.—It was still dark when the 7-year-old boy was awakened by rustling mice beneath the tattered sofa that served as his bed. His little sister, still groggy and struggling with the zipper on her coat, lurched past. Judging from the wind hissing through the window cracks, the outhouse seat would be cold.

"Look at this place," the father muttered, as the seven-member family stirred to life in the condemned two-bedroom house just before dawn.

Imagine how dull Shaw's lead would have been if he had used dismal verbs:

MESQUAKIE SETTLEMENT, IA.—Mice under his bed woke up the 7-year-old boy. His tired sister went past him. There was wind coming through the window cracks, which meant the outhouse seat would be cold.

"Look at this place," their father said as the seven-member family got up in their two-bedroom house before dawn.

In a story in the *Kenosha* (Wis.) *News* on an authorization by the Wisconsin Public Service Commission to withdraw party-line telephone service in areas where it seldom is used, the lead was:

Wisconsin Bell is hanging up on the party line.

And a colorful verb was used in the lead on this story in the *Milwaukee Sentinel* about a possible tax increase in Wisconsin on packages of cigarettes. (The unusual spelling of *cigarette* in the story is *Sentinel* style.)

> There's a catch in Gov. Earl's new budget that will have Wisconsin cigaret smokers continuing to cough up 41 cents a pack in taxes even if 8 cents of the federal tax expires as scheduled Oct. 1.

When writing the lead, or any other paragraph in a story, it is important to pick the most precise verb, the one that enhances each sentence and makes the scene clearer to an audience. That does not mean writers should try to surprise or shock their audiences with a spectacular verb in each sentence. When a 17-year-old boy is shot and killed by a shotgun blast, the lead simply should say he was shot and killed, not, "A 17-year-old boy was blown away today."

Be accurate and colorful, not cute, sensational or shoddy.

WHICH ONE AND WHEN?

The nice, and sometimes most annoying, thing about lead writing is that there really is no best lead or most correct lead for a news or feature story. Tradition, the time people spend reading news and the space in which journalists have to present it still dictate that summary leads are the best on hard news stories. Still, there are exceptions.

Writers do not sit at their video display terminals or typewriters and say to themselves, "I'm going to write a summary lead on this story" or "This story deserves a contrast lead or a narrative lead." They usually write the lead before the story, but sometimes, they construct the story before writing what they think is the best lead. Several things help writers decide on the lead:

- *Their own creativity.* It always is nice to be different from everyone else, as long as the audience understands the final product.
- *What their sources said.* Writers have to work with what their sources said or did. They cannot make up quotes or narrative to enhance their stories.
- *Their observations.* Writers are limited by what they see, hear, smell and touch during an interview. They are not allowed to embellish or obfuscate.
- *Tradition.* Reporters usually know when to write a summary lead and when to steer away from it.
- *Their editors.* Face it. Reporters write for editors. Some bosses like only summaries; some will accept narrative and contrast but no others; some think quote leads are fine.
- *Space.* A reporter may come up with a terrific three-paragraph lead that takes up two inches. But if an editor says, "You only have 8 inches of space," that wonderful lead probably will be abandoned.

SPECIAL LEADS

ONE STORY, SEVERAL LEADS

To illustrate how it is possible to write different leads on a single story, here is part of a news story from the *Chicago Tribune*:

BRADFORD, England—Police said Sunday that the final death toll could exceed 85 in a fire that engulfed the main grandstand at a soccer stadium in this city in northern England Saturday.

On a day that civic celebrations had been planned to honor the championship Bradford City soccer club, flags flew at half-staff to mourn what Sports Minister Neil Macfarlane called "the worst tragedy we have ever seen in English football (soccer)."

Prime Minister Margaret Thatcher said she was "dumbfounded" on seeing footage of the fire on television. "It was one of the worst things I've ever seen. It was a day of agony for Bradford and a day of torture for people who have lost someone. Everything is being done to find the cause of the fire."

Some spectators died in their seats as the flames jumped through the wooded stands within four minutes. Other spectators, their clothes and hair aflame, were crushed to death in a stampede to escape through padlocked gates.

As police began trying to identify 52 bodies recovered so far from the charred wreckage, a spokesman said 24 people remained unaccounted for and 12 of the 211 injured in the blaze were fighting for their lives.

Although the cause of the fire remained unknown, West Yorkshire Chief Constable Colin Sampson said that arson could not be ruled out. But he added, "The early indication is that it was not a deliberate criminal act."

The fire began late in the first half of a game between Bradford City and Lincoln City, of the English Football League's Third Division.

Many bodies were burned beyond recognition and Sampson said they would have to be identified through teeth and personal possessions.

Members of the crowd of 12,000 told horrifying stories of how spectators were burned.

"The place was full of children, families and old people. I saw a man on fire and I don't want to see anything like that again," said John Waite.

This story is a *follow-up*, which provides the latest news of a story that broke—was reported—earlier. In this case, the breaking story on Saturday would have reported, probably with a summary lead, the fire and given the preliminary death count. The follow-up, also with a summary lead, says the final toll may reach 85.

The story also could have started with any of the special leads except none of the above, which simply would not have been appropriate on such a hard news story. Here are some examples:

Narrative

The flags flew at half-staff in Bradford City Sunday as West Yorkshire Chief Constable Colin Sampson and others dug through the rubble of the burned soccer club and hunted for clues and bodies.

Contrast

It started as a day of celebration to honor the championship Bradford City soccer club in its game against Lincoln City.

It ended in tragedy as fire engulfed the main grandstand in the city's soccer stadium, killing as many as 85 and injuring 211.

Staccato

Soccer on Saturday. A tradition. A celebration. Now, a nightmare.

Direct Address

You cannot comprehend the nightmare of Bradford City until you have walked through the charred wreckage, where spectators, their clothes and hair aflame, were crushed to death in a stampede.

Question

Was it arson or was it an accident that sparked the tragic fire at the Bradford City soccer stadium?

Quote

"I saw a man on fire and I don't want to see anything like that again," spectator John Waite said Sunday as he recalled the horror of the fire at the Bradford City soccer stadium.

News can happen anytime and anyplace. It can be anything from a major disaster to an animal rights protest. (Photo by Don B. Stevenson)

14 / Features

Features are not meant to deliver the news firsthand. They do contain elements of news, but their main function is to humanize, to add color, to educate, to entertain, to illuminate. They often recap major news that was reported in a previous news cycle or elsewhere in the same edition.

In this chapter you will be introduced to the following terms:

immediate news value
Jell-O journalism
sidebar
mainbar
personality profile
human-interest story
trend story

in-depth story
backgrounder
analysis piece
thread
transition
voice

For Mary Gillespie, a general assignment feature writer at the *Chicago Sun-Times,* feature writing is news writing with a heart. "News writers love the rush they get when they run out and cover a breaking news story," she said. "That's their challenge. My challenge is to grab readers and not let them go until they finish the story, to take them beyond what they may have read in the newspaper the day before."

Gillespie writes for the daily Living section of the *Sun-Times,* its main feature section. She writes anything except hard news and arts and entertainment. Her beat is wherever the story is.

She has spent a day on a barge in Lake Michigan, interviewing the men who drop buoys into harbors in preparation for the summer boating season; she has been to the Miss America pageant to find out what the contestants do before and after the contest; she has traveled to Luxembourg to rekindle memories of the Battle of the Bulge.

"I've also written a feature on napping," she said. "Who naps, who doesn't nap. Voluntary and involuntary nappers. Famous nappers in history.

"There is an infinite number of features out there. To me the best place to find a feature is to look at what's happening around you. Look at the news. Talk to people in the supermarket. In other words, live.

"A feature involves readers on the level of, 'This could happen to you.' You are teaching people something about themselves. You are telling them, 'Look what this did to this guy. Here's what we can learn from this.' It's like holding up a mirror."

Gillespie's first job out of college was as a news writer at the *Suburban Sun-Times.* "You have to learn your ABCs of writing news before you can write features," she said. "The two are intertwined. You should begin as a news writer, but you cannot forever evolve with who, what, where, why, when, period. The feature writer's challenge is to go farther."

THE IMPORTANCE OF FEATURES

There is no firm line between a news and feature story, particularly today when many news events are "featurized." For instance, Monday may have been the warmest day so far this year. A news story may begin: Record heat toasted the city Monday, and there's no relief in sight. A featurized story may begin: John Hilkevich did what everyone in the city wanted to do Monday. He spent the day getting a tan at the beach.

Most newspapers offer a mix: hard news stories that chronicle the significant events that occurred since the last edition, and features that:

- Illuminate the people who made the news
- Explain the events that moved or shook the news
- Analyze what is happening in the world, nation or community
- Teach an audience how to do something
- Suggest better ways to live in a complicated world
- Examine trends in constantly changing societies
- Entertain

Despite today's interest in feature stories, hard news still fills most of a newspaper's front page. However, inside the newspaper and often on the lower half of the front page, the stories become softer.

Newspapers use many factors to determine what events they will report, including timeliness, proximity, consequence, the perceived interest of the audience, competition, editorial goals and even influence of advertisers. All of these factors put pressure on newspapers to give their readers both news and features. Readers want hard news that tells them the who, what, where, when, why and how of events that are occurring constantly in their world, nation and community. They also want to be entertained, to smile or cry, to learn and to sit back and truly enjoy a story.

HARD AND SOFT NEWS

People get up in the morning and they want to know what happened since they went to bed. They read a morning newspaper or turn on the morning news. They switch their car or office radios to the news during the day to find out the latest happenings. When they get home, they turn on the evening news or read an evening newspaper for a recap of what happened during the day.

A news story can be *hard*, chronicling as concisely as possible the who, what, where, when, why and how of an event. It can be *soft*, standing back to examine the people, places and things that shape the world, nation or community.

Hard news events, such as school board meetings and bond elections, affect many people, and journalists report them as they happen. Soft news, such as the re-emerging popularity of soft-top automobiles or how people are coping with cold weather, also is reported by the media. Feature stories often are written on these soft news events.

One newspaper that seems to have found the successful formula for mixing hard and soft news is *The Wall Street Journal*. Every day, the *Journal* prints sober business and finance reports. It also reports a "What's News" column that summarizes the top news stories. Mixed in with these are feature stories that center on the business world.

Sometimes, the distinction between hard and soft news is clear. When people are killed in a fire, there is *immediate news value*. The breaking stories will be written in typical inverted pyramid form that puts the most important points at the beginning. However, when the governor visits town just so he can eat chili at his favorite downtown restaurant, the writer may choose an alternative to the inverted pyramid. Here is where the distinction becomes hazy between hard and soft news. The story on the governor can be written as hard news, reporting that the official is in town to eat chili at his favorite restaurant. It can be written as a soft news feature, letting the governor and others explain what makes this chili and this restaurant so good. Either way, the story must be written as objectively as possible in easy-to-understand language.

In another story, a student reporter is assigned to write about the increasing burglary rate in the apartment buildings near her university. She calls the police department and sets up an interview with the officer in charge of the burglary detail. She finds out that the increase is alarming. The officer tells her that unless his department is given additional funding, his staff can do little to check the skyrocketing rate.

The reporter can handle the story as hard news and write it in inverted pyramid form, or she can write it as a soft news feature. Here is an example of each.

Inverted Pyramid

Burglaries have increased in apartment buildings here by more than 200 percent in the last year, and police say there is little they can do about it.

"Without a bigger budget and more manpower, we are powerless to reduce the wave of crime," Lt. Felix Ramirez of the burglary detail said. "The best we can do is hope witnesses will come forth and help us capture the criminals."

Ramirez blamed much of the increase on a climbing unemployment rate. He said another major reason is that most apartments in the area are occupied by students, who are at school all day long.

Soft News Feature

It was 5 p.m. Tuesday when Herbert V. Williamson walked in on three men who were burglarizing his apartment.

Panicking, the three thieves ran out and took off in their car. Williamson called the police immediately and then started to cry as he stared at his possessions dumped on the floor.

Fifteen minutes later, three men were arrested by police near the Saxton Street Mall after their car stalled. On the back seat were three paintings and hundreds of dollars worth of silver coins and clothing taken from Williamson's apartment.

Williamson and the three suspects are only a small part in the city's skyrocketing burglary rate, which has increased more than 200 percent near the university in the last year. Police blame much of the increase on a rising unemployment rate, and they say there is little they can do about it.

FEATURES   287

"JELL-O JOURNALISM"

When a hard news story breaks, such as a major development in a continuing story, a killing or a fire, it should be topped with a hard news lead. Soft leads and stories are more appropriately written when a major news event is not being reported for the first time. Some editors decry an overemphasis on soft writing and refer to it as *Jell-O journalism.*

In a story on the prosecutions of a motorcycle gang for allegedly raping and beating two women in a national forest in southeastern Illinois, the *St. Louis Post-Dispatch* did not report until the 11th paragraph that the court costs could plunge a rural county into a financial crisis. The lead paragraph said:

> The two-lane road winds through the hills of Hardin County deep into the Shawnee National Forest in southeastern Illinois, carrying visitors far from the interstate highways and backward in time.

The next nine paragraphs built up to the paragraph that gave the news. Even the headline was written on the 11th paragraph. It said, "Cycle Gang Violence Jars Rural County's Budget."

There was no reason to take the reader through 10 paragraphs before giving the thrust of the story. A hard news story such as this deserved a summary lead. A soft lead would have been more appropriate on a feature on the psychological effects of the attack on the two women. And even in a feature story, the news peg should have been given in the third or fourth paragraph.

TYPES OF FEATURES

Feature is an umbrella term for a number of soft-news stories that humanize, add color, educate, entertain or illuminate. A feature is not meant to deliver news firsthand. It usually recaps major news that was reported in a previous news cycle. It can stand alone or it can be a *sidebar* to the main story, the *mainbar.* A sidebar runs next to the main story or elsewhere in the same edition, providing an audience with additional information on the same topic.

Types of features include:

- Personality profile
- Human-interest story
- Trend story
- In-depth story
- Backgrounder

PERSONALITY PROFILE

A *personality profile* is written to bring an audience closer to a person in or out of the news. Interviews and observations, as well as creative writing, are used to paint a vivid picture of the person. People enjoy reading about other people, which makes a personality profile one of the most popular features in today's media.

Examples include an interview with a judge in a sensational murder trial and the story of a man in a wheelchair who just completed a cross-country trek to raise funds for handicapped children. Mary Gillespie once wrote a personality profile on her father, who was a prisoner of war during World War II. Her lead was, "I didn't expect to cry."

HUMAN-INTEREST STORY

A *human-interest story* is written to show a subject's oddity or emotional or entertainment value. Examples include what Atlantic City does each year to prepare for the Miss America pageant, how to repair a washing machine and how people are surviving in the town with the nation's highest unemployment rate.

TREND STORY

A *trend story* examines people, things or organizations that are having an impact on society. People are excited to read or listen about the latest fads, which makes trend stories popular. Examples include a look at summer fashions, a new religion or the language of teen-agers.

IN-DEPTH STORY

An *in-depth story,* through extensive research and interviews, provides a detailed account well beyond a basic news or feature story. It can be a lengthy news feature that examines one topic extensively; an investigative story that reveals wrongdoing by a person, agency or institution; or a first-person article in which the writer relives a happy or painful experience.

Examples include stories on cancer and how it has affected three families, how illegal aliens get into the United States and how one rock group made it to the top and another failed.

BACKGROUNDER

A *backgrounder*—it's also called an *analysis piece*—adds meaning to current issues in the news by explaining them further. These stories bring readers up to date, explaining how this country, organization, person or whatever got to be where it is now.

Examples include an analysis of the state death penalty shortly after a murderer is sentenced to death or a story explaining how the university food service won its exclusive contract.

FINDING A THEME AND DEVELOPING A STORY

Before a feature is written it should have a theme or a purpose. Writers do not simply sit down and write features. They determine the feature's purpose—to teach something, to reveal something, to illuminate something—and then they do their research and organize their stories to help them achieve it. Each section of the story—the beginning, body and end—should revolve around the theme.

Writers also narrow their themes as much as possible. No one writes a feature on cancer. That would take volumes. The feature would be on the latest medicine, how certain foods reduce the risk or one person's valiant fight.

Once the theme is determined, all research, interviewing and writing should support it. Of course, something may come up during the research or interviewing process that alters the focus of the story, but writers try to stick to their original themes as much as possible. They determine their themes based on several factors:

• *Has the story been done before?* Writers look for something fresh or unusual. Even an old topic, such as cancer, can have a new theme.

• *The audience.* The story should be of interest to the audience. If people cannot relate to the piece, they will not read it, no matter how well written it is.

• *Holding power.* The story has to keep readers interested. Emotional appeal is important here. Will the story make an audience laugh or cry?

• *Worthiness.* Writers also must ask themselves (or their editors may ask them): "Is this story worth anything? Is the theme so narrow or so broad that it has no value?"

FEATURE LEADS

Lead possibilities for features are endless. Feature writers generally write narrative, contrast, staccato, direct address or none-of-the-above leads. They usually avoid summary leads because it is not necessary or practical to summarize an entire feature in a single opening paragraph.

"You can't underestimate the importance of the lead," Gillespie said. "If you don't get them in the lead, you won't get them. The lead has to convey urgency, something so provocative that they'll want to read the story. You're like a carny, saying, 'Hey, don't pass me by. Stop and read me.' But you're in trouble if you can't back up your lead. You have to follow the fireworks with something just as big."

A *lead block* of two or more paragraphs often begins a feature. Rather than putting the news elements of the story in the lead, the feature writer uses the first two or three paragraphs to set a mood, to arouse readers, to invite them inside. Then the news peg or the significance of the story is provided in the third or fourth paragraph, the *nut graph*. Because it explains the reason the story is being written, the nut graph—it also is called the *so-what graph*—is a vital paragraph in every feature.

FROM START TO FINISH

When Victoria Malmer of Western Kentucky University wrote a trend story on break dancing, her purpose was not only to explain the fad but to teach her readers the language of the streets that goes with the dancing. She packaged her story around her theme: the movements and language of break dancing.

THE BEGINNING

Malmer's story appeared in *The State Journal,* the community daily in Frankfort, Ky. It began with a two-paragraph lead block:

Bust this, man. Break dancing is the most deaf, most chilly, most awesome thing going. Just grab your home slice, put on your freshest kicks, and get down to the serious business of poppin', lockin' and boppin'.

Confused? The translation: "Look at this critically, friend. Break dancing is the most hip, most cool thing around. Just grab your best friend, put on your most "in" sneakers, and start dancing. Tense the muscles in a section of your body, and rhythmically pop one joint out of line and then back in. Then, freeze your body and expression, sculpture-like in a dance move, for effect and comic relief. Or, walk as though one leg is two inches shorter than the other Chaplin-style."

Malmer used the first two paragraphs to entice her readers, to reach out and grab them. Her colorful lead block not only dangled a carrot in front of readers, but it revealed to them the theme of the story.

THE BODY

The first two paragraphs invited readers inside; the third paragraph, the nut graph, told them the reason the story was written:

Sounds like fun? Doctors and parents think breakin' is whack (bad). But to the teen-age population, it's fresh (new, original, different). You need a permit to do it at a shopping mall in San Bernardino, Calif. But in school gymnastics, or cement street corners, break dancing seems to have replaced all other forms of dancing.

FEATURES

Features often are written this way. They begin with a narrative or anecdote, which describes an amusing or interesting incident or event that is not necessarily news. Then, the third or fourth paragraph becomes the nut, or so what, graph, in which the writer gives the story's news peg. Stories in *The Wall Street Journal* often follow this form.

The body of a feature story should entertain and educate. A news story informs people of events that have occurred within the last day or hours; a feature should teach them something and tie them emotionally to the subject. To do that, the body of a feature must be written so that it provides vital information and is easy and fun to read.

As in a news story, transitions, paraphrases and quotes are used to connect paragraphs and move from one area to another. Because a feature generally runs longer than a news story, it also is effective to weave a *thread* throughout the story, which connects the lead to the body and to the conclusion. This thread can be a single person, an event or a thing, and it usually highlights the theme of the story.

A feature on how people fight heart disease could begin with a 13-year-old child in a hospital bed, waiting for a heart transplant and facing the deadline of death. The body of the story would explore heart disease, how many people it affects and what is being done to help those who have it. Throughout the body of the story, the writer would keep coming back to the 13-year-old, the thread. The feature also should conclude with the child, waiting.

The same feature on heart disease could begin with an event, such as an auto accident in which a 20-year-old man dies. He is rushed to a hospital, where his heart is removed and transplanted into the chest of a 13-year-old child. The event becomes the thread. Throughout the story, the writer refers to the accident that brought death to one person and life to another.

In the break dancing story, the thread was the language of the dancers. The lingo began the story, it was sprinkled throughout to keep readers involved and it concluded the story. The body contained instructions on how to do some of the dances, quotes from youths who break dance for fun and/or profit and warnings from a hospital on its dangers. And throughout the story there was the language, as in this paragraph:

> The rap (rhythmically spoken with and over an instrumental part of a song, talking with the beat of the music) of Electric Kingdom, performed by Twilight 22, illustrate break dancing roots. "Deep in the city, people live in the streets. You got to be careful of everyone you meet. There's lootin', there's shootin', people stabbin' and grabbin'. The innocent bystander the police are grabbin'. Ain't it a pity, 'cause you hate the city, but the way you feel ain't no big deal. You've got to survive . . ."

THE CONCLUSION

Like a news story, a feature often is concluded with a quote, which lets the story trail off with a source talking directly to the reader. Ending with narrative also is effective. Some features build up to the conclusion, which contains an exciting or surprising climax.

Malmer concluded her story by tracing the roots of break dancing. Although it contained some of the lingo, it probably would have been stronger if it contained a quote from one of the dancers.

> The originator of the violence-channeled-to-art movement is Afrika Bambaataa, founder of the Zulu Nation, a group of South Bronx street gang members. He encouraged them to rechannel their frustration into the creative forms of art (graffiti), dance (break dancing) and music (rap music and words). Zulu Nation is a non-violent organization discouraging the use of alcohol or drugs by its members.

STEPS TO FOLLOW

Here are the steps typically followed in organizing a feature story:

- *Pick the theme.* Make sure it is not too broad or too narrow.
- *Write a lead that invites readers into the story.* A summary may not be the best lead for a feature. A two- or three-paragraph lead block may be better. The nut graph should be high in the story. Do not make readers wait until the 10th or 11th paragraph before telling them what the story is about.
- *Provide vital background information.* If appropriate, a paragraph or two of background should be placed high in the story to bring readers up to date.
- *Write clear, concise, sentences.* Sprinkle direct quotes and additional background throughout the story. Paragraphs can be written in order of importance or chronologically.
- *Use a thread.* Connect the beginning, body and conclusion of the story.
- *Use transition.* Connect paragraphs with transitional words, paraphrases and direct quotes.
- *Conclude with a quote or another part of the thread.* A feature can trail off like a news story or it can be concluded with a climax.

THE MECHANICS OF A FEATURE

Feature writers seldom use the traditional inverted pyramid form. Instead, they may write a chronology that builds to a climax at the end, a narrative, a first-person article about one of their own experiences or a combination of these. Their stories are held together by the thread, and they often end where the lead started, with a single person or event.

In an in-depth series on the Miss America pageant, Mary Gillespie of the *Chicago Sun-Times* began one story with a narrative lead block that described Ruth Booker, Miss Illinois.

FEATURES

It's a late-summer Sunday designed for luscious languor—bright but cool, with a silky breeze that just riffles the luxurious old trees of West Dundee.

But as much as she loves the outdoors, 21-year-old Ruth Booker is spending this glorious day in a borrowed studio in the sleepy Fox Valley suburb, patiently being put through her paces.

By noon, she has sung "Kiss Me in the Rain" what seems like 100 times. She has been grilled on current events and made to state specific views on abortion, nuclear war and Geraldine Ferraro. She's been critiqued on her posture ("Glide!"), her eye contact (or lack of it) and the pitch of her voice (a little low, says the voice coach).

By 3 p.m., her red, white and blue outfit is rumpled, her matching high heels have long since been kicked aside and her haute couture body is momentarily draped across a folding director's chair. But Ruth Booker is still smiling. She has to. Smiling is paramount for a newly crowned Miss America, and that's what this long-legged American beauty hopes to be on Saturday night.

Booker is the story's thread. It branches out into several areas: It is about other beauty queens from Illinois; it is about beauty pageants in general and the Miss America pageant in particular. It is also about Booker, and because she is the thread, Gillespie uses her as an example throughout. The story also ends with Booker, talking directly to the reader:

"I've learned to be thankful for my strong core when everyone is picking me apart, telling me to wear my hair up instead of down or walk differently or whatever. I've learned that the point is not so much to win; it's to grow. It's to become confident in your own abilities.

"And," she adds with a perfect runway smile, "to have a good time."

In between the lead and the ending, the story must be organized so that it is easy to follow and understand. The body provides vital information while it educates, entertains and emotionally ties an audience to the subject. The ending wraps up the story and comes back to the lead, often with a quote or a surprising climax.

"Many times, I'll be sitting in an interview and I'll know the lead," Gillespie said. "I'll hear the person say something or he'll do something, and I'll think, that's great. That's the lead. Your goal in the lead is to grab readers. You're trying to tell the reader, 'I'm going to tell you a story. I'm going to tell you something you don't know. Come in here, look at this, examine this person or situation.'"

Gillespie said the story's body should not jar the reader. "The middle should flush out the provocative statement in the lead. It should analyze and dig deeper. It should illuminate the lead," she said.

Then, she added, the ending should complete the circle and come back to the lead. "I like to end with a quote," Gillespie said. "The story then says, here's this guy, here's why he's neat, here's his final statement to the reader. By using a quote at the end, you eliminate the feeling of a chopped off story."

TRANSITION

Transition holds paragraphs together and allows them to flow into each other. Transition is particularly important in a long feature examining several people or events because it is the tool writers use to move subtly from one person or area to the next. Transition keeps readers from being jarred by the writing. It guides them through the story and keeps them comfortable until the end. Like the thread, it helps connect the beginning, middle and end of a story.

Transition can be a word or phrase at the beginning or end of a sentence, or it can be a sentence or paragraph that connects other sentences or paragraphs. With transition, the writer says, "Now, reader, the writing is going to move smoothly into another area." Words commonly used as transitions include: meanwhile, therefore, sometimes, also, and, but, meantime, nevertheless and however. Phrases include: at 8 p.m., in other action, despite the promises or in the time that followed. Sentences include: Police gave the following account of the accident. The witness described how the crime occurred.

How It's Used

Here is a personality profile that Gillespie wrote on the Illinois State Lottery superintendent. Try to pick out her transitions.

The T-shirts, posters, buttons and huge dollar-bill mural in the high-rise conference room all promise one thing—big, easy money. This is indeed the stuff of dreams, and Michael Jones feels right at home. His is the job of chief dream weaver. It's an occupation he takes seriously.

Jones is the cinema handsome, 35-year-old wunderkind superintendent of the Illinois State Lottery. In less than three years, he has upped annual lottery revenues from $334 million to more than $900 million. He's increased the number of ticket-selling agents statewide by about 5,000. Between $20 million and $21 million in dream chits are now sold every week in Illinois.

But it's not just big bucks that Jones has brought to the lottery (and thus to the general revenue fund—a sort of checking account for the state—where the currency of hope is deposited). It's also image. A higher profile. And, Jones is quick to point out, fun.

"It can be wonderful, buying a ticket and entertaining a little daily or weekly fantasy," says Jones, who admits he loves to gamble on lotteries in other states. He's especially fond of New York's Lotto game—after which ours is patterned. "I always think I'm going to win," he says with a grin that can only be described as All-American boyish. "The superintendent of the New York lottery hates me because I call him on Sunday mornings to get the winning numbers.

"But I think it's possible to overdraw the idea that people's hopes and dreams are totally tied up in winning the lottery," he adds. "I think people's hopes and dreams are probably more complex than that. The lottery is not life and death for most people; it's an escape, a fun dream that they like to believe just might come true someday."

It was "plain business sense"—which he honed in such diverse early career endeavors as managing the "late, lamented" Oakland Stompers soccer team and directing marketing for WMET radio—that led Gov. James Thompson to seek him out to oversee the lottery, Jones believes.

"I think he saw the lottery could be much more than it was, and he wanted to see it run like a business," he says. "That approach has, quite literally, paid off."

One of the key catalysts for the lottery's stunning success since Jones' arrival is his emphasis on catchy, light-hearted advertising. From prime-time TV spots to arresting L placards, impertinent Ping-Pong balls and other disarming characters and props have persuaded thousands of the previously blase to ante up a dollar or two.

Jones works closely with Bozell and Jacobs ad agency in formulating new campaigns to convince consumers to hitch their dreams to a fame ticket. They introduced a new pitch June 18 for the latest instant game, "Pay Day."

With the fun of being lottery superintendent goes serious responsibility. "I am very careful about the lottery's image and we try to be extremely careful in explaining to people exactly what they can expect from it," he says. "Remember those ads a while back about various ways to make a million? One said, 'You can marry a millionaire,' and there were other humorous examples. But one you never saw was a guy in a funny old striped prison uniform with a ball and chain and the message, '. . . or, you could rob a bank.' That just wasn't a message we wanted to send to the public. So although it was funny, it was canned."

An Army brat, Jones grew up in various spots around the country. His high school and college years were spent in Florida, where he attended Satellite High School in the shadow of Cape Kennedy during the heyday of the space race. Now, though, he's an avowed Chicagoan. He, his wife and their 2-year-old son live on the North Side.

While he is unabashedly in love with his job, Jones says he'll not make a lifetime pursuit of it. For now, though, he says he's content in the lottery's catbird seat.

"There are still a couple more personal goals I have for the lottery that I'd like to fulfill," he says. "I've always craved work that is a challenge, and I've been very lucky so far. I can only hope that luck will continue."

Behind him, on his credenza, sits a replica of the Maltese Falcon of film fame. It was a gift from his wife, who shares his passion for movies, he says. But it also has another meaning for him.

"You have to remember at the end of the 'Maltese Falcon,' when the guy asks Bogie what the statuette is? He says, 'That's the stuff dreams are made of.' In my job and my life, it's turned out to be very appropriate."

Gillespie first used transition in the third paragraph, when she moved readers from the finances of the lottery to Jones' stamp on the lottery:

But it's not just big bucks that
Jones has brought to the lottery . . .

To take the reader from Jones' impression of how much fun playing the lottery can be (third through fifth paragraphs) Gillespie made her sixth paragraph transitional:

It was "plain business sense"—which he honed in such diverse early career endeavors as managing the "late, lamented" Oakland Stompers soccer team and directing marketing and advertising for WMET radio—that led Gov. James Thompson to seek him out to oversee the lottery, Jones believes.

Gillespie began the eighth paragraph with a transitional sentence to move readers from Jones' selection as lottery chief to what he has done during his tenure:

One of the key catalysts for the lottery's stunning success since Jones' arrival is his emphasis on catchy, lighthearted advertising.

After two paragraphs on the funny advertising, transition was used again:

With the fun of being lottery superintendent goes serious responsibility.

In her 11th paragraph, Gillespie told readers a little about Jones' upbringing. She begins with a transitional phrase:

An Army brat, Jones grew up in various spots around the country.

Then in the 14th paragraph, Gillespie used transition to switch readers to Jones' office and the ending of the story:

Behind him, on his credenza, sits a replica of the Maltese Falcon of film fame.

USING VOICE

Another key element that holds a feature together is *voice*, the "signature" or personal style of each writer. Yes, there is a byline on the top of the story to tell readers who the writer is, but voice inside the story allows writers to put their individual stamps on their writing. It reveals their personality and subtly tells readers that this story is not by any writer; it is by this writer.

"I think if given the chance, all writers have something unique in the way they tell a story," Gillespie said. "They all bring their style, their ego and all of their baggage to whatever they do. That's the voice. Therein lies the creativity and the real challenge. There is a formula for writing feature

FEATURES

stories like there is for news stories. But good feature writers take the basic formula and expand it. They use their own voice. When I write a story, I want readers to say this is Mary Gillespie writing about something, not just anyone who happened to be available to cover a story."

Remember, though, voice is used subtly; it is not meant to scream at readers. And it also can fall victim to an editor.

Gillespie's voice pops up whenever she writes. She did not simply call the state lottery director handsome—she called him cinema handsome. That's voice; that's Mary Gillespie drawing a conclusion and putting it into the story. When she wrote a Christmas feature about families who have had to spend the holidays at home while loved ones were fighting wars or stationed overseas, Gillespie revealed some of her personality when she wrote:

> The ache is familiar to those who remember the irony of war at Christmas—those who, while their hairlines may be beginning to recede as their bellies expand, have memories of holiday duty as sharp as blood on snow.

In his story on a championship boxing match in which the two fighters brutalized each other, *Chicago Tribune* sportswriter Bob Verdi used voice when he said:

> You didn't just walk away from this fight; you sat in your chair awhile.

San Jose (Calif.) *Mercury News* writer Michael Zielenziger clearly let his voice pop up in a story he wrote about Warren Buffett, a major owner of Berkshire Hathaway Inc. The company is a principal investor in scores of companies, including Time Inc., Washington Post Co. and General Foods Corp.:

> There's no hint of marble, no glint of gold in Buffett's modest-size office just outside downtown Omaha. There's no stock ticker, no ornamental fountain, not even a sweeping staircase in the corporate headquarters of Berkshire Hathaway, which houses all of six people. Berkshire Hathaway doesn't even have a corporate logo.

Because voice is a subjective expression of a writer, it often is challenged by editors, who may edit it out or even insert some voice of their own. It is best used in feature stories, where writers are given more license to reveal their opinions and personality.

"Features offer potentially a far greater chance to put in voice, but you have to be careful," Gillespie said. "There's always an editor; there's always a copy desk. In writing features, everyone has to find his voice.

Every writer has it, too. You just have to find it. The only way to grab someone is if you have been grabbed."

WHAT AN EDITOR LOOKS FOR IN A FEATURE

Topy Fiske, editor of the Style section of the *San Francisco Examiner*, continually evaluates feature stories. As editor of the *Examiner*'s daily feature section, she heads a staff of 38 reporters, critics and editors. She said the best features are those written in simple, colorful language that are to the point, shocking or thought provoking. "The writing should take readers into subsequent paragraphs so quickly that they've read the entire story without even realizing it," she said. "They drink it up."

Fiske said a good feature story "has to grab me and keep me with it, even when the phone is ringing, the kids are crying and food is burning on the stove. It has to be on a subject that makes me think I am going to learn something about myself and the world around me."

Ideas for features come from many sources, Fiske said. Often, people will write to the *Examiner* suggesting ideas. Many times, staff members are the best sources. "I meet with each reporter once a week to see what's going on," Fiske said. "Lots of ideas for the section come out of the meetings."

Magazine articles and books also provide ideas for Fiske and her staff. For example, a feature on clothes worn by professional men and women began when a recently published book about putting together a wardrobe was sent to the Style section. Fiske said she read the book and wondered how "we can do it better and give it local application."

The assignment went to the *Examiner*'s fashion writer, Gladys Perint Palmer. Her idea was to use well-known people to illustrate an issue that affects all career men and women.

So began a trend story on dressing television news anchors. The story had two purposes:

- To tell readers about the wardrobes of Sylvia Chase and Jim Paymar, the news coanchors of KRON-TV in San Francisco.
- To let readers know that they could use the same clothing designs in their daily wardrobes.

"The story had to appeal to both men and women," Fiske said. "It had to be broad enough to attract a woman at home by giving her tips on what to wear when she goes out to dinner. It had to show men and women how to make a good impression on the job as well as off the job. It needed to give a lot of specific information and a lot of 'how to.'"

A SAN FRANCISCO STORY

Here is how Palmer's story began:

Professional men and women may dread making a fashion statement every time they get dressed, but whether they like it or not, they are judged by their appearance.

The result is that many people end up wearing a uniform, often a boring one.

Into this mine field comes tall, willowy Suzanne Newcome, an image and wardrobe consultant with private and corporate clients. A teacher of fashion image and retailing in Bay Area colleges, she frequently appears on television shows to discuss the subject. Most intriguing of all, she dresses the news and sports anchors at KRON-TV (Channel 4), including Sylvia Chase and Jim Paymar.

Newcome, 30ish, a graduate of Ohio State University, is vice president of the Association of Image Consultants. Although she looks like an East Coast socialite and dresses like a Gianfranco Ferre model, she is aware of the delicate dynamics of business dressing for professional men and women.

Chase and Paymar have a very high profile, but they share every business person's goal—an image that's attractive but not intimidating.

Palmer used clear and colorful language in the first five paragraphs of her 59-paragraph story to set the stage for readers. Her story did not begin with a summary lead; instead, the opening paragraphs mapped out what was to follow and invited readers inside. Such writing is common in feature stories. Palmer's five-paragraph lead block told readers that the story would be about wardrobes that are attractive but not boring or intimidating; the sources would be wardrobe consultant Suzanne Newcome and TV anchors Sylvia Chase and Jim Paymar.

After the lead block, the story moved to Chase's wardrobe. Readers were told:

Sylvia Chase has beautiful gray-green eyes and fair complexion. Excitement comes from the use of vivid colors. The styles are traditional.

Chase looks well in a brilliant cyclamen suit and a violet satin blouse. And in turquoise. And bright yellow.

The two paragraphs about Chase's eyes, complexion and best colors illustrate a fundamental difference between feature stories and news stories. The feature writer, who usually has more space than the news writer, also has more license to use observation and voice. Because the feature writer is not reporting the news firsthand, writing flair must draw the reader through the story.

After a discussion of Chase's wardrobe, the story moved to Paymar. It told readers how Paymar looks and what clothes he should wear. Here are three paragraphs:

He begins by trying on an $800 cashmere Armani suit ("I'm getting used to the cost of clothes pretty well"). The second suit is also by Armani. A 40-regular Armani and Paymar are made for each other.

(Although Paymar and Chase would not disclose their clothing allowances, it is a common practice for television networks to pay all or part of the working wardrobe.)

"I like (suit jackets) snug on camera," he explains, "or sports coats, which I can leave open and not monkey around with. Off-screen I prefer loose and baggy clothes. Relaxed."

Palmer tried to describe the two anchors as real people, not as television personalities, in an effort to show her readers that they, too, can dress for success. The story ends with a set of tips from Newcome on how to put together an effective and professional wardrobe.

Palmer was able to paint many pictures for her readers. She had the space to develop each source carefully. If her story had been used on a tighter news page, it might have started:

Two top San Francisco television personalities pay a clothes expert big money to make them look good in front of the camera.

Sylvia Chase and Jim Paymar, news anchors at KRON-TV (Channel 4), say that Suzanne Newcome is worth every dime they pay her.

A LOVE AFFAIR WITH WORDS

Fiske said the toughest part of any feature usually is the beginning. "I believe that once you have your lead it all comes together," she said. "How you start is the hardest part. That's where a good editor comes in. If the writer and editor can talk about the story it usually comes out better."

Fiske gave the following tips to aspiring feature writers:

- You must know how to spell.
- You must know grammar.
- You have to love the language. You have to love words.
- You have to be a quick study who can go into any subject area and learn about it fast. Then you have to be able to create a vivid picture with words while sitting at a video display terminal.
- You have to have a sense of fair reporting. You have to be able to get comments from people on both sides of an issue.

"If you love words, know the basics and have a feeling for people, the good writing will be there," Fiske said. "Life experience is also very important."

Retired Gen. William C. Westmoreland is escorted out of federal district court after listening to testimony in his libel case against CBS. The case was settled out of court. (Photo by A. Tannebaum/Sygma)

15 / Law and Ethics

Reporters should have a working knowledge of the legal framework within which they operate. It is not necessary for journalists to be authorities on First Amendment theory, but it is essential that they know enough about the law to freely and aggressively report within constitutional and court-sanctioned boundaries. The First Amendment gives journalists the freedom to report and edit, but it does not mandate responsibility in return. Society, however, is calling for journalistic accountability.

In this chapter you will be introduced to the following terms:

libel
actual malice
public official
public figure
negligence
journalists' privilege
shield law

authoritarian system
libertarian system
social responsibility theory
ombudsman
press critic
code of ethics

A quarter-century ago, when the U.S. Supreme Court considered cases that involved the mass media, reporters and editors predictably climbed their soapboxes and pointed majestically to the First Amendment, smugly assured that the Constitution provided them with ironclad protection to print and gather news as they wished.

Most journalists today are less confident and certainly more realistic. Lyle Denniston, veteran U.S. Supreme Court reporter who covers legal affairs for *The Baltimore Sun,* vividly capsulized what a lot of journalists think. He wrote in the *Sun:* "Reporters, editors, publishers and broadcasters can be less sure than ever before about their constitutional freedom. The law has discovered the press in a big and threatening way, and as a result the 'free press' clause is not as strongly protective as the press has thought . . . that it was."

Henry Kaufman, general counsel for the Libel Defense Resource Center, New York, called America's press freedom climate "tumultuous." He said: "There is a lot of attention being paid to journalism, the power of the press and the influence of controversial stories in a wide variety of contexts. Everything goes in cycles. We seem to be in a cycle where the public questions media methods and is less willing to question what the media are exposing."

The depth of press freedom indeed runs in cycles. The late Zechariah Chafee Jr., a Harvard law professor, summarized press freedom in the first half of the 20th century. He labeled the World War I years as a "period of struggle and criminal prosecutions"; the 1920s as a "period of growth"; the era from 1930 to 1945 as a "period of achievement"; and the Cold War years as a "period of renewed struggle and subtle suppressions." Press freedom blossomed under the liberal Earl Warren Court in the 1960s, but if there has been no erosion, there has been scant expansion during the 1970s and 1980s.

THE FIRST AMENDMENT: NOT AN ABSOLUTE

Very simply, the First Amendment does not mean literally what it says: Congress shall make no law abridging the freedom of speech, or of the press. There are exceptions to its seemingly ironclad language. Only seven years after ratification of the First Amendment, Congress passed the Alien and Sedition Laws of 1798, the latter designed to stifle criticism of the government. Those laws expired when the Thomas Jefferson administration took office in 1801, but more than a century later, in 1918, Congress approved another Sedition Act for basically the same reason.

In 1919 Justice Oliver Wendell Holmes wrote that "the First Amendment while prohibiting legislation against free speech as such cannot have been, and obviously was not, intended to give immunity for every possible use of language."

In 1942 Justice Frank Murphy wrote: "It is well understood that the right of free speech is not absolute at all times, and under all circumstances.

There are certain well-defined and narrowly limited classes of speech, the prevention and punishment of which have never been thought to raise any Constitutional problem."

The courts repeatedly have held that the First Amendment is not an absolute. Thus, they constantly are called upon to decide whether actions taken by the press are legally permissible. As the courts consider issues on a case-by-case basis, journalists are obligated to stay abreast of significant decisions.

A national survey reported in *Journalism Quarterly* showed that editors are increasingly cognizant of the need to keep pace with communication law developments. Student journalists—as well as professionals—certainly need to be aware of the effects of court decisions on reporters and editors. Applicable court decisions should not be looked on as esoteric ramblings by scholarly justices; working journalists should view the decisions as fragments of wisdom that help them to function effectively—day by day.

Areas of particular concern to reporters are libel and protection of sources.

LIBEL

Libel—holding someone up to public hatred, ridicule or scorn—is the communication of information that damages an individual in his profession, business or calling. This tort has become "politicized," according to Kaufman. "Libel litigation was intended to bring about the vindication of an individual at an individual level," he said. "But it has moved into the political arena where people are vying for more power. This is a troubling development. The press, being a powerful institution itself, inherently always has been subject to this tugging and pulling within the political process. But putting libel into the political process is coercive and threatening."

Kaufman was referring to two libel suits decided in the mid-1980s: the $50 million action former Israeli Defense Minister Ariel Sharon brought against Time Inc., and the $120 million action brought by Gen. William Westmoreland against CBS. Neither public figure was able to recover monetary damages, but in both cases the media defendants were forced to spend millions of dollars to defend themselves.

"It is odd that, because of the *Sharon* and *Westmoreland* cases, in an unusual, unexpected way, an arcane legal issue has struck a responsive chord with the public, and the battle over these legal issues has become part of a much broader trend," Kaufman said.

In an article in the *Los Angeles Times,* reporters Philip Hager and Thomas B. Rosenstiel said "the battlefield of libel law is still swarming with combatants." They said the *Sharon* and *Westmoreland* cases were "only the most prominent of a flurry of libel cases on court dockets. From major public figures to obscure local leaders, the unhappy subjects of news reports are going to court in mounting numbers."

LIBEL LAW BOUNDARIES

Three requirements must be met before a libel action can be successfully brought: (1) publication (communication to a third party); (2) identification (though not limited to calling an individual by name); and (3) harmful effect.

William Prosser, the late dean of the Hastings College of the Law, wrote: "There is a great deal of the law of defamation which makes no sense. It contains anomalies and absurdities for which no legal writer ever has a kind word." Indeed, libel law is complex. Large-circulation newspapers have the luxury of retaining attorneys with special expertise in this area; most smaller-circulation papers retain lawyers, but they probably do not specialize in communication law. Knowing that virtually every story is potentially libelous is enough to make any reporter timid. It is imperative, therefore, that reporters have at least a basic understanding of libel law. Reporters then can free themselves from the albatross of calling an attorney—particularly one who does not specialize in communication law—every time a controversial story is written.

In fact, Denniston thinks that reporters are too dependent on attorneys. Though possibly an overstatement, Denniston wrote in *Quill* magazine that lawyers in the newsroom are "as much of a threat to the press as judges sitting on the bench deciding what we can print. I think you have to go hell for election with your stories and then take the consequences—and I do mean prepare to go to the slammer." Translation: Newspaper attorneys are retained to keep their newspapers out of court; the easiest way to do so is to avoid printing controversial stories.

Most libel suits, however, do not grow from hard-hitting, aggressive reporting of monumental importance. Instead, the majority of suits evolve from—to use the newsroom vernacular—stupid, idiotic mistakes, such as failure to copy information correctly from public records. For example, John Jones is found *not guilty* of aggravated assault, but the reporter hurriedly skims the court records and writes that he was found *guilty* of aggravated assault.

Bruce Sanford, a reporter-turned-attorney who represents the Society of Professional Journalists, Sigma Delta Chi, and Scripps-Howard, said at the First Amendment Survival Seminar held in Washington, D.C., that the "chief cause of libel suits is plain old unromantic carelessness." Sanford estimated that 80 percent of all libel suits flows from "the simple, routine story that nobody would have missed if it hadn't appeared in the newspaper or been broadcast." Sanford cautioned that reporters must be very careful with rewrites, condensations and summaries.

WORDS TO HANDLE WITH CARE

Sanford listed the following "Red Flag" words in "Synopsis of the Law of Libel and the Right of Privacy." Reporters and editors should handle these words carefully; potentially they are legally explosive and could lead to libel litigation.

LAW AND ETHICS

adulteration of products	drug addict	perjurer
adultery	drunkard	plagiarist
altered records	ex-convict	pockets public funds
ambulance chaser	false weights used	price cutter
atheist	fascist	profiteering
attempted suicide	fawning sycophant	rascal
bad moral character	fool	rogue
bankrupt	fraud	scandalmonger
bigamist	gambling house	seducer
blackguard	gangster	sharp dealing
blacklisted	gouged money	short in accounts
blackmail	grafter	shyster
blockhead	groveling office seeker	skunk
booze-hound	humbug	slacker
bribery	hypocrite	smooth and tricky
brothel	illegitimate	sneak
buys votes	illicit relations	sold his influence
cheats	incompetent	sold out to a rival
collusion	infidelity	spy
communist (or red)	intemperate	stool pigeon
confidence man	intimate	stuffed the ballot box
correspondent	intolerance	suicide
corruption	Jekyll-Hyde personality	swindle
coward	kept woman	unethical
crook	Ku Klux Klan	unmarried mother
deadbeat	liar	unprofessional
deadhead	mental disease	unsound mind
defaulter	moral delinquency	unworthy of credit
disorderly house	Nazi	vice den
divorce	paramour	villain
double-crosser	peeping Tom	

Reporters can steer clear of many libel suits by scrutinizing the meaning of the words and sentences they write. A warning bell should sound any time that a reporter writes a story that contains any of the "Red Flag" words. In certain contexts, these words could damage a person's reputation.

RESPONSIBILITY FOR QUOTING OTHERS

Remember: The reporter and the newspaper are responsible for statements printed—even if someone is being quoted directly or indirectly. Assume, for example, that a reporter interviews the neighbor of a man who has just been charged with murder. The neighbor says that the man is a "no good drunken bum who beats his kids regularly and belongs to the Communist Party." The fact that the neighbor made the observation does not reduce the newspaper's level of liability; *the media outlet must assume responsibility for the statement if it is used.*

Always keep in mind the following points:

• **Just because a source provides the information does not necessarily mean it is correct.** Assume, for example, that a nurse tells a reporter that Dr. John Jones was the only physician who practiced at Memorial Hospital who had been sued successfully for malpractice during the preceding year. The reporter could sit at his video display terminal and type:

Dr. John Jones is the only physician who practices at Memorial

Hospital to be sued successfully for malpractice during the past year,

according to a nurse.

The lead sounds like the start to a great story. The problem: The reporter did not verify the information. Jones had been sued, but he won his case. The nurse had him confused with another doctor. Lesson: Do not rely on second-hand information when printing accusations of such gravity. Check and double-check. And then go to the doctor for his side of the story. By failing to do so, the reporter invites a libel action.

• **Beware of off-the-record tips passed along by sources, even high-ranking officials or law enforcement officers.** Always confirm potentially libelous accusations. Prefacing an accusation with the word *alleged* generally will not help when you get to court. Do not, for example, write:

Police said the alleged crook is in custody.

Instead, write:

Police said the man charged with the crime is in custody.

CLASSES OF LIBELOUS WORDS

When writing sensitive stories, always be alert for potentially libelous statements. Libel in the state of Illinois, for example, includes these classes of words: (1) words imputing the commission of a criminal offense; (2) words that impute infection with a communicable disease of any kind which, if true, would tend to exclude one from society; (3) words that impute inability to perform, or want of integrity in the discharge of, duties of office or employment; and (4) words that prejudice a particular party in his or her profession or trade. Classes of libelous words can, of course, vary slightly among the states, but the Illinois list is representative.

Here are examples of each:

• **Words imputing the commission of a criminal offense.** Avoid statements such as this:

LAW AND ETHICS

John Crandall was taken into custody Wednesday for murdering Sally Smith Tuesday night.

Think again. Is that really what happened? Remember: Choose your words carefully. Crandall is not guilty of murder until a court says he is. It would be better to write:

John Crandall was taken into custody Wednesday in connection with (or in the investigation of) the Tuesday night slaying of Sally Smith.

• **Words that impute infection with a communicable disease of any kind which, if true, would tend to exclude one from society.** Don't write:

John Crandall, who was elected Wednesday to be president of the local chapter of the Fellowship of Christian Athletes, was treated last summer for a venereal disease, the Daily Bugle has learned.

Such an accusation is hardly a major scoop. There is no reason to publish it. It is an example of going out on a legal limb for the type of story that Sanford mentioned earlier: one that "nobody would have missed if it hadn't appeared in the newspaper or been broadcast." The lesson is clear: The danger of libel constantly lurks; if you are going to tempt fate, do so with a story that is worth the risk.

• **Words that impute inability to perform, or want of integrity in the discharge of, duties of office or employment.** Don't write:

Public school groundskeeper John Crandall is unfit by temperament and intelligence to adequately perform his duties, sources who wish to remain anonymous said Wednesday.

This lead paragraph is another example of using a verbal sledge hammer to bludgeon an ant. Why risk a suit for such a revelation? Again: Be aggressive when you report, but make sure the story justifies the potential harm to your subject and to your employer's pocketbook.

• **Words that prejudice a particular party in his or her profession or trade.** Don't write:

Attorney John Crandall, who will represent the widow in the embezzlement case, is the most incompetent lawyer in town, according to courthouse observers.

Obviously, Crandall is not going to take kindly to the accusation. Can the reporter document the charge and is there sufficient justification for making it? The reporter who wrote the paragraph better hope so.

The examples and suggestions outlined above illustrate one principle: Handle stories that could injure a person's reputation with care. This does not mean you should back off of a story that should be told. But it does mean you should choose your words carefully. Ask yourself: Am I being fair? Am I being accurate? Is this story worth the legal risk?

No matter how careful a good reporter is, though, libel suits can materialize.

LIBEL DEFENSES

If a libel suit is filed, a defendant can use a number of defenses. Some defenses are conditional (they are viable if certain conditions or qualifications are met); others are absolute (if proven, there are no conditions or qualifications).

Conditional Defenses

In their book, "Libel: Rights, Risks, Responsibilities," Robert H. Phelps and E. Douglas Hamilton, two authorities on libel law, discuss complete but conditional defenses that have evolved through the common law (judge-made law based on prior court decisions) and statutory law. These defenses include:

- **Privilege of reporting.** This defense flows from fair and accurate reporting of official proceedings—city council meetings, state legislative sessions, congressional hearings and so forth—and the fair and accurate reporting of information contained in official documents and court records. Obviously, this defense is often cited by reporters. As emphasized, however, the defense is limited to fair and accurate reporting. Extraneous libelous matter cannot be intertwined. If, for example, during a city council meeting the mayor accuses the council president of embezzling city funds, the reporter is free to report that the charges were made—so long as the story accurately conveys what the mayor said. Any elaboration or interpretation of the mayor's remarks by the reporter would not necessarily be protected.

- **Fair comment and criticism.** This defense applies only when writing opinions about matters of public concern. The defense does not protect erroneous factual reporting. It must be clear that the allegedly libelous statement—whether it appears in an editorial, book review or personal viewpoint column—is a statement of opinion, not an expression of fact. This defense is not available to the reporter who covers an event and then writes a factual news account. However, if a reporter were to comment on the news event and offer an analysis of it in a personal column, this defense could then be utilized.

• **Neutral reportage.** In 1977 the 2nd U.S. Circuit Court accepted neutral reportage as a conditional defense; that is, it is defensible to report charges made by one responsible person or organization about another when both parties are involved in a public controversy. This defense has not been widely accepted, however, and at least one circuit has specifically rejected it. Where it applies, though, it makes available additional protection to the libel suit defendant. Check to see if it applies in your state.

The defense was cited in *Edwards* v. *National Audubon Society* where a *New York Times* reporter wrote a story concerning accusations by officials of an Audubon Society periodical, *American Birds,* that scientists who contended that the insecticide DDT did not have a negative impact on bird life were being paid to lie. The *Times* story included a short denial by some of the named scientists who had sent to the reporter extensive research material to refute the charges. The 2nd U.S. Circuit Court said that even when a newspaper seriously doubts the truth of the charges, the publication is protected under the defense of neutral reportage—objective and dispassionate reporting of the charges.

Absolute Defenses

The following are absolute defenses:

• **Statute of limitations.** This is the most ironclad of the defenses. If a suit is brought after a specified period—in most states the statute of limitations on libel is one, two or three years—the plaintiff has no standing to sue.

• **Truth.** Truth is an absolute defense in most states. In a few states, truth is a conditional defense, the conditions being that the article must have been published for justifiable ends and with good motives. Don R. Pember wrote in "Mass Media Law," however, that "appellate courts are overturning these laws as being in violation of the First Amendment." It is, of course, sometimes difficult to prove in a court of law that statements are true. Check to see if truth is an absolute or a conditional defense in the state in which you work.

• **Privilege of participant.** This defense applies to participants in official proceedings: a city councilman's remarks during a meeting, testimony of a witness during a trial, a U.S. senator speaking on the protected floor of the Senate. This, then, is not a defense reporters generally would be able to use. Reporters normally report the news—not make it.

• **Consent or authorization.** If a reporter writes a libelous passage, calls the individual in question and gets his or her permission to publish it, this defense can be used. Obviously, this situation is not likely to happen.

• **Self-defense or right of reply.** If publicly criticized, the recipient of the criticism has a privilege to respond. He or she must be careful, however, to keep the response within the framework of the original accusation. Journalists would not often have occasion to use this defense. An example of its use would be if a newspaper's drama critic treats the opening of a play harshly. The star of the play could respond, but the privilege covers his response to the original criticism. The star, in other words, could not launch a salvo critical of the reviewer's home life.

Partial Defenses

If conditional or absolute defenses cannot be used successfully (including the conditional *New York Times* actual malice defense, which will be discussed in the next section), the defendant probably will be assessed damages. He or she can, however, cite partial defenses to mitigate the damages. Partial defenses represent good faith on the part of the defendant, and a judge can take them into consideration when levying damages. Partial defenses include publication of a retraction (a clear admission of erroneous reporting) or of facts showing that, though the newspaper erred, there was no gross neligence or ill will or that the reporter relied on a usually reliable source.

THE *NEW YORK TIMES* RULE

Clearly, then, the reporter is not without common law and statutory defenses. However, these defenses are severely limited compared with the federal rule (commonly called the *actual malice* defense), a constitutional defense first articulated by the U.S. Supreme Court in 1964. In the landmark *New York Times Co.* v. *Sullivan* case, the court nationalized the law of libel to provide a constitutional defense when *public officials* are plaintiffs. Suit was brought against the *Times* for publication of an advertisement in 1960 that, in essence, said that the civil rights movement in the South was being met with a wave of aggression by certain Southern officials. L.B. Sullivan, a Montgomery, Ala., commissioner, filed the suit. Portions of the advertisement were false and under existing statutory and common law, a defendant had to prove the literal truth of the statements. The Alabama courts awarded Sullivan $500,000 in damages.

   The U.S. Supreme Court, however, reversed this ruling. It held that, to collect damages, a public official—which Sullivan clearly was—would have to prove that the defendant acted with "actual malice." Justice William Brennan said this would constitute disseminating information "with knowledge that it was false or with reckless disregard of whether it was false or not." Brennan wrote that the advertisement, "as an expression of grievance and protest on one of the major public issues of our time, would seem clearly to qualify for the constitutional protection." The media would be protected against suits brought by public officials, even when the statements were false—so long as the statements were not made with actual malice. Essentially, the case put to death the concept of seditious libel in America.

FIRST CONSIDERATION: PUBLIC OR PRIVATE?

The conditional actual malice defense provides reporters with a primary defense to add to their arsenal of common law and statutory defenses. The condition on which the *Times* rule was based, of course, is that the publication must concern a public official. From 1964 on, the status of the plaintiff—whether public or private—has been the first consideration a defendant makes when formulating possible defenses against a libel action. In 1967 the U.S. Supreme Court said that *public figures*—in addition to public officials—also have to show actual malice to recover libel damages.

The message is clear: As a reporter, you don't want to get tied up in a libel action, but if you do, there is more protection if the plaintiff is a public person.

Libel protection again was extended in 1971. The court said in *Rosenbloom* v. *Metromedia* that private persons involved in events of general or public interest also have to show actual malice to recover libel damages. The press was elevated to its most protected position ever regarding libel defenses. In 1974, however, the press was dealt a setback. In *Gertz* v. *Robert Welch*, the court said that it had gone too far in *Rosenbloom* and that unless a libel suit plaintiff were to be awarded punitive damages, private persons involved in events of general or public interest need only prove a lower fault standard—presumably *negligence*—to receive damages. Negligence certainly would be easier to prove than actual malice, the standard still required with public officials and public figures.

IMPACT OF THE *GERTZ* CASE

In addition to stripping the press of some of the protection it had grown to enjoy as a result of *Rosenbloom*, *Gertz* also restructured the definition of a public figure. The court said that to be categorized as a public figure, an individual must "voluntarily thrust" himself or herself into the vortex of the particular controversy that gave rise to the litigation with the intention of influencing its outcome (for example, leading a movement to recall a city council member) or he or she must assume a role "of especial prominence" to the extent that, for all purposes, he or she is to be considered a public figure (for example, Henry Kissinger).

The court also said that each state would define the appropriate level of liability—negligence—when suits were brought by non-public persons involved in events of general or public interest. Approximately half the states have since defined negligence, but few definitions are uniform. Some states define it as "gross negligence," others as the "failure to act as a reasonable person."

In 1985 Professor W. Nat Hopkins of the University of Arkansas at Little Rock wrote in *Journalism Monographs:* "Negligence is a nebulous word. And other nebulous words—reasonable, prudent, ordinary, careful, proper—are being used to define it."

The article focused on the various standards of negligence that had been established in 26 states. Hopkins concluded: "While courts may not have always agreed on the legal definition of negligence, most courts, thus far anyway, have recognized sloppy reporting. And the best protection from the finding of negligence is the elimination of sloppy reporting."

It is important that reporters check to see the definition that applies in the states in which they work. Some state supreme courts agreed to review cases for the sole purpose of defining the standard of liability for libel of private persons involved in public events. In reviewing such a case, for example, the Arizona State Supreme Court said that negligence is "conduct which creates an unreasonable risk of harm. It is the failure to use that amount of care which a reasonably prudent person would use under like circumstances."

As emphasized earlier, with the status of the plaintiff an all-important consideration when defending against libel actions, *Gertz* took away some of the certainty editors and reporters had when deciding who might be categorized as a public figure. In *Gertz*, for example, the plaintiff was a well-known Chicago attorney who had been reasonably active in civic affairs. But the court reasoned that his reputation as a lawyer was not pervasive enough to stamp him as a public figure for all purposes and in this particular case, he had not thrust himself to the forefront of the controversy.

In another far-reaching case, in 1976 (*Time Inc.* v. *Firestone*), it became even more apparent that reporters and editors would have difficulty distinguishing between public figures and private individuals. The Supreme Court said that the wife of a prominent wealthy industrialist who held press conferences during the course of her divorce proceedings, who subscribed to a press clipping service to keep pace with articles written about her and who was well-known in Palm Beach, Fla., society was, for purposes of libel law, to be considered a private person.

In 1979 the U.S. Supreme Court continued its flow of conservative libel decisions that went against the media. The court said that to show that a defendant acted in reckless disregard for the truth, a libel plaintiff could probe the state of mind of the defendant and inquire into the "predecisional communications" between editors and reporters (*Herbert* v. *Lando*).

Justice White, who wrote the opinion for a six-member majority, said that courts have "traditionally admitted any direct or indirect evidence relevant to the state of mind of the defendant . . . necessary to defeat a conditional privilege or enhance damages." White said that he was aware of the First Amendment rights of the press but that the courts were obligated also to consider the individual's interest in his reputation.

Also in 1979 the court ruled that a man—a research director at a state mental hospital and an adjunct professor at a university—who had received hundreds of thousands of dollars in federal grant money was not, for libel purposes, a public figure (*Hutchinson* v. *Proxmire*). That same term the court held that persons engaged in criminal conduct do not automatically become public figures for purposes of libel law application (*Wolston* v. *Reader's Digest*).

As we have seen, the press has most protection when sued by either public officials or public figures; if the plaintiffs are so categorized, they must prove the defendant acted with actual malice to recover damages. When plaintiffs are private persons involved in events of public concern, in order to collect general damages, they must prove the defendant acted with negligence—a less stringent standard to meet. Reporters naturally do not want to become embroiled in libel suits. If they are, however, the chance of a successful defense is greater if the plaintiff is a public official or public figure.

This was apparent in the mid-1980s when well-financed public figure Ariel Sharon, former Israeli defense minister, was unable to collect damages from Time Inc., despite the fact that the jury said the paragraph in question was *false* and *defamatory*. The jury held for the magazine when it decided that *Time* had not acted with actual malice.

The Associated Press quoted Sharon's attorney, Milton Gould, who said: "The only thing we don't get is money, and the reason we don't get any money is that we're dealing with a peculiar law of actual malice which makes it almost impossible for a public figure to prove."

The AP also reported that the jury issued a statement saying that certain *Time* employees, even though they had not published the story in reckless disregard for the truth, had acted "negligently and carelessly in reporting and verifying the information which ultimately found its way" into the paragraph.

Both sides claimed victory, but one fact emerges: *Time* did not have to pay damages. The case illustrates that the protection flowing from the actual malice standard is considerable. Clearly, it is not enough for a public figure to show that a media defendant carelessly published a defamatory or false report—even when the report caused significant damage to reputation. The public person also must show that the defendant published the report knowing it to be false or with a high degree of awareness of probable falsity—a stringent standard to overcome.

ADVICE FOR REPORTERS

- **Be aggressive—but don't take foolish risks.** Fear of losing a libel suit most likely chills the reporting process. Denniston advised reporters not to take "foolish risks" but also not to be overly cautious. "Reporters should not compromise," he said. "Journalists must take chances when reporting stories. They have to be aggressive.

"Reporters should not consider legal ramifications as they gather information and as they write a story. They should go after the story and worry about the law later. It is a risk, but when reporters and editors operate on legal premise, they inhibit the reportorial processes.

"If reporters follow ethical restraints, they should be within legal bounds. Reporters shouldn't try to gauge in advance what will fly legally. They aren't equipped to think legally—they inhibit themselves too much."

- **Be fair—keep an open mind.** First Amendment scholar Marc A. Franklin of the Stanford Law School noted that reporting "involves substantial responsibility on the part of the journalist." He advised: "No reporter acts without a hypothesis. But that hypothesis must be open to change and modification continually. The reporter should not seek facts that support a strongly held hypothesis. Instead, reporters should seek as much information as will shed light on the situation. This requires an open mind, but not necessarily one that is unable to draw conclusions. If the reporter honestly concludes, after careful research and investigation, that the facts support a conclusion that is negative about someone—perhaps even defamatory—the reporter should lean over backwards to make sure that he or she has been reasonably careful in acquiring the facts and reasonably fair in considering them.

"Reporters should recognize that the fairness with which a story is published may go a long way in avoiding the filing of a lawsuit. Working to be fair does not compromise the reporter's integrity in any way whatsoever. The point is that many subjects of defamation, though obviously unhappy, will respond to fair treatment in an article.

"This kind of press behavior is in no way inconsistent with the notion of a strong, aggressive and inquiring media."

• **Seek advice if you are unsure of your turf.** Kaufman pointed out that legal rules are complex. "Reporters should take advantage of advice from legal counsel and from editors, and they should draw on what they learned in school," he said. "No matter how well advised you are or how much you know, though, you can't completely guarantee that you are going to avoid litigation. A claim always can be filed, even if it is not meritorious. In fact, it would probably be a negative thing if the focus of reporters was on trying to guarantee a 100 percent libel-proof story. The only way to guarantee that would be to make a story completely unoffensive to public people. I don't think that would be good for journalism or in the public interest. The best thing reporters can do is to be good journalists. That means be careful and hope that you have a good lawyer if it comes down to defending the story."

GUIDELINES FOR POTENTIAL LIBEL DEFENDANTS

Concern over libel actions is real enough that the New York State Newspapers Foundation, in its "Survival Kit for Reporters, Editors and Broadcasters," provided this advice for the potential defendant:

• **Be courteous and polite.** Nothing is gained by antagonizing the individual who claims to have been libeled.

• **Do not admit an error when a person initially claims that he or she has been libeled.** Take advantage of the complexity of the law. Even though you conceivably have libeled the individual, the wrong may not be sufficient to sustain a libel suit.

• **Agree to look into the matter.** If nothing else, this will get the caller to leave you alone at least temporarily.

• **If an attorney calls you about the potential libel, refer the call to your attorneys.** Libel law is full of traps for the unwary; do not assume that you can discuss a case on an attorney's turf. The attorney probably knows the territory; you do not.

• **Notify your editor or attorney at the first mention of libel.** Reporters should not attempt to resolve the problem without proper advice or counsel.

REPORTERS AND THEIR SOURCES

Reporters historically have guarded the identities of anonymous sources. It is theorized that once a reporter betrays a confidential source, the reporter's other anonymous contacts soon will vanish. Why, after all, would sources who wished to remain unnamed give information to reporters if the sources thought they might be betrayed?

Attorneys and police have turned with increasing frequency to reporters for information. The problem is real. To date, the U.S. Supreme Court has considered only one case that focuses on *journalists' privilege.* In 1972 the court held that the First Amendment does not provide a testimonial privilege to reporters who have witnessed a crime if they are called upon to testify during a criminal investigation (*Branzburg* v. *Hayes*).

THE *BRANZBURG* CASE

Paul Branzburg, a reporter for the *Courier-Journal* in Louisville, Ky., had witnessed illegal drug use and had written articles about it. He was subpoenaed and asked to testify before a grand jury. He refused, claiming a First Amendment privilege. Justice Byron White, who wrote the majority decision, when the case was reviewed by the Supreme Court, said that to contend that it is better to write about a crime than to do something about it is absurd. White's opinion, though not well received by the press, did provide some hope. He emphasized that official harassment of the press in an effort to disrupt the reporter's relationship with his or her sources would not be tolerated. White also said that states were free to implement statutory laws—*shield laws*—to protect reporters.

Justice Lewis F. Powell Jr., in a concurring opinion, attempted to put *Branzburg* in perspective. He said that the ruling was "limited"; courts still would be available to reporters who think that their First Amendment rights have been violated. Furthermore, he said the press could not be annexed as an "investigative right arm" of the government or judiciary, and if the requested testimony was "remote," news reporters could move to quash the subpoena. The information sought had to be relevant and go to the heart of the issue; it could not be a fishing expedition by the authorities.

George Killenberg, a professor of journalism at Southern Illinois University–Edwardsville, has emphasized the flexibility of *Branzburg;* though the decision went against the Louisville reporter, portions of the opinion did provide the rationale for lower courts to halt any blatant abuses of a reporter's First Amendment rights. Killenberg wrote in *Journalism Quarterly,* "Judicial developments have shown that *Branzburg* was not a death knell for press freedom."

Partly because of Justice Powell's carefully worded concurring opinion, a number of state and lower federal courts have upheld the right of news reporters to protect their sources under certain conditions. In other circumstances, however, several lower courts have not upheld the reporter's rights. Courts consider questions of testimonial privilege on a case-by-case basis.

SHIELD LAWS

Though the Supreme Court made it plain that the First Amendment would not provide absolute protection for journalists called to testify, it did leave the door open for states to pass laws that would shield reporters from testifying. More than half the states have done so. Some states have relatively stringent shield laws that provide a great deal of protection, whereas others have qualified shield laws. It is important to remember, however, that even the most stringent laws probably have some loopholes.

Nebraska has one of the country's more stringent laws. The Nebraska law is designed to ensure the free flow of news and other information to the public and to protect the reporter against direct or indirect governmental restraint or sanction. The statute states that "compelling such persons to disclose a source of information or to disclose unpublished information is contrary to the public interest and inhibits the free flow of information to the public." The law protects reporters from testifying before any federal or state judicial, legislative, executive or administrative body.

No matter how ironclad shield laws appear, however, they are subject to interpretation by the judiciary. The constitutionality of most shield laws never has been contested, and even if their constitutionality were upheld, hostile judicial interpretation could strip protection from the reporter. In essence, reporters never should make the assumption that the law always will keep them out of jail.

RESPONSIBILITY OF THE PRESS TO SOCIETY

Media critics constantly evaluate the role of the press as an American institution. Privately owned newspapers understandably have resisted any type of governmental control, but during recent decades critics of the press increasingly have called for codes of ethics and greater professionalism on the part of reporters.

Reporters must recognize that today's society expects them to behave responsibly. This expectation fits in with the "social responsibility" theory outlined by Theodore Peterson in "Four Theories of the Press," a book he wrote more than three decades ago with Wilbur Schramm and Fred S.

Siebert. Peterson wrote that "freedom carries concomitant obligations; and the press, which enjoys a privileged position under our government, is obliged to be responsible to society for carrying out certain essential functions of mass communications."

THEORIES OF PRESS SYSTEMS

Siebert, Peterson and Schramm grouped the press systems of the world under four headings: authoritarian, Soviet Communist (which, because of its inapplicability to the American system, will not be discussed here), libertarian and social responsibility.

THE AUTHORITARIAN SYSTEM

In an *authoritarian system*, which is the oldest of the four, criticism of the government is not tolerated. Although most newspapers are privately owned, their content is controlled by the state through licensing or the issuance of patents. If newspapers want to be unceremoniously shut down, they criticize the government. If newspapers want to stay in business, they print what the state wants them to print. Some colonial American newspaper editors went along with the system; they were content to publish innocuous newspapers that did not offend or check on the government. Other more courageous colonial American journalists sought to escape suppression under the authoritarian system.

THE LIBERTARIAN SYSTEM

As authoritarian controls on the press were resisted, the *libertarian system* developed. Under this philosophy, humans are rational thinking beings capable of separating truth from falsehood, good from evil. Thus, newspapers must provide information on a variety of topics—particularly government—so that citizens are in a position to make enlightened decisions. This romantic concept flourished during the early 1800s and has continued into this century.

As might have been expected, the libertarian philosophy opened the door for unscrupulous reporters to be blatantly irresponsible. Some 19th-century American newspapers were particularly vicious. They were, however, regarded as the primary instrument for checking on the government and its officials.

SOCIAL RESPONSIBILITY THEORY

In reaction to perceived press shortcomings under the libertarian system, the Commission on Freedom of the Press was formed shortly after World War II. Made up of scholars and philosophers, it was particularly concerned about the shrinking newspaper marketplace (the number of daily newspapers had been declining since shortly after the turn of the century) and the accompanying loss of potential philosophies. The commission said that the press should exercise more responsibility; it should make a concerted effort to discuss divergent views, even if the views were not compatible with those of management. The commission said that it was the responsibility of the press not only to present diverse viewpoints but also to interpret them responsibly.

What has been labeled the *social responsibility theory* of the press emerged from the commission's report. According to this philosophy, everyone who wants to express views should be given access to the press, which is bound by professional ethics. Community opinion helps to keep the press in check. And if the press fails to live up to its obligations of social responsibility, the government can step in to ensure public service.

In exploring the evolution of the social responsibility theory, Peterson wrote:

> A rather considerable fraction of articulate Americans began to demand certain standards of performance from the press. . . . Chiefly of their own volition, publishers began to link responsibility with freedom. They formulated codes of ethical behavior, and they operated their media with some concern for the public good—the public good as they regarded it, at least.

Today's reporters, then, find themselves working in a libertarian system that is making increasingly strong demands for journalistic responsibility. The challenge is formidable.

The courts, however, have not been willing to impose a responsibility standard on the press. In 1974 Chief Justice Warren Burger wrote in a court opinion: "A responsible press is an undoubtedly desirable goal, but press responsibility is not mandated by the Constitution and like so many virtues it cannot be legislated. . . . A newspaper is more than a passive receptacle or conduit for news, comment and advertising. The choice of material to go into a newspaper . . . constitutes the exercise of editorial control and judgment."

AN INCREASE IN PRESS CRITICISM

Americans have grown increasingly outspoken in their criticism of perceived media irresponsibility. A national opinion poll conducted at the beginning of this decade by the Public Agenda Foundation showed that the majority of Americans surveyed support laws requiring fairness in newspaper coverage of controversial stories or political races.

The message to the media is clear: Society is demanding responsibility. In an article published in *Editor & Publisher*, pollster George Gallup wrote: "The press in America is operating in an environment of public opinion that is increasingly indifferent—and to some extent hostile—to the cause of a free press in America."

LAW AND ETHICS

Many Americans feel that journalists should exercise greater restraint in choosing the stories to publish or to air. A Gallup poll showed that Americans think the media "exaggerate the news in the interest of making headlines and selling newspapers," and that the media "rush to print without first making sure all facts are correct."

THE PRESS RESPONDS

Many newspapers have looked inward to determine, address and find solutions to the shortcomings for which they have been criticized. Some have appointed *ombudsmen* to see that readers' complaints are acted upon. An ombudsman is a "middle person"—a theoretically objective employee of the newspaper—who listens to complaints from readers and, when they are justified, passes them on to the appropriate reporters or editors. A few metropolitan newspapers, such as the *Los Angeles Times*, have hired *press critics*—reporters who write stories about the strengths, weaknesses and trends of daily media coverage.

THE PRESS CRITIC

David Shaw, national press reporter, has been media critic for the *Times* since 1974. *Times* editor William H. Thomas asked Shaw, who then was a general assignment reporter, to write in "exhaustive fashion" about the American press and the *Times*. Shaw was somewhat unsure of his turf.

But Thomas quickly cleared the air. In his book, "Journalism Today," Shaw wrote that Thomas told him that "the one thing the press covers more poorly today than anything else is the press." Shaw paraphrased Thomas: "We don't tell our readers what we do or how we do it. We don't admit our mistakes unless we're virtually forced to under threat of court action or public embarrassment. We make no attempt to explain our problems, our decisions, our fallibilities, our procedures." Thomas wanted the press critic to confront these issues directly.

Shaw wrote that his job was unique—he was to function neither as beat reporter nor ombudsman. Thomas wanted him "to provide long, thoughtful overviews on broad issues confronting the press today, to analyze, criticize and make value judgments, to treat my own newspaper as I would any other."

Shaw's pieces are not always greeted with enthusiasm by fellow journalists who come under scrutiny, but the *Times* has been a pacesetter in media introspection.

THE OMBUDSMAN

The Washington Post has been a leader in the use of ombudsmen. Most newspapers that have ombudsmen instruct reporters and editors to respond to, not ignore, complaints or suggestions forwarded by the ombudsman. These responses take several forms—argument, agreement, disagreement, rebuttal, frustration or even anger—but the reporters and editors must respond to the independent positions of the ombudsman. To establish rapport with and gain respect from these reporters and editors, each ombudsman must be scrupulously fair and unbiased. It is not an easy job.

The *Post* created the position in 1970—one year after *The Courier-Journal* in Louisville, Ky., did. Today about two-dozen dailies have full-time ombudsmen.

Robert J. McCloskey, a retired ambassador who for 10 years was the State Department's press spokesman, served as an ombudsman at the *Post* in the early 1980s. According to McCloskey, an ombudsman can funnel complaints primarily in three ways: (1) go directly to the editor or reporter involved, say that an issue has been raised that should be considered and pose a possible solution; (2) write memos, which are distributed to senior editors and the publisher, outlining complaints and possible solutions; or (3) write a column outlining shortcomings and posing solutions. The column is published.

THE ETHICS OF JOURNALISM

Professors John Merrill of Louisiana State University and Ralph D. Barney of Brigham Young University, noting that journalistic ethics had received scant attention in the literature between the 1930s and the early 1970s, decided to edit a book of readings that they titled "Ethics and the Press." The book, published in 1975, featured a variety of ethical topics.

Merrill said the resurging interest in journalistic ethics at that time was the result of people becoming increasingly critical of press excesses such as leak journalism—where anonymous sources provide presumably confidential information to reporters. "A better informed, more critical, more skeptical population began to question many of the things the press does," Merrill said. "Before this time, the general public was more or less naive and trusting of the press."

Merrill put the issue of journalistic ethics in perspective in another of his books, "The Imperative of Freedom." He wrote:

> Ethics is that branch of philosophy that helps journalists determine what is right to do in their journalism; it is very much a normative science of conduct. Ethics has to do with "self-legislation" and "self-enforcement"; although it is, of course, related to law, it is of a different nature. Although law quite often stems from the ethical values of a society at a certain time (i.e., law is often reflective of ethics), law is something that is socially determined and socially enforced. Ethics, on the other hand, is personally determined and personally enforced—or should be. Ethics should provide the journalist certain basic principles

or standards by which he can judge actions to be right or wrong, good or bad, responsible or irresponsible.

It has always been difficult to discuss ethics; law is much easier, for what is legal is a matter of law. What is ethical transcends law, for many actions are legal, but not ethical. And there are no "ethical codebooks" to consult in order to settle ethical disputes. Ethics is primarily personal; law is primarily social. Even though the area of journalistic ethics is swampy and firm footing is difficult . . . , there are solid spots which the person may use in his trek across the difficult landscape of life.

First of all, it is well to establish that ethics deals with voluntary actions. If a journalist has no control over his decisions or actions, then there is no need to talk of ethics. What are voluntary actions? Those which a journalist could have done differently had he wished. Sometimes journalists, like others, try to excuse their wrong actions by saying that these actions were not personally chosen but assigned to them—or otherwise forced on them—by editors or other superiors. Such coercion may indeed occur in some situations (such as a dictatorial press system) where the consequences to the journalist going against an order may be dire. But for an American journalist not to be able to "will" his journalistic actions—at least at the present time—is unthinkable; if he says that he is not able and that he "has to" do this-or-that, he is only exhibiting his ethical weaknesses and inauthenticity.

The journalist who is concerned with ethics—with the quality of his actions—is, of course, one who wishes to be virtuous.

Merrill once said that there often is no general agreement on what is right or what is wrong. "It always boils down to an individual journalistic concept," he said. "In life, if the journalist believes anything goes to get a story—that the ends justify the means—he will apply that concept in journalism. Some people, for example, believe that it is ethical to surreptitiously tape an interview; this is a personal belief, a belief the person came to on his own. There are others, however, who believe that it is dishonest because it is not being frank or forthright with the source. Ultimately, it boils down to personal ethics—personal values applied to the work of journalism."

CODES OF ETHICS

As the growing concern about media ethics and responsibility gathered steam in the 1970s, The Associated Press Managing Editors Association; the American Society of Newspaper Editors; the Society of Professional Journalists, Sigma Delta Chi; the National Conference of Editorial Writers; and The Associated Press Sports Editors were among groups that revised existing codes. The American Society of Newspaper Editors Statement of

Principles, for example, was adopted in 1975. It replaced a code of ethics that was about a half-century old.

The *codes of ethics* developed by national groups that sincerely wished to strengthen the profession were broad statements of principle. However, Merrill wrote in "Existential Journalism": "Acting journalistically is the main thing; having a theory about journalism is another, and of much lesser import. A code of ethics hanging on the wall is meaningless; a code of ethics internalized within the journalist and guiding his actions is what is meaningful."

Merrill said he did not know how helpful a code of ethics drawn up by a committee could be. "The codes do indicate a desire on the part of organizations to be ethical—whatever that means to them," Merrill said. "But ethics always boils right back to the individual. Ethical values are acquired all through life from a number of sources, such as church, family and friends. Reporters can't separate the ethics of journalism from the values they hold as individuals."

Although individual journalists need to assume personal responsibility for ethical decisions they make, it is important to examine codes of ethics that have been structured by various media organizations.

Examples of codes are in Appendix C.

THE ISSUE OF ENFORCEMENT

The formulation and updating of codes show an awareness by individual newspapers that ethical matters are a growing concern. A former managing editor of the no-longer-published *Washington Star*, however, contended that most codes "share a weakness—they are toothless." Charles B. Seib wrote in *Presstime*:

> My belief that codes of ethics are of limited value is based on examination of a number of codes and my own experience. I have come to the conclusion that while codes have some use as broad statements of standards and as prior restraints on disgraceful conduct and bases for action in response to such conduct, their natural resting place is the back of the desk drawer.

Casey Bukro, environment writer for the *Chicago Tribune* and head of the Society of Professional Journalists, Sigma Delta Chi, Ethics Committee, wrote in the 1985–86 journalism ethics report: "The Society of Professional Journalists has turned wimpish toward its code of ethical standards, adopted in 1973."

Bukro wrote that "the society still cannot say whether its members or chapters honor the code in a meaningful way, though compliance is a condition of membership."

No matter how transparent some codes are, they do represent legitimate attempts by the industry to police its own ranks. The codes often are helpful—particularly to the working reporter—but journalists regularly are confronted with ethical and moral dilemmas that must be reacted to on a case-by-case basis.

ETHICAL ISSUES

Do reporters adhere to the same stringent ethical standards for which they hold public officials accountable? Journalists are trained to report the first hint of governmental impropriety. Government officials, after all, have a responsibility to their constituents. Reporters should remember, however, that they too have a responsibility to their readers. Should reporters:

- Jump at the chance for free movie tickets?
- Stock personal libraries with review books sent out by publishers?
- Look forward to gulping down free liquor from friendly sources?
- Expect—and accept—small favors in return for complimentary stories?

Though the acceptance of "freebies" often is the first thing that comes to mind when discussing media ethics, dilemmas faced by journalists sometimes are considerably more complicated.

Nearly 100 editors of daily newspapers across America responded to a survey that explored their opinions about and their handling of ethical dilemmas. Among other things, editors were asked to discuss what they considered to be the most pressing ethical issues facing journalists today. A synthesis of their responses results in the following list:

- Fairness and objectivity
- Reporter misrepresentation
- Privacy rights vs. the public's right to know
- Conflicts of interest
- Anonymous sources
- "Freebies"
- Ticklish times: When compassion collides with policy

FAIRNESS AND OBJECTIVITY

Approximately one-fourth of the editors listed the quest for fairness and objectivity as being the most pressing ethical issue facing journalists today. This concern far outdistanced the others.

Gilbert M. Savery, the managing editor of the *Lincoln* (Neb.) *Journal*, explored the issue in some detail. He wrote:

> To answer the question of what I would consider to be the most pressing ethical issues facing reporters and editors today, I have to ask: "What is unethical and why should it be avoided?"
>
> Presumably when reporters or editors accept favors of magnitude, they are beholden to the donor. The question then arises as to whether that donor or his personal or corporate interests will be given more favorable treatment than other persons, businesses or institutions.
>
> Ethics, under this interpretation, translates into fairness. Therefore, the major ethical issues facing journalists today are those dealing with fair and balanced treatments of all viewpoints expressed on such issues as abortion, nuclear arms, nuclear power, a host of national issues including fiscal policy, education, religion and economics.

Journalistically, the challenge is to deliver to readers, listeners and viewers a fair and balanced representation of viewpoints held by persons who differ markedly in their perceptions of what public policy should be.

Mitch Kehetian, managing editor of *The Macomb Daily* in Michigan, said he "cringed at some of the holes in so-called in-depth stories and the famous: 'could not be reached for comment.'" He said he worried about editors who allow the phrase "according to sources" to dominate stories. "We continue to hide behind the 'we were on deadline' excuse," Kehetian said. "That doesn't go with me. In essence: accuracy, credibility and fairness rank uppermost with me in pressing ethical issues."

Professor Merrill of Louisiana State University, who has written extensively in the area of journalistic ethics, wrote in *Journalism Quarterly* that acceptance of the assumption that "objective reporting is ethical reporting" raises interesting questions. He said such acceptance would "mean that a journalist who was objective—or tried diligently to be objective—could forget about additional ethical decisions per se; for the journalist would have already entered the ethical field simply by applying technique. In short, the journalist accepting objective reporting-is-ethics as a valid concept would have to concentrate on the technique of being objective, thereby satisfying any journalistic ethical demands which might be placed upon him."

Merrill pointed out, however, that the terms *objectivity* and *ethics* "are filled with semantic noise, and when they are brought together in tandem in this objectivity-as-ethics sense, the abstractness is greatly increased." Merrill wrote that we are "immediately aware of the intriguing question as to the possibility of ever reaching 'objective' news coverage" because of the many variables that go into story selection, writing and presentation.

REPORTER MISREPRESENTATION

Should reporters misrepresent themselves when working on stories? Yes? No? Sometimes? According to editors who responded to the survey, this is a major ethical issue facing journalists today.

Tim Harmon, managing editor of *The Journal-Gazette,* Fort Wayne, Ind., said he saw ethical problems in misrepresentation tactics "and any of the various other ways journalists foster the stereotype of the callous, get-the-story-at-any-price reporter or editor." Harmon said journalists "don't put enough thought into how we get the information for our stories or whether we should use all of it."

Tim Wood, managing editor of *The Weatherford* (Texas) *Democrat,* emphasized the care reporters must take to be open with sources. "Reporters must clearly identify themselves as reporters when they contact a source and make it clear that anything the source says may end up in the newspaper," he wrote. "Anyone being interviewed for publication must be aware of the purpose of the interview. Even asking vague questions without revealing the context in which the answers will be put is a practice that borders on being unethical. Sources should not be surprised when the story appears in print."

James E. Shelledy, editor of the *Idahonian* in Moscow, Idaho, noted that it is important for reporters to allow subjects to respond "to the thrust of the story." He said, "We often seek responses to a specific question which would be answered somewhat differently if the thrust of the story were known." Shelledy said he considered this issue to be part of the broader concern of reporter misrepresentation.

An example of reporter misrepresentation occurred in Chicago when *Sun-Times* reporters grew frustrated when gathering information for a story focusing on corruption in small business. They reasoned that because small businessmen were hesitant to talk about extortion and payoffs to ensure protection, the best way to write the story would be to start a small business. The newspaper bought a tavern and renamed it the Mirage. *Sun-Times* reporters worked as tavern employees. A revealing story of city inspector payoffs was written. The story was significant—one that should have been told.

Critics, though, questioned the reporting method. Had the newspaper gone too far?

Many editors do not allow this type of investigative journalism at their newspapers—ever. They view undercover journalism as a form of entrapment.

David Shaw, after conducting a non-random survey of reporters across the country, wrote in the *Los Angeles Times*: "Most journalists argue that it is unethical for a reporter to pretend he is not a reporter—or to fail to identify himself as a reporter—when interviewing someone."

The fact remains, however, at some metropolitan newspapers undercover journalism occasionally is practiced. Generally, it is only after editors and reporters have concluded that the story is extremely significant and that there would be no other means of obtaining it. Many journalists widely criticize undercover journalism, whereas others view it as a necessary means of gathering information, particularly when criminal activity is being investigated. In those situations, some newspaper editors and reporters contend that the ends justify the means.

The *Lincoln Journal*'s Savery said that, in general, he is opposed to journalists misrepresenting themselves to get a news story. "Yet I would never say 'never,'" he said. "Such techniques should be used only when all normal channels of information gathering are closed and when the information sought is of such overriding public importance that failure to get it would permit continuation of inhumane practices or fraudulent public acts."

Certainly, most editors and reporters realize that purposeful misrepresentation to gain information should be considered only as a last resort, if ever.

PRIVACY RIGHTS VS. THE PUBLIC'S RIGHT TO KNOW

We all have seen the scenes on television or read the stories in the newspaper: A man has just died in a traffic accident caused by a drunken driver. The victim's widow, barely able to compose herself, is confronted by reporters who want to know how she feels and whether there should be stiffer sentences for those found guilty of driving while intoxicated.

To what extent should reporters invade the privacy of people in an effort to get a story? Wickliffe R. Powell, the managing editor of *The Daily Independent* in Ashland, Ky., said he thinks the dilemma is most sensitive when seeking interviews with "people who are thrust into the public eye due to circumstances beyond their own control."

Does the public always have a right to know?

Rod Deckert, managing editor of the *Missoulian*, in Missoula, Mont., was confronted with such a problem. His dilemma was explored in a *Quill* article by Jack Hart and Janis Johnson.

When a 21-year-old Missoula native was stabbed to death on the streets of Washington, D.C., the *Missoulian* carried the story on the front page. At the time, the circumstances of the death were not known. Most of the community remembered the girl as a model student, member of the All-State Orchestra, recipient of a scholarship to Radcliffe (though she dropped out in her freshman year) and member of a respected local family.

Shortly after the death, *The Washington Post* carried a front-page story that described the girl as a "$50-a-trick prostitute" who had worked the city's streets. Editors and reporters undoubtedly handled the story carefully, but they probably lost little sleep in deciding whether to publish it. *Missoulian* editors were alerted to the *Post*'s story; because the article was to be distributed by the *Post*'s news service, it was apparent that its contents soon would filter to Missoula.

Should the *Missoulian* carry the story? The girl's mother and father pleaded that the story not be run. The girl, an honors graduate of a local high school was, after all, more than a name in a news story. She was a real person who had hundreds of friends and acquaintances in Missoula. What purpose would the story serve? She was dead. Her family was hurt.

But did the newspaper have a responsibility to its readers—to parents of local teen-age girls? When Deckert discovered that the girl had been recruited out of a Missoula bar by an East Coast pimp, he decided to publish the story. *Missoulian* editors deleted the "$50-a-trick prostitute" description and carried the article on an inside page. Despite efforts to humanize the story as much as possible, editors and reporters at the *Missoulian* were struck by a torrent of adverse public opinion. Why did the paper print such "garbage"? What good did it do now? Had the newspaper no ethical standards?

What do you think?

CONFLICTS OF INTEREST

Mike Foley, managing editor of the *St. Petersburg* (Fla.) *Times*, sees conflicts of interest as a major ethical issue facing journalists. Foley said that these conflicts—real or perceived—can involve such things as club memberships, friendships or even a spouse's political involvements.

These potential conflicts cover a variety of areas.

Harry J. Reed, editor of the *Jackson* (Mich.) *Citizen-Patriot* recalled the time, at another newspaper, when a reporter called a business and said she no longer would give them her personal business because of the position the owner had taken on a political issue. "The reporter's primary job was writing business news, and the owner she alienated was one she had to contact for news," Reed said. "I fired the reporter for compromising herself and the newspaper for personal reasons. The newspaper guild grieved it, I denied the grievance, they took it to arbitration and my action was upheld."

Thomas Nielson, executive news editor of *The News & Courier* in Charleston, S.C., noted that one of his reporters "took payment for freelancing in a competing magazine-type publication in our immediate circulation area." He said the "reporter didn't agree with our policy prohibiting such action and refused to stop." The reporter was fired.

Reporters and editors cannot be expected to live like hermits and to develop no friendships. But friendships can pose potential problems. Arthur C. Gorlick, assistant managing editor of the *Seattle Post-Intelligencer*, called it "cronyism." He said: "It seems manifested in many ways at various levels of news organizations. Reporters, editors and publishers establish friendships with many of the people involved with things news organizations are expected to report about fairly. It is difficult for reporters or editors to maintain the impression of being impartial in a news report about a legislator if they have been socializing the previous evening or have a weekend golf date. It is difficult for journalists to function easily in reporting about a business leader knowing the publisher has invited the business leader to join on the board of a civic fund-raising effort, however good the cause."

Reporters also can feel an ethical squeeze when they are asked by organizations to which they belong to write newsletters for the groups. Media policies vary on the level of outside involvement its reporters and editors can have. New reporters should familiarize themselves with the ethics codes of organizations for which they work.

ANONYMOUS SOURCES

"The anonymous source—its use or misuse—is an issue of growing concern for us and other newspapers, particularly as it relates to the issue of newspaper credibility and public confidence in the media," said William T. Newill, editor of the *Burlington* (N.J.) *County Times*. "There are times when it is absolutely necessary to guarantee anonymity in exchange for vital information. But the process has been abused by politicians and reporters up and down the system to the point where readers must certainly believe that the anonymous sources quoted in so many stories are none other than the reporters themselves. And who can blame our readers for thinking that way?"

A national survey of daily newspaper managing editors that was reported in *Journalism Quarterly* in the early 1980s found that more than four-fifths of the editors said their newspapers had published staff-written articles based on unnamed sources. The survey also found that a majority of the editors felt that the press generally overuses unidentified sources in stories, that the use of unnamed sources leads to more distortion or hyperbolic statements in stories and that newspaper editors in the future will scrutinize stories that rely on unnamed sources more carefully.

Newspaper policies on the use of unnamed sources vary, but most prohibit publication of material in which sources are not shared with at least one key editor. A sampling of policies and an extended discussion of the use of anonymous sources can be found in Chapter 5.

"FREEBIES"

Presumably all editors and reporters agree that it is unethical to accept any gift of value from a news source. Some editors contend that it is unethical to accept any gifts—period. There are, however, some gray areas.

Tim Wood of *The Weatherford Democrat* said: "Accepting gifts usually is a judgment call. For example, several organizations bring food to our office during the holiday season. Is it unethical to accept this food? The food has little monetary value. Turning it down could be interpreted as an insult. The people who give us the food don't expect anything in return. However, if an organization wanted to treat the staff to a nice dinner at a local restaurant, that would be a different matter."

Many of the national and individual newspaper codes deal with the matter of gifts. The code of the Society of Professional Journalists says "nothing of value should be accepted." The Associated Press Sports Editors' code says: "Gifts of insignificant value—a calendar, pencil, key chain or such—may be accepted if it would be awkward to refuse or return them. All other gifts should be declined. A gift that exceeds token value should be returned immediately with an explanation that it is against policy. If it is impractical to return it, the gift should be donated to a charity by your company." *The Washington Post*'s code says: "We accept no gifts from news sources. Exceptions are minimal (tickets to cultural events to be reviewed) or obvious (invitations to meals). Occasionally, other exceptions might qualify. If in doubt, consult the executive editor or the managing editor or his deputy."

Codes also often address the matter of free travel. The code of the *Chicago Sun-Times* says: "As a general principle, we will continue to pay for all travel. If an exception is required, a decision will be made on the merits of each case, with the understanding that conditions of any free travel are to be fully explained in connection with the subsequent news coverage."

The issue of free travel usually surfaces in sports departments. The AP Sports Editors' code addresses this question: "The basic aim for members of this organization and their staffs is a pay-your-own-way standard. It is acceptable to travel on charter flights operated by teams and organizations, but the newspaper should insist on being billed."

Brian Walker, managing editor–news of *The Muncie Evening Press*, said the issue of freebies—travel more often than gifts—is the most discussed ethical issue at his newspaper. "The matter is hotly debated here and both

LAW AND ETHICS

sides remain unmoved by one another's arguments," he said. "The company has not forbidden travel, and, although at one time there was a rule against accepting any gift that could not be eaten in one sitting, that issue has come up seldom in recent years. Of course, if acceptance of gifts or travel affected or appeared to affect someone's news judgment, it would become a very serious matter."

The *Lincoln Journal*'s Savery said, "Ethical journalists are not influenced by free lunches or minor extensions of courtesy, yet we are better off paying our own way and discouraging these kinds of gifts."

TICKLISH TIMES: WHEN COMPASSION COLLIDES WITH POLICY

Reporters and editors of smaller dailies and weeklies are most likely to encounter those ticklish, awkward day-to-day situations when a subscriber, an acquaintance or a friend walks in the front door of the newsroom and asks, for example, that his name be kept out of the court news.

Most journalists have been threatened with, "Do you want to be responsible for the consequences if you print this story?" The threats occur with frequency, but even veteran reporters never grow completely calloused to them.

It is not uncommon for court reporters—particularly those who work for smaller newspapers—to be confronted by people charged with criminal offenses. One would be surprised at how many of them have relatives with heart trouble or other medical problems—conditions that would quickly worsen if a story were published. Most reporters have received telephone calls from ministers, Boy Scout leaders or other community leaders urging that a drunken-driving story not be printed because of the disastrous effects such a story would have on the family of the accused. Sometimes, policies are in place to handle such matters. Other times, reporters or editors must make individual decisions.

"The real ethical issues are the hard choices faced in reporting day-to-day news," said Bill Williams, editor of *The Paris* (Tenn.) *Post-Intelligencer*. "Do I publish the name of the rape victim? Do I wait until the defendant appears in court before publishing news of his arrest? Do I allow the mayor to provide information off the record? Does my birth column list illegitimate children?"

Williams told of an incident that occurred at his newspaper. It illustrates that, particularly in small-town journalism, an editor sometimes is darned if he does and darned if he doesn't.

"The child of divorced parents won an honor," he said. "The mother reported the information, and we identified the child with her mother's name. The father called to object, said he was proud of the kid, too, even though the mother had custody, and he wanted to be identified as father. So we ran a correction. The mother stormed in [subscribers don't have to get by security guards at small dailies and weeklies], said the father was a louse who had forfeited any claim. The child had subsequently been adopted by the stepfather, she said, and he should be identified as the father. I agreed with her that the guy was a louse, but I said he was still the biological father and we didn't see we had any choice. She slapped me in the face and stalked out. That's how I 'solved' the issue."

T. J. Hemlinger, editor of the *Hartford City* (Ind.) *News-Times*, said that, at his small-town (population: 7,600) newspaper, staffers don't face some of the ethical problems encountered by larger newspapers. "'Free travel' [for us] means riding a bus to the state capital with the Farm Bureau members to attend the state convention. Our ethics questions are: Should we run a picture of a suicide victim covered by a sheet, or a picture of someone injured in a traffic accident? Should we run a picture of a woman who probably is mentally ill as she goes into court to face charges of murdering her 9-month-old infant? My answers all are 'yes,' by the way."

Thad Poulson, editor of the *Daily Sitka Sentinel* in Alaska, said: "We are regularly asked, by acquaintances and strangers alike, to 'keep my name out of the paper' in connection with the police news we publish. We often would prefer to comply, but we never do. Everyone on the staff, editorial and in other departments, knows that exceptions cannot be made even for them."

Policies often provide ironclad guidance for journalists, but is it clear that sometimes difficult decisions must be made on the spot. As Professor Merrill pointed out, ethics involves personal values. Journalists must decide what, under the circumstances, is the correct course of action.

"A SWAMPLAND OF PHILOSOPHICAL SPECULATION"

Clearly, there are no sure-fire answers to many of the ethical concerns that regularly confront journalists. As Professor Merrill noted, "Ethics has to do with 'self-legislation' and 'self-enforcement.'" Merrill vividly summarized the issue of ethics and journalism in his book, "The Imperative of Freedom": "When we enter the area of journalistic ethics, we pass into a swampland of philosophical speculation where eerie mists of judgment hang low over a boggy terrain. In spite of the unsure footing and poor visibility, there is no reason not to make the journey. In fact, it is a journey well worth taking for it brings the matter of morality to the individual person; it forces the journalist, among others, to consider his basic principles, his values, his obligations to himself and to others. It forces him to decide for himself how he will live, how he will conduct his journalistic affairs, how he will think of himself and of others, how he will think, act and react to the people and issues surrounding him.

"Ethics has to do with duty—duty to self and/or duty to others. It is primarily individual or personal even when it relates to obligations and duties to others."

Journalists bear an awesome responsibility to themselves and to their audience; this they should never forget.

Appendix A
STORY PROCESSING

Before a story is given to an editor, the reporter must copy edit it to make certain that there are no writing, grammatical, style, spelling, usage or typographical errors. Some reporters still write hard copy. That means they compose their stories on typewriters rather than computers (video display terminals). In these cases, they "clean" their copy with a pencil, using standard copy editing symbols. At most newspapers, however, reporters compose their stories on VDTs, which have eliminated paper and editing with a pencil.

VIDEO DISPLAY TERMINALS

Twenty years ago, everything in the newsroom was done on paper. Reporters put copy paper in their typewriters and pounded out a story. The story was sent to the copy desk, where it was edited by a copy editor with a heavy, black pencil. The editor also wrote a headline for the story by inserting a head sheet in a typewriter. Then the story was sent to the composing room, where a printer at a Linotype or other typesetting machine "set the story." Then a proofreader backread a proof of the story to make certain it was set the way the editors wanted and that it was free of typos—typographical errors.

Newspaper newsrooms were computerized in the 1970s, however, and the typewriters, editing pencils, glue pots and typesetting machines became relics. Video display terminals took their places, and with the new technology came profound changes in how stories were processed. Journalists became reporters, editors, typesetters and proofreaders. Stories could move from idea to reality to type by keystrokes on a VDT.

There are many different computer systems in today's newsrooms. Because the technology continues to change so rapidly, many newsrooms are finding that the equipment they bought several years ago is outdated. The VDT of 10 years ago, an electronic keyboard attached to a television tube, was a machine that cost thousands of dollars. It was big and complicated.

Journalists who always had used typewriters had to attend training sessions to figure out how the things worked.

Today's VDT can be a hand-held machine that costs hundreds of dollars. Most VDTs are user friendly, which means little training is required to use them. Because there is so much available, newsrooms now can be designed around software, the programs that run computers, and hardware, the physical components of the machines themselves. Much of the work done at a newspaper now can be done on portable computers in remote locations or even from reporters' and editors' homes.

EDITING

COPY EDITING SYMBOLS

Because most news stories now are written on VDTs, reporters also can do their editing on a screen. They do not need to mark symbols on paper. They merely move their cursor, the flashing light on the screen, then make the necessary changes. Paragraphs can be moved, sentences eliminated or new words inserted simply by using the correct keys on the keyboard.

Where paper is still being used, writers must use a standard set of copy editing symbols to clean their copy. These symbols, which can be used in newsrooms everywhere, are an effective means of communication between reporters and editors and between the newsroom and composing room. The most common symbols include:

New paragraph:
⌐

⌐A Wheeling woman missing for

more than a week was found

unharmed Thursday in a Seat-

tle hotel.

Capitalize the letter or letters:
F̲

Elena Delgado, of 2323 W. fifth

ave., was found after she used a

credit card to rent the room,

police said.

APPENDIX A STORY PROCESSING 335

Make the letter or letters lowercase:

/

Wheeling *P*olice Sgt. Gary Gollwitzer said Delg*AD*o went to Seattle "on her own accord."

Insert a hyphen:

-‌
∧

Gollwitzer said he is happy the eight-day search has ended.

Insert a dash:

--
∧

The search, conducted by police in three states, began when Delgado's invalid mother reported her missing on Nov. 8.

Run together the copy:

⌒

"She caused a lot of worry in her family," Gollwitzer said.

Insert a letter, a word, words or punctuation. (Usually accompanied with a caret or circle): ⌄ ∧ ⊙

"We're always afraid that cases like *this* can end tragically."

Delete letters, punctuation or figures and don't close the space:

/

Besides/ 155 officers from Wheeling, police in Montana and Washington hunted for/ Delgado after she was reported seen in those states.

Delete the letter or letters and close the space (arc above and below):	"She led us on quite a chase," Gollwitzer said. "No one knew she was doing this on her own accord."
Let the copy stand as orginally written: *stet*	When she was found in the hotel, she told police "~~she just wanted to get away;~~" Gollwitzer said. (stet) (stet)
The copy is correct as written: CQ	Lt. Jon Smyth of the Seattle Police Department concurred that Delgado left Wheeling on her own accord. (CQ)
Delete the word and leave a space (arc above only):	"A lot of people come to Seattle because ~~because~~ they are fed up with their situations," Smyth said.
Make a space: #	"I'm never surprised when we find someone here."
Transpose letters, words or phrases:	Delgado's had mother reported that she had bene kidnapped, Gollwitzer said.

APPENDIX A   STORY PROCESSING

Spell out, abbreviate or use numerals. A circle means that the copy should conform to correct newspaper style:

◯

End mark. The story is complete:

㉚

"Her mother is ⓢeventy-nine years old and she has been an invalid for ⑨ years, the ⓢgt. said. "Her daughter just wanted to get away."

Gollwitzer said no charges would be filed against Delgado.

㉚

EXAMPLE OF AN EDITED STORY

Here is an example of a copy edited story. It illustrates the typical editing that a story goes through from the time it leaves the typewriter to when it is set into type. The story was cleaned up by the reporter before it went to the city editor. The city editor worked on it before it went to the copy editor. The copy editor gave it the final editing and sent it to the composing room.

After 10 years of neglect, the university's women's dorms and men's dorms are getting a much needed facelift.

Dr. Lee Cowherd, director of residential life, said a 15 percent room and board rate increase will fund the changes.

"It looks like a hospital," remarked a number of residents of Beste Hall.

Student reactions have been generally favorable, although most students who live in the dorms would like to see more done.

Beste Hall resident Danny Morris said that the changes have been gradual. "The biggest improvement has been the mirrors in the bathrooms," he said.

Rosemarie Ortega (CQ), a sophomore and Wilson Hall resident, said, "I don't like the way our heater works. It's always too warm in our room. I wish they'd do something about that."

WRITING THE NEWS

The work includes
Painted ceilings and hallways, full-length mirrors in Beste and Wilson Hall rooms and florescent lighting in the Wilson Hall hallways. ~~are just a small sampling of the work being done to update the condition of the dorms. According to~~ Dr. Sharon Ashton, vice president and dean of student services, said the improvements have been planned for six years but have not been done because of funding problems.

"With the exception of the lounge areas," ~~said Dr. Ashton,~~ Ashton said, "there have not been major changes in six years. The bathroom fixtures have been there since the dorms were built."

~~Dr. Lee~~ Cowherd, ~~director of residential life,~~ said he is happy to see the improvements. ~~"I'm happy to see the improvements," he said.~~

"In the next month or so we hope to replace sink fixtures and we'll be looking more at the lighting," ~~Cowherd~~ he said. "Presently we're working out a plan to determine what we're going to be doing when."

"These improvements are just the beginning of what we hope to do," ~~Cowherd~~ added.

~~Cowherd said a 15 per cent room and board increase will fund the changes.~~

OTHER EDITING SUGGESTIONS

Copy editing is more than putting in the correct marks. It also is making sure that the story is readable, accurate, fair and worthy of publication. When editing copy, always ask yourself:

- Is the lead appropriate and concise?
- Does it make sense?
- Does it contain all essential information?
- Are the transitions logical?
- Is there enough attribution?
- Does the story contain superfluous words or phrases?

APPENDIX A STORY PROCESSING

- Is it free of clichés, double meanings and redundancies?
- Are there grammatical, punctuation or spelling problems?
- Are there possible legal ramifications?

Here are some additional guidelines to follow when editing copy:

- **Use a pencil.** The temptation always exists to edit with a pen, particularly when working with cheap paper, but because erasing often is necessary, editing should be done with a pencil.

- **Make straight lines through deleted passages.** Don't scratch out the copy with bold strokes of the pencil. If the copy needs to be reinstated, the editor should be able to simply mark "stet" in the margin. That enables the typesetter to follow the original version.

- **Do not scrawl in the margins.** When inserting words or phrases, use the caret to guide the typesetter. Write the edited version neatly above the original. Don't stretch a long insert into and down the margin. If the insert is extensive, it should be retyped and pasted over the original.

- **Avoid excessive arrows and lines when transposing paragraphs or sentences.** If they are limited and clear, arrows are efficient shortcuts. If they begin to look like the rough draft of a road map, retype the copy.

- **Don't split paragraphs from one page to the next.** Occasionally, a story will be distributed to more than one typesetter. Problems are created if paragraphs are not completed on each page.

- **Make clear changes.** More time is wasted by having the typesetter confused over scribbled editing than is saved by an editor who is hurrying.

Appendix B
THE ASSOCIATED PRESS STYLE RULES

Here is a summary of the major rules from The Associated Press Stylebook and Libel Manual. These rules are only a sampling of what can be found in the stylebook, which you should have and refer to often.

abbreviations and acronyms The notation *abbrev* is used in this book to identify the abbreviated form that may be used for a word in some contexts.

A few universally recognized abbreviations are required in some circumstances. Some others are acceptable depending on the context. But in general, avoid alphabet soup. Do not use abbreviations or acronyms which the reader would not quickly recognize.

Guidance on how to use a particular abbreviation or acronym is provided in entries alphabetized according to the sequence of letters in the word or phrase.

Some general principles:

BEFORE A NAME: Abbreviate the following titles when used before a full name outside direct quotations: *Dr., Gov., Lt. Gov., Mr., Mrs., Rev., the Rev., Sen.,* and certain military designations listed in the **military titles** entry. Spell out all except *Dr., Mr., Mrs.,* and *Ms.* when they are used before a name in direct quotations.

AFTER A NAME: Abbreviate *junior* or *senior* after an individual's name. Abbreviate *company, corporation, incorporated* and *limited* when used after the name of a corporate entity.

WITH DATES OR NUMERALS: Use the abbreviations *A.D., B.C., a.m., p.m., No.* and abbreviate certain months when used with the day of the month.

Right: *In 450 B.C.; at 9:30 a.m.; in room No. 6; on Sept. 16.*

Wrong: *Early this a.m. he asked for the No. of your room.* The abbreviations are correct only with figures.

Right: *Early this morning he asked for the number of your room.*

IN NUMBERED ADDRESSES: Abbreviate *avenue, boulevard* and *street* in numbered addresses: *He lives on Pennsylvania Avenue. He lives at 1600 Pennsylvania Ave.*

addresses Use the abbreviations *Ave., Blvd.* and *St.* only with a numbered address: *1600 Pennsylvania Ave.* Spell them out and capitalize when part of a formal street name without a number: *Pennsylvania Avenue.* Lowercase and spell out when used alone or with more than one street name: *Massachusetts and Pennsylvania avenues.*

All similar words (*alley, drive, road, terrace,* etc.) always are spelled out. Capitalize them when part of a formal name without a number; lowercase when used alone or with two or more names.

Always use figures for an address number: *9 Morningside Circle.*

Spell out and capitalize *First* through *Ninth* when used as street names; use figures with two letters for *10th* and above: *7 Fifth Ave., 100 21st St.*

Abbreviate compass points used to indicate directional ends of a street or quadrants of a city in a numbered address; *222 E. 42nd St., 562 W. 43rd St., 600 K St. N.W.* Do not abbreviate if the number is omitted: *East 42nd Street, West 43rd Street, K Street Northwest.*

capitalization In general, avoid unnecessary capitals. Use a capital letter only if you can justify it by one of the principles listed here.

Many words and phrases, including special cases, are listed separately in this book. Entries that are capitalized without further comment should be capitalized in all uses.

If there is no relevant listing in this book for a particular word or phrase, consult Webster's New World Dictionary. Use lowercase if the dictionary lists it as an acceptable form for the sense in which the word is being used.

As used in this book, *capitalize* means to use uppercase for the first letter of a word. If additional capital letters are needed, they are called for by an example or a phrase such as *use all caps.*

Some basic principles:

PROPER NOUNS: Capitalize nouns that constitute the unique identification for a specific person, place or thing: *John, Mary, America, Boston, England.*

Some words, such as the examples just given, are always proper nouns. Some common nouns receive proper noun status when they are used as the name of a particular entity: *General Electric, Gulf Oil.*

PROPER NAMES: Capitalize common nouns such as *party, river, street* and *west* when they are an integral part of the full name for a person, place or thing: *Democratic Party, Mississippi River, Fleet Street, West Virginia.*

Lowercase these common nouns when they stand alone in subsequent references: *the party, the river, the street.*

Lowercase the common noun elements of names in all plural uses: *the Democratic and Republican parties, Main and State streets, lakes Erie and Ontario.*

POPULAR NAMES: Some places and events lack officially designated proper names but have popular names that are the effective equivalent: *the Combat Zone* (a section of downtown Boston), *the Main Line* (a group of Philadelphia suburbs), *the South Side* (of Chicago), *the Badlands* (of North Dakota), *the Street* (the financial community in the Wall Street area of New York).

The principle applies also to shortened versions of the proper names for one-of-a-kind events: *the Series* (for the World Series), *the Derby* (for the Kentucky Derby). This practice should not, however, be interpreted as a license to ignore the general practice of lowercasing the common noun elements of a name when they stand alone.

DERIVATIVES: Capitalize words that are derived from a proper noun and still depend on it for their meaning: *American, Christian, Christianity, English, French, Marxism, Shakespearean.*

Lowercase words that are derived from a proper noun but no longer depend on it for their meaning: *french fries, herculean, manhattan cocktail, malapropism, pasteurize, quixotic, venetian blind.*

SENTENCES: Capitalize the first word in a statement that stands as a sentence.

In poetry, capital letters are used for the first words of some phrases that would not be capitalized in prose.

COMPOSITIONS: Capitalize the principal words in the names of books, movies, plays, poems, operas, songs, radio and television programs, works of art, etc.

TITLES: Capitalize formal titles when used immediately before a name. Lowercase formal titles when used alone or in constructions that set them off from a name by commas.

Use lowercase at all times for terms that are job descriptions rather than formal titles.

comma The following guidelines treat some of the most frequent questions about the use of commas.

For more detailed guidance, consult "The Comma" and "Misused and Unnecessary Commas" in the Guide to Punctuation section in the back of Webster's New World Dictionary.

IN A SERIES: Use commas to separate elements in a series but do not put a comma before the conjunction in a simple series: *The flag is red, white and blue. He would nominate Tom, Dick or Harry.*

Put a comma before the concluding conjunction in a series, however, if an integral element of the series requires a conjunction: *I had orange juice, toast, and ham and eggs for breakfast.*

Use a comma also before the concluding conjunction in a complex series of phrases: *The main points to consider are whether the athletes are skillful enough to compete, whether they have the stamina to endure the training, and whether they have the proper mental attitude.*

WITH EQUAL ADJECTIVES: Use commas to separate a series of adjectives equal in rank. If the commas could be replaced by the word *and* without changing the sense, the adjectives are equal: *a thoughtful, precise manner; a dark, dangerous street.*

Use no comma when the last adjective before a noun outranks its predecessors because it is an integral element of a noun phrase, which is the equivalent of a single noun: *a cheap fur coat* (the noun phrase is *fur coat*); *the old oaken bucket; a new, blue spring bonnet.*

WITH INTRODUCTORY CLAUSES AND PHRASES: A comma normally is used to separate an introductory clause or phrase from a main clause: *When he had tired of the mad pace of New York, he moved to Dubuque.*

The comma may be omitted after short introductory phrases if no ambiguity would result: *During the night he heard many noises.*

But use the comma if its omission would slow comprehension: *On the street below, the curious gathered.*

WITH CONJUNCTIONS: When a conjunction such as *and, but* or *for* links two clauses that could stand alone as separate sentences, use a comma before the conjunction in most cases: *She was glad she had looked, for a man was approaching the house.*

As a rule of thumb, use a comma if the subject of each clause is expressly stated: *We are visiting Washington, and we also plan a side trip to Williamsburg. We visited Washington, and our senator greeted us personally.* But no comma when the subject of the two clauses is the same and is not repeated in the second: *We are visiting Washington and plan to see the White House.*

The comma may be dropped if two clauses with expressly stated subjects are short. In general, however, favor use of a comma unless a particular literary effect is desired or it would distort the sense of a sentence.

INTRODUCING DIRECT QUOTES: Use a comma to introduce a complete, one-sentence quotation within a paragraph: *Wallace said, "She spent six months in Argentina and came back speaking English with a Spanish accent."* But use a colon to introduce quotations of more than one sentence.

Do not use a comma at the start of an indirect or partial quotation: *He said his victory put him "firmly on the road to a first-ballot nomination."*

BEFORE ATTRIBUTION: Use a comma instead of a period at the end of a quote that is followed by attribution: *"Rub my shoulders," Miss Cawley suggested.*

Do not use a comma, however, if the quoted statement ends with a question mark or exclamation point: *"Why should I?" he asked.*

WITH HOMETOWNS AND AGES: Use a comma to set off an individual's hometown when it is placed in apposition to a name: *Mary Richards, Minneapolis, and Maude Findlay, Tuckahoe, N.Y., were there.* However, the use of the word *of* without a comma between the individual's name and the city name generally is preferable: *Mary Richards of Minneapolis and Maude Findlay of Tuckahoe, N.Y., were there.*

If an individual's age is used, set it off by commas: *Maude Findlay, 48, Tuckahoe, N.Y., was present.* The use of the word *of* eliminates the need for a comma after the hometown if a state name is not needed: *Mary Richards, 36, of Minneapolis and Maude Findlay, 48, of Tuckahoe, N.Y., attended the party.*

NAMES OF STATES AND NATIONS USED WITH CITY NAMES: *His journey will take him from Dublin, Ireland, to Fargo, N.D., and back. The Selma, Ala., group saw the governor.*

Use parentheses, however, if a state name is inserted within a proper name: *The Huntsville (Ala.) Times.*

WITH YES AND NO: *Yes, I will be there.*

IN DIRECT ADDRESS: *Mother, I will be home late. No, sir, I did not do it.*

SEPARATING SIMILAR WORDS: Use a comma to separate duplicated words that otherwise would be confusing: *What the problem is, is not clear.*

IN LARGE FIGURES: Use a comma for most figures higher than 999. The major exceptions are: street addresses (*1234 Main St.*), broadcast frequencies (*1460 kilohertz*), room numbers, serial numbers, telephone numbers, and years (*1976*).

PLACEMENT WITH QUOTES: Commas always go inside quotation marks.

courtesy titles In general, do not use the courtesy titles *Miss, Mr., Mrs.* or *Ms.* with first and last names of the person: *Betty Ford, Jimmy Carter.*

Do not use *Mr.* in any reference unless it is combined with *Mrs.*: *Mr. and Mrs. John Smith, Mr. and Mrs. Smith.*

On sports wires, do not use courtesy titles in any reference unless needed to distinguish among persons of the same last name.

On news wires, use courtesy titles for women on second reference, following the woman's preference. Some guidelines:

MARRIED WOMEN: The preferred form on first reference is to identify a woman by her own first name and her husband's last name: *Susan Smith.* Use Mrs. on the first reference only if a woman requests that her husband's first name be used or her own first name cannot be determined: *Mrs. John Smith.*

On second reference, use *Mrs.* unless a woman identified by her own first name prefers *Ms., Ms. Hills;* or no title: *Carla Hills, Mrs. Hills, Hills.*

If a married woman is known by her maiden last name, precede it by *Miss* on second reference unless she prefers *Ms.*: *Jane Fonda, Miss Fonda, Ms. Fonda;* or no title, *Jane Fonda* or *Fonda.*

UNMARRIED WOMEN: For women who have never been married, use *Miss* or *Ms.* or no title before a woman's last name, depending on her preference.

For divorced women and widows, the normal practice is to use *Mrs.* or no title, if she prefers. But if a woman returns to the use of her maiden name, use *Miss, Ms.* or no title, if she prefers it.

MARITAL STATUS: If a woman prefers *Ms.* or no title, do not include her marital status in a story unless it is clearly pertinent.

dates Always use Arabic figures, without *st, nd, rd* or *th.*

directions and regions In general, lowercase *north, south, northeast, northern,* etc. when they indicate compass direction; capitalize these words when they designate regions.

Some examples:

COMPASS DIRECTION: *He drove west. The cold front is moving east.*

REGIONS: *A storm system that developed in the Midwest is spreading eastward. It will bring showers to the East Coast by morning and to the entire Northeast by late in the day. Warm temperatures will prevail throughout the Western states.*

The North was victorious. The South will rise again. Settlers from the East went west in search of new lives. The customs of the East are different from those of the West. The Northeast depends on the Midwest for its food supply.

She has a Southern accent. He is a Northerner. Nations of the Orient are opening doors to Western businessmen. The candidate developed a Southern strategy. She is a Northern liberal.

The storm developed in the South Pacific. Leaders of Western Europe met leaders of Eastern Europe to talk about supplies of oil from Southeast Asia.

WITH NAMES OF NATIONS: Lowercase unless they are part of a proper name or are used to designate a politically divided nation: *northern France, eastern Canada, the western United States.*

But: *Northern Ireland, East Germany, South Korea.*

WITH STATES AND CITIES: The preferred form is to lowercase compass points when they describe a section of a state or city: *western Texas, southern Atlanta.*

But capitalize compass points:

—When part of a proper name: *North Dakota, West Virginia.*

—When used in denoting widely known sections: *Southern California, the South Side of Chicago, the Lower East Side of New York.* If in doubt, use lowercase.

IN FORMING PROPER NAMES: When combining with another common noun to form the name for a region or location: *the North Woods, the South Pole, the Far East, the Middle East, the West Coast* (the entire region, not the coastline itself, *the Eastern Shore, the Western Hemisphere.*

doctor Use *Dr.* in first reference as a formal title before the name of an individual who holds a doctor of medicine degree: *Dr. Jonas Salk.*

The form *Dr.*, or *Drs.* in the plural construction, applies to all first-reference uses before a name, including direct quotations.

If appropriate in the context, *Dr.* also may be used on first reference before the names of individuals who hold other types of doctoral degrees. However, because the public frequently identifies *Dr.* only with physicians, care should be taken to assure that the individual's specialty is stated in first or second reference. The only exception would be a story in which the context left no doubt that the person was a dentist, psychologist, chemist, historian, etc.

In some instances it also is necessary to specify that an individual identified as *Dr.* is a physician. One frequent case is a story reporting on joint research by physicians, biologists, etc.

Do not use *Dr.* before the names of individuals who hold honorary doctorates.

Do not continue the use of *Dr.* in subsequent references.

house of representatives Capitalize when referring to a specific governmental body: *The U.S. House of Representatives, the Massachusetts House of Representatives.*

Capitalize shortened references that delete the words *of Representatives: the U.S. House, the Massachusetts House.*

Retain capitalization if *U.S.* or the name of a state is dropped but the reference is to a specific body:

BOSTON (AP)—*The House has adjourned for the year.*

Lowercase plural uses: *the Massachusetts and Rhode Island houses.*

Apply the same principles to similar legislative bodies such as *the Virginia House of Delegates.*

hyphen Hyphens are joiners. Use them to avoid ambiguity or to form a single idea from two or more words.

Some guidelines:

AVOID AMBIGUITY: Use a hyphen whenever ambiguity would result if it were omitted: *The president will speak to small-business men.* (*Businessmen* normally is one word. But *The president will speak to small businessmen* is unclear.)

Others: *He recovered his health. He recovered the leaky roof.*

COMPOUND MODIFIERS: When a compound modifier—two or more words that express a single concept—precedes a noun, use hyphens to link all the words in the compound except the adverb *very* and all adverbs that end in *ly*: *a first-quarter touchdown, a bluish-green dress, a full-time job, a well-known man, a better-qualified woman, a know-it-all attitude, a very good time, an easily remembered rule.*

Many combinations that are hyphenated before a noun are not hyphenated when they occur after a noun: *The team scored in the first quarter. The dress, a bluish green, was attractive on her. She works full time. His attitude suggested that he knew it all.*

But when a modifier that would be hyphenated before a noun occurs instead after a form of the verb *to be*, the hyphen usually must be retained to avoid confusion: *The man is well-known. The woman is quick-witted. The children are soft-spoken. The play is second-rate.*

The principle of using a hyphen to avoid confusion explains why no hyphen is required with *very* and *ly* words. Readers can expect them to modify the word that follows. But if a combination such as *little-known man* were not hyphenated, the reader could logically be expecting *little* to be followed by a noun, as in *little man*. Instead, the reader encountering *little known* would have to back up mentally and make the compound connection on his own.

TWO-THOUGHT COMPOUNDS: *seriocomic, socio-economic.*

COMPOUND PROPER NOUNS AND ADJECTIVES: Use a hyphen to designate dual heritage: *Italian-American, Mexican-American.*

No hyphen, however, for *French Canadian* or *Latin American.*

AVOID DUPLICATED VOWELS, TRIPLED CONSONANTS: Examples: *anti-intellectual, pre-empt, shell-like.*

WITH NUMERALS: Use a hyphen to separate figures in odds, ratios, scores, some fractions and some vote tabulations.

When large numbers must be spelled out, use a hyphen to connect a word ending in *y* to another word: *twenty-one, fifty-five,* etc.

SUSPENSIVE HYPHENATION: The form: *He received a 10- to 20-year sentence in prison.*

legislative titles

FIRST REFERENCE FORM: Use *Rep., Reps., Sen.* and *Sens.* as formal titles before one or more names in regular text. Spell out and capitalize these titles before one or more names in a direct quotation. Spell out and lowercase *representative* and *senator* in other uses.

Spell out other legislative titles in all uses. Capitalize formal titles such as *assemblyman, assemblywoman, city councilor, delegate,* etc., when they are used before a name. Lowercase in other uses.

Add *U.S.* or *state* before a title only if necessary to avoid confusion: *U.S. Sen. Herman Talmadge spoke with state Sen. Hugh Carter.*

FIRST REFERENCE PRACTICE: The use of a title such as *Rep.* or *Sen.* in first reference is normal in most stories. It is not mandatory, however, provided an individual's title is given later in the story.

Deletion of the title on first reference is frequently appropriate, for example, when an individual has become well known: *Barry Goldwater endorsed President Ford today. The Arizona senator said he believes the president deserves another term.*

SECOND REFERENCE: Do not use legislative titles before a name on second reference unless they are part of a direct quotation.

CONGRESSMAN, CONGRESSWOMAN: *Rep.* and *U.S. Rep.* are the preferred first-reference forms when a formal title is used before the name of a U.S. House member. The words *congressman* or *congresswoman*, in lowercase, may be used in subsequent references that do not use an individual's name, just as *senator* is used in references to members of the Senate.

Congressman and *congresswoman* should appear as capitalized formal titles before a name only in direct quotation.

legislature Capitalize when preceded by the name of a state: *the Kansas Legislature.*

Retain capitalization when the state name is dropped but the reference is specifically to that state's legislature: *TOPEKA, Kan. (AP)—Both houses of the Legislature adjourned today.*

Capitalize *legislature* in subsequent specific references and in such constructions as: *the 100th Legislature, the state Legislature.*

Although the word *legislature* is not part of the formal, proper name for the lawmaking bodies in many states, it commonly is used that way and should be treated as such in any story that does not use the formal name.

If a given context or local practice calls for the use of a formal name such as *Missouri General Assembly*, retain the capital letters if the name of the state can be dropped, but lowercase the word *assembly* if it stands alone. Lowercase *legislature* if a story uses it in a subsequent reference to a body identified as a general assembly.

Lowercase *legislature* when used generically: *No legislature has approved the amendment.*

Use *legislature* in lowercase for all plural references: *The Arkansas and Colorado legislatures are considering the amendment.*

In 49 states the separate bodies are a *senate* and a *house* or *assembly.* The *Nebraska Legislature* is a unicameral body.

military titles Capitalize a military rank when used as a formal title before an individual's name.

See the lists that follow to determine whether the title should be spelled out or abbreviated in regular text. Spell out any title used before a name in a direct quotation.

On first reference, use the appropriate title before the full name of a member of the military.

In subsequent references, do not continue using the title before a name. Use only the last name of a man. Use *Miss, Mrs., Ms.* or no title before the last name of a woman depending on her preference.

Spell out and lowercase a title when it is substituted for a name: *Gen. John J. Pershing arrived today. An aide said the general would review the troops.*

In some cases, it may be necessary to explain the significance of a title: *Army Sgt. Maj. John Jones described the attack. Jones, who holds the Army's highest rank for enlisted men, said it was unprovoked.*

In addition to the ranks listed, each service has ratings such as *machinist, radarman, torpedoman,* etc., that are job descriptions. Do not use any of these designations as a title on first reference. If one is used before a name in a subsequent reference, do not capitalize or abbreviate it.

ABBREVIATIONS: The abbreviations, with the highest ranks listed first:

MILITARY TITLES

Rank	Usage before a name
ARMY	
Commissioned Officers	
general	Gen.
lieutenant general	Lt. Gen
major general	Maj. Gen.
brigadier general	Brig. Gen.
colonel	Col.
lieutenant colonel	Lt. Col.
major	Maj.
captain	Capt.
first lieutenant	1st Lt.
second lieutenant	2nd Lt.
Warrant Officers	
chief warrant officer	Chief Warrant Officer
warrant officer	Warrant Officer

APPENDIX B THE ASSOCIATED PRESS STYLE RULES

Enlisted Personnel

sergeant major of the Army	Army Sgt. Maj.
command sergeant major	Command Sgt. Maj.
staff sergeant major	Staff Sgt. Maj.
first sergeant	1st Sgt.
master sergeant	Master Sgt.
platoon sergeant	Platoon Sgt.
sergeant first class	Sgt. 1st Class
specialist seven	Spec. 7
staff sergeant	Staff Sgt.
specialist six	Spec. 6
sergeant	Sgt.
specialist five	Spec. 5
corporal	Cpl.
specialist four	Spec. 4
private first class	Pfc.
private 2	Pvt. 2
private 1	Pvt. 1

NAVY, COAST GUARD

Commissioned Officers

admiral	Adm.
vice admiral	Vice Adm.
rear admiral	Rear Adm.
commodore	Commodore
captain	Capt.
commander	Cmdr.
lieutenant commander	Lt. Cmdr.
lieutenant	Lt.
lieutenant junior grade	Lt. j.g.
ensign	Ensign

Warrant Officers

chief warrant officer	Chief Warrant Officer
warrant officer	Warrant Officer

Enlisted Personnel

master chief petty officer	Master Chief Petty Officer
senior chief petty officer	Senior Chief Petty Officer
chief petty officer	Chief Petty Officer
petty officer first class	Petty Officer 1st Class
petty officer second class	Petty Officer 2nd Class
petty officer third class	Petty Officer 3rd Class
seaman	Seaman
seaman apprentice	Seaman Apprentice
seaman recruit	Seaman Recruit

MARINE CORPS

Ranks and abbreviations for commissioned officers are the same as those in the Army. Warrant officer ratings follow the same system used in the Navy. There are no specialist ratings.

Others

sergeant major	Sgt. Maj.
master gunnery sergeant	Master Gunnery Sgt.
master sergeant	Master Sgt.
first sergeant	1st Sgt.
gunnery sergeant	Gunnery Sgt.
staff sergeant	Staff Sgt.
sergeant	Sgt.
corporal	Cpl.
lance corporal	Lance Cpl.
private first class	Pfc.
private	Pvt.

AIR FORCE

Ranks and abbreviations for commissioned officers are the same as those in the Army.

Enlisted Designations

chief master sergeant of the Air Force	Chief Master Sgt. of the Air Force
senior master sergeant	Senior Master Sgt.
master sergeant	Master Sgt.
technical sergeant	Tech. Sgt.
staff sergeant	Staff Sgt.
sergeant	Sgt.
senior airman	Senior Airman
airman first class	Airman 1st Class
airman	Airman
airman basic	Airman

PLURALS: Add *s* to the principal element in the title: *Majs. John Jones and Robert Smith; Maj. Gens. John Jones and Robert Smith; Specs. 4 John Jones and Robert Smith.*

RETIRED OFFICERS: A military rank may be used in first reference before the name of an officer who has retired if it is relevant to a story. Do not, however, use the military abbreviation *Ret.*

Instead, use *retired* just as *former* would be used before the title of a civilian: *They invited retired Army Gen. John Smith.*

FIREFIGHTERS, POLICE OFFICERS: Use the abbreviations listed here when a military-style title is used before the name of a firefighter or police officer outside a direct quotation. Add *police* or *fire* before the title if needed for clarity: *police Sgt. William Smith, fire Capt. David Jones.*

Spell out titles such as *detective* that are not used in the armed forces.

numerals A numeral is a figure, letter, word or group of words expressing a number.

Roman numerals use letters *I, V, X, L, C, D* and *M*. Use Roman numerals for wars and to show personal sequence for animals and people: *World War II, Native Dancer II, King George VI, Pope John XXIII.*

Arabic numerals use the figures *1, 2, 3, 4, 5, 6, 7, 8, 9* and *0*. Use Arabic forms unless Roman numerals are specifically required.

The figures *1, 2, 10, 101,* etc. and the corresponding words—*one, two, ten, one hundred one,* etc.—are called cardinal numbers. The term ordinal number applies to *1st, 2nd, 10th, 101st, first, second, tenth, one hundred first,* etc.

Follow these guidelines in using numerals:

LARGE NUMBERS: When large numbers must be spelled out, use a hyphen to connect a word ending in *y* to another word; do not use commas between other separate words that are part of one number: *twenty; thirty; twenty-one; thirty-one; one hundred forty-three; one thousand one hundred fifty-five; one million two hundred seventy-six thousand five hundred eighty-seven.*

SENTENCE START: Spell out a numeral at the beginning of a sentence. If necessary, recast the sentence. There is one exception—a numeral that identifies a calendar year.

Wrong: *993 freshmen entered the college last year.*

Right: *Last year 993 freshmen entered the college.*

Right: *1976 was a very good year.*

CASUAL USES: Spell out casual expressions:

A thousand times no! Thanks a million. He walked a quarter of a mile.

PROPER NAMES: Use words or numerals according to an organization's practice: *20th Century-Fox, Twentieth Century Fund, Big Ten.*

FIGURES OR WORDS? For ordinals:

—Spell out *first* through *ninth* when they indicate sequence in time and location—*first base, the First Amendment, he was first in line.* Starting with *10th,* use figures.

—Use *1st, 2nd, 3rd, 4th,* etc. when the sequence has been assigned in forming names. The principal examples are geographic, military and political designations such as *1st Ward, 7th Fleet* and *1st Sgt.*

SOME PUNCTUATION AND USAGE EXAMPLES:
—*Act 1, Scene 2*
—*a 5-year-old girl*
—*DC 10* but *747B*
—*a 5-4 court decision*
—*2nd District Court*
—*the 1970s, the '70s*
—*The House voted 230–205.* (Fewer than 1,000 votes)
Jimmy Carter defeated Gerald Ford 40,827,292 to 39,146,157 (More than 1,000 votes)
Carter defeated Ford 10 votes to 2 votes in Little Junction. (To avoid confusion with ratio)
—*5 cents, $1.05, $650,000, $2.45 million*
—*No. 3 choice,* but *Public School 3*
—*0.6 percent, 1 percent, 6.5 percent*
—*a pay increase of 12 percent to 15 percent*

Or: *a pay increase of between 12 percent and 15 percent*
Also: *from $12 million to $14 million*
—*a ratio of 2-to-1, a 2–1 ratio*
—*a 4–3 score*
—*(212) 262-4000*
—*minus 10, zero, 60 degrees*

OTHER USES: For uses not covered by these listings: Spell out whole numbers below 10, use figures for 10 and above. Typical examples: *The woman has three sons and two daughters. He has a fleet of 10 station wagons and two buses.*

IN A SERIES: Apply the appropriate guidelines: *They had 10 dogs, six cats and 97 hamsters. They had four four-room houses, 10 three-room houses and 12 10-room houses.*

party affiliation Let relevance be the guide in determining whether to include a political figure's party affiliation in a story.

Party affiliation is pointless in some stories, such as an account of a governor accepting a button from a poster child.

It will occur naturally in many political stories.

For stories between these extremes, include party affiliation if readers need it for understanding or are likely to be curious about what it is.

GENERAL FORMS: When party designation is given, use any of these approaches as logical in constructing a story:
—*Democratic Sen. Hubert Humphrey of Minnesota said* . . .
—*Sen. Hubert Humphrey, D-Minn., said* . . .
—*Sen. Hubert Humphrey also spoke. The Minnesota Democrat said* . . .
—*Rep. Morris Udall of Arizona is seeking the Democratic presidential nomination.* Not: *Rep. Morris Udall, D-Ariz., is seeking the Democratic.* . . .

In stories about party meetings, such as a report on the Republican National Convention, no specific reference to party affiliation is necessary unless an individual is not a member of the party in question.

SHORT-FORM PUNCTUATION: Set short forms such as *D-Minn.* off from a name by commas, as illustrated above.

Use the abbreviations listed in the entries for each state. (No abbreviations for *Alaska, Hawaii, Idaho, Iowa, Maine, Ohio, Texas* and *Utah.*)

Use *R-* for Republicans, *D-* for Democrats, and three-letter combinations for other affiliations: *Sen. James Buckley, R-Con-N.Y., spoke with Sen. Harry Byrd, D-Ind-Va.*

FORM FOR U.S. HOUSE MEMBERS: The normal practice for U.S. House members is to identify them by party and state. In contexts were state affiliation is clear and home city is relevant, such as a state election roundup, identify representatives by party and city: *U.S. Reps. Thomas P. O'Neill Jr., D-Cambridge, and Margaret Heckler, R-Wellesley.* If this option is used, be consistent throughout the story.

FORM FOR STATE LEGISLATORS: Short-form listings showing party and home city are appropriate in state wire stories. For trunk wire stories, the normal practice is to say that the individual is a *Republican* or *Democrat.* Use a short-form listing only if the legislator's home city is relevant.

periods Follow these guidelines:

END OF DECLARATIVE SENTENCE: *The storybook is finished.*

END OF A MILDLY IMPERATIVE SENTENCE: *Shut the door.*

Use an exclamation point if greater emphasis is desired: *Be careful!*

END OF SOME RHETORICAL QUESTIONS: A period is preferable if a statement is more a suggestion than a question: *Why don't we go.*

END OF AN INDIRECT QUESTION: *He asked what the score was.*

INITIALS: *John F. Kennedy, T.S. Eliot.* (No space between *T.* and *S.*, to prevent them from being placed on two lines in typesetting.)

Abbreviations using only the initials of a name do not take periods: *JFK, LBJ.*

ENUMERATIONS: After numbers of letters in enumerating elements of a summary: *1. Wash the car. 2. Clean the basement.* Or: *A. Punctuate properly. B. Write simply.*

PLACEMENT WITH QUOTATION MARKS: Periods always go inside quotation marks.

plurals Follow these guidelines in forming and using plural words:

MOST WORDS: Add *s*: *boys, girls, ships, villages.*

WORDS ENDING IN CH, S, SH, SS, X AND Z: Add *es*: *churches, lenses, parishes, glasses, boxes, buzzes.* (*Monarchs* is an exception.)

WORDS ENDING IN IS: Change *is* to *es*: *oases, parentheses, theses.*

WORDS ENDING IN Y: If *y* is preceded by a consonant or *qu*, change *y* to *i* and add *es*: *armies, cities, navies, soliloquies.* (See PROPER NAMES below for an exception.)

Otherwise add *s*: *donkeys, monkeys.*

WORDS ENDING IN O: If *o* is preceded by a consonant, most plurals require *es*: *buffaloes, dominoes, echoes, heroes, potatoes.* But there are exceptons: *pianos.*

WORDS ENDING IN F: Change *f* to *v* and add *es*: *leaves, selves.*

LATIN ENDINGS: Latin-root words ending in *us* change *us* to *i*: *alumnus, alumni.*

Most ending in *a* change to *ae*: *alumna, alumnae* (*formula, formulas* is an exception).

Those ending in *on* change to *a*: *phenomenon, phenomena.*

Most ending in *um* add *s*: *memorandums, referendums, stadiums.* Among those that still use the Latin ending: *addenda, curricula, media.*

Use the plural that Webster's New World lists as most common for a particular sense of a word.

FORM CHANGE: *man, men; child, children; foot, feet; mouse, mice;* etc.

Caution: When *s* is used with any of these words it indicates possession and must be preceded by an apostrophe: *men's, children's,* etc.

WORDS THE SAME IN SINGULAR AND PLURAL: *corps, chassis, deer, moose, sheep,* etc.

The sense in a particular sentence is conveyed by the use of a singular or plural verb.

WORDS PLURAL IN FORM, SINGULAR IN MEANING: Some take singular verbs: *measles, mumps, news.*

Others take plural verbs: *grits, scissors.*

COMPOUND WORDS: Those written solid add *s* at the end: *cupfuls, handfuls, tablespoonfuls.*

For those that involve separate words or words linked by a hyphen, make the most significant word plural:

—Significant word first: *adjutants general, aides-de-camp, attorneys general, courts-martial, daughters-in-law, passers-by, postmasters general, presidents-elect, secretaries general, sergeants major.*

—Significant word in the middle: *assistant attorneys general, deputy chiefs of staff.*

—Significant word last: *assistant attorneys, assistant corporation councils, deputy sheriffs, lieutenant colonels, major generals.*

WORDS AS WORDS: Do not use *'s*: *His speech had too many ifs, ands and buts.* (Exception to Webster's New World.)

PROPER NAMES: Most ending in *es* or *z* add *es*: *Charleses, Joneses, Gonzalezes.*

Most ending in *y* add *s* even if preceded by a consonant: *the Duffys, the Kennedys, the two Germanys, the two Kansas Citys.* Exceptions include *Alleghenies* and *Rockies.*

For others, add *s*: *the Carters, the McCoys, the Mondales.*

FIGURES: Add *s*: *The custom began in the 1920s. The airline has two 727s. Temperatures will be in the low 20s. There were five size 7s.* (No apostrophes, an exception to Webster's New World guideline under "apostrophe.")

SINGLE LETTERS: Use 's: *Mind your p's and q's. He learned the three R's and brought home a report card with four A's and two B's. The Oakland A's won the pennant.*

MULTIPLE LETTERS: Add *s*: *She knows her ABCs. I gave him five IOUs. Four VIPs were there.*

possessives Follow these guidelines:

PLURAL NOUNS NOT ENDING IN S: Add 's: *the alumni's contributions, women's rights.*

PLURAL NOUNS ENDING IN S: Add only an apostrophe: *the churches' needs, the girls' toys, the horses' food, the ships' wake, states' rights, the VIPs' entrance.*

NOUNS PLURAL IN FORM, SINGULAR IN MEANING: Add only an apostrophe: *mathematics' rules, measles' effects.* (But see INANIMATE OBJECTS below.)

Apply the same principle when a plural word occurs in the formal name of a singular entity: *General Motors' profits, the United States' wealth.*

NOUNS THE SAME IN SINGULAR AND PLURAL: Treat them the same as plurals, even if the meaning is singular: *one corps' location, the two deer's tracks, the lone moose's antlers.*

SINGULAR NOUNS NOT ENDING IN S: Add 's: *the church's needs, the girl's toys, the horse's food, the ship's route, the VIP's seat.*

Some style guides say that singular nouns ending in *s* sounds such as *ce*, *x*, and *z* may take either the apostrophe alone or 's. See SPECIAL EXPRESSIONS below, but otherwise, for consistency and ease in remembering a rule, always use 's if the word does not end in the letter *s*: *Butz's policies, the fox's den, the justice's verdict, Marx's theories, the prince's life, Xerox's profits.*

SINGULAR COMMON NOUNS ENDING IN S: Add 's unless the next word begins with *s*: *the hostess's invitation, the hostess' seat; the witness's answer, the witness' story.*

SINGULAR PROPER NAMES ENDING IN S: Use only an apostrophe: *Achilles' heel, Agnes' book, Ceres' rites, Descartes' theories, Dickens' novels, Euripides' dramas, Hercules' labors, Jesus' life, Jules' seat, Kansas' schools, Moses' law, Socrates' life, Tennessee Williams' plays, Xerxes' armies.*

SPECIAL EXPRESSIONS: The following exceptions to the general rule for words not ending in *s* apply to words that end in an *s* sound and are followed by a word that begins with *s*: *for appearance' sake, for conscience' sake, for goodness' sake.* Use 's otherwise: *the appearance's cost, my conscience's voice.*

PRONOUNS: Personal, interrogative and relative pronouns have separate forms for the possessive. None involve an apostrophe: *mine, ours, your, yours, his, hers, its, theirs, whose.*

Caution: If you are using an apostrophe with a pronoun, always double-check to be sure that the meaning calls for a contraction: *you're, it's, there's, who's.*

Follow the rules listed above in forming the possessives of other pronouns: *another's idea, others' plans, someone's guess.*

COMPOUND WORDS: Applying the rules above, add an apostrophe or 's to the word closest to the object possessed: *the major general's decision, the major generals' decisions, the attorney general's request.*

Also: *anyone else's attitude, John Adams Jr.'s father, Benjamin Franklin of Pennsylvania's motion.* Whenever practical, however, recast the phrase to avoid ambiguity: *the motion by Benjamin Franklin of Pennsylvania.*

JOINT POSSESSION, INDIVIDUAL POSSESSION: Use a possessive form after only the last word if ownership is joint: *Fred and Sylvia's apartment, Fred and Sylvia's stocks.*

Use a possessive form after both words if the objects are individually owned: *Fred's and Sylvia's books.*

DESCRIPTIVE PHRASES: Do not add an apostrophe to a word ending in *s* when it is used primarily in a descriptive sense: *citizens band radio, a Cincinnati Reds infielder; a teachers college, a Teamsters request, a writers guide.*

Memory Aid: The apostrophe usually is not used if *for* or *by* rather than *of* would be appropriate in the longer form: *a radio band for citizens, a college for teachers, a guide for writers, a request by the Teamsters.*

An *'s* is required, however, when a term involves a plural word that does not end in *s: a children's hospital, a people's republic, the Young Men's Christian Association.*

DESCRIPTIVE NAMES: Some governmental, corporate and institutional organizations with a descriptive word in their names use an apostrophe; some do not. Follow the user's practice: *Actors Equity, Diners Club, the Ladies' Home Journal, the National Governors' Association, the Veterans Administration.*

QUASI POSSESSIVES: Follow the rules above in composing the possessive form of words that occur in such phrases as a *day's pay, two weeks' vacation, three days' work, your money's worth.*

Frequently, however, a hyphenated form is clearer: *a two-week vacation, a three-day job.*

DOUBLE POSSESSIVE: Two conditions must apply for a double possessive—a phrase such as *a friend of John's*—to occur: 1. The word after *of* must refer to an animate object, and 2. The word before *of* must involve only a portion of the animate object's possessions.

Otherwise, do not use the possessive form on the word after *of: The friends of John Adams mourned his death.* (All the friends were involved.) *He is a friend of the college.* (Not *college's*, because college is inanimate).

Memory Aid: This construction occurs most often, and quite naturally, with the possessive forms of personal pronouns: *He is a friend of mine.*

INANIMATE OBJECTS: There is no blanket rule against creating a possessive form for an inanimate object, particularly if the object is treated in a personified sense. See some of the earlier examples, and note these: *death's call, the wind's murmur.*

In general, however, avoid excessive personalization of inanimate objects, and give preference to an *of* construction when it fits the makeup of the sentence. For example, the earlier mentioned references to *mathematics' rules* and *measles' effects* would better be phrased: *the rules of mathematics, the effects of measles.*

quotation marks The basic guidelines for open-quote marks (") and close-quote marks("):

FOR DIRECT QUOTATIONS: To surround the exact words of a speaker or writer when reported in a story:

"*I have no intention of staying,*" he replied.

"*I do not object,*" he said, "*to the tenor of the report.*"

Franklin said, "*A penny saved is a penny earned.*"

A speculator said the practice is "*too conservative for inflationary times.*"

RUNNING QUOTATIONS: If a full paragraph of quoted material is followed by a paragraph that continues the quotation, do not put close-quote marks at the end of the first paragraph. Do, however, put open-quote marks at the start of the second paragraph. Continue in this fashion for any succeeding paragraphs, using close-quote marks only at the end of the quoted material.

If a paragraph does not start with quotation marks but ends with a quotation that is continued in the next paragraph, do not use close-quote marks at the end of the introductory paragraph if the quoted material constitutes a full sentence. Use close-quote marks, however, if the quoted material does not constitute a full sentence. For example: *He said,* "*I am shocked and horrified by the incident.*

"*I am so horrified, in fact, that I will ask for the death penalty.*" But:

He said he was "*shocked and horrified by the incident.*"

"I am so horrified, in fact, that I will ask for the death penalty," he said.

DIALOGUE OR CONVERSATION: Each person's words, no matter how brief, are placed in a separate paragraph, with quotation marks at the beginning and the end of each person's speech:
"Will you go?"
"Yes."
"When?"
"Thursday."

NOT IN Q-AND-A: quoation marks are not required in formats that identify questions and answers by Q: and A.

NOT IN TEXTS: Quotation marks are not required in full texts, condensed texts or textual excerpts.

IRONY: Put quotation marks around a word or words used in an ironical sense: The "debate" turned into a free-for-all.

UNFAMILIAR TERMS: A word or words being introduced to readers may be placed in quotation marks on first reference:
Broadcast frequencies are measured in "kilohertz."
Do not put subsequent references to *kilohertz* in quotation marks.

AVOID UNNECESSARY FRAGMENTS: Do not use quotation marks to report a few ordinary words that a speaker or writer has used:
Wrong: *The senator said he would "go home to Michigan" if he lost the election.*
Right: *The senator said he would go home to Michigan if he lost the election.*

PARTIAL QUOTES: When a partial quote is used, do not put quotation marks around words that the speaker could not have used.
Suppose the individual said, "*I am horrified at your slovenly manners.*"
Wrong: *She said she "was horrified at their slovenly manners."*
Right: *She said she was horrified at their "slovenly manners."*
Better when practical: Use the full quote.

QUOTES WITHIN QUOTES: Alternative between double quotation marks (" or ") and single marks (' or '):
She said, "*I quote from his letter, 'I agree with Kipling that "the female of the species is more deadly than the male," but the phenomenon is not an unchangeable law of nature,' a remark he did not explain."*
Use three marks together if two quoted elements end at the same time: *She said, "He told me, 'I love you.' "*

PLACEMENT WITH OTHER PUNCTUATION: Follow these long-established printers' rules:
—The period and the comma always go within the quotation marks.
—The dash, the semicolon, the question mark and the exclamation point go within the quotation marks when they apply to the quoted matter only. They go outside when they apply to the whole sentence.

semicolon In general, use the semicolon to indicate a greater separation of thought and information than a comma can convey but less than the separation that a period implies.
The basic guidelines:

TO CLARIFY A SERIES: Use semicolons to separate elements of a series when individual segments contain material that also must be set off by commas:
He leaves a son, John Smith of Chicago; three daughters, Jane Smith of Wichita, Kan., Mary Smith of Denver, and Susan, wife of William Kingsbury of Boston; and a sister, Martha, wife of Robert Warren of Omaha, Neb.
Note that the semicolon is used before the final *and* in such a series.

TO LINK INDEPENDENT CLAUSES: Use a semicolon when a coordinating conjunction such as *and, but* or *for* is not present: *The package was due last week; it arrived today.*
If a coordinating conjunction is present, use a semicolon before it only if extensive punctuation also is required in one or more of the individual clauses: *They pulled their boats from the water,*

sandbagged the retaining walls, and boarded up the windows; but even with these precautions, the island was hard-hit by the hurricane.

Unless a particular literary effect is desired, however, the better approach in these circumstances is to break the independent clauses into separate sentences.

PLACEMENT WITH QUOTES: Place semicolons outside quotation marks.

senate Capitalize all specific references to governmental legislative bodies, regardless of whether the name of the nation or state is used: *the U.S. Senate, the Senate; the Virginia Senate, the state Senate, the Senate.*

Lowercase plural uses: *the Virginia and North Carolina senates.*

The same principles apply to foreign bodies.

Lowercase references to non-governmental bodies: *The student senate at Yale.*

state names Follow these guidelines:

STANDING ALONE: Spell out the names of the 50 U.S. states when they stand alone in textual material. Any state name may be condensed, however, to fit typographical requirements for tabular material.

EIGHT NOT ABBREVIATED: The names of eight states are never abbreviated in datelines or text: *Alaska, Hawaii, Idaho, Iowa, Maine, Ohio, Texas* and *Utah*.

Memory Aid: Spell out the names of the two states that are not part of the continental United States and of the continental states that are five letters or fewer.

ABBREVIATIONS REQUIRED: Use the state abbreviations listed at the end of this section:

—In conjunction with the name of a city, town, village or military base in most datelines.

—In conjunction with the name of a city, county, town, village or military base in text. See examples in punctuation section below.

—In short-form listings of party affiliation: *D-Ala., R-Mont.* See **party affliation** for details.

The abbreviations, which also appear in the entries for each state, are:

Ala.	Md.	N.D.
Ariz.	Mass.	Okla.
Ark.	Mich.	Ore.
Calif.	Minn.	Pa.
Colo.	Miss.	R.I.
Conn.	Mo.	S.C.
Del.	Mont.	S.D.
Fla.	Neb.	Tenn.
Ga.	Nev.	Vt.
Ill.	N.H.	Va.
Ind.	N.J.	Wash.
Kan.	N.M.	W. Va.
Ky.	N.Y.	Wis.
La.	N.C.	Wyo.

PUNCTUATION: Place one comma between the city and the state name, and another comma after the state name, unless ending a sentence or indicating a dateline: *He was traveling from Nashville, Tenn., to Austin, Texas, en route to his home in Albuquerque, N.M. She said Cook County, Ill., was Mayor Daley's stronghold.*

MISCELLANEOUS: Use *New York state* when necessary to distinguish the state from New York City.

Use *state of Washington* or *Washington state* when necessary to distinguish the state from the District of Columbia. (*Washington State* is the name of a university in the state of Washington.)

time element Use *today, this morning, this afternoon, tonight,* etc., as appropriate in stories for afternoon editions. Use the day of the week elsewhere.

Use *Monday, Tuesday,* etc., for days of the week within seven days before or after the current date.

Use the month and figure for dates beyond this range.

Avoid such redundancies as *last Tuesday* or *next Tuesday*. The past, present or future tense used for the verb usually provides adequate indication of which *Tuesday* is meant: *He said he finished* the job Tuesday. *She will return on Tuesday.*

Avoid awkward placements of the time element, particularly those that suggest the day of the week is the object of a transitive verb: *The police jailed Tuesday.* Potential remedies include the use of the word *on*, rephrasing the sentence or placing the time element in a different sentence.

titles In general, confine capitalization to formal titles used directly before an individual's name.

The basic guidelines:

LOWERCASE: Lowercase and spell out titles when they are not used with an individual's name: *The president issued a statement. The pope gave his blessing.*

Lowercase and spell out titles in constructions that set them off from a name by commas: *The vice president, Nelson Rockefeller, declined to run again. Paul VI, the current pope, does not plan to retire.*

COURTESY TITLES: See the courtesy titles entry for guidelines on when to use *Miss, Mr., Mrs.* and *Ms.*

The forms *Mr., Mrs., Miss* and *Ms.* apply both in regular text and in quotations.

FORMAL TITLES: Capitalize formal titles when they are used immediately before one or more names: *Pope Paul, President Washington, Vice Presidents John Jones and William Smith.*

A formal title generally is one that denotes a scope of authority, professional activity or academic accomplishment so specific that the designation becomes almost as much an integral part of an individual's identity as a proper name itself: *President Carter, Gov. Ella Grasso, Dr. Marcus Welby, Pvt. Gomer Pyle.*

Other titles serve primarily as occupational descriptions: *astronaut John Glenn, movie star John Wayne, peanut farmer Jimmy Carter.*

A final determination on whether a title is formal or occupational depends on the practice of the governmental or private organization that confers it. If there is doubt about the status of a title and the practice of the organization cannot be determined, use a construction that sets the name or the title off with commas.

ABBREVIATED TITLES: The following formal titles are capitalized and abbreviated as shown when used before a name outside quotations: *Dr., Gov., Lt. Gov., Rep., Sen.* and certain military ranks listed in the **military titles** entry. Spell out all except *Dr.* when they are used in quotations.

All other formal titles are spelled out in all uses.

ROYAL TITLES: Capitalize *king, queen,* etc., when used directly before a name.

TITLES OF NOBILITY: Capitalize a full title when it serves as the alternate name for an individual.

PAST AND FUTURE TITLES: A formal title that an individual formerly held, is about to hold or holds temporarily is capitalized if used before the person's name. But do not capitalize the qualifying word: *former President Ford, deposed King Constantine, Attorney General-designate Griffin B. Bell, acting Mayor Peter Barry.*

LONG TITLES: Separate a long title from a name by a construction that requires a comma: *Charles Robinson, undersecretary for economic affairs, spoke.* Or: *The undersecretary for economic affairs, Charles Robinson, spoke.*

UNIQUE TITLES: If a title applies only to one person in an organization, insert the word *the* in a construction that uses commas: *John Jones, the deputy vice president, spoke.*

women Women should receive the same treatment as men in all areas of coverage. Physical descriptions, sexist references, demeaning stereotypes and condescending phrases should not be used.

To cite some examples, this means that:

—Copy should not assume maleness

when both sexes are involved, as in *Jackson told newsmen* or in *the taxpayer . . . he* when it easily can be said *Jackson told reporters* or *taxpayers . . . they*.

—Copy should not express surprise that an attractive woman can be professionally accomplished, as in: *Mary Smith doesn't look the part but she's an authority on . . .*

—Copy should not gratuitously mention family relationships where there is no relevance to the subject, as in: *Golda Meir, a doughty grandmother, told the Egyptians today . . .*

—Use the same standards for men and women in deciding whether to include specific mention of personal appearance or marital and family situation.

In other words, treatment of the sexes should be even-handed and free of assumptions and stereotypes. This does not mean that valid and acceptable words such as *mankind* or *humanity* cannot be used. They are proper.

Appendix C
CODES OF ETHICS

SPJ'S CODE OF ETHICS

The Society of Professional Journalists, Sigma Delta Chi, believes the duty of journalists is to serve the truth.

We believe the agencies of mass communication are carriers of public discussion and information, acting on their constitutional mandate and freedom to learn and report the facts.

We believe in public enlightenment as the forerunner of justice, and in our Constitutional role to seek the truth as part of the public's right to know the truth.

We believe those responsibilities carry obligations that require journalists to perform with intelligence, objectivity, accuracy and fairness.

To these ends, we declare acceptance of the standards of practice here set forth:

Responsibility:

The public's right to know of events of public importance and interest is the overriding mission of the mass media. The purpose of distributing news and enlightened opinion is to serve the general welfare. Journalists who use their professional status as representatives of the public for selfish or other unworthy motives violate a high trust.

Freedom of the press:

Freedom of the press is to be guarded as an inalienable right of people in a free society. It carries with it the freedom and the responsibility to discuss, question and challenge actions and utterances of our government and of our public and private institutions. Journalists uphold the right to speak unpopular opinions and the privilege to agree with the majority.

Ethics:

Journalists must be free of obligation to any other interest other than the public's right to know the truth.

1. Gifts, favors, free travel, special treatment or privileges can compromise the integrity of journalists and their employers. Nothing of value should be accepted.

2. Secondary employment, political involvement, holding public office and service in community organizations should be avoided if it compromises the integrity of journalists and their employers. Journalists and their employers should conduct their personal lives in a manner which protects them from conflict of interest, real or apparent. Their responsibilities to the public are paramount. This is the nature of their profession.
3. So-called news communications from private sources should not be published or broadcast without substantiation of their claims to news value.
4. Journalists will seek news that serves the public interest, despite the obstacles. They will make constant efforts to assure that the public's business is conducted in public and that public records are open to public inspection.
5. Journalists acknowledge the newsman's ethic of protecting confidential sources of information.
6. Plagiarism is dishonest and is unacceptable.

Accuracy and objectivity:

Good faith with the public is the foundation of all worthy journalism:

1. Truth is our ultimate goal.
2. Objectivity in reporting the news is another goal which serves as the mark of an experienced professional. It is a standard of performance toward which we strive. We honor those who achieve it.
3. There is no excuse for inaccuracies or lack of thoroughness.
4. Newspaper headlines should be fully warranted by the contents of the articles they accompany. Photographs and telecasts should give an accurate picture of an event and not highlight a minor incident out of context.
5. Sound practice makes clear distinction between news reports and expressions of opinion. News reports should be free of opinion or bias and represent all sides of an issue.
6. Partisanship in editorial comment which knowingly departs from the truth violates the spirit of American journalism.
7. Journalists recognize their responsibility for offering informed analysis, comment and editorial opinion on public events and issues. They accept the obligation to present such material by individuals whose competence, experience and judgment qualify them for it.
8. Special articles or presentations devoted to advocacy or the writer's own conclusions and interpretations should be labeled as such.

Fair play:

Journalists at all times will show respect for the dignity, privacy, rights and well-being of people encountered in the course of gathering and presenting the news.

APPENDIX C   CODES OF ETHICS

1. The news media should not communicate unofficial charges affecting reputation or moral character without giving the accused a chance to reply.
2. The news media must guard against invading a person's right to privacy.
3. The media should not pander to morbid curiosity about details of vice and crime.
4. It is the duty of news media to make prompt and complete correction of their errors.
5. Journalists should be accountable to the public for their reports and the public should be encouraged to voice its grievances against the media. Open dialogue with our readers, viewers and listeners should be fostered.

Pledge:

Journalists should actively censure and try to prevent violations of these standards, and they should encourage their observance by all newspeople. Adherence to this code of ethics is intended to preserve the bond of mutual trust and respect between American journalists and the American people.
Adopted 1973. Revised 1984.

THE *LOS ANGELES TIMES'* CODE OF ETHICS

Guidelines established by national organizations, though helpful, are inherently vague. Recognizing this, individual newspapers have formulated more concrete policies.

In 1982 William F. Thomas, editor of the *Los Angeles Times,* distributed to members of the editorial staff this code:

Members of the Times staff are being offered increasing opportunities these days to use their expertise for outside publications or the electronic media. These offers can bring career enhancement and personal satisfaction, and we do not seek to discourage either.

But, to try to avoid embarrassment or conflicts with your responsibilities to the Times, and to answer questions which arise from time to time, here are some general guidelines to confirm and clarify our existing practices.

Since they are general, possibly the most important of them is the recommendation that any question of definition or applicability can be settled by a discussion of specifics. So if the slightest doubt is sparked by any situation, talk it over with a supervisor.

Outside Writing

1. No articles for competing publications.
2. No articles for business or trade publications, or any others which

might fit the category of house organs, by writers or editors involved in coverage of their special areas.
3. No paid sports scoring.
4. No record or book jacket reviews which have not been published in the Times, with rare exceptions.

Gifts

1. Shun gifts from news sources or subjects of coverage, except those gifts of insignificant value.
2. Books or records received for review should not be sold by staffers.

Junkets

1. Within the bounds of common sense and civil behavior, staffers should not accept free transportation or reduced rate travel, or free accommodations or meals. Exceptions can occur in such areas as political coverage, when convenience or access to news sources dictate. Again: if there are any questions, ask.

Meals

1. As before, common sense and good manners should guide. A meal or a drink with a news source may be perfectly acceptable with the understanding that they will be reciprocated at company expense when appropriate.
2. A staffer in most cases may accept a meal ticket when covering a political or civic event.

Tickets, Admission

1. Staff members covering a sports or entertainment event can accept admission or preferred or press box seating. When attending an event upon which you will not report, but is judged by a supervisor to be useful to your work, pay the price and submit an expense report.
2. In all other situations, ask.

Business Dealing

1. Staff members may not enter into a business relationship with their news sources.
2. Staff members with investments or stockholdings in corporations should avoid making news decisions that involve these corporations. If it is impossible to avoid them, these potential conflicts should be disclosed to a supervisor.

Political Activities

1. Staff members should not take part in political or governmental activities they may be called upon to cover, or whose coverage they supervise.
2. No staff member should work for pay in any political campaign or organization.

3. Only in cases where there is no possibility of conflict should a staff member run for public office or assist in a political campaign or organization.
4. If a staff member has a close relative or personal friend working in a political campaign or organization, the staffer should refrain from covering or making news judgments about that campaign or organization.

Broadcasting and Other Outside Appearances

1. All such appearances for pay should be carefully examined from the aspect of possible conflicts and embarrassment to yourself or the newspaper. In general, regularly scheduled appearances or those under any other circumstances which might confuse the staffer's primary identification as a Times person should be avoided.

Glossary

A wire The main news wire of The Associated Press and United Press International that transmits the most significant national and international stories of the day. The wire is sometimes written as **AAA** or **Aye**.

Absolute defenses In libel suits, defenses that, if proven, are viable when defending against such actions. There are no conditions or qualifications. For example, under the statute of limitations, suit must be brought within a specified period or the plaintiff has no standing to sue.

Abstracts Brief summaries of articles or books that are contained in some computer reference searches.

Accident forms Reports available in police stations that outline the circumstances surrounding accidents investigated by the department. Larger-circulation newspapers generally cover only spectacular accidents. Smaller-circulation dailies and weeklies routinely report all accidents, no matter how minor.

Action line column A consumer-oriented column that helps people solve their problems. People write or call in their problems, and a reporter tries to solve them.

Active voice When the subject of a sentence acts upon an object. For example: *The mayor denied the charge.* Active voice generally is preferred in journalistic writing because it is more vigorous.

Actual malice A fault standard in libel law, first articulated by the U.S. Supreme Court in 1964, that must be met by plaintiffs who are public officials or figures. These plaintiffs must prove that the information was communicated "with knowledge that it was false or with reckless disregard of whether it was false or not."

Add Each subsequent page of a story written on hard copy. For example, the second page of a story is the first add, the third page is the second and so forth. When wire copy is electronically transmitted, an add is additional information to a story that is filed under the same keyword as the original story.

Advance A story announcing an upcoming event.

Advance text A copy of the speech a source is expected to deliver. Reporters use advance texts to help them prepare for covering stories. They do not write stories from advance texts, however, because speakers often wander from their prepared remarks.

Advocacy journalism The type of news writing practiced by a reporter who defends or maintains a proposal or cause.

Agate Smaller than regular text type, generally 6 points or 7 points in size. (A **point** is 1/72nd of an inch.) Sports statistics and public-record items commonly are set in this type size.

Agenda An outline of matters to be considered by a government body.

AM A morning newspaper.

AM cycle Generally the time from noon to midnight. Usually morning newspapers report news that breaks on the AM cycle.

Analysis piece A feature story, also called a **backgrounder**, that adds meaning to current issues in the news by explaining them further.

Anonymous sources People who are willing to provide information on the condition that their names not be used in the story.

AP members Newspapers and broadcast stations that receive news from The Associated Press (see below). The organization is a not-for-profit cooperative.

Arraignment The step in the judicial process involving the reading of the charge to the accused. The arraignment often is held in a lower court, where a plea typically is entered.

Associated Press Generally referred to as the

363

AP, it is the world's oldest cooperative news-gathering service.
Attribution   Telling readers the source of the information.
Authoritarian (press) system   System in which criticism of the government is forbidden. Most newspapers in countries that operate under this philosophy are privately owned, but their content is controlled by the state through licensing or the issuance of patents.
"Aw-nuts" school   Premise subscribed to by some sports reporters that even great games and gifted athletes should be treated with near disdain.

B wire   News wire of The Associated Press and United Press International that transmits national and international news of secondary importance.
Background   Sentences in a news story that explain important elements. Background can explain something technical or provide details that were reported in earlier stories.
Backgrounder   See **analysis piece**.
Banner   A headline that stretches across a newspaper page.
Beat reporter   A reporter who covers a specific geographic or subject area each day. Beats include police and fire; county and federal courts; and city, county and state government.
Body   The portion of a news or feature story between the lead and conclusion. The body should keep readers interested in the story and hold them until the conclusion.
Bold face   Dark type that is thicker and blacker than ordinary text type. Also: **boldface caps**, which are capital letters set in blacker than ordinary type. Bold face or boldface caps often are used for bylines.
Box score   Statistical summary for various sports.
Breaking news   News that is available for publication.
Brief   A written report in which a lawyer sets forth facts that support his or her position.
Brightener   A short, often humorous story that emphasizes quirks in the news. Brighteners are used to give an audience a break from hard news. They allow people to sit back and smile.
Bulldog   A newspaper's first edition of the day.
Bulletin   Priority designation used by wire services. A bulletin contains at least one publishable paragraph but not more than two; it alerts newsrooms that a major story is developing.

Bullets   Bold dots that introduce and highlight items in a news or feature story.
Bureau   A geographically removed extension of a media outlet's headquarters. The Associated Press, for example, has its headquarters in New York, but it has bureaus in every state and in scores of foreign countries.
Buried lead   The term for a news story's most important point that is not in the opening paragraph, where it belongs.
Byline   A line at the top of a story that names the author.

Caps   Media shorthand for **capital letters**.
Change of venue   Moving a trial to another location to reduce the possibility that prejudicial opinions, emotions and publicity will deprive the accused of a fair, impartial hearing.
City editor   The editor who runs the city (or metropolitan) desk and is in charge of the city-side general-assignment, beat and specialty reporters. The city editor makes certain that news in the city (or metropolitan area) is covered and as many local stories as possible get in each edition.
Civil case   A case that involves arriving at specific solutions to legal strife between individuals, businesses, state or local governments or agencies of government. Civil cases include suits for breach of contract and for libel.
Closed-ended question   A question that is structured to elicit a short, precise answer. Reporters often ask closed-ended questions that require only "yes" or "no" responses. Sometimes, such questions build answers into them. For example: *John Johnson and Bill Blodgett are candidates for mayor. Which of these candidates will you vote for?*
Clutter lead   An awkward and difficult-to-understand lead that contains too many elements.
Codes of ethics   Guidelines developed by national groups and some individual media outlets to provide guidance to journalists. Codes often discuss matters such as the responsibilities of journalists, the use of unnamed sources, accuracy, objectivity, reporter misrepresentation, acceptance of gifts and favors from sources, political activities journalists should or should not take part in and business dealings that could present conflicts of interest.
Color   Observations, narrative or anecdotes in a story that give an audience a clearer picture of a person or event.
Column inch   One column wide, one inch deep.

Stories in a newspaper often are measured in column inches.

Commission government Municipal government system in which a committee of city leaders assumes both executive and legislative functions.

Complaint In law, a document that is filed by a plaintiff against a defendant in a civil suit. The complaint usually contains a precise set of arguments against the defendant.

Complete direct quote A source's exact words, set off by quotation marks.

Complex sentence A sentence that has but one independent clause and at least one dependent clause. For example, *Johnson is the coach who will be elected to the hall of fame. Johnson is the coach* is an independent clause because it would make complete sense when left standing alone; *who will be elected to the hall of fame* is a dependent, or subordinate, clause.

Composing room The production area of a newspaper where each edition's pages are put together according to an editor's instructions on layout sheets.

Computer reference services Services provided by many libraries to search for information via computer. The search is similar to a volume-by-volume search of a printed index, except that the requested information is returned electronically.

Conditional defense A defense against libel suits that involves certain conditions or qualifications. For example, the defense of privilege of reporting may be used when reporting information from official proceedings, public documents and court proceedings. The defense is limited, however, to *fair* and *accurate* reporting that does not intertwine extraneous libelous matter.

Contrast lead A lead that compares or contrasts one person or thing with another or several people or things.

"Cooling off" period A relatively short time, generally 10 to 15 minutes, set aside by coaches after a game during which the locker room is off limits to reporters who seek interviews with players.

Cop shop An old-time journalism term for police station that still is used today by many reporters.

Copy The written material produced by journalists.

Copy desk The desk inside a newsroom where copy editors process copy written by journalists and write headlines.

Copy editor The editor who checks stories to make certain they follow proper style, usage, spelling and grammar rules. The copy editor also makes certain a story is well organized and not libelous. After editing the story, the copy editor writes a headline for it.

Copy paper The paper on which a story is typed. Copy paper often is newsprint trimmed to 8 1/2 by 11 inches.

Correction Material that corrects something in a previously disseminated story.

Correspondent A journalist who contributes news stories to a media outlet that is located elsewhere. Metropolitan newspapers, for example, normally have correspondents stationed in the nation's capital as well as in countries around the world.

Council-manager government A municipal government system in which the city manager controls the administrative apparatus of the city. The main source of city government expertise is the city manager, a trained professional adept at administering a community's affairs.

Counts In law, parts of a complaint or indictment claiming a specific wrong done.

Courtesy titles Titles such as Mr., Mrs. or Miss that precede names. Most newspapers limit courtesy titles to second references in obituaries.

Criminal case A case that involves the enforcement of a criminal statute. Actions are brought by the state or federal government against an individual charged with committing a crime, such as murder or armed robbery.

Criss-cross directory A directory that lists a city's residents by names and addresses. By looking up an address in the directory, a reporter can find the identity and phone number of the person at the address.

Crop A mark on a photograph or other piece of art indicating that it will not be used full frame. Art is cropped to eliminate unneeded material or to make it fit into a predetermined hole.

Cursor The flashing light on a computer screen that indicates where the next character would appear.

Cut Another term for a printed photograph or other piece of art. Stories also are cut, trimmed or sliced.

Cut the fluff To eliminate superfluous, overwritten and untimely information from a press release.

Cutline The copy accompanying a photograph or other piece of art that explains what is occurring or being shown.

Damages In law, the monetary value for the injury allegedly sustained through the unlawful act or negligence of another.
Dangling modifiers Grammatical errors that occur when a phrase used to begin a sentence is not followed by a subject, or when the subject is not correctly connected to the phrase or modifier. For example: *By working diligently, the job was accomplished.*
Dateline The opening line of an out-of-town story that gives the place of origin.
Death notice A story or listing of information about someone who has died. Many newspapers consider death notices to be synonymous with **obituaries.**
Defendant The party against whom a lawsuit is brought.
Dependent clauses Clauses that would not make complete sense if left standing alone. For example: *John studies hard before he takes a test.* The clause *before he takes a test* is dependent upon *John studies hard* in order to make sense. It cannot be left standing alone.
Deposition An out-of-court statement made by a witness under oath.
Direct address lead A lead that communicates directly with an audience by including the word *you.*
Docket Court record that documents progress in a specific case. All complaints filed, motions made and other developments in a case are recorded chronologically.
Double truck A story or advertisement that covers two facing pages of a newspaper or magazine, including the **gutter** (the space down the center of the two pages).
Dummy A mock-up of a newspaper or magazine page that has advertisements with specific sizes keyed in. News stories, features and photographs are laid out around the ads.
Dupe An abbreviation for duplicate and a designation for a carbon copy of a story.

Editor The person in charge of the editorial function of a newspaper. The role of the editor changes depending on the size of the newspaper.
Editorial news hole The space on a newspaper page that does not contain an advertisement and is reserved for stories or art. The ads are laid out on the page first; the editorial news hole consists of the column inches remaining.
Electronic carbons Designation by The Associated Press for the transmission of stories directly from newspapers' computers to regional AP bureaus.
Enterprise journalism Stories that require reporters to go beyond their daily routine. For example, a police reporter routinely writes stories from accident logs. An enterprise story would examine why a particular intersection has more accidents than any in the city and would require multiple sources, statistical information and extensive quotations.
Executive session A meeting at which no official actions can be taken by government officials and at which members of the press and public are excluded.

Feature story A story that analyzes the news; entertains an audience; or describes people, places or things in or out of the news.
Federal judicial system The branch of the federal government that is responsible for interpreting the law. The U.S. Supreme Court is the nation's highest court.
Felony A serious crime for which punishment normally is imprisonment in a penitentiary.
Filing In law, formal lodging of a complaint in a civil action.
Filler A short story of less importance that is used to fill a small open space on a newspaper page.
Financial editor The editor in charge of handling the business news that goes into a newspaper. Most papers have a business page or section each day, and many have a staff of financial reporters who cover area businesses.
Financial wire A news wire of The Associated Press that transmits business news stories, some stock tables and other market data.
Fire reports Daily reports of activity involving the fire department.
Five W's and H The *who, what, where, when, why* and *how* of an event. These are the six primary elements of a news story.
Flash Top-priority designation used by wire services. It usually contains only a few words and may not be a complete sentence. A classic flash: *DALLAS (AP)—Kennedy shot.*
Focal point The thrust of a summary lead. A reporter determines the focal point of the lead by choosing which of the five W's and H to emphasize.
Follow Sometimes referred to as a **second-day story,** a second or later story written about a

newsworthy event. A follow provides the latest news in the lead or early in the story, but it also repeats the major news that was reported earlier.

Follow-up question A rearticulated or new question that a reporter asks to elicit a new or more specific response from a source.

Foreign editor The editor who supervises reporters who cover news events outside the United States.

Fragmentary quotes Extremely small parcels of the precise words of a source that are spread throughout a sentence or paragraph. Fragmentary quotes look confusing when set in type and generally should not be used.

Free ad Information in a press release that clearly is of no news value and tries to seek free publicity for a person, business or organization.

Free-lance To produce news stories for several publications, none of which is a full-time employer.

Funnel interview The most common type of interview, in which the reporter begins with non-threatening background and open-ended questions. The toughest questions, those that may put the source on the spot, are saved for near the end of the interview.

Gag order A judicial mandate, sometimes called a **protective order,** that requires the press to refrain from disseminating specific information or that restricts those associated with the trial or investigation from discussing the case with the press.

Gang interview A press-conference interview in which every reporter is given the same information and the source refuses to meet with reporters individually.

Gatekeepers People in positions to make news decisions. Editors and reporters, on a story-by-story basis, decide items to include and angles to emphasize.

"Gee-whiz" school The premise of some sportswriting stories that athletes perform nothing but heroic feats.

General assignment reporter A reporter who covers a breaking news or feature story that has been assigned by an editor. A general assignment reporter does not cover a specific beat.

Grand jury A jury of citizens convened to determine if there is probable cause that a crime has been committed and that the person charged with the crime committed it. A grand jury is so labeled because it has more members than a trial jury.

Graph Media shorthand for **paragraph.** Also spelled **graf.**

Guild A union of journalists formed to bargain collectively over such things as wages and benefits. For example, many newspaper journalists belong to the Newspaper Guild.

Handout Another term for **news release** or **press release.** Corporations, businesses, universities, organizations and political parties send handouts to alert the media to something they are doing.

Hard copy The product of a story composed on a typewriter or printed out from a computer (video display terminal).

Hard news Events that are timely and are covered almost automatically by print and electronic media. A speech by a ranking public official is an example.

Hardware Physical components of a computer such as the terminal, cables, disk drives and so forth.

Head sheet The paper on which a headline is written or typed. Computerized newsrooms no longer use head sheets.

Hoaxes Deceptive or fraudulent calls or letters that dupe a newspaper into disseminating an obituary for someone who has not died or does not exist.

Hostile source An uncooperative, close-lipped source who does not want to talk to reporters.

Hourglass style A style of writing in which the major news of a story is reported in the first few paragraphs and then a transitional paragraph introduces a chronology of the events of the story.

House ad An advertisement that promotes a publication.

Human angles Approaches to stories that readers can relate to. This is common on weather-related stories that reporters write to emphasize how the weather will affect people.

Human-interest story A feature story that shows a subject's oddity or emotional or entertainment value.

Hyperbolic adjectives Overused references most common to sportswriting that stretch beyond controlled, accurate description. Phrases such as *phenomenal freshman, sensational sophomore* and *game of the century* are examples.

Immediate news value Descriptive of a breaking story, such as a fire, an accident or an election, that reporters try to cover as quickly as possible.

Immediate release A line at the top of a press release informing the media that the information in the release can be used immediately.

In-camera inspection A judge's examination of materials in a private room or with all spectators excluded from the courtroom.

Independent clauses Clauses that make complete sense when left standing alone. For example: *John studies hard before he takes a test.* The clause *John studies hard* could stand alone; it expresses a complete thought.

In-depth story A story that, through extensive research and interviews, provides a detailed account well beyond a basic news story. An in-depth story can be a lengthy news feature that examines one topic extensively; an investigative story that reveals wrongdoing by a person, an agency or an institution; or a first-person article in which the writer relives a happy or painful experience.

Indictment A written accusation by a grand jury charging that a person has committed a public offense.

Indirect quote Paraphrase of a source's statement that retains its meaning. Attribution must be provided.

Individual statistics Data compiled for each player in an athletic contest. For example, field goals made, free throws made, fouls, rebounds and total points are important individual statistics for basketball players.

Information In law, a written accusation, presented by a public officer such as a prosecuting attorney instead of a grand jury, that charges a person with committing a public offense.

Initial appearance The step in the judicial process at which the charge is read to the accused. In most states, this is referred to as an **arraignment**.

Insert Copy that is placed, or inserted, into a story to make the story more complete or to clarify what has been written already.

Interview from the outside in An interviewing process, used mainly by investigative reporters, in which the source most critical to the story is interviewed last, after the reporter knows many of the answers to the questions he or she will ask.

Inverted-funnel interview A type of interview in which the key questions, often the toughest, are asked immediately. This style of interview is used when sources are experienced in fielding closed-ended or adversary questions or when there is little time to ask questions.

Inverted pyramid A traditional news writing form in which the key points of a story are put in the opening paragraph and the news is stacked in the following paragraphs in order of descending importance.

Issues reporting Reporting that examines complex matters of interest rather than simply providing the who, what, where, when, why and how of a newsworthy event.

Italics Type that slants to the right.

"Jell-O journalism" News reporting that over-emphasizes soft writing, which is decried by some editors.

Journalists' privilege The assertion that journalists have a privilege, under certain conditions, not to reveal information sought by a court or grand jury. No such absolute privilege exists.

Jump To continue a story from one newspaper page to another.

Kid quotes In sportwriting, quotations gathered from junior high and high school athletes.

Lay out To position stories and art elements on a newspaper page. A **layout,** or **dummy,** is an editor's plan of how the page will look when it is printed.

Lead The opening paragraph of a story.

Lead block A multiparagraph lead that builds up to the major point of the story.

Leak journalism The practice of relying on "leaks" from unnamed sources to construct a story. Most editors discourage such a practice.

Libel The legal offense of publishing a story in which a person's reputation is damaged by holding him or her up to public ridicule, hatred or scorn.

Libertarian (press) system Developed in America beginning early in the 19th century, the system in which the media flood the marketplace with information so citizens can make enlightened decisions. The press is regarded as a primary instrument for checking on government and its officials.

Lifestyle editor The person, also called **features editor,** who leads what usually is a newspaper's main features section. The section may include articles by lifestyle writers, a food editor, an entertainment writer, a drama critic, a television writer and other reviewers and critics.

GLOSSARY

Limited access Designation for police reports that cannot be examined in their entirety, under all circumstances, by members of the public or by journalists.

Localizing Putting a local emphasis on a story with broader ramifications. For example, if a wire service report datelined Washington mentions a local or state official in the body of the story, the local newspaper may rework the story to move the local reference to the top of the story.

Local news value Characteristic of a story of particular interest to local readers.

Local weather forecasts Stories that discuss and predict upcoming weather for a local area.

Lower case Small letters of type, in contrast to capital letters.

Mainbar The main story in a group of articles about the same topic in a single edition of a newspaper.

Makeup editor The person who dummies (lays out) pages of a newspaper.

Managing editor The top editor in most newspaper newsrooms. This editor makes certain the paper is out on time each day and that costs are kept within a budget. The managing editor is responsible for hiring and firing newsroom personnel and usually is involved in story, photo and graphics selection.

Masthead The box that appears inside a newspaper, often on the editorial page, that identifies its top executives.

Mayor-council government A municipal government system in which the mayor can be categorized as "weak" or "strong," depending on the powers assigned to the position. In a "strong" mayor system, the mayor has the power to draw up budgets and to make and administer policy. In a "weak" mayor system, the mayor is, in essence, the chairperson of the city council, with most managerial functions divided among other elected officials and the council.

Media event A news occurrence, such as a presidential press conference, in which both the interviewee and the reporters are in the limelight.

Memorials Gifts that are given in honor of a person who has died. In obituaries, most newspapers note when families suggest memorials to a specific cause or organization.

Minor sports Non–revenue-producing sports such as gymnastics, volleyball, cross country and swimming.

Misdemeanor A crime considered to be less serious than a felony. Punishment normally is a fine or imprisonment in a facility other than a penitentiary.

More The word written at the end of a page to indicate another page is following.

Morgue The common name for a newspaper library where clippings files and reference books are kept. Reporters do much of their research in the morgue. Stories (clips) generally are filed under subject and reporters' bylines.

Mugshot A head-only photograph of a source. One-column mugshots of primary sources often accompany news stories. They are used to show readers what the sources look like, as well as to break up long pieces of gray type.

Multiple-element lead A lead, also called a **double-barreled lead,** that gives two or more of the primary elements of a news story equal rating and informs an audience immediately that more than one major event is occurring.

Nameplate The name of a newspaper on Page One. It is also called the **flag.**

Narrative lead A lead that uses narrative to draw people into a story by putting them in the middle of the action. A narrative lead is the most popular lead on features and non-breaking news stories.

National editor The editor who supervises reporters covering news events in cities other than the city in which the newspaper is published.

Negligence A fault standard in libel law articulated by the U.S. Supreme Court in 1974 that can vary from state to state. In some states, the level of liability is "gross negligence"; in others, it is the "failure to act as a reasonable person" when gathering information for and writing a story.

New lead Updated information that replaces the original lead. The wire services, during a 12-hour cycle, constantly are transmitting new leads to developing stories.

News editor The editor who decides which news is put in the newspaper and where. This editor is in charge of the copy desk, where makeup editors and copy editors work.

News huddle A daily meeting of a newspaper's editors, also called a **doping session,** a **news conference,** an **editors' meeting** or an **editorial conference.** In this meeting the editors discuss and then decide which of the top foreign, national, state and local stories and photographs will make it into the paper.

News mix A combination of hard news stories and feature pieces. The news mix also can include a blend of longer and shorter local, regional, national and international stories.

News peg A sentence or paragraph linking a story to a news occurrence.

News release See **handout**.

News story A write-up that chronicles the who, what, where, when, why and how of timely occurrences.

Newsworthy element Peg of a story that often should be reported in the lead paragraph. In stories based on survey research, for example, the most significant statistical finding would be the newsworthy element that belongs in the lead.

No bill The finding returned by a grand jury if it determines a sufficient probability does not exist that the accused committed the crime with which he or she is being charged.

Nose for news A reporter's instinct, which is used to gather information and make news decisions as quickly as possible.

Nut graph An explanatory paragraph, also called a "**so-what**" **paragraph,** that follows the introductory lead block and explains the significance of a story.

Obit The common journalism term for **obituary**, a story about someone who has died.

Objective verbs of attribution Verbs of attribution such as *said* or *added* that reporters can use when quoting sources, thus avoiding the interjection of personal feelings or perceptions about the way the source sounded.

Observation What a reporter sees, hears, smells, tastes or touches while working on a story. Observations add color to news and feature stories.

Off the record An agreement reached by a reporter and source prior to an interview that disallows use of the material revealed. Often, reporters refuse to accept information off the record, choosing instead to try to find it from another source.

Ombudsman A "middle person," or theoretically objective employee of a newspaper, who listens to complaints from readers and, when they are justified, passes them on to appropriate reporters or editors. About two dozen newspapers employ ombudsmen.

On background An agreement reached by a reporter and source prior to an interview that the material can be used, but attribution by name cannot be provided.

On deep background An agreement reached by a reporter and source prior to an interview that the material can be used, but not in direct quotations and not accompanied by attribution.

On the record An agreement reached by a reporter and source prior to an interview that the material can be used, complete with the name of the source and identification.

Op-ed page The page that runs next to an editorial page, giving readers a mix of opinion columns and illustrations.

Open-ended question A question that is structured to allow a source time to develop an answer. Open-ended questions are a good way to break the ice between a reporter and source because they give the source time to expand at length. For example: *What do you think about the quality of sports coverage in your local daily?*

Open-meeting laws Statutes in all 50 states that provide for public access to meetings of government bodies. The laws are not uniform, and all list exceptions to access.

Open-records laws Statutes that provide for access to state-level information. Most of these statutes, which also list specific exceptions to public records, specify that the laws should be construed liberally in favor of persons seeking the records.

Open sentences Clearly constructed sentences that present no confusing ambiguities to the reader. Open sentences normally contain a straight subject-verb sequence and seldom are introduced with distracting dependent clauses and phrases.

Organizational structures Chains of command that outline the titles and duties of executives and employees. Beat reporters, for example, must master the organizational structures of the agencies they cover.

Paper of record A newspaper that offers comprehensive straightforward news accounts of what happened in the world, nation, state and community since the last edition. A paper of record also is a source for future historical reference.

Partial defense A defense, sometimes called a **mitigating factor,** that can be employed against libel suits if conditional or absolute defenses cannot be used successfully. Partial defenses, such as publication of a retraction, represent good faith on the part of the defendant and can be taken into consideration when damages are assessed.

GLOSSARY

Partial quotes Specific portions of a lengthier complete direct quotation, which are reported and set off by quotation marks.

Passive voice When the subject of a sentence is acted upon by the object. For example: *The child was hit by the car.* Passive voice should be used in news writing only when the person or thing receiving the action is more important than the person or thing doing the acting.

Personality profile A feature story that brings an audience closer to a person in or out of the news. Interviews, observations and creative writing are used to paint a vivid picture of the person.

Petition In law, a document that asks a court to take a particular action.

Photo editor The editor who supervises a newspaper's photographers. This editor also may write the captions that run with photographs that appear in the newspaper.

Plaintiff The party bringing a lawsuit.

Play-by-play charts Tables produced at sports events such as football and basketball games to help reporters piece together important sequences in the contests. In basketball, for example, the chart would note who scored, on what kind of shot and what the score was at the time of the play.

Plea bargaining Negotiation between the prosecutor and defense lawyers over the kind of plea a suspect might enter on a specific charge. Prosecutors often propose that, in exchange for a plea of guilty, the state would bring a lesser charge against the suspect.

Pleadings In law, a written statement by all the parties setting forth assertions, denials and contentions.

PM An evening newspaper.

PM cycle Generally the time from midnight to noon. Usually evening newspapers report news that breaks on the PM cycle.

Police log A daily report of activity involving the department.

Precision journalism The practice of using social science research methods—such as methodologically sound sampling procedures and computer analysis—to gather facts, thus leading to more precise, accurate news stories.

Preliminary hearing The step in the judicial process at which the state must present evidence to convince the presiding judge that there is probable cause to believe the defendant committed the crime with which he or she is being charged.

Press critic A reporter who writes stories about the strengths and weaknesses of and trends in daily media coverage. David Shaw of the *Los Angeles Times* probably is the best known.

Proof A copy of a typeset story.

Proofreader The person who reads a proof of a story to ensure that it is set the way the editors wanted and that it is free of typographical errors.

Public figure In libel cases, one who must "voluntarily thrust" himself or herself into the vortex of a particular controversy to resolve that controversy, or one who must assume a role "of especial prominence" to the extent that, for all purposes, he or she is to be considered a public figure.

Public official In libel cases, a government employee who has substantial responsibility for or control over the conduct of governmental affairs.

Public relations people People who work for public relations firms and whose job it is to gain media atttention for the businesses, organizations, people or institutions they represent.

Queue A file in a newsroom computer system. Stories and other information are stored in and pulled out of queues.

Question lead A lead that asks a question. The key to writing a question lead is to answer the question as quickly as possible.

Quote lead A lead that allows a central character to begin a news or feature story by talking directly to the audience. The quote may be the most powerful one in the story, or it may set the tone for what is to follow.

Rambling quotes Long, drawn-out direct quotations that journalists can avoid reporting by paraphrasing or by using indirect quotes when possible.

Release date A date at the beginning of a press release or wire story that informs the media of the earliest time they can use the information. Many press releases are stamped *for immediate release*, which means the information can be used as soon as it is received.

Same-day obits Obituaries, written on the day of a person's death, in which the lead paragraph features the fact that the person has died.

Scanner A multichannel radio that monitors police and fire dispatches.

Search warrant A court document issued in the name of the state that directs a law-enforcement officer to search specified premises.

Second-day obits Obituaries, written one or

more days after a person dies, in which the lead paragraph features the time of services.
Second-day story A follow-up story written after the breaking news has been reported.
Settlement In law, an agreement reached by the parties, often before the case goes to trial.
Shield laws Statutes in about half the states that allow journalists and other specified people who are questioned by grand juries or under other circumstances to protect their sources under certain conditions.
Shotgun interview See **smoking gun interview.**
Sidebar A story that runs with a mainbar. A sidebar isolates a person, place or thing usually mentioned in a mainbar and further explains, examines or illustrates it.
Simple sentence A sentence that has but one independent clause. For example: *The high jumper won.*
Slot editor The person who supervises copy editors. The slot editor distributes stories to copy editors and then checks their editing and headlines.
Slug A one- or two-word label on a story. The slug identifies a story and keeps it separate from other stories.
Smoking gun interview Also called a **shotgun interview,** a question-and-answer session in which a reporter, armed with videotape or other evidence of wrongdoing, asks direct questions about specific incidents. When the source denies any wrongdoing, the reporter shows the incriminating evidence in the hope that the source will admit guilt.
Social responsibility theory The philosophy, which emerged as a theory in America in the post–World War II years, that all views should be disseminated through the media, which is bound by professional ethics. The theory holds that if the press fails to live up to its obligations to present diverse views and to interpret them responsibly, the government can step in to ensure public service.
Soft news Events that usually are not considered immediately important or timely to a wide audience. Many of these events still merit coverage. A math fair at an elementary school or a faculty member's prize-winning rose garden might be covered as soft news, for example.
Software A program that tells the computer how to carry out specific functions such as word processing.
Source Written material or a person that a reporter uses for information.

Source file A file a reporter keeps that shows names, phone numbers, addresses and the expertise of useful sources.
Specialty reporter A reporter who covers breaking news or feature stories in a highly specialized area, such as transportation, energy, education, religion, aviation, the arts and legal affairs. Like the sources they cover, specialty reporters must be experts in a particular field.
Sports editor The editor in charge of sportswriters and the desk people who process their copy. The sports editor often writes a column.
Sportswriting clichés Phrases such as *brilliant field generals* or *sparkplug guards* often overused by reporters.
Spot news A news event covered by reporters as it is occurring.
Staccato lead A lead made up of a short burst of phrases that carry readers into a story by dangling some of its key elements in front of them. It is meant to tease readers and set the mood for the story.
Standard offense forms Available at police and sheriff's departments, these forms provide information such as the time an alleged offense took place, where it occurred, the names of any victims and a brief synopsis of what reportedly transpired.
State editions Those issues of a metropolitan daily newspaper that have earlier deadlines than other editions and are delivered to counties and towns outside the metro area.
State editor Alternatively called the **area** or **suburban editor,** the person who supervises reporters covering communities and areas outside the city in which the newspaper is published.
State judicial systems The third branch of government for each of the 50 states. State judicial systems usually have three layers: trial courts, intermediate courts and supreme courts.
State news only (SNO) wire A news wire that carries virtually all of the state news and sports produced by The Associated Press or United Press International for a particular state.
State weather forecasts Stories that discuss and predict upcoming weather for a state.
Steady advance A term used to describe writing that flows smoothly and logically. Sentences are constructed in such a way that readers glide efficiently from the first word to the last.
Story budget A list of stories that have been written or are to be written. Individual reporters sometimes keep their own budgets. The wire services move international, national and state

GLOSSARY

budgets that contain overviews of the most important stories to move on each day's cycles.

Stringer A part-time newspaper or broadcast correspondent who covers a specific subject or geographical area for a media outlet often located elsewhere.

Sub A substitute. Reporters often are asked to write subs, which may provide later information or be better written than the original material.

Subpoena A court order for an individual to give testimony or to supply documents.

Summary lead A terse opening paragraph that provides the gist of a story and lets an audience decide right away if it is interested enough in the story to continue.

Summons In law, a writ informing a person that an action has been filed against him or her in court and that he or she must answer the complaint.

Supplemental news services More limited in scope and resources than The Associated Press and United Press International, services that, for a fee, provide media outlets with materials ranging from cartoons to in-depth political analysis. An example is the Newspaper Enterprise Association.

Survivors Those persons who live after the death of another. In obituaries, most newspapers list names of surviving spouses, children, sisters, brothers and parents.

Team statistics Data computed by totaling individual statistics for sports contests. For example, if a team used eight basketball players in a game and each accumulated three fouls, the team total would be 24.

Text type The type in which newspaper stories are set. Text type generally is 8-, 9-, or 10-point. (One point equals 1/72 inch.)

-30- Symbol used to indicate the story has ended.

Thread A common element, usually a narrative about a person or event, that is sprinkled throughout a story to connect the beginning, body and conclusion.

Tight pages Pages on which there are so many advertisements that comparatively little space is available for news stories and features.

Time element The *when* of a news story. Generally, the time element is included in the lead paragraph.

Tort In civil law, a wrongful act committed against a person or his or her property.

Transition A word, phrase, sentence or paragraph that ushers an audience from one area of a story to another. Transition alerts an audience that a shift or change is coming.

Trend story A type of feature story that examines people, things or organizations having an impact on society.

True bill An indictment returned by a grand jury if it determines there is probable cause that a person charged with a crime committed it and should stand trial for it.

Turn word A transitional word that moves readers from one area to another. Some of the most common turn words are *now, today, but* and *meanwhile*.

Typo A typographical error.

Undercover journalism A type of reporting in which the journalist does not reveal to a source that he or she is working on a story.

United Press International Generally referred to as **UPI,** it is a privately held corporation formed in 1958 when United Press and International News Service merged.

Unrestricted access A term for the unlimited availability of police reports to members of the public or to journalists. The types of reports permitted unrestricted access vary among cities and states, but accident reports often are unrestricted.

UPI clients Newspapers and broadcast stations that recieve news from United Press International (see above). These media outlets are called clients because UPI, unlike the AP, is a private corporation.

User friendly A term for a computer that is easy to use and requires little training by anyone using it.

VDT A **video display terminal,** or electronic keyboard attached to a television monitor that flickers white letters on a black—or sometimes green—background.

Verdict The decision of a trial jury after it has considered the directions given to it by the judge and after it has weighed the evidence presented.

Visitations Hours established for viewing the decedent at a funeral home. Most newspapers provide visitation details in obituaries.

Voice The "signature" or personal style of every writer. Using voice in a story allows writers to put their individual stamps on their work. Voice reveals a reporter's personality and subtly tells readers that this story is not by any writer, but by *this* writer.

Warrant A writ issued by a magistrate or other appropriate official to a law enforcement officer that directs that officer to arrest a person and bring him or her before a court to answer a charge.

Weather forecasting services Sources of information for journalists working on weather-related stories. The National Weather Service is a primary source although some larger newspapers also contract with private weather forecasting services.

Wide-open pages Pages on which there are comparatively few advertisements.

"Words-in-your mouth" technique A method used occasionally by journalists when interviewing inarticulate or tight-lipped sources. For instance, the reporter asks: *Did you feel ecstatic when you won the race?* and the source says, *Yes*. The journalist reports: *Jones said he felt ecstatic when he won the race*.

Writethru The designation wire services use to tell newsrooms that a story replaces all earlier stories on the same news event.

Year-end weather summaries Stories routinely published by newspapers on Jan. 1 that recap the weather for the previous year and present the most relevant statistics, such as rainfall amounts.

INDEX

Abstracts, 139
Accidents, coverage of, 229–232
Accuracy, in obituaries, 150
Address Book, 140
Addresses, in obituaries, 155–156
Adjectival clauses, 41
Advance texts, 205
Advertisements
　editorial news hole and, 8
　newspapers influenced by, 27
　press releases as, 183–184
Aeschliman, Roger, 218, 219, 220–232
Afternoon newspapers, 10–11
　sports writing for, 173
Ages, in obituaries, 155–156
Alien and Sedition Laws (1798), 304
Allen, Michael, 40, 46
American Digest System, 144
American Hospital Association Guide to the Health Care Field, 141
American Jurisprudence, 143
American Library Directory, 141
American Society of Newspaper Editors Statement of Principles, 323–324
American Statistics Index (ASI), 139
AMs, 10–11
　sports writing for, 171–173
Anderson, Jack, 80
Anonymous sources, 90–93, 317–318
　ethics and, 329–330

Area editors, 8
Arizona Republic, 12, 40, 46, 84, 172–173
Arraignment, definition of, 247
Arrests, coverage of, 227–228
Associated Press (AP), 7, 19, 22, 66, 80, 83, 84
　ethics code of, 330
Associated Press Stylebook and Libel Manual, 49, 79, 166–167
　excerpts from, 340–356
Attribution, 79–90
　in beat reporting, 225
　in court reporting, 253
　guidelines for handling, 84–86
　hearsay, 83
　identification in, 82–83
　placement of, 84
　punctuation for, 86–90
　quotes interrupted by, 89–90
　verbs of, 80–82
Authoritarian systems, 319
Authorization, as defense to libel, 311
"Aw nuts" school, 167

Background, 106
Backgrounders, 288–289
Bangor (Maine) *Daily News*, 93, 157
Barfield, Chet, 22–23
Barfknecht, Lee, 167
Barney, Ralph D., 322–323
Beat reporting, 6, 217–258
　accident coverage, 229–232
　arrest stories, 227–228
　attribution in, 225

city government, 234–243
courtroom, 243–258
deadlines in, 223–224
description of scene in, 225–226
follow-up interviews in, 228–229
hostile sources in, 232–233
leads in, 224
police and fire, 218–234
preparation in, 241
source development in, 219–221
sources in, 232–233
taste in, 226–227
Beaumont (Texas) *Enterprise*, 20, 28, 84
Bedell, Sally, 256
Berkshire (Mass.) *Eagle*, 148
Bingham, Maren S., 124, 125–126, 130–131
Biographies, as research material, 138
Biography Index, 138
Black's Law Dictionary, 143, 246, 254
Blodgett, Tom, 265–266
Blue books, as research material, 138
Book of the States, 142
Book Review Digest, 139
Book Review Index, 139
Books in Print, 139
Boone, Jeff, 165–166
Branzburg, Paul, 317–318
Breed, Warren, 26
Brennan, William, 312
Briefs, in civil court, 254
Brotman, Barbara, 264
Bukro, Casey, 324

375

Bullets, 105, 239, 240
Burger, Warren, 320
Buried leads, 61–62
Business Periodicals Index, 139
Bylines, definition of, 7

Capps, Kris, 161–162
Carelessness, libel and, 306
CBS (broadcast network), 305
Chafee, Zechariah, Jr., 304
"Changing Needs of Changing Readers" (study), 16–17
Chase's Annual Events, 141
Chicago Sun-Times, 66, 267–268, 284, 292–298, 327, 330
Chicago Tribune, 57, 58, 65, 150, 264, 267–268, 279
 stylebook of, 49
 suicide coverage policy of, 97
Christensen's Ultimate Movie, TV and Rock Directory, 141
Chronologies, 106
City council meetings, 238–241
City desk, 4
City directories, as research material, 137–138
City editors, 8
City government, coverage of, 234–243
Civil cases, coverage of, 254–257
Civil suits, newsworthiness of, 256–257
Clark, Roy Peter, 32, 107–109
 good writing traits delineated by, 33–34
Clark, Ruth, 16–17
Cliches, in sports writing, 173
Climates of the States, 140
Clippings
 press conferences and, 195, 197–199
 as research material, 136–137
Close-ended questions, 116
Clutter leads, 60–61
Cohn, Bob, 172–173
College Heights Herald (Western Kentucky University), 274–275
Colons
 after quotation marks, 87
 in attribution, 85–86
Colorado Springs Gazette Telegraph, 20, 25, 82, 83
Commas, 36–37
 quotes and, 86–87
Commission on Freedom of the Press, 319–320
Competition, 28–29
Complaint, definition of, 255
Complex sentences, 40–41
Conflict, as news, 20–21
Conflicts of interest, 328–329
Congress, research materials on, 142–143
Congressional Digest, 142
Congressional Directory, 142
Congressional Information Service (CIS) Index, 142
Congressional Quarterly Weekly Report, 136, 142
Congressional Record, 142
Congressional Staff Directory, 142
Conjunctions, 36
Consent, as defense to libel, 311
Consequences of news, 22
Conte, Christopher, 273
Contemporary Authors, 141
Contrast leads, 266–269
Conway, John, 74
Copy desks, 7
Copy editing symbols, 334–337
Copy editors, 7
Corpus Juris Secundum, 143
Court coverage, 243–258
 case types, 246
 challenge of, 257–258
 civil cases, 254–257
 criminal cases, 246–253
 demands of job, 244
 judicial system, 244–246
 steps to follow, 253–254
Courtesy titles, in obituaries, 155
Court of Claims, 245
Court of Customs and Patent Appeals, 245
Creed, John, 161–162

Criminal cases, 246–253
Current Biography, 136, 138
Current World Leaders, 138
Customs Court, 245

Daily Kansan, 75
Daily Nebraskan (University of Nebraska), 167
Daily Northwestern (Northwestern University), 66–67, 262–263, 274
Daily Pioneer (Bimidji, Minn.), 159–160
Daily Reveille (Louisiana State University), 74, 75
Daily Tar Heel (University of North Carolina), 74
Daily Texan, 75
Dallas Morning News, 62–63, 65, 120–121
Damages, definition of, 255
Dangling modifiers, 38
Dashes, 37–38
Daytona Beach (Fla.) *News-Journal*, 153, 155
Deadlines, 4
 of beat reporters, 223–224
Death notices. *See* Obituaries
Deckert, Rod, 328
DeGalan, Matt, 75
Democracy, press conferences and, 195
Denniston, Lyle, 247, 248, 304, 306, 315
Denver Post, 93
Dependent clauses, 36, 40–41
Depositions, definition of, 255
Des Moines Sunday Register, 277
Development, of feature stories, 289
Dialect, in quotes, 79
Dialogue
 direct quotes and, 75
 paragraphs and, 90
Diamondback (University of Maryland), 70
Dictionaries
 legal, 143
 as research material, 137
Dictionary of American Biography, 138
Dillon, Marie, 124–125

INDEX

Direct address leads, 271–273
Directory of Medical Specialists, 140
Direct quotes, 71
   guidelines for use, 73–76
Dodd, Monroe, 150
Dorlund's Illustrated Medical Dictionary, 140
Downey, Dave, 46, 152–153
Dress, for interviews, 116
Dummy, definition of, 7
Dvorchak, Bob, 22

Editing, symbols and process in, 334–339
Editorial conferences, 10
Editorializing, 107
Editorial news hole, 25
   definition of, 8
   inverted pyramid and, 52
   press releases and, 179–180
Editorial Research Reports, 136, 138
Editorials on File, 140
Editors
   features and, 298–300
   functions of, 7–10
   instincts of, 23–24
   See also specific types of editors
Edwards v. *National Audubon Society,* 311
Eisenhower, Dwight, 195
Eissman, Mark, 96, 97–98, 99–100
Eminence of news, 21
Encyclopedia of American Crime, 141
Encyclopedia of Associations, 141
Encyclopedias
   legal, 143
   as research material, 137
Essay and General Literature Index, 139
Essential Guide to Prescription Drugs, 140
Ethics, 322–332
   anonymous sources and, 329–330
   codes of, 323–324, 357–361
   compassion and, 331–332
   conflicts of interest and, 328–329

   enforcement of, 324
   fairness and, 325–326
   "freebies" and, 330–331
   issues involved in, 325–332
   Los Angeles Times code of, 359–361
   objectivity and, 325–326
   privacy and, 327–328
   reporter misrepresentation and, 326–327
   Society of Professional Journalists code of, 357–359
Evansville (Ind.) *Press*, 19, 21, 22, 80, 187–188
Evening newspapers, 10–11
   sports writing for, 173
"Existential Journalism" (Merrill), 324

Facts about Presidents, 140
Facts on File, 136, 138
Fairbanks (Alaska) *Daily News-Miner*, 80, 82, 83, 160–162
Fairness
   in court reporting, 254
   as ethical issue, 325–326
   libel and, 315–316
Fargo (N.D.) *Forum*, 156
Features, 5, 283–300
   conclusions, 291–292
   definition of, 5
   editors and, 298–300
   importance of, 284–285
   leads in, 289–290
   mechanics of, 292–298
   steps in, 292
   story development in, 289
   transitions in, 294–296
   types, 287–289
   voice in, 296–298
Federal government, research materials on, 142–143
Federal judicial system, 245
Federal Register, 142
Financial editors, 10
Findlay (Ohio) *Courier*, 158
Fire beats, 218–234
First Amendment, 304–305, 317–318
   obscenity and, 16
Fisher, Simon, 214–215
Fiske, Toby, 298–300

Five W's and H, 53–55
Flesch, Rudolf, 39
Flynn, Adrianne, 234–241
Focal points, in summary leads, 62–63
Foley, Mike, 328
Follow-up questions, 127–128
Foreign editors, 8
"Four Theories of the Press" (Peterson *et al.*), 318–319
Fox, Kym, 6
Frankeny, Kelly, 75
Franklin, Marc. A., 315–316
"Freebies", 330–331
Friendship, job vs., 242
Fry, Donald, sentence clarity guide of, 34–39
Fry, Steve, 219, 221
Funnel interviews, 117

Gallup, George, 320–321
Gallup Opinion Index, 140
Gang interview, definition of, 194
Gannet news service, 26
Gatekeepers, 17–18
Gateway, The (University of Nebraska), 73
"Gee whiz" school, 167
Geiselman, Art, 117, 118, 125, 129–130
General assignment reporters (GAs), 5
Geography, newsworthiness influenced by, 16
Gertz v. *Robert Welch*, 313–314
Gillespie, Mary, 284, 292–298
Gleaner, The (Henderson, Ky.), 20, 21, 22, 25, 28, 165–166
Glossary, 363–373
Gorlick, Arthur C., 329
Gould, Milton, 315
Governments, forms of, 235–236
Grammar
   errors in, 72–73
   quotes and, 78
Grand juries, 247
Greensboro (N.C.) *News and Record*, 41
Guibor, Jerry, 121
Guide to Congress, 142–143

INDEX

Guinness Book of World Records, 136
Gunning, Robert, writing clarity guide of, 39–48

Hager, Philip, 305
Haines Criss-Cross Directory, 97
Hamilton, E. Douglas, 310
Hammer, James E., 159–160
Han, Andrea, 215
Handouts. *See* Press releases
Haney, Jim, 159
Hard news, 16
   contrast leads in, 269
Harmon, Tim, 326
Harris, Benjamin, 16
Headlines, 8
Hearsay attribution, 83
Heath, Harry E., Jr., 43
Hemlinger, T.J., 332
Henion, Terry, 44
Henry, Nicholas L., 235
Herbert v. *Lando*, 314
Hoaxes, in obituaries, 150
Hogan, Alfred R., 70
Holmes, Oliver Wendell, 304
Hoover, Herbert, 194
Hopkins, W. Nat, 313–314
Hourglass style, 107–109
Human interest stories, 22–23, 288
Hutchinson v. *Proxmire*, 314

Identification, in attribution, 82–83
Impact of news, 22
IMS/Ayr Directory of Publications, 141
Inaccuracies, in quotes, 76–77
Independent clauses, 36, 40–41
Independent Florida Alligator, 43–44, 70
Independent News Network, 270
In-depth stories, 288
Indexed Periodicals, 139
Indexes, 139
   legal, 143
   newspaper, 139
Index to Legal Periodicals, 143

Indianapolis Star, 63
Indictment, definintion of, 246
Indirect quotes, 72
Information, gathering of. *See* Research
Initial appearance, definition of, 247
International Who's Who, 138, 141
Interviews, 111–133
   anonymous sources in, 90–93
   close-ended questions, 116
   dressing for, 116
   end of, 132–133
   establishing rapport in, 121–122
   follow-up questions, 127–128
   funnel, 117
   gang interviews, 194
   with hostile sources, 128–130
   inverted-funnel, 118
   "no comment" in, 128–130
   note-taking during, 130–132
   observation during, 122–124
   open-ended questions, 116–117
   personal questions in, 124–127
   question framing, 119–121
   setting up, 114–116
   by telephone, 97–98, 118–119
Inverted-funnel interviews, 118
Inverted pyramids, 52
   alternatives to, 107–109
   features using, 286
   organization and, 96–97, 105–107
Iowa City (Iowa) *Press Citizen*, 157

Jamestown (N.Y.) *Post-Journal*, 158
Jefferson, Thomas, 304
"Jell-o journalism", 287
Jenkins, Ron, 25, 28
Johnson's World Wide Chamber of Commerce Directory, 140

Journalism Quarterly, 305, 326, 329–330
Judicial system, 244–246

Kanaley, Reid, 108–109
Kansas City Times, 63, 150
Kaufman, Henry, 304, 305, 316
Kehetian, Mitch, 326
Kenosha (Wis.) *News*, 275, 277
Killenberg, George, 317–318
Knight-Ridder news service, 26
Krasnow, Iris, 273

Lamm, Greg, 43–44, 70
Law, 303–332
   research materials on, 143–144
"Law and the Courts" (American Bar Association), 246
Lead blocks, 289–290
   definition of, 262
Leads
   in beat reporting, 224
   contrast, 266–269
   development of, 265–266
   direct address, 271–273
   in features, 289–290
   miscellaneous types, 276
   narrative, 262–266
   in obituaries, 153–157
   observation in, 264
   in press releases, 181
   question, 273–274
   quote, 274–275
   rewriting of, 272–273
   special, 261–280
   staccato, 269–271
   strong verbs in, 276–278
   summary. *See* Summary leads
   teasing with, 274
   turn words in, 268–269
   type selection, 278–280
Libel, 228, 234, 244, 249, 275, 305–317
   carelessness as factor in, 306
   defendants' guidelines, 316–317
   defense to, 310–312
   definition of, 305
   fair comment and citicism and, 310

INDEX

fairness and, 315–316
legal boundaries, 306
negligence and, 313–314
neutral reportage and, 311
public v. private figures in, 313–315
quotes and, 307–308
Red Flag words, 306–307
reporting privilege and, 310
statute of limitations and, 311
truth as defense in, 311
word classes in, 308–310
Libertarian systems, 319
Libraries, 113
   computer reference services in, 138–139
   obituary information in, 149
   research materials in, 138–143
Lifestyle editors, 10
Los Angeles Times, 58, 139, 255, 321
   ethical code of, 359–361
   stylebook of, 49
Louisville (Ky.) *Courier-Journal*, 322

McCloskey, Robert J., 322
McConnell, Doug, 173
Makeup editors, 7, 8
Malmer, Victoria, 290–292
Managing editors, 7
Massa, Mark, 187–188
Media events, press conferences as, 194–195
Mehler, Neil H., 122
Merrill, John, 322–323, 326, 332
Mesa (Ariz.) *Tribune*, 22–23, 248–253
Metropolitan editors, 8
Milwaukee Sentinel, 267, 276, 277–278
Minors, policies on use of names of, 234
Mock, William, 23–24, 28
Mohave Valley News (Bullhead City, Ariz.), 65, 271–272, 274–275
Monthly Catalog of U.S. Government Publications, 139
Montrose (Calif.) *Ledger*, 264
Morgues, 112–113

Morning newspapers, 10–11
   sports writing for, 171–173
Moscardini, Mike, 24
Moss, Donna, 75
Murder, use of term, 252
Murphy, Frank, 304–305
Murphy, Michael, 12

Narrative leads, 262–266
National Directory of Addresses and Telephone Numbers, 139
National editors, 8
National Reporter System, 144
National Weather Service, 159, 162, 164
Negligence, libel and, 313–314
New Haven (Conn.) *Register*, 149, 150, 152, 156, 157
Newill, William T., 329
News
   anonymous sources and, 90–93
   availability of, 25–26
   conflict and, 20–21
   consequences of, 22
   criteria for determining, 18–23
   definition of, 16
   eminence of, 21
   evolution of treatment of, 16–17
   factors affecting treatment of, 23–29
   geography in determination of, 16
   hard, 16
   human interest angles on, 22–23
   impact of, 22
   ingredients of, 15–29
   prominence of, 21
   proximity of, 20
   soft, 16
   story angles, 12
   timeliness of, 19
   weather as, 165
News editors, 7–8
News hole. *See* Editorial news hole
News huddles, 10
News mix, 27–28
Newspaper indexes, 139

Newspapers
   advertisers' influence on, 27
   AMs, 10–11, 171–173
   competition, 28–29
   evolution of, 16–17
   as paper of record, 11, 26
   PMs, 10–11, 173
   publishers' pressures on, 26–27
   readership of, 16–17, 24
   styles of, 48–49
News releases. *See* Press releases
Newsrooms, 3–12
   chart of, 9
   editorial functions in, 7–10
   research sources in, 136–138
News stories
   basic writing, 147–174
   definition of, 5
   organizing. *See* Organization
   processing of, 333–339
   weather, 158–167
News-Sun, The (Waukegan, Ill.), 269
New York Daily News, 63, 276
New York Times, 84, 122–123, 139, 153–154, 256, 270, 311–312
   libel ruling concerning, 312
   as paper of record, 26
New York Times Biographical Edition, 138
New York Times Book Review Index, 139
New York Times Co. v. Sullivan, 312
New York Times Manual of Style and Usage, 49
   quotation of dialect rules in, 79
New York Times News Service, 26
Nielson, Thomas, 329
Notes, 207–210
   in court reporting, 254
   during interviews, 130–132
   during speeches, 206
Nut graph, 263, 290
Nykanen, Mark, 125, 128, 129

Obituaries, 148–158
   ages and addresses in, 155–156

INDEX

Obituaries *(cont.)*
  basic information in, 149
  cause of death in, 156–157
  courtesy titles in, 155
  hoaxes in, 150
  information sources for, 149–150
  leads in, 153–157
  nicknames in, 154–155
  same-day, 151
  second-day, 151–152
  selection of, 148–149
  styles for, 150–152
  suicides, 157
  terminology in, 158
Obituaries on File, 138
Objectivity, as ethical issue, 325–326
Obscenity, Supreme Court's ruling on, 16
Observation
  in contrast leads, 268
  during interviews, 122–124
  narrative leads and, 264
  at speeches, 206
Observer, The (La Grande, Ore.), 164, 165
Offensive language, 72, 75, 78–79
Official Museum Directory, 141
Off the record, use of term, 91
Okeson, Sarah, 262–263
Omaha (Neb.) *World-Herald*, 44, 167
Ombudsmen, 321–322
On background, use of term, 91
On deep background, use of term, 91
On the record, use of term, 91
Open-ended questions, 116–117
Open sentences, 35
Organization
  body of, 99–100
  conclusions, 101
  hourglass style of, 107–109
  inverted pyramid in, 96–97
  of news stories, 95–109
  of press conference and speech stories, 211–214
  rewrites, 101–105
Orlando (Fla.) *Sentinel*, 44, 47, 270–271

Padgett, Mike, 244, 250–253
Paper of record
  New York Times as, 26
  use of term, 11
Paragraphs
  dialogue and, 90
  nut graph, 263, 290
  quotation marks in, 89
Paraphrasing, 72
Partial quotes, 71–72
Passive voice, 35–36
Perron, Michelle, 74
Persistence, 242
Personality profiles, 288
Personal questions, 124–127
Petchel, Jacquee, 12
Peterson, Theodore, 318–319, 320
Pett, Saul, 33
Phelps, Robert H., 310
Philadelphia Inquirer, 63, 108–109
Phoenix Gazette, 12, 173
Photo editors, 8–10
Places Rated Almanac, 141
Plaintiff, definition of, 255
Plea bargaining, definition of, 247
Pleading, definition of, 255
PMs, 10–11
  sports writing for, 173
Police beats, 218–234
Polls, 5
Poulson, Thad, 332
Povtak, Tim, 44, 47
Powell, Lewis F., Jr., 317–318
Powell, Wickliffe R., 328
Poynter, Nelson, 32
Preliminary hearing, definition of, 247
Preparation, in beat reporting, 241
Prescher, Dan, 73
Press
  criticism of, 320–321
  self-criticism, 321–322
Press conferences, 193–204
  as media events, 194–195
  news value of, 202–204
  preparations for, 195–199
  press releases to announce, 195, 196–197
  questions and answers at, 199–202
Press freedom, 304–305

Press releases, 177–190
  as advertisements, 183–184
  leads in, 181
  news value of, 184–187
  press conferences and, 195, 196–197
  rewriting of, 187–190
  selection of, 179–180
  value of, 179
Press systems, theories of, 319–320
Privacy, ethics and, 327–328
Privilege of participant, as defense to libel, 311
Profanities, in quotes, 72, 75, 78–79
Prominence of news, 21
Prosser, William, 306
Proximity of news, 20
Publick Occurrences Both Forreign and Domestick, 16
Public relations people, 178
Publishers, newspapers pressured by, 26–27
Punctuation, 36–38
  for quotes and attribution, 86–90

Question leads, 273–274
Question marks, quotation marks and, 87–88
Questions
  close-ended, 116
  follow-up, 127–128
  framing of, 119–121
  funnel interviews, 117
  inverted-funnel interviews, 118
  memorizing of, 118
  open-ended, 116–117
  personal, 124–127
  at press conferences, 199–202
  after speeches, 207
Queue, definition of, 49
Quill (magazine), 92, 306
Quotation marks, punctuation and, 86–90
Quote leads, 274–275
Quotes, 69–79, 106
  attribution in interruption of, 89–90
  coherence of, 77–78

INDEX

dialect in, 79
direct, 71
fragmentary, 78
grammatical errors in, 72–73, 78
guidelines for use, 73–76
inaccuracies in, 76–77
indirect, 72
libel and, 307–308
partial, 71–72
pitfalls, 76–78
profanities in, 72, 75, 78–79
punctuation for, 86–90
quotes within, 88–89
rambling, 77
reconstruction of, 78
repeating of, 132
in sports writing, 174
types, 71–72

Raines, Howell, 32
Random House College Dictionary, 159
Rapport, during interviews, 121–122
Rawitch, Robert, 244, 255, 257–258
Reader's Guide to Periodical Literature, 139
Readership
  changing habits of, 16–17
  news treatment affected by, 24
Reed, Harry J., 328–329
"Reporter and the Law, The" (Denniston), 247, 248
Reporters
  anonymous sources and, 90–93
  beat, 6, 217–258
  editorializing by, 107
  ethics and. *See* Ethics
  general assignment (GAs), 5
  instincts of, 23–24
  libel and. *See* Libel
  qualities of, 4
  sources for. *See* Sources
  specialty, 6–7
  tasks of, 4–5
Reporting privilege, libel and, 310
Research, 135–144
  computer reference services, 138–139

in court reporting, 253
for interviews, 112–114
legal, 143–144
library sources in, 138–143
newsroom sources for, 136–138
obituary, 149–150
prior to press conferences, 195–199
Reverse Acronyms, Initialisms and Abbreviations Dictionary, 140
Rewriting, 101–105
  of direct address leads, 272–273
  of press releases, 187–190
Right of reply, in libel cases, 311–312
Roosevelt, Theodore, 194
Rosenbloom v. Metromedia, 313
Rosenstiel, Thomas B., 305

"Said", as verb of attribution, 80–81
St. Petersburg (Fla.) *Times*, 32
Sanford, Bruce, 306–307
San Francisco Examiner, 298–300
San Jose (Calif.) *Mercury News*, 297
Santa Ana (Calif.) *Register*, 271
Savery, Gilbert M., 325–326, 327, 331
Scanlon, Cynthia, 140
Schramm, Wilbur, 318–319
Sedition Act (1918), 304
Seib, Charles B., 324
Self-defense, in libel cases, 311–312
Semicolons, after quotation marks, 87
Sentences
  clarity of, 34–39
  length of, 40
  quotes and attribution in multiple, 84–86
  simplicity of, 40–41
  word familiarity in, 41–42
Settlements, in civil court, 255
Sharon, Ariel, 305, 315
Shaw, Bob, 277

Shaw, David, 321, 327
Sheehan, Susan, 80
Shelledy, James E., 327
Shepard's Federal and State Acts and Cases by Popular Names, 143
Shield laws, 317, 318
Siebert, Fred S., 318–319
Silverman, Lauren, 96, 99
Simple sentences, 40–41
Slot editors, 8
Smith, Red, 33
Social responsibility theory, 319–320
Society, press responsibility to, 318–319
Society of Professional Journalists, ethical code of, 357–359
Soft news, 16
  feature articles concerning, 285–286
Sources
  anonymous, 90–93, 317–318, 329–330
  in beat reporting, 219–221
  in city government reporting, 242
  hostile, 128–130, 232–233
  interviewing of, 111–133
  reporter misrepresentation and, 326–327
So-what graph, 290
Specialty reporters, 6–7
Speeches, 204–215
  advance texts of, 205
  coverage of, 205–207
  preparation for, 204–205
  tape recorders for, 205
Spelling, in sports writing, 174
Sports editors, 10
Sports writing, 167–174
  cliches in, 167–168, 173
  contest stories, 170–173
  for evening newspapers, 173
  for morning newspapers, 171–173
  spelling in, 174
  statistics deciphered in, 168–170
  summary leads in, 173
  tips, 173–174
Spot news, 5
Spratt, Tom, 256–257
Staccato leads, 269–271

INDEX

Standard and Poor's Register, 140
Standard Directory of Advertisers, 140
Standard Periodical Directory, 141
Star-Herald (Scottsbluff, Neb.), 20
State directories, as research material, 138
State editors, 8
State Information Book, 142
State Journal, The (Frankfort, Ky.), 290–292
State judicial systems, 245–246
State Press (Arizona State University), 215, 265–266
States, research materials on, 141–142
Statesboro (Ga.) *Herald*, 159
Statistical Abstract of the United States, 140
Statistical Reference Index (SRI), 139
Statistics, in sports writing, 168–170
Statute of limitations, libel and, 311
Stewart, Potter, 16, 23
Stonecipher, Harry W., 136
Story angles, 12
Strunk, William, Jr., 39
Stylebooks, 48–49
Subject and verb, 38
Subject Guide to Books in Print, 139
Subjectivity, attributive verbs and, 80
Suburban editors, 8
Suicides, 97
  obituary coverage of, 157
Sullivan, L.B., 312
Summary leads, 51–67, 98
  active voice in, 66–67
  definition of, 51, 52
  focal point in, 62–63
  improvement of, 59–63, 105
  multiple elements in, 57
  number of words in, 58–59
  primary elements in, 53–55
  in sports writing, 173
  terseness of, 106
  thought process behind, 54–55

  time element in, 64–66
  uniqueness of, 64
  writing of, 55–57
Summons, definition of, 255
Sumter (S.C.) *Daily Item*, 159
Supreme Court, U.S., 244, 245
  conservative libel decisions of, 314
  New York Times ruling of, 312
  obscenity ruling of, 16
  press freedom and, 304–305
  research materials concerning, 144
Supreme Court Reporter, 144
Swope, Karen, 148
Sylvester, Edward, 77–78
Symbols
  copy editing, 334–337
  in note taking, 132
Symbols of America, 141

Taber's Cyclopedic Medical Dictionary, 140
Tape recorders, 130–131
  for speeches, 205
Taste, in fire reporting, 226–227
Telephone directories, as research material, 137
Telephones
  interviews by, 118–119
  news gathering using, 97–98
Television, competition with, 28–29
Tempe (Ariz.) *Daily News Tribune*, 21, 45, 46, 81–82, 152–153, 214–215, 234–241
Terminology, in court reporting, 254
Thomas, Helen, 195
Thomas, William, 321, 359
Thompson, Phyllis H., 159
Tight, definition of, 25
Tilley, Greta, 41
Time Inc., 305, 314, 315
Time Inc. v. *Firestone*, 314
Timeliness of news, 19
Topeka (Kan.) *Capital-Journal*, 218, 219, 220–232
Transitions, 106, 240
  in features, 294–296

Trend stories, 288
Trentonian, The (Trenton, N.J.), 150, 156, 158
Truman, Harry, 195
Truth, as defense to libel, 311
Turn words, 268–269
Twichell, Tonia, 248–250

United Press International (UPI), 7, 19
  stylebook of, 49
United States Code, 143
U.S. Court of Appeals, 245
U.S. District Courts, 245
U.S. Government Organizational Manual, 142
United States Law Week, 144
United States Reports, 144
United States Supreme Court Reports, 144
USA Today, 62, 158–159

Variety, in writing style, 46–47
Venere, Emil, 45, 81–82
Verb modifiers, 38–39
Verbs
  action in, 44
  of attribution, 80–82
  in leads, 276–278
  modifiers, 38–39
Video display terminals, 333–334
Voice, in features, 296–298

Walker, Brian, 330
Wall Street Journal, 139, 273, 285, 291
Ward, Kent H., 157
Warrant, definition of, 247
Warrick County (Ind.) *Press*, 187, 188–190
Washington Information Directory, 141
Washington Post, 65, 139, 321–322, 330
  stylebook of, 79
Weather, 158–167
  forecasts, 163–165
  as hard news, 165
  local coverage, 159–162
  seasonal and year-end stories, 166

INDEX

steps to follow when writing about, 162–163
story types, 163–166
terms, 166–167
travel condition reports, 165–166
Webster's Biographical Dictionary, 141
Welch, Robert, 313–314
Westmoreland, William, 305
White, Brian, 164, 165
White, Byron, 314, 317
White, David M., 17
White, E. B., 39
Who's Who (reference books), 138, 140, 141
Wide open, definition of, 25
Williams, Bill, 331–332
Williams, Jack, 158–159
Williston (N.D.) Daily Herald, 58–59, 67, 266–269
Wire services, 7–8
Wolston v. Reader's Digest, 314
Wood, Tim, 326, 330
Woodward, Stanley, 167–168
Words
familiarity of, 41–42
libelous, 306–307
libelous classes of, 308–310
World Almanac, 140
Writing
active voice in, 66–67
of basic stories, 147–174
colloquial styles in, 45
inverted pyramid in, 52
of obituaries, 148–158
punctuation, 36–38
quality of, 31–49
readers' experiences tied in with, 46
sentence clarity, 34–39
sports. *See* Sports writing
of summary leads, 55–57
transitions in, 240
variety in, 46–47
weather stories, 158–167
See also Sentences

Year Book of Higher Education, 140

Zielenziger, Michael, 297
Zinsser, William, 39, 40, 47

ABOUT THE AUTHORS

DOUGLAS A. ANDERSON is a professor and director of the Walter Cronkite School of Journalism and Telecommunication at Arizona State University. He is author or co-author of *A "Washington Merry-Go-Round" of Libel Actions*, *Contemporary Sports Reporting*, *Electronic Age News Editing*, *Contemporary News Reporting*, and *News Writing and Reporting for Today's Media*. He has written articles that have appeared in such academic and professional publications as *Journalism Quarterly*, *Newspaper Research Journal*, *American Journalism*, *APME News* and *Grassroots Editor*. His teaching specialties are reporting, editing and communication law. Formerly managing editor of the *Hastings* (Neb.) *Daily Tribune*, Professor Anderson was a graduate fellow at Southern Illinois University, where he received his Ph.D.

BRUCE D. ITULE is the director of student publications at Arizona State University and a faculty associate in the Walter Cronkite School of Journalism and Telecommunication. Before moving to ASU, he was night city editor of the *Chicago Tribune*. He is the co-author of *Contemporary News Reporting* and *News Writing and Reporting for Today's Media*. He has been a reporter and copy editor at the *Arizona Daily Star* in Tucson, *The Phoenix* (Ariz.) *Gazette*, the *Boulder* (Colo.) *Daily Camera*, the *Denver Post*, the *Minneapolis Star* and the *Montrose* (Calif.) *Ledger*. Mr. Itule has written articles on journalism for professional journals, including *The Quill*, *Journalism Educator*, *Grassroots Editor* and *APME News*, and often conducts seminars for journalists who want to improve their writing.